With Justice for All?

The Nature of the American Legal System

Michael Ross Fowler
University of Louisville

Prentice Hall, Upper Saddle River, New Jersey 07458

Library of Congress Cataloging-in-Publication Data

FOWLER, MICHAEL
With justice for all? : the nature of the American legal system / Michael Ross Fowler

Includes bibliographical references and index.
1. Justice, Administration of—United States. 2. Law reform—United States. I. Title.
KF384.F69 1997
347.73—dc21 96–49653
CIP

ISBN 0-13-618349-2 (alk. paper)

Editorial director: Charlyce Jones Owen
Editor in chief: Nancy Roberts
Acquisitions editor: Michael Bickerstaff
Editorial/production supervision and
interior design: Barbara Reilly
Copyeditor: Stephen C. Hopkins
Editorial assistants: Anita Castro, Kathryn Sheehan
Prepress and manufacturing buyer: Robert Anderson
Marketing manager: Christopher DeJohn
Cover art director: Jayne Conte

This book was set in 10/12 ITC New Baskerville by ElectraGraphics, Inc., and was printed and bound by RR Donnelley & Sons Company. The cover was printed by Phoenix Color Corp.

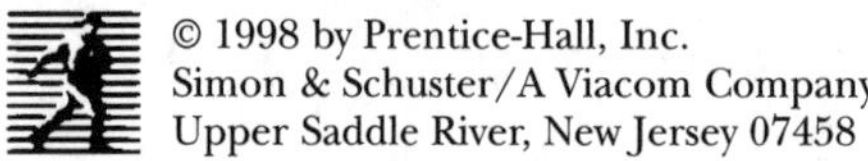

Printed in the United States of America
10 9 8 7 6 5 4 3 2 1

ISBN 0-13-618349-2

Prentice-Hall International (UK) Limited, *London*
Prentice-Hall of Australia Pty. Limited, *Sydney*
Prentice-Hall Canada Inc., *Toronto*
Prentice-Hall Hispanoamericana, S.A., *Mexico*
Prentice-Hall of India Private Limited, *New Delhi*
Prentice-Hall of Japan, Inc., *Tokyo*
Simon & Schuster Asia Pte. Ltd., *Singapore*
Editora Prentice-Hall do Brasil, Ltda., *Rio de Janeiro*

Dedicated
to the memory of

Colonel S. Nelson Drew of Virginia
(1948–1995)
Died on a U.S. Peace Mission to Bosnia, August 19, 1995

and

Robin Lee Little of Kentucky
(1957–1994)

Warm friends, formidable intellects, and gentlemen both

Contents

PART II
KEY PARTICIPANTS IN THE AMERICAN LEGAL SYSTEM

PART III
THE ADVERSARIAL SYSTEM IN ACTION

PART IV
ASSESSING THE AMERICAN LEGAL SYSTEM

Abbreviations

ABA	American Bar Association
ACLU	American Civil Liberties Union
ATLA	Association of Trial Lawyers of America
CPSC	Consumer Product Safety Commission
DEA	Drug Enforcement Administration
DNA	Deoxyribonucleic Acid
DUI	Driving Under the Influence
DWI	Driving While Intoxicated
EEOC	Equal Employment Opportunity Commission
EPA	Environmental Protection Agency
FAA	Federal Aviation Administration
FBI	Federal Bureau of Investigation
FCC	Federal Communications Commission
FDA	Food and Drug Administration
FTC	Federal Trade Commission
GNP	Gross National Product
IBM	International Business Machines
ICC	Interstate Commerce Commission
IRS	Internal Revenue Service
J.D.	Juris Doctorate
JUSEC	Japan–United States Educational Commission
LL.M.	Master of Law
LSAT	Law School Aptitude Test
NAACP	National Association for the Advancement of Colored People
NLRB	National Labor Relations Board
OSHA	Occupational Safety and Health Administration
SEC	Securities and Exchange Commission
SWAT	Strategic Weapons and Assault Team

✥ ✥ Preface ✥ ✥

With assorted editorial additions and subtractions, this book contains the substance of a lecture series I delivered while serving as Fulbright Scholar at the College of Law and Letters of the University of the Ryukyus in Okinawa, Japan, in 1992 and 1993. In suggesting that I focus my remarks on the American judicial process, the Ryudai faculty invited me to reflect on my experiences as a practicing attorney as well as my studies as a political scientist and legal scholar. Thus, this work attempts to introduce and evaluate American law by combining something of the theoretical with something of the practical.

The chapters that follow do not purport to explain in any detailed or comprehensive manner the content of American law in any particular field or the rules and procedures of American courts. Rather, I have tried to paint an impressionistic picture, in a very few strokes of the brush, of the nature of modern American justice. Naturally, in an introductory text many important matters will be dealt with in a cursory fashion or omitted altogether. I have, however, attempted to draw the reader's attention to a few fundamental aspects of the legal system, as I understand it, and to additional sources that may fill in the gaps—the areas that this book does not cover.

The impetus for turning the Ryudai lectures into a book came first from faculty colleagues in Okinawa who noted the scarcity of Japanese-language texts written to introduce students, professionals, and other interested groups in Japan to the American legal system. Later, various American scholars suggested that students at U.S. universities might also be interested in this analysis, especially since it examines the American legal system through a comparative lens.

In seeking to explain and analyze the administration of justice, both civil and criminal, in the United States, this book is organized around a handful of principal questions: How is the American system of justice supposed to work? How does it really function in practice? What role does law play in American society? And, what are the most salient problems and the most marked successes of the American legal system?

After preliminary thoughts on the historical development of American law and the functioning of the courts, I consider the chief participants in the American judicial system: judge, lawyer, jury, and police. I then reflect upon the adversarial system in action—criminal and civil cases. I conclude by examining training and regulation within the legal profession and by outlining how the current legal system serves and denies justice.

Several themes recur throughout my analysis, including the ambivalence with which Americans view their legal system, the breadth of tasks that the legal system performs in American society, and the tension between tradition and evolution that so often characterizes American law. That I have titled the book in the form of a question is meant to imply that there is much within the American legal system to be criticized and much that might usefully be reformed. Nevertheless, I find much of the bitter popular rhetoric about the American system to be overblown and misinformed. One objective of this book is to provide a comprehensible and balanced introduction that unveils the inner workings of the legal system. Above all, I aim to portray the American legal system realistically: neither shying away from its many warts, nor passing over its quite attractive features.

Incidentally, those readers unfamiliar with American culture may wonder about the title of the book: *With Justice for All?* turns a well-known phrase from the pledge of allegiance, customarily learned and recited by American schoolchildren, into a question. The full pledge reads as follows: "I pledge allegiance to the flag of the United States of America, and to the Republic for which it stands, one nation, under God, indivisible, *with liberty and justice for all.*"

I happily acknowledge my debt to the many friends who assisted me in turning these thoughts, initially presented in informal lectures, into a global introduction to American law. First, I thank Professor Tetsumi Takara of the University of the Ryukyus, not only for encouraging me to pursue this project, but also for attending and summarizing the original lectures in the spring and summer of 1992. Professor Takara then edited and helped to translate the lectures some years thereafter. During my year in Okinawa, I owed more than can readily be imagined to his initiative, guidance, and cheerful support. His daily acts of kindness could never be enumerated, much less replicated, and I will always treasure our friendship. I am grateful as well to the Fulbright Scholarship Program, the Japan–United States Educational Commission (JUSEC), and for the special attention I received from the former director, Caroline Matano Yang, and her able deputy, Ms. Kazuko Kamimura.

I would also like to single out Professor Hojun Kakinohana of the University of the Ryukyus for his tireless assistance in arranging and overseeing my visit to Japan. Although space does not permit me to thank all who graciously offered their time and hospitality during my stay in Okinawa, I am also particularly grateful to the president of the University, Dr. Keisha Sunigawa, the former dean of the Junior College, Dr. Yoshimitsu Higa, and the dean of the College of Law and Letters, Dr. Tetsuo Shimabukuro. In addition, several Okinawan friends—Professor Keitetsu Ishimine, Professor Toshiaki Nakahara, and Professor Masaaki Gabe, and his wife, Masako Gabe—and several American friends teaching in Okinawa—Professor Donald Seekins, Professor Eric Shaffer, and Veronica Winegarner—contributed sage advice and unfailing good cheer throughout the delivery of these lectures and the preparation of the manuscript. I deeply appreciate their support.

Years ago I had an English teacher who would require each of his students to write an essay describing as accurately as possible the functioning of an ordinary mousetrap. When the task was completed, he would hold a mousetrap in front of him, reading aloud from each essay to demonstrate how imprecisely we had described the trap and the manner in which it functions. Writing an introduction to

American law, I have found, is uncomfortably comparable to describing a mousetrap: The most obvious features are also the most easily ignored or mischaracterized when one tries to describe them.

Fortunately, I have been able to draw on a wealth of friends and colleagues who have listened to the original lectures or read drafts of the manuscript and pointed out the many times that I had neglected to give the audience the basic information necessary to hold the mousetrap right side up and bait it properly without having it spring shut on the fingers. Thus, to all who contributed a helping hand in reading the manuscript and offering suggestions on clarifications and improvement, I offer special thanks.

In particular, Orm W. Ketcham, a retired judge of the D.C. Juvenile Court and the D.C. Superior Court, offered a series of cogent suggestions for improving Chapter 3. Paul Brosnahan, graduate of the University of Notre Dame Law School and a lawyer representing injured clients in Winona, Minnesota, gave freely of his time and expertise in reviewing a preliminary draft of the manuscript. Bob Morris, graduate of the University of Chicago Law School and a labor attorney in the Boston law offices of Morgan, Brown, and Joy, painstakingly critiqued multiple drafts of each chapter, and offered thorough and trenchant criticisms. Moreover, as is true of much of my written work, the hand of Inis L. Claude, Jr., Professor Emeritus of Government and Foreign Affairs at University of Virginia, is apparent in the writing and ideas in many of the chapters.

Those familiar with American legal scholarship will soon sense that I owe an intellectual debt to a number of important figures in the field. Although none has had a direct hand in this manuscript, each has shaped my thinking in significant ways. First, I commend to the reader the works of Professor Henry J. Abraham of the University of Virginia, especially *The Judicial Process: An Introductory Analysis of the Courts of the United States, England and France,* now in its sixth edition. I also drew heavily upon the work of Professor Lawrence Friedman of Stanford University Law School, especially his towering study *A History of American Law.* Although I never had the privilege of being a student, in the formal sense, of professors Abraham and Friedman, I did study criminal process under Professor Lloyd Weinreb of Harvard Law School. I owe much to his classroom analysis and his pathbreaking work entitled *Denial of Justice: Criminal Process in the United States.*

I am also especially indebted to a slender but insightful volume entitled *What Every Lawyer Knows* by Walter Fisher, who was for many years a distinguished attorney in Chicago working in private practice and state government service and who also contributed to American law two influential sons: Frank Fisher, academic, diplomat, and attorney for various federal government agencies, and Roger Fisher, now professor emeritus of law at Harvard Law School. The Fisher family has contributed much to my legal education.

I should tip my hat as well to my research assistant at University of Louisville Law School, Rachelle Laisnez, and my undergraduate and graduate students at Ryudai, particularly the members of my two seminars on American law. Most especially, I am much obliged to Ms. Kyoko Tamaki, who translated many of my lectures and helped to create a stimulating classroom environment. The curious and provocative questions posed by students in Okinawa freshened my own approach to American law.

Of course, there would be no book to acknowledge were it not for Michael Bickerstaff, political science editor at Prentice Hall. I appreciate his patience and support and all the technical assistance offered by copyeditor Stephen C. Hopkins and production editor Barbara Reilly.

Special thanks are also due the many family members and friends who cheerfully and conscientiously looked after my responsibilities in the United States while I was enjoying a year lecturing in Japan. In this regard, I should gratefully mention Russell Riley, on-site Director of the Semester-in-Washington Program for the University of Pennsylvania, and Monique van Landingham of the National Park Service, who took care of an extraordinary number of personal and professional matters that I really should have been attending to myself.

Finally, I am especially thankful for the many contributions of my wife, political scientist Julie Marie Bunck of the University of Louisville, who accompanied me to Japan and helped immensely in preparing the lectures and manuscript. Julie is the sort of stalwart traveler who delights in hardships, handily defeats crises, and enriches all who meet her. Her adept editing and insights into American culture have corrected and improved this book, just as her incisive classroom comments corrected and improved the original lecture series. To echo the words of the biblical Book of Proverbs, "with the fruit of her hands she has planted much in these vineyards."

To all others who joined in this project, I offer sincere thanks. Naturally, those who added something to the contents should in no way be taken to endorse the views expressed in the pages that follow.

M.R.F.

1

The Development of the American Legal System

According to an ancient Chinese saying, even the longest of journeys must begin with a single step. A first step in gaining a better understanding of the legal system in the United States is to focus upon what Americans think of the way their country administers justice. What are popular attitudes toward the legal system? What aspirations do Americans have for their legal system? How has the legal system developed, and how does it differ from other systems? What roles do law and lawyers play in society? How has American law evolved?

POPULAR ATTITUDES TOWARD AMERICAN JUSTICE

Perspectives on the Legal System

Americans have curiously ambivalent feelings about their system of administering justice. The average citizen is proud of the U.S. Constitution, its timeless principles, unparalleled longevity, carefully crafted prose, and protection of property and individual liberties. Although they certainly disagree with particular judicial decisions, Americans also tend to believe that, on the whole, their courts dispense justice by unbiased methods. Many feel that their legal system administers justice more equitably than do the systems of other countries, especially those in Communist societies and the Third World.

Most Americans also find themselves fascinated by the drama of their courtrooms. A lawyer seeking justice for a client is sometimes cast in heroic dimensions. The media closely follow the trials of celebrities, notorious criminals, and others in the public spotlight. Fair-minded Americans would likely concede that lawyers have played prominent roles in civil rights, prisoner rights, and other movements that have eventually brought into being a more equitable society than had hitherto existed.

The most visible attorneys in the United States often become nationally recognizable public figures and are hailed for their devotion to each client, no matter how unpopular. Many educated Americans would have no difficulty identifying such attorneys as Daniel Webster[1] and Clarence Darrow,[2] John W. Davis[3] and Clark Clifford,[4] Edward Bennett Williams[5] and Lloyd Cutler,[6] Melvin Belli,[7] and William Kunstler,[8]

[1] Daniel Webster, one of the finest trial lawyers in early American history, is even better known for his political career, in which he served as a senator from two states, a frequent contender for the presidency, and a respected secretary of state. A famous American short story, "The Devil and Daniel Webster" by Stephen Vincent Benét, immortalized his oratorical skills by portraying Webster defeating the Devil in legal debate. For works on Webster's legal career see Maurice G. Baxter, *Daniel Webster and the Supreme Court* (Amherst, MA: University of Massachusetts Press, 1966), and his "Daniel Webster: The Lawyer," in Kenneth E. Shewmaker, ed., *Daniel Webster: The Completest Man,* foreword by William H. Rehnquist (Hanover, NH: University Press of New England, 1990), pp. 138–202.

[2] Clarence Darrow gained a reputation for accepting highly unpopular or poor clients facing difficult problems, and for winning their cases at trial. In his most famous case, known as the "Scopes Monkey Trial," *State of Tennessee v. John Thomas Scopes,* 154 Tenn. 105, 289 S.W. 363 (1927), Darrow convinced the court that scientists had proven that mankind had evolved from apes. For works on Darrow see his autobiography, *The Story of My Life* (New York: Charles Scribner's Sons, 1932), and biographies by Irving Stone, *Clarence Darrow for the Defense* (Garden City, NY: Doubleday, Doran, 1941), Kevin Tierney, *Darrow: A Biography* (New York: Crowell, 1979), and Arthur Weinberg, ed., *Attorney for the Damned,* foreword by William O. Douglas (New York: Simon & Schuster, 1957).

[3] Founder of Davis Polk & Wardwell, John W. Davis used his exceptional skills as an oral advocate to move from a small law practice in West Virginia to Congress. Eventually, he became a solicitor general of the United States, an ambassador to England, a Democratic presidential candidate, and a successful Wall Street lawyer. Justice Oliver Wendell Holmes once remarked: "Of all the persons who appeared before the Court in my time, there was never anybody more elegant, more clear, more concise, or more logical than John W. Davis." William H. Harbaugh, *Lawyer's Lawyer: The Life of John W. Davis* (New York: Oxford University Press, 1973), p. 128.

[4] Founder of Clifford and Warnke, a prestigious Washington law firm, Clark Clifford gained a reputation as a Washington insider with experience spanning five decades and a special talent for advising presidents of both parties. In his later years, Clifford's indictment in a banking fraud scandal involving the sale of First American Bankshares to the Bank of Credit and Commerce International tarnished his reputation; however, he proclaimed his innocence and was never convicted of any alleged crime.

[5] Edward Bennett Williams founded Williams and Connolly, a well-known law firm in Washington, DC, and became known as one of the most successful and celebrated defense attorneys of his time. In his later years he became a celebrity, owning sports teams and advising presidents.

[6] Lloyd Cutler, senior partner in the Washington law firm of Wilmer, Cutler, and Pickering, moved from private practice to government service throughout his legal career. Co-chairman of the Lawyers Committee for Civil Rights Under Law, Cutler gained national recognition as legal advisor to presidents Jimmy Carter and Bill Clinton. Not only is Cutler's firm well known for its ***pro bono*** representation of the poor, but during the rioting after the Martin Luther King assassination Cutler personally led a group of private attorneys who offered their services to those arrested.

[7] Melvin Belli, a flamboyant attorney in San Francisco, long specialized in personal-injury cases. Author of numerous popular books, Belli won large sums of money for persons injured in various types of accidents. Belli is the author, among other works, of *Belli for Your Malpractice Defense,* 2d ed. rev. (Oradell, NJ: Medical Economics Books, 1989) and *The Belli Files: Reflections on the Wayward Law* (Englewood Cliffs, NJ: Prentice-Hall, 1983).

[8] William Kunstler gained fame as a controversial attorney who earned a living defending radical defendants, who were often scorned by the public. His clients ranged from the "Chicago Seven" of the Chicago riots of 1968 to the Arab suspects in the World Trade Center bombing in New York City in 1993. He is the author of *My Life as a Radical Lawyer.* (Secaucus, NJ: Carol, 1994).

Gerry Spence,[9] Richard "Racehorse" Haynes,[10] and Alan Dershowitz.[11] In the murder trial of football star O. J. Simpson, defense lawyers Johnnie L. Cochran, Jr. and Robert Shapiro became national celebrities; even prosecutors Marcia Clark and Christopher Darden gained national fame. And the elder statesman of the defense team, F. Lee Bailey,[12] added to his already illustrious resume.

Americans customarily applaud the role of a jury of ordinary citizens determining guilt or innocence in a criminal case, and many view with surprise and suspicion foreign legal systems in which a judge both investigates a criminal complaint and renders a decision regarding the validity of that complaint. Public opinion in the United States also broadly supports the idea that no one, however powerful, should be above the law and that a legal system should serve the legal interests of the poor as well as the wealthy, the ordinary person as well as the well connected. When a poverty-stricken or unpopular individual is charged with a crime, most would consider it un-American as well as unconstitutional to deprive that person of legal counsel. In 1974, while many citizens of liberal democracies looked on in bemusement at all the fuss made over a minor break-in and ensuing political coverup, most Americans would have been disturbed had the Watergate affair been quietly swept aside.[13]

At the same time, Americans often bitterly criticize the length of time their legal system takes to administer justice. They regularly feel confused, intimidated, or constrained by the number and complexity of national, state, and local laws and administrative regulations. Some cynics believe that the government is in the business of manufacturing **red tape,*** and that crafty lawyers are paid to create dense legal jargon (known by the slang terms **legalese** or "mumbo jumbo") and to find **loopholes** that allow wealthy clients to avoid jailtime or taxes.

* All boldface legal terms are also defined in the Glossary.

[9] A notable defense lawyer from Wyoming with an engaging courtroom presence, Gerry Spence represented clients ranging from the former Philippine First Lady Imelda Marcos, to the family of antinuclear activist Karen Silkwood. He wrote *With Justice For None: Destroying an American Myth* (New York: Times Books, 1989) and *The Making of a Country Lawyer* (New York: St.Martin's Press, 1996).

[10] Founder of the Houston law firm Haynes and Fullenweider, Richard "Racehorse" Haynes became widely known for his uncanny ability to influence juries with his homespun style. Perhaps his most notable case involved representing multimillionaire Texas businessman T. Cullen Davis, acquitted of murder and attempted murder.

[11] Alan Dershowitz, Felix Frankfurter Professor of Law at Harvard Law School, gained national fame for the remarkable success he enjoyed in defending unpopular clients. Among his most well-known works are *The Best Defense* (New York: Random House, 1982), recounting some of his most interesting cases and *Reasonable Doubts: The O. J. Simpson Case and the Criminal Justice System* (New York: Simon & Schuster, 1996).

[12] A well-known defense lawyer and author of *For the Defense* (New York: Atheneum, 1975), among other works, F. Lee Bailey helped to defend Dr. Sam Shepherd, heiress Patty Hearst, and football star O. J. Simpson, among many other prominent clients. Bailey also served as a lead counsel in the lawsuits after the Soviet Union shot down Korean Airlines Flight 007 and in suits filed after the pesticide plant disaster in Bhopal, India.

[13] Mary Ann Glendon, *A Nation Under Lawyers: How the Crisis in the Legal Profession Is Transforming American Society* (New York: Farrar, Straus & Giroux, 1994), p. 8.

People from all walks of life resent the high fees that the legal profession charges ordinary citizens. A common and bitter complaint is that America is extraordinarily litigious. People are amazed that a woman would sue McDonald's for serving scalding coffee, that an accountant would bring a lawsuit for $38 in expenses against a woman who stood him up on a planned date,[14] that one investment banker would sue a colleague for failing to warn him of an errant golf shot by yelling "Fore" before the ball struck him,[15] that a three-year-old girl and her mother would take a three-year-old boy and his mother to court over a minor altercation in a sandbox![16]

Many people scorn the so-called **ambulance-chasers,** lawyers who aggressively file lawsuits to recover money for claims of dubious merit. Others deride lawyers who act as **hired guns,** that is, who offer themselves to the highest bidder like unscrupulous cowboys in the old West. Many dismiss the legal profession as one that feeds on the misfortunes of others. While Americans applaud doctors for serving society, whatever the unpopularity or dubious moral character of their patients, Americans frequently identify lawyers with their clients and blame them for their clients' sins.[17] Increasingly, citizens link rising crime rates, in part, to an inefficient legal system that in too many cases neither promptly nor sufficiently punishes criminals.

Yet, while Americans may criticize their country's administration of justice, they look even more skeptically upon legal systems in which the prosecution almost always prevails and appeals normally go nowhere. In that regard most Americans would not trade their legal system, for all its faults, for that in China or Cuba or even for the systems in Asian democracies like Japan or Singapore, in which respect for the authority of the state often places the defense counsel at a considerable disadvantage even when he or she has a strong argument to advance.

Moreover, while Americans tend to be suspicious, skeptical, and cynical about the role of lawyers in their legal system, they tend to view judges much more positively. Of course, since judges make weighty and difficult decisions, they too are sometimes bitterly criticized. A judge who frees a criminal suspect after the police have violated the U.S. Constitution in collecting evidence may be said to be too soft on crime. Another, who sentences the convicted harshly, may be dismissed as part of a biased "Establishment" by the friends, family, neighbors, or others who share class or racial bonds with the defendant. Still another judge who rules against a long-battered wife who finally struck back and injured her abusive husband might be called reactionary or out of step with modern society. Despite such continuing controversies, however, many view the judiciary as a whole as one of the more respectable, admirable, and incorruptible American professions. In the United

[14] Ibid., pp. 257–258, 264. A judge threw this claim out of court.

[15] See "Golfer Didn't Speak Up, May Have to Pay Up," *Washington Post,* Mar. 13, 1996, p. D2.

[16] See "Stacey Versus Jonathan: Once in the Sandbox, Now in Court," *Washington Post,* Mar. 9, 1996, p. A1.

[17] See Lloyd Paul Stryker, *The Art of Advocacy: A Plea for the Renaissance of the Trial Lawyer* (New York: Simon & Schuster, 1954), pp. 214–215.

States, the lawyer has long since lost social dignity; the judge has maintained an aura of honor.

Today, a psychologist might conclude that Americans have a "love-hate" relationship with their legal system. Despite frequent and acerbic criticism, one widely popular television series followed the professional and personal lives of attorneys working at a fictional law firm in Los Angeles. Indeed, the drama of an actual courtroom attracts Americans for all it can reveal about society. One trial lawyer wrote:

> Except perhaps for the confessional of a priest, there is no better vantage ground for the study of mankind than a court of justice. There is no seat where humanity reveals itself more clearly than in the witness chair. There is no better laboratory for the dissection of human character and motives than the crowded scene that daily is unfolded before some judge and jury . . . [who must try] to distinguish between sincerity and sham, the genuine and the spurious, truth and falsity, half-truths and those undiluted.[18]

Years ago, American humorist Damon Runyon perceptively observed: "A big murder trial possesses some of the elements of a sporting event. I find the same popular interest . . . that I find . . . on the eve of a big football game, or . . . [boxing match], or a baseball series. There is the same conversational speculation on the probable result, only more of it."[19] Certainly, from 1994 through 1996 the investigation and criminal and civil trials of O. J. Simpson dominated the news for month after month.

Under the influence of Hollywood and the media, as well as through personal experience, the average American seems to view lawyers and the legal system as simultaneously glamorous and repulsive. Each year another 50,000 university students take the Law School Aptitude Test in hopes of becoming a lawyer, and each year American law schools confer degrees on more than 35,000 graduating students.[20] While many Americans shake their heads in disbelief at the steadily growing ranks of American lawyers, many of them are also employing those lawyers to carry out a wide variety of tasks. And, while many rue the extent to which the tentacles of American law enter and disrupt their lives, they are quick to suggest that society use new laws to cure its ills. One scholar observed: "The same citizens who want to get annoying regulations out of their own lives often believe that the way to deal with a broad range of social problems is to bring a lawsuit, to criminalize unwanted activity, or to augment the power of police and prosecutors."[21]

[18] Ibid., p. 85.

[19] Jerome Frank, *Courts on Trial: Myth and Reality in American Justice* (Princeton, NJ: Princeton University Press, 1973), p. 91.

[20] From 1980 to 1991 law schools conferred between 35,000 and 37,900 law degrees annually. *Statistical Abstract of the United States* (Washington, DC: U.S. Government Printing Office, 1994), p. 191.

[21] Glendon, p. 262. Glendon went on to observe: "One day we complain of suffocating in a regulatory miasma; on the next we ransack the legal cupboard for nostrums to rectify every wrong, to ward off every risk, and to cure every social and economic ill." Ibid., p. 270.

Popular perspectives on the American legal system thus take on a contradictory, perhaps even paradoxical, nature. Exploring why that might be the case is one continuing theme of this book.

The Aspirations of American Society

Over the centuries Americans have come to view fairness and justice as entitlements owed them by their society.[22] Nineteenth-century Americans went without insurance and bankruptcy protection, disaster-relief funds, and the many protections offered by a welfare state. When accidents occurred, crops failed, and untimely deaths occurred, people blamed fate and, often, turned to religion for succor. American society had not yet developed the urge to immediately try to ascertain what caused the tragedy, determine who might be held legally responsible, and fully compensate the victims or survivors.

In addition, many Americans seem increasingly to view the personal decency, discretion, and good judgment of all those they interact with to be something to which they are legally entitled. In some eras of American history insults, rudeness, discourtesy, and lack of respect might be ignored; in others they might invite a punch in the nose; in still others an insult might bring on efforts by friends, neighbors, educators, police, or religious leaders to bring about an apology or an effort to "talk it out." These days too many Americans expect a lawsuit or a new law to resolve such situations and to deter others from so acting in the future. If many want to use the law as a salve for hurt feelings,[23] even more want to employ it to redress grievances, however petty, that arise from the mistakes, bad manners, or poor judgment of others.

Today, Americans have much higher expectations for how law might be used to bring justice into people's lives. The American people set high goals for their legal system—some would say "impossibly high goals"—and, consequently, they are often disappointed by the extent to which the system falls short of their expectations. Yet even those who most strongly condemn the legal system often find themselves relying on an attorney to accomplish complex legal tasks that the ordinary citizen lacks the requisite expertise to accomplish alone. To list just a few of the myriad tasks that lawyers routinely perform, Americans customarily call on an attorney when starting a business, buying or selling real estate, firing an employee, appealing an adverse decision regarding their taxes, writing a will or **probating** it

[22] This point echoes that made by Lawrence Friedman in Steven Keeva, "Demanding More Justice: Whether Americans Get What They Want from the Legal System Depends on Its Ability to Stretch Limited Resources," *ABA Journal* 80 (Aug. 1994): 49. See also Inis L. Claude, Jr., "Compensatory Justice and Multinational Corporations," in R. S. Khare, ed., *Issues in Compensatory Justice: The Bhopal Accident,* Working Paper no. 2 (Charlottesville, VA: Center for Advanced Studies, University of Virginia, 1987), pp. 44–47.

[23] Judith Martin, better known as the columnist Miss Manners, perceptively observed: "People who find rude but legally permitted behavior intolerable have attempted to expand the law to outlaw rudeness." Judith Martin, "The World's Oldest Virtue," *First Things* (May 1993): 25, cited in Glendon, p. 266.

(that is, proving its validity), arranging a **prenuptial agreement,** settling a divorce, or adopting a child.

Much more than many other political cultures, the American democratic tradition, with its extensive roots in English history, strongly emphasizes formalities, tradition, and order. Americans have long found law and lawyers, courts and judges to be essential to help an increasingly complex society and an ever more heterogeneous population deal with its many diverse problems without resorting to violence. Of all the modern technologically advanced societies that have developed since World War II, the United States combines one of the largest, wealthiest, and most transient populations with an extremely sophisticated economy. One result of this, perhaps, has been that the American method of administering justice, confusing even at the birth of the nation, has grown exceedingly complicated over time. As U.S. citizens marry, buy houses, go to work, suffer illnesses, have traffic accidents, fall victim to crime, and divide up **estates** at death, they have long characterized lawyers as "a necessary evil."[24]

The United States has also traditionally been a relatively open society that permits large numbers of foreigners to settle in the country. Indeed, by 1995 nearly 23 million Americans had been born in another country, almost 9 percent of the entire population.[25] At least ten countries—countries with remarkably diverse cultures—have recently contributed at least half a million persons to the present American population: Mexico, the Philippines, Cuba, El Salvador, Canada, Germany, China, the Dominican Republic, Korea, and Vietnam.

The American legal system attempts to create an orderly society in which people with widely diverse values and beliefs and from very different backgrounds might live together harmoniously. Law is used to try to provide a common social framework for families whose roots extend to cultures in virtually every continent. It aims to add a measure of cohesion and guidance to a society that lacks the natural order provided by an ancient civilization or a single common religion.

THE HISTORICAL DEVELOPMENT OF AMERICAN LAW

The ideal of the rule of law, as opposed to lawlessness or rule by a tyrannical minority, lies at the heart of American legal theory.[26] When the rule of law is supreme, the legal system guarantees individual rights and protects individuals from the actions of others and from abuse by the state. In a society that values law so highly, individuals can assert and defend their legal rights, and laws will define and limit the powers of the state. In such a system law guides daily life: bestowing benefits, forbidding harmful activity, providing rules and predictability, and ensuring security

[24] See Robert A. Carp and Ronald Stidham, *Judicial Process in America,* 3d ed. rev. (Washington, DC: Congressional Quarterly Press, 1996), p. 98.

[25] The statistics are drawn from the U.S. Census Bureau. See Spencer Rich, "U.S. Immigrant Population at Postwar High," *Washington Post,* Aug. 29, 1995, p. A1.

[26] For a sophisticated analysis of different views of the rule-of-law ideal see Ronald Dworkin, *A Matter of Principle* (Cambridge, MA: Harvard University Press, 1985), especially pp. 11–12.

and remedies for the citizens it protects. Thus, it establishes the authority of the state, but also limits that authority.

Constructing and maintaining a rule of law entails fashioning a legal framework, establishing effective law enforcement, and developing an independent judiciary. A rule-of-law system creates fair and predictable rules to govern interactions between private parties and to define the obligations of all citizens and of the government. Ideally, law is to be applied evenhandedly to all. Above all else, the legal system ought to provide a secure and safe environment in which citizens can freely pursue their interests and goals. Indeed, creating rules that establish a comfortable equilibrium between the rights and obligations of citizens and the requirements and responsibilities of the state stands as the most fundamental role that law plays in democratic societies.

If one understands that in the United States, and before that in England, people have historically used law to settle a wide spectrum of disputes, then it seems to be a natural development that modern Americans interacting in an exceptionally complicated society should look to law to resolve so many different matters. How does the American legal system differ from other systems around the world? How have America's legal institutions evolved?

Types of Legal Systems

Scholars customarily divide legal systems into **civil law systems** and **common law systems.** In civil law systems, such as those in continental Europe, Latin America, Scotland, and Japan, courts apply very extensive codes of laws to particular legal disputes. Rather than relying on how judges have customarily resolved similar legal issues on past occasions, civil law judges focus primarily upon applying the relevant portion of the code to the dispute. Thus, from at least the time that the Roman Emperor Justinian issued his historic code in A.D. 528, civil law systems have emphasized the responsibility of the government to pass all-encompassing codes and the duty of the courts to apply those codes faithfully to disputes before them.

Civil law systems are also marked by a very active and ultimately decisive role for the judge. Although the steps of a trial differ from country to country, normally an investigating judge in a civil law system receives a complaint about some unlawful act. If the complaint appears to be true and the illegal activity is significant, the judge calls upon a police force to investigate the case. If the facts call for a criminal trial, the first judge—called the **judge of instruction**—passes on the evidence to a **penal judge.**

During the trial, the penal judge confronts the accused person. Although the lawyers may suggest witnesses, the judge decides who shall testify in accordance with the objective of determining the truth in the matter. The judge then leads the questioning of the witnesses and oversees the gathering of relevant facts. During the proceedings the judge often comments on the weight of the evidence and the credibility of witnesses.[27]

[27] Henry J. Abraham, *The Judicial Process: An Introductory Analysis of the Courts of the United States, England, and France,* 6th ed. rev. (New York: Oxford University Press, 1993), p. 126.

Although the role of the **prosecutor** and **defense counsel** varies from one civil law system to another, and may include supplementary questioning of witnesses, the judge is ultimately in charge of discovering what actually happened and deciding whether the person on trial has committed an unlawful act and should be punished or has been unjustly accused and should be acquitted. Whereas one schooled in a common law system might object that a judge who takes such a leading part in a trial could not possibly conduct a trial impartially,[28] one schooled in a civil law system might respond that since the judge should have the most experienced perspective in the courtroom it makes eminently good sense for the judge to take responsibility for making the ultimate decision of guilt or innocence.

Commentators often say that a typical civil law legal system operates in an **inquisitorial manner,** that is, the accused person is put on trial after substantial incriminating evidence has already been collected. At that point, the accused must convince the court that he or she actually did not commit the crime. Rather than advancing the interests of the client, the lawyer in a civil law system is chiefly concerned with seeing that justice is done. Moreover, the civil law process of proving guilt or innocence is not typically subject to the many detailed rules of civil and criminal procedure and evidence that one finds governing trials in most common law systems. A civil law trial is not so much a legal contest as an endeavor to discover the truth.

A typical civil law legal system contrasts markedly with a typical common law legal system such as those found in many English-speaking countries: the United States and England, Australia and New Zealand, India, and those Caribbean islands with an English heritage. Although both systems aim to find the truth, to apply the relevant law, and to punish wrongdoers, a common law system sets up an adversarial contest between the lawyers on each side. The lawyers bear the chief responsibility for drawing out the facts and legal issues in the case by investigating the allegations, calling, examining, and cross-examining **witnesses** at trial, and filing **briefs** when appropriate. In a criminal proceeding the government prosecutor squares off against the accused person, called the criminal **defendant,** and his or her defense lawyer. In a civil trial, the **plaintiff** faces the civil defendant, against whom a **civil complaint** or **suit** has been brought, both sides being represented by legal counsel.

In common law adversarial systems the prosecutor decides whether to charge an individual with a crime. In the United States, the prosecutor, at both state and federal levels, is granted the power to determine whether or not to bring criminal charges against an individual. Such **prosecutorial discretion** is a weighty responsibility that contributes to making the prosecutor a very powerful individual in any American **county** or state. Although prosecutors are usually selected with regard for their integrity and qualifications, prosecutorial discretion is occasionally abused. For the most part, this happens in politically sensitive cases in which the prosecutor refrains from filing charges despite substantial evidence of guilt or hurries to file charges even without the evidence necessary to prove guilt beyond a rea-

[28] Prominent defense attorney Lloyd Paul Stryker made this point. See Stryker, p. 75.

sonable doubt. Although the defendant in such a case is often ultimately vindicated, the costs in legal fees and in damage to the person's reputation can be staggering.

In this type of common law adversarial system, after initiating charges, the prosecutor, not the judge, works with police to investigate the case. And, the prosecutor and the defense lawyer, not the judge, question witnesses at trial.[29] Because of these characteristics, common law legal systems are said to determine guilt by an **accusatorial** method, rather than an inquisitorial one. The government through a prosecutor accuses a person of committing a crime. The defense counsel is charged with saying all that could honestly be said on behalf of the client's legal position.[30] The decision maker, either judge or jury, then assumes that the person on trial is innocent, unless the state can prove guilt **beyond a reasonable doubt.**

Incidentally, the term *common law legal system* is not used literally to mean a legal system that relies solely, or even primarily, on the common law. Rather, whether the proceeding is a civil or a criminal trial, judges in a common law country concern themselves with the laws (or **statutes**) passed by the legislature, and with the constitution, if the country has one, along with the common law. Civil law judges, by contrast, refer solely to codes of law. Perhaps the key distinction is that common law judges apply the law, or instruct the **jury** as to the law, only after inquiring into **precedent,** that is, determining how other judges resolved similar issues in the past. Civil law judges are far less concerned with such matters.

One scholar wrote:

> [T]he common law judge is supposed to be a virtuoso of practical reason, weaving together the threads of fact and law, striving not only for a fair disposition of the dispute at hand but to decide each case with reference to a principle that transcends the facts of that case—all with a view toward maintaining continuity with past decisions, deciding like cases alike, and providing guidance for other parties similarly situated; and all in the spirit of caring for the good of the legal order itself and the polity it serves."[31]

Separation of Powers and Federalism

Since the American legal system encompasses state courts as well as national courts, it is called a **dual court system.** This feature sharply distinguishes the American judicial system from the **unitary court system** that is found in many other countries, in which a single network of courts hears all the legal disputes that arise. Rather than relying upon the more common and simple unitary system, the United States

[29] Judges do occasionally question a witness, for instance, when they feel a trial is going awry or a jury is lost, but they typically leave the course of the examination to the attorneys.

[30] Stryker, p. 277. Stryker further observed: "No man or woman is so bad that something good could not honestly be said about him. Even the very bad may not be guilty of the crime of which they are charged."

[31] Glendon, pp. 180–181.

developed its complicated dual court system for both historical and philosophical reasons.

Before the United States gained its independence from Great Britain, the King of England through his governors ruled the colonies strung along the east coast of the continent. Although each colony attracted immigrants and tended to develop its own customs and style of law enforcement and limited self-government, the governors exercised ultimate executive, legislative, and judicial authority. After the American Revolution, the new states loosely bound themselves together under the **Articles of Confederation,** a weak system of national government that failed to provide for a national judicial branch. Within a decade, however, a political consensus favored a constitutional arrangement that would unite the states more closely than had been possible in a mere **confederation,** and that would thus provide a stronger national government.

Nevertheless, the abiding fear of an unduly powerful national government led the Founding Fathers to create a decentralized system in which the distinctive political and legal traditions of the states might be respected. The Founders sensed that a single court system would concentrate judicial power in the hands of the U.S. Supreme Court. But public sentiment favored the idea that each state would rely on its own judicial system to govern its legal affairs. Thus, in order to nurture the different approaches to law and politics that had already developed in the various states since the colonial period, the U.S. Constitution permitted each state to retain its own state court system, with different responsibilities from the national court system.

The courts instituted by the Founders thus featured two important principles of early American political philosophy: the **division of powers** (that is, dividing power between the state and federal governments) and the **separation of powers** (that is, separating power among executive, legislative, and judicial branches). Each was derived from lessons of American colonial history.

During the colonial era the British had granted each American colony its own legislature with strictly limited powers. Yet, despite this measure of self-government, American politicians in those colonial legislatures soon began to quarrel with representatives of the British king over taxes and other public-policy issues. The colonists eventually demanded direct representation in British politics through the election of American politicians to the British Parliament. When the King refused this demand, American leaders began to call for outright independence, rather than mere representation in the British government.

After the Revolutionary War secured independence for America, the Founding Fathers remembered clearly how English kings and their governors had acted arbitrarily and unreasonably in governing the American people. As a result, the Founders wanted to be sure to divide and separate political power in the new country. They believed that government would be more accountable to the people and less subject to abuse if no single individual, indeed, no single center of governmental authority, held ultimate power.

This historical experience helped to frame for Americans the philosophical principle that political power in a democracy ought to be split among different levels of government, local, state, and federal, and among different political units or institutions.[32] Consequently, the U.S. Constitution divides political power between the federal government and the state governments and grants different sets of rights and duties to the president, the Congress, and the judiciary. The creation of separate state and national court systems may be viewed as yet another method used to allocate power among different centers of authority to ensure that no single branch of government becomes too powerful.

In the United States, the government of each state exists separate from and independent of the federal government. While local governments exist separate from the state governments, they depend upon the states for their existence and, in certain respects, can be considered instrumentalities of the states. Nevertheless, each level of American government—national, state, and local—can raise money through taxes and spend that money as it wishes. This form of government is called **federal,** a system of divided political power in which different governments exercise different realms of authority over the same territory.

While Americans often argue over questions of political philosophy such as the extent to which the national government should encroach on traditional state powers, few question the basic scheme of a government divided into different levels. Under federalism the national government in Washington, DC focuses much of its attention on matters that concern the entire United States. At the same time, each state has a capital city of its own, with its own state government and its own sphere of responsibility. State governments have delegated many important powers to the thousands of local governments that attend to purely local matters.

So, the laws passed by the national government in Washington, DC will determine certain matters for a person who lives in the city of Los Angeles in the state of California. The state government in Sacramento will decide other highly significant issues, and the city government in Los Angeles will make laws that affect that person's life in still other ways. The central idea of America's complicated scheme of **federalism** is that the national, state, and local governments will each share legislative power.

Those being introduced to the American system of government often marvel at the confusion of such a federal system. In fact, although a federal system of government can be quite complex, certain rules help to eliminate some of the confusion by designating when one level of government is supreme. For instance, only the federal government can sign treaties with foreign countries,[33] and only state governments can tax a property owner's real estate. Thus, California is not permitted to conclude a treaty with Japan, and no American pays a property tax to the national government.

[32] For a work exploring the early development of federalist principles see Stanley Elkins and Eric McKitrick, *The Age of Federalism: The Early American Republic, 1788–1800* (New York: Oxford University Press, 1993).

[33] For other prohibitions regarding the authority of states see Article I, Section 10 of the U.S. Constitution.

Yet, while each level of government lacks authority in certain areas, both the state and the federal governments are permitted to pass laws regarding most subjects. This, of course, raises problems when a federal law and a state law overlap or conflict. Two rules help to determine which law takes precedence. First, when a state law does not meet certain minimum standards of fairness found in the U.S. Constitution, perhaps by failing to provide citizens with **due process of law** or **equal protection of law,**[34] the U.S. Supreme Court can find that state law to be unconstitutional. Thus, the words of the U.S. Constitution take precedence over a conflicting state law.

In addition, the **federal preemption doctrine** may dictate that federal legislation supersedes state legislation.[35] The U.S. Supreme Court has held that federal laws will take precedence over state laws on matters that are primarily national, rather than local, in nature. Consequently, the federal preemption doctrine bars a state from passing a law that is inconsistent with a federal law regarding a national matter. As these examples illustrate, while federalism is not a simple method of governing a country, certain rules—broadly familiar to educated Americans—help to minimize the confusion by determining which authority takes precedence under particular circumstances.

Today, federalism has developed into one national government, fifty state governments, tens of thousands of local governments, and a handful of odd cases such as those found in the territories of Puerto Rico, Guam, American Samoa, the Virgin Islands, and the Northern Mariana Islands. One might ask: Why did Americans decide to create all these governments, each with a different budget to spend and with different tasks to perform? Is this what early American political philosophers had in mind? Or, would they be astonished to see how federalism has developed?

Certainly, the division of responsibilities among all these different government bodies is not wholly illogical. Some small governments, like a local public school board, focus on political problems that affect a relatively small number of citizens, like choosing the proper books for the school children of that particular school district to read. Thus, the federal system grants people who may be suspicious of the national government the leeway to solve at least some of their own problems. At the same time, some larger government bodies, like the U.S. Congress, confront political problems that affect far more Americans, such as how to write national legislation that protects the national environment while disrupting American lives and businesses as minimally as possible.

[34] The Fourteenth Amendment to the U.S. Constitution states: "No State shall make or enforce any law which shall abridge the privileges and immunities of the citizens of the United States; nor shall any State deprive any person of life, liberty, or property, without due process of law; nor deny to any person within its jurisdiction the equal protection of the laws." U.S. Constitution, Amendment XIV.

[35] The U.S. Constitution states: "This Constitution, and the Laws of the United States which shall be made in Pursuance thereof; and all Treaties made, or which shall be made, under the Authority of the United States, shall be the supreme Law of the Land; and the Judges in every State shall be bound thereby, any Thing in the Constitution or Laws of any State to the Contrary notwithstanding." U.S. Constitution, Article VI, Section 2.

Yet, while the scope of the task to be accomplished may help to explain why this government structure emerged, the current scheme of American government came about primarily as a result of historical experience.[36] Citizens trying to solve problems, politicians competing for power, and vast historical movements sweeping over the country—these important forces shaped the division of power among the different governments that make up America's federal system.

Throughout American history states and the federal government have competed for power. As time passed, most major political crises were eventually resolved in favor of national power. Today, the federal government has become deeply involved in matters that many Americans once considered solely the business of individual states. For example, since state governments traditionally took responsibility for protecting the health and safety of their citizens, they frequently built and operated public hospitals, like the well-known Massachusetts General Hospital in Boston. However, as hospitals became more expensive to construct and to run, states began to ask the national government for financial assistance. Although the federal government often agreed to fund such state projects, the Congress then forced the states to agree to follow national regulations and guidelines.

So, by controlling funds, the national government continually increased its political power in fields as diverse as highway construction and environmental protection, and the states consequently lost some of the power they traditionally held. Since the strengths of a federal form of government include decentralized decision making and the freedom given to states and localities to experiment with their own schemes of government, this steady expansion of federal power has become increasingly controversial. How far should the power of the national government reach? How much power should be reserved to the states? While liberals tend to view the consolidation of national power as a natural response to problems that are national in scope, conservatives tend to believe that national decisionmakers already have too much power at the expense of their state counterparts.

While the long-term trend in American politics has clearly been in the direction of more and more national power, that trend has slowed and it may even be reversed should the national government prove incapable of solving problems that might better be handled at the state or local levels. Certainly, for decades a significant political movement has aimed to scale back the size and power of the national government. And, in recent years the states have gained control over matters ranging from setting speed limits to directing welfare programs.

One should remember, however, that states and localities were never powerless: They have long exercised many duties essential to their citizens. These smaller government bodies issue licenses, regulate businesses, supervise professions, administer education systems, and oversee state and county law enforce-

[36] This argument is drawn from Lawrence M. Friedman, *A History of American Law,* 2d ed. rev. (New York: Simon & Schuster, 1985), pp. 656–662.

ment.[37] The national government has never attempted to regulate and control all antisocial behavior by citizens and groups or to manage all government services. State and local governments, although declining in importance relative to the national government through much of the twentieth century, have always passed and enforced or implemented legislation affecting critical facets of life in the United States.

LAW, LAWYERS, AND AMERICAN SOCIETY

To become familiar with the nature of the legal system in the United States, one must know something of American law, the role of the participants, and the history of legal institutions. How is law actually used in American society? What different bodies of law exist, and what are their sources?

To understand better how we use law in daily life, I will next sketch out several legal issues that a lawyer in the United States might consider in the course of a day's work. Since laws differ substantially from state to state, I offer the following examples simply to illustrate the varieties of common legal problems and to give the reader the flavor of typical legal advice. Anyone actually confronting similar legal circumstances would, of course, need to check carefully their own state law to determine the best approach to their problem.

A Real Estate Question

A typical day for an attorney starts with the phone ringing. A **client**—that is, someone who hires a lawyer to help with a legal problem—is calling for advice. Suppose that the client is a woman whom the lawyer helped to write a **will** some months before. Now, she would like legal counsel concerning a real estate question.

Two months ago this client spoke with her neighbor and promised to sell him a piece of land that he could use for a baseball field for his child's team. Since the neighbor did not yet have sufficient funds to buy the property, the two agreed to all the terms of the property sale, shook hands to seal the deal, and scheduled a meeting for next week to exchange the agreed sum for title to the land.

As time has passed, however, the client has changed her mind. She wants to give that land to a family member who would like to build a house there, rather than sell it to her neighbor. However, she is concerned that her oral agreement

[37] Friedman noted:

> State law remains vigorous. The states continue to have the last word in much . . . private law: the law of ordinary commerce, tort law, property law, the law of marriage and divorce. States and cities make up and enforce thousands of simple, ordinary rules that affect the daily life of the average person. They draft building codes, plumbing codes, and electrical codes for cities and towns. They devise speed limits and set out parking zones. They regulate dry cleaners, license plumbers, and dictate the open hunting season. . . . They control the right to marry, to own a dog, to sell vegetables, to open a [bar]. . . . [T]hey share with the federal government rule-making responsibility over schools. . . . They also . . . [run] the welfare system." Ibid., p. 660.

with her neighbor might be considered legally binding. The client asks her attorney: "Can I give the land to my nephew, or do I have to sell the land to my neighbor as previously agreed?"

The lawyer will advise that the client is not obligated to sell the land to her neighbor, but can give it to her nephew instead.[38] In counselling this client, the lawyer relies on an old English law, which has been codified in the states and which American judges have cited in more or less modified form for many years, known as the **Statute of Frauds.** This ancient rule states that a valid contract regarding the sale of land must be in written form. In order for a buyer to enforce a promise to buy or sell land, the agreement must be written and signed.

The rationale for this rule is that an agreement as important as that governing the purchase of land should be written down, so that the parties clearly understand all the terms of the sale. Since the client and her neighbor never wrote down their oral agreement concerning the sale of the woman's land, no legally binding contract exists. Although the lawyer might counsel the client to consider carefully her future relations with her neighbor and her reputation in the neighborhood before she comes to a final decision, the lawyer will conclude that the client is free to give the land to a family member so long as no prior written agreement exists to sell it to someone else.

A Prisoner's Rights Question

The lawyer might well be jotting down the time spent explaining the Statute of Frauds to the first client, in order to send out a bill later in the week, when the phone rings again.

This time the caller is an official from the local **bar association,** that is, the group that supervises the professional conduct of attorneys in that state. The official had called earlier to ask the lawyer to volunteer to help prisoners with legal problems. She tells the lawyer that an interesting prisoner's rights case has just arisen, and she asks if the prisoner might call right away for legal counsel.

When the prisoner calls, he reports: "A year ago, a jury convicted me of robbing a grocery store, and I got a sentence of six years in jail. But the prison guards pick on me, and a month ago, for no reason, two of them said they were going to teach me a lesson. They put me in **solitary confinement** for two weeks. Isn't that against the law? Can you help me?"

The lawyer might well advise that the prisoner should consider suing the prison guards and the government, as their employer, for the injuries suffered. One possible ground for such a **prisoner's rights lawsuit** would be the Eighth Amendment to the U.S. Constitution, which states that no person shall suffer "cruel and unusual punishment." Such an arbitrary decision by prison guards,

[38] Under exceptional circumstances, the neighbor might be able to use the doctrine of **promissory estoppel** to compel enforcement of the oral agreement. For the doctrine to apply, an individual must have made a promise which he or she should have expected to induce some definite and substantial action by another. If the other person did so act, and if serious injustice would otherwise result, a court may declare the promise to be binding.

without according the prisoner due process of law, probably constitutes a constitutionally prohibited penalty. The court might award money damages to the prisoner to compensate him for being harmed by the guards. Equally important, the prison authorities might themselves respond to the case by disciplining, or even dismissing, the guards for their callous behavior. In the future the authorities might supervise all the guards more closely. Thus, even a prisoner could find a lawsuit to be quite beneficial to his or her interests.

An Environmental Question

After a "working lunch"—perhaps with a client negotiating the sale of her business to a large corporation—the lawyer sits down for the afternoon and the phone rings again. This time, perhaps, the client is a businessman who owns an underground storage tank containing gasoline used to fuel his company's trucks.

The businessman tells the lawyer: "Late last night an employee at the company discovered that a tank holding a very large amount of gasoline had developed a serious leak. He told me about the problem this morning, and I called the government office to report the leak right away. I thought the authorities would be happy to hear that I was reporting this accident, but the person I spoke with acted as though my company had done something wrong." The businessman wants his lawyer to advise him as to whether his company complied with the law in informing authorities of the leak.

The lawyer will respond that the company had not acted properly. Environmental laws obligate someone responsible for a leaking fuel tank to report the leak to the government's emergency office immediately so that the authorities can ensure that no danger exists for the community or the environment. Certain government offices are open every hour of every day to respond to such emergencies, and anyone working with fuel should know whom to contact if a leak occurs. Thus, the employee failed to abide by the law because he went home to sleep and waited until the following morning to report the leaking tank.

The lawyer would also be likely to advise the businessman to do everything possible to ensure that the fuel leak does not cause any further environmental damage. For instance, in some states the company might send to the site a state-authorized environmental cleanup firm to contain and remove the leaked gasoline. To minimize its liability to future lawsuits, the company should take appropriate steps to ensure that the employee's mistake causes no additional harm. The businessman might also be well advised to determine whether the costs of the accident might be ameliorated by the insurance company with which his business carries a comprehensive **general liability policy.**

A Divorce Question

In the course of the afternoon our attorney would be likely to field various other calls. The president of a small company might want to know about new laws that the state legislature just passed. She asks her lawyer: "In order to comply with the new laws, do I need to change the way my factory operates?" A second call might be from a partnership that is trying to settle a problem with its insurance company. The insurance company has offered a cash settlement of the dispute, perhaps $30,000. The managing partner wants the lawyer to advise whether the partnership should accept the $30,000 settlement or try to win $100,000 in court. A third call might come from a well-known author, who has been offered a contract on a new book from a major publishing house. The author wants his attorney to review the proposed contract and advise whether he should accept its terms or negotiate revisions.

Late in the afternoon, while investigating the caselaw that might be relevant to his new prisoner's rights lawsuit, the lawyer finds the phone ringing once more. This time the client, a man whose marriage is failing, says his wife has treated him and their children very badly. Since the marriage, she has never worked outside the home. She criticizes him constantly, drinks heavily, and ignores most of the housework.

The client reports that he no longer loves his wife and has temporarily separated from her. He is now considering divorce. But he wonders whether a judge would be likely to award her one-half of their property. The client, now a very wealthy man, had almost no money at the time of his marriage, but has now earned millions of dollars. He certainly does not want his wife to gain half of his earnings in a divorce judgment. He asks his lawyer: "If I decide to divorce my wife, will a court automatically award her one-half of all the property I earned during the marriage?"

The answer to this question depends upon where the parties are living. Certain states, mostly in the western and southwestern parts of the United States, have enacted **community property laws.**[39] These laws state, in essence, that at the time of a divorce one-half of the property that the couple gained during the course of the marriage belongs to the husband and one-half to the wife, regardless of which partner actually earned the income or otherwise brought in the assets.[40] Only property acquired before the marriage or inherited by, or given to, one spouse during the marriage would not be subject to the fifty-fifty split. The rationale for such community property laws is that normally the spouse who is not increasing the couple's assets is working within the home and providing logistical and moral support that should help the income-producing spouse to succeed.

In most states, however, each spouse owns whatever he or she earned. Typically, the judge decides how to divide the property by considering what the husband and the wife each contributed during the course of the marriage. If one of them worked hard inside and outside the home while the other contributed little, the one who put forth the most effort is entitled to receive most of the property. In

[39] States that have passed community property laws include Arizona, California, Idaho, Louisiana, Nevada, New Mexico, Oregon, Texas, Washington, and Wisconsin.

[40] For an overview of modern reforms in this corner of family law see Herbert Jacob, *Silent Revolution: The Transformation of Divorce Law in the United States* (Chicago: University of Chicago Press, 1988).

making that determination, the court will consider not just who earned the most money, but also who spent the most time raising the children, cleaning the house, and attending to the other matters that enabled the salary earner to prosper.

The lawyer will advise this client (assuming that they are not in a community-property state) that the court will not automatically divide the property in half during the divorce. If the husband can prove that his wife contributed very little to the marriage, the court is not likely to require him to give her anywhere near one-half of the property.

So ends a more or less typical day for our lawyer.

DIVERSE BODIES OF LAW

This typical day in an American lawyer's life illustrates several ideas about the legal system. Plainly, many Americans bring law into diverse areas of their daily lives, and many American lawyers deal with a wide range of problems during the course of a day's work. Although attorneys in large **law firms** have become increasingly specialized at ever earlier stages in their careers, most American lawyers do not concentrate exclusively on one area of law. Rather, they practice in firms of five or fewer lawyers and, hence, must be prepared to handle a spectrum of legal disputes.

One might also note that the answer to each of the questions posed by the lawyer's clients came from a different body of law. In fact, American law is derived from various sources: statutes, the common law, and the U.S. Constitution. The American legal system draws on a fascinating mixture of laws. Just as the English language has adopted words from many foreign languages, in much the same way American law has adopted ideas from the legal traditions of many different countries.[41] To illustrate that idea, one might think back to the four primary phone calls that the lawyer received.

The Common Law

The first client called her lawyer to find out whether she could give land to her nephew or had to sell it to her neighbor, as had been previously agreed to orally. The answer depended on an old English law called the Statute of Frauds, a law that requires people buying and selling land to put their agreements in writing. The Statute of Frauds illustrates one important source of American law: the common law.

The **common law** may be thought of as the traditional law of England. The English people did not have extensive **codes of law,** that is, systematic collections of written laws, such as the French *Code civil* initially organized by Napoleon

[41] Friedman wrote (p. 18) that American English is a fascinating mixture of sounds and phrases: very old English mixes with modern slang, words with roots in Latin find themselves in the same sentence with French phrases or Spanish words. Indeed, despite the vast differences between language, culture, and history in Japan and the United States, an educated American is likely to be familiar with such Japanese words as "samurai," "honcho," "haiku," "karaoke," "kimono," and "hibachi."

Bonaparte, or the civil, commercial, and criminal codes found in Japan. Instead, English law courts depended heavily on legal customs common to the English people. From one generation to the next, judges handed down customary principles of law in written decisions. When a legal dispute arose, the lawyers would decide how to argue their side of the case by reading how judges had dealt with similar issues in the past.

In deciding how to resolve the dispute, the judge would focus on the traditional principles of law relied upon by other judges in similar circumstances and on the writings of legal scholars who explained the logic behind those decisions. One observer recently noted: "Application of the common law always depends on the circumstances: The accident caused by swerving to avoid the child is excusable; falling asleep at the wheel is not. The most important standard is what a reasonable person would have done. Every principle has exceptions. More than anything else, the common law glorifies the particular situation and invites common sense."[42]

To this day, common law judges rely heavily on precedent—legal principles derived from prior decisions in cases resembling the dispute at hand. The doctrine of ***stare decisis,*** or "stand by what has been decided," states that when a court has finally ruled that some principle of law should properly be interpreted as applying to a particular dispute in a particular manner, it should apply that same reasoning to future cases involving similar disputes. Respect for *stare decisis* is thought to encourage law-abiding behavior by helping people to specify precisely and consistently what the law is and by demonstrating that the law is applied in the same way to all.

Since the common law develops through decisions in one case after another, common law legal principles tend to be narrowly drawn and closely bound to particular facts. While the body of common law changes over time, it normally does so pragmatically in an unhurried, incremental, evolutionary manner. One scholar explained: "Over centuries that saw the rise and fall of feudalism, the expansion of commerce, and the transition to constitutional monarchy and representative government, judges and lawyers adapted English law to each new circumstance, neither erasing prior arrangements completely nor becoming captives of them. Parliament made relatively few efforts to hasten or force the process. Its enactments, for the most part, were like patches here and there against the background of the judge-made law . . ."[43]

However, when courts ignore *stare decisis* and act unpredictably, the law loses coherence. Judges face conflicting precedents, and lawyers find it difficult to "give reliable advice to clients who are trying to plan for the future, or to decide whether to prosecute, [bring], defend, or settle claims."[44] Although judges in a

[42] Philip K. Howard, *The Death of Common Sense: How Law Is Suffocating America* (New York: Warner Books, 1994), p. 23. Howard continued: "Justice Benjamin Cardozo, considered the greatest common law judge of this century, said in the 1920s that the common law 'is at bottom the philosophy of pragmatism. Its truth is relative, not absolute.'" Ibid.

[43] Glendon, p. 180.

[44] Ibid., p. 166.

common law system do sometimes overturn precedents that they believe were wrongly decided, in the United States such **reversals** are unusual matters that may eventually be considered by the ultimate **court of appeals**—either the U.S. Supreme Court or the highest court of a particular state. In any event, that process of legal decision making in which a judge looks back toward ancient legal principles to guide his or her actions in a current dispute constitutes the basis of the common law.

A student being introduced to American law might next ask: If the common law was the law of England, why is it now important in the United States? The first large influx of early immigrants came to America from England: some were lawyers; all spoke English; many were steeped in the common law tradition. Thus, as English immigrants settled in this new land, they organized their societies on the basis of the familiar legal concepts of their former home. Even in the decades just before the American Revolution many young American lawyers received their training at the **Inns of Court** in London.[45]

Modern American law has thus incorporated many principles that may be traced to English common law roots. Although statutes have overridden certain common law precepts, as when modern consumer protection laws nullified the common law doctrine of **caveat emptor,**[46] meaning "let the buyer beware," to this day American lawyers rely upon some of the most important legal customs of England. The common law, with legal principles like those found in the Statute of Frauds, remains one important source of American law.

The U.S. Constitution

The second case our lawyer considered concerned the prisoner placed in solitary confinement at the whim of two prison guards. The advice given by the lawyer in that case depended upon yet another source of American law—the U.S. Constitution.

Originally English colonists, Americans declared themselves independent in 1776. But this Declaration of Independence and the accompanying Revolutionary War against Great Britain led to a troublesome period. Over time, the most perceptive American politicians came to believe that the security of the thirteen states would improve and substantial economic and political benefits might also accrue if they were bound together in a more cohesive unit. In 1787 a group of prominent Americans met in Philadelphia to write a constitution that would bind together the states in order to form a single unified nation and to lay out essential ground rules to govern political, commercial, and security matters within the country.

[45] One authority noted: "Between 1760 and the Revolution, a hundred and fifteen American students were educated at the Inns of Court. Five signers of the Declaration of Independence, five delegates to the Continental Congress which adopted the Articles of Confederation, and six of the signatories of the United States Constitution were graduates of the Middle Temple." Stryker, p. 264.

[46] James V. Calvi and Susan Coleman, *American Law and Legal Systems,* 2d ed. (Englewood Cliffs, NJ: Prentice Hall, 1992), p. 14.

Those who frame a constitution, including America's Founding Fathers, aim to describe the structure of the new government, its powers, important qualifications and limits to its powers, the most fundamental rights and duties of the citizens, and the process by which the document might be amended in the future. Over time, of course, the body of constitutional law grows far beyond the words of any constitution and its amendments to encompass all the caselaw developed by judges applying the constitution to particular legal issues. In 1791, Congress added to the U.S. Constitution the Eighth Amendment: the constitutional prohibition against inflicting cruel and unusual punishment on prisoners. Within the caselaw interpreting that provision are decisions calling for the protection of the due process rights of a prisoner before he or she is placed in solitary confinement.

So, the second phone call illustrated that, along with the common law, the U.S. Constitution provides another very significant source of American law directly relevant to resolving actual disputes.

Statutory Law

The third case involved the owner of a company whose employee discovered a petroleum leak but who went home to bed and reported the leak to the authorities the following morning. The lawyer concluded that the employee had violated American law by not immediately reporting the accident to the government's emergency office. Plainly, the resolution of that legal problem depended upon some source of law other than the English common law. No centuries-old English legal custom could possibly concern gasoline leaks, since gasoline was not used before the late nineteenth century.[47]

Instead, the lawyer in the third case relied on what is called **statutory law.** In the United States statutory laws are passed by the Congress or by state governments. While the bills passed by state and federal legislators are called **statutes,** laws passed by cities and counties are usually referred to as **ordinances.** Both statutes and ordinances are part of American statutory law. Although often organized into collections for indexing purposes, statutory law differs from the codes of civil law countries. For the most part, legislators in the United States pass law in a piecemeal fashion, rather than attempting to frame an entire code of laws that comprehensively covers a broad subject, such as the rights and duties of property and business owners.

Moreover, frequently legislators drafting a statute will prohibit certain conduct in general terms. They will then leave to **administrative agencies** the task of filling in the details of the law with appropriate **regulations.** In this case the rules

[47] It is true that broadly analogous circumstances did occur in the distant past when activities on one landowner's property had adverse consequences for some neighboring landowner. For instance, one farmer might dam a stream, and an ensuing flood might ruin crops on some other farmer's land. Such developments may well have helped to shape the responsibilities that legislatures imposed upon property owners involved in gasoline leaks and other such difficulties.

regarding leaking underground storage tanks would likely be derived from regulations issued by the particular state's department of environmental protection or similar agency.

So, alongside the venerable principles and evolving interpretations of the common law and the Constitution, American law also includes much statutory law, law passed by the U.S. Congress and state legislatures. In addition, federal and state agencies and local governing bodies are often granted important rule-making powers. The third phone call illustrated, therefore, the statutory source of much of American law and the manner in which lawyers must be familiar with national and state laws and administrative regulations.

Foreign Influences on American Law

The final problem that faced our attorney involved the question of property in a divorce case. In states that have adopted community property laws, the possessions acquired by a husband and wife during their marriage are divided equally after a divorce. In states without such laws, the statutes dealing with divorce typically rely upon the court to determine how much each spouse contributed to the marriage and, hence, how the property should be divided.

Community property laws furnish one example of the legal traditions brought by immigrants to the United States. The American idea of community property grew out of laws regarding marriage and divorce in Mexico. Since many millions of Mexican people settled in Texas, New Mexico, Arizona, and California, these western states came to adopt certain principles of Mexican law, such as the idea of community property.[48]

This same process of adopting foreign legal traditions has occurred elsewhere in the United States. As different nationalities came to live in America, leaving their former homes in England, France, the Netherlands, and many other countries, each group of immigrants arrived with its own legal traditions. Over time, legislators incorporated certain of these traditions into American statutes, as with the Mexican and Latin American community property laws. Other foreign notions influenced federal and state constitutions. Indeed, the very notion of a constitution may be traced, not to England, but to European political philosophy in the Enlightenment period of the seventeenth and eighteenth centuries.

A host of foreign legal ideas has thus influenced the way that the American system functions. Louisiana, originally a French possession, still uses a civil code that resembles one found in France. The idea of a **district attorney,** one type of prosecutor, came from Dutch emigrants to the United States.[49] In certain significant respects the preliminary **information** hearing, which has replaced the

[48] Friedman, pp. 19–20. In *A History of American Law,* Friedman traces the influence of Spanish, Mexican, French, and Dutch law on the development of American law. For an earlier version of this same argument see Roscoe Pound, *The Formative Era of American Law* (Boston: Little, Brown, 1938), pp. 94–95.

[49] Friedman, pp. 19–20.

grand jury in many states, resembles hearings before investigating judges in continental Europe.[50] The increasing specialization of American trial practice may be coming to resemble the British system in which a different category of attorneys, the **barristers,** argue all important cases. Thus, just as American popular cuisine now includes "pizza" and "spaghetti" from Italy, "sauerkraut" and "wienerschnitzel" from Germany, "nachos" and "tacos" from Mexico, "sushi" and "teriyaki" from Japan, and "lo mein" and "wontons" from China, so American law now includes distinct ingredients from various cultures.[51]

THE EVOLUTION OF AMERICAN LAW

Scholars often refer to the Anglo-American legal tradition, and rightly so: American law is linked closely to English law in many respects. Yet, to suit the changing needs of the people, American law has grown in its own ways through statutes passed by legislatures and through the writing, amending, and interpreting of the U.S. Constitution. While the development of American law has been influenced by a variety of legal traditions, its English roots have proven to be the most lasting and consequential. Daniel Webster put it this way: "We [Americans] have seen . . . copious and salutary streams turning and running backward, replenishing their original fountains, and giving a fresher and brighter green to the fields of English jurisprudence."[52]

Certainly, to foreign and domestic observers alike the contents of American law often seem extraordinarily, and perhaps unnecessarily, complicated. However, the federal system of government and the acceptance by Americans of various sources of law have had important benefits. The states have served as laboratories in which their citizens have been permitted to try out new laws that might not yet or might never have national support. The gambling laws of Nevada need not be identical with those of Alabama, nor must the handgun regulations in Wyoming mirror those applicable in New York City. The federal system has allowed diverse laws and procedures to flourish, so long as they conformed with the basic precepts of the U.S. Constitution.

The American system of government also helps to explain why law has evolved gradually in the United States, rather than being subject to sudden revolutionary changes. Article V of the U.S. Constitution discourages impulsive or sweeping changes by requiring that any constitutional amendment be proposed by a two-thirds majority of both the Senate and the House of Representatives, then be ratified by legislatures or conventions in three-quarters of the states. Thus, within a relatively rigid constitutional framework the federal scheme of government has

[50] See Lloyd L. Weinreb, *Denial of Justice: Criminal Process in the United States* (New York: The Free Press, 1977), p. x.

[51] See Friedman, p. 18.

[52] Glendon, p. 182, citing Daniel Webster, *Remarks at the Meeting of the Suffolk Bar on Moving the Resolutions Occasioned by the Death of the Hon. Mr. Justice Story* (Boston: James Munroe, 1845), pp. 9–10.

permitted new legal ideas to displace old ones in a flexible, incremental fashion. And, while the complicated federal system of government has its drawbacks, Americans tend to be pleased with the way in which it has contributed to the development of American law. The legal system has developed in an effort to meet the aspirations of American society to provide justice for all. The degree to which those aspirations have been met is an issue for future chapters.

SELECTED ADDITIONAL READINGS

DWORKIN, RONALD. *A Matter of Principle.* Cambridge, MA: Harvard University Press, 1985.

FRIEDMAN, LAWRENCE M. *A History of American Law.* 2d ed. rev. New York: Simon & Schuster, 1985.

———. *American Law.* New York: W. W. Norton, 1984.

GILMORE, GRANT. *The Ages of American Law.* New Haven, CT: Yale University Press, 1977.

HALL, KERMIT L. *The Magic Mirror: Law in American History.* New York: Oxford University Press, 1989.

HOLMES, OLIVER WENDELL, JR. *The Common Law.* Boston: Little, Brown, 1881; new edition, Mark DeWolfe Howe ed. Cambridge, MA: Harvard University Press, 1963.

HORWITZ, MORTON J. *The Transformation of American Law, 1780–1860.* Cambridge, MA: Harvard University Press, 1977.

———. *The Transformation of American Law, 1870–1960: The Crisis of Legal Orthodoxy.* New York: Oxford University Press, 1992.

LLEWELLYN, KARL N. *The Common Law Tradition: Deciding Appeals.* Boston: Little, Brown, 1960.

NOONAN, JOHN T., JR. *Persons and Masks of the Law: Cardozo, Holmes, Jefferson, and Wythe as Makers of the Masks.* New York: Farrar, Straus & Giroux, 1976.

SARAT, AUSTIN, AND KEARNS, THOMAS R., eds. *The Rhetoric of Law.* Ann Arbor: University of Michigan Press, 1994.

2

The Courts

In the United States, as in other countries, courts consider and determine the facts in a dispute and apply the relevant law to those facts. Courts thus aim to answer three principal questions: What are the facts in the case? What is the relevant law to be applied? How is the law to be applied to the factual circumstances? Courts thus resolve legal disputes by deciding which party wins and which loses. An American court also typically reports its decision to provide a formal written record of the proceedings for the parties and to help others to decide similar future cases. All these are ordinary matters that occupy many tribunals elsewhere in the world. However, particular characteristics differentiate the American system from its counterparts elsewhere. This chapter describes the American court system and identifies certain outstanding differences and similarities with other court systems.

THE COURT SETTING

Although most American courthouses are located in buildings that are either modern and comfortable or dignified and historic, increasing exceptions to this generalization exist among small local courts or rundown urban courts in which facilities are clearly inadequate. Courthouses are ordinarily located in the center of cities or in the case of state courts in the most influential town in each county (the *county seat*). Courthouses include courtrooms for trials, staff offices for administrators, conference rooms for jurors and others, and **judge's chambers,** which are offices in which judges can research and write or conduct private meetings with lawyers.

At the front of each courtroom, which is customarily wood-paneled, the lawyers sit behind two long tables facing the judge. In criminal cases the defendant sits quietly at one of these tables with his or her defense counsel. The jury sits over on the side in the **jury-box**—two rows of seats enclosed by a wooden fence. The judge, seated behind a large wooden desk raised above the courtroom floor and facing the lawyer's tables, presides over the action. The judge's desk is traditionally termed the **bench,** and when an individual is **called to the bench** that signifies that he or she has been offered employment as a judge. Placed before the judge is the **gavel,** a wooden mallet that he or she strikes on the bench to initiate or dismiss proceedings, signal for attention, or restore order. The public watches court proceedings from rows of seats behind the lawyers.

A low wooden fence, traditionally called **the bar,** separates the spectators in the rear of the courtroom, who are to remain quiet, from the lawyers, who may speak in turn when the judge signals them that the appropriate time has arrived. Curiously, this wooden fence has had linguistic repercussions of far greater note than any practical value it may have contributed toward keeping order in the court. The term **the bar** forms the root of the terms **bar association, bar examination,** and **bar organization,** of the common phrases *admitted to the bar* and *practicing before the bar* (that is, being employed as an active attorney), and of the word used in Great Britain to refer to a trial lawyer—a *barrister.*

Next to the judge, who looks down on the action in his or her court, is another fenced-in area where a witness can sit while answering questions. This is called the **witness stand** (or *the stand*). During the trial the lawyer who is addressing the court rises from the table and, on occasion, paces around the open space between the bar, jury-box, and bench to ask questions of witnesses and make arguments to the jury or judge.

Also present is the **court reporter,** who has the responsibility for producing an official record of all legally significant statements that occur during the proceedings. Using stenography, audiotape, or videotape, the court reporter records testimony by witnesses, objections and statements by lawyers, and rulings by the judge. He or she will also list, mark for identification, and file for the record all papers, maps, charts, and other objects that the attorneys wish to introduce into evidence as **exhibits.** Depending on the type of court and the type of proceeding—and in some states whether the parties have granted their permission or not—television cameras may also be present in the courtroom.[1] Federal criminal trials, however, have never been televised.

Within the court, the judge, always dressed in a flowing black robe, receives special formal respect. The lawyers refer to the judge as "Your Honor," and all those present in court rise when the judge enters or leaves the room. When a lawyer disputes something a judge says in court, he or she customarily prefaces the statement by saying: "with all due respect." A lawyer who must challenge a judge's authority normally takes pains to do so in a properly deferential and formal manner: "Your Honor, respectfully, the plaintiff believes that the court lacks **jurisdiction** in this matter for the following reasons." All such traditions are intended to preserve the dignity of the court and to emphasize to the public, the parties, and their lawyers the special majestic role that the judiciary is supposed to play in American society.

[1] See Susanna Barber, *News Cameras in the Courtroom: A Free Press–Fair Trial Debate* (Norwood, NJ: Ablex, 1987).

In turn, the judge has the responsibility of ensuring that court proceedings are expeditious, yet thorough and dignified. A judge, with the help of two chief assistants, must first keep proceedings orderly. A **bailiff**[2] calls a court to order, maintains decorum in the courtroom, and performs various other tasks such as helping to keep time during **oral argument** in appeals cases. **Marshals**[3] or sheriff's deputies ensure courtroom security, deliver legal documents, guard and transport prisoners, and protect witnesses.

As the final authority within his or her courtroom, a judge should ideally be patient with and courteous to the parties as well as their lawyers, the jurors, and the witnesses. One experienced judge remarked: "The trial judge ought to be neutral, detached, kindly, benign, reasonably learned in the law, firm but fair, wise, knowledgeable about human behavior, and in lesser respects as well, somewhat superhuman."[4] Above all, the judge assumes the duty of making certain that the parties, through their lawyers, have enjoyed their right to be fully heard. Although people often refer to this principle by saying that "everybody is entitled to their day in court," in fact, a full opportunity to be heard usually requires considerably longer than a single day in the courtroom.

THE VARIETY OF AMERICAN COURTS

The celebrated French scholar Alexis de Tocqueville visited America in the late 1830s and concluded: "Scarcely any political question arises in the United States that is not resolved, sooner or later, into a judicial question."[5] Even today, Americans seem to feel especially comfortable in pursuing legal resolutions to their problems, whether political, social, business, or personal. People often settle in court issues that in other countries might be ignored or dealt with by a political group, a neighborhood committee, a religious leader, or a person-to-person discussion.[6]

Courts in the United States, as elsewhere, may be divided into **trial courts,** which decide a dispute by examining the facts, and **appellate courts,** which review the manner in which the trial court applied the law to the facts. However, the sheer number and variety of American courts can bewilder foreign and domestic observers alike. Even well-educated Americans find the judicial system extraordinar-

[2] The term *bailiff* came to the United States from England where it originally signified the deputy to a sheriff. People speaking old English called the territory patrolled by a deputy sheriff the bailiff's *wic* from which modern English derives *bailiwick.*

[3] See Robert A. Carp and Ronald Stidham, *Judicial Process in America,* 3d ed. rev. (Washington, DC: Congressional Quarterly Press, 1996), p. 92, and Ethan Nadelmann, *Cops Across Borders: The Internationalization of U.S. Criminal Law Enforcement* (University Park: Pennsylvania State University Press, 1993), especially pp. 167–170.

[4] Marvin Frankel, "The Adversary Judge: The Experience of a Trial Judge," in Mark W. Cannon and David M. O'Brien, eds., *Views From the Bench* (Chatham, NJ: Chatham House, 1985), p. 47, cited in G. Alan Tarr, *Judicial Process and Judicial Policymaking* (St. Paul, MN: West, 1994), p. 66.

[5] Alexis de Tocqueville, *Democracy in America,* Vol. I (New York: Random House, 1945), p. 290.

[6] Chapter 9 takes up the issue of why this might be the case.

ily confusing with its many **state courts** and **federal courts,** not to mention such specialized tribunals as **drug courts, water courts, juvenile courts, small claims courts, workers' compensation boards,** even **foreign intelligence surveillance courts!**

Experienced lawyers may not know whether the court in a neighboring state that decides issues regarding inheritance and administration of estates and the guardianship of minors and incompetents is known as the **probate court,** the **surrogate's court,** or the **orphan's court.** Indeed, the American court system is so large and complicated that a practicing attorney might not be able to distinguish between **constitutional courts** and **legislative courts,** and might well be wholly ignorant of the dimensions of the **tribal court system** or even the **military court system.**[7] Thus, it is no wonder that the complexities of the American court system often intimidate observers who are not lawyers.

American federalism contributes to this public confusion. Since legal practices in the states differ significantly, quite fundamental terminology can vary substantially from one court system to the next. What is called the **county court** in one part of the country might be termed the **circuit court, district court, chancery court, superior court,** or **court of common pleas** in another. Some states even label institutions *courts* that are really not courts at all. For instance, an elected executive official known as a *county judge/executive* directs the *fiscal courts* of Kentucky. These institutions have no judicial function; instead, the judge/executive is an administrator and legislator who chairs a **county** legislative body. Since these bodies were once often headed by judges, they took on and have long retained the misleading label *court.*

Despite the evident complexities of the state court systems, all court reform efforts have failed that aimed at establishing one uniform court scheme to be adopted by every state. Indeed, none has approached success. Even neighboring states that share many characteristics have jealously guarded their prerogative to utilize somewhat different network of courts. Indeed, even those intent on reforming the court system within a single state to eliminate overlapping or redundant jurisdictions have often struggled in vain. As was once said of changing a university curriculum, reforming the American courts is like moving a graveyard!

Since a first step toward understanding the nature of modern American justice is to become familiar with the court system, this chapter describes and distinguishes among the most prominent tribunals, using a handful of cases to explore how the several levels of courts function.

The Historical Development of American Courts

All those attempting to understand something of the nature of law and politics in the United States should bear in mind the difference between the affairs of the single national government, with its headquarters in Washington, DC, and the affairs

[7] For a useful synopsis of the military court system, see Henry J. Abraham, *The Judicial Process: An Introductory Analysis of the Courts of the United States, England, and France,* 6th ed. rev. (New York: Oxford University Press, 1993), pp. 145–148.

of the fifty state governments, each with its own headquarters in a state capital city. Just as the national and state governments have independent responsibilities under the federal scheme of American government, so too have the national and state courts taken on divergent tasks under the scheme of American law. The historical development of the United States helps to explain the divided responsibilities that are found within the court system.

From the birth of the country, Americans distrusted uniformity in laws and courts. When the delegates to the Constitutional Convention of 1787 drafted the U.S. Constitution, these Founding Fathers attempted to bind together fledgling states that already had established laws, legislatures, and legal traditions from the colonial period. Each state wanted the freedom to continue to develop a legal system tailored to its own needs. Just as the states were reluctant to give up political power to one another or to a central government, so they were leery of creating a national court system that might overwhelm existing state legal institutions.

In addition, each state wanted to retain the ability to design and enforce its own laws. To this day, conduct that is proscribed in one state may be perfectly legal in another. For instance, prostitution violates state laws across the United States, except in Nevada where under state law it remains legal in certain counties. Even when states prohibit the same act, the definition of that illegal behavior may vary substantially from state to state. While two states might prohibit the installation of secret video cameras by persons other than police officers, the issue of whether the police, at the request of a department store, could lawfully install secret videocameras in dressing rooms to thwart shoplifters would depend upon the details of how each state legislature limited such surveillance.

In discussing how to create an American court system that would accommodate the interests of the different states and the newly strengthened national government, the Founders tended to agree that the system created by the Articles of Confederation, featuring no judicial branch whatsoever, was inadequate.[8] A consensus developed that the new national government ought to rely on a more extensive legal system than that offered by the existing state courts. Disputes would inevitably arise regarding national laws. Since state courts might resolve issues of national law differently, creating excessive confusion and controversy and weakening the national government, these national issues might best be decided in a national court system or at least in a national court of last resort. Moreover, in a more tightly unified country, citizens of different states could be expected to become embroiled in legal disputes with one another. Settling such disputes in the courts of one state or the other might put the out-of-state party at a disadvantage.

However, the Founders' opinions differed sharply on precisely which model of a national judicial branch ought to be adopted. On the one hand, some advocates of states' rights argued that only a single national court was necessary: a "supreme court" to hear appeals from state courts on questions of national law.[9]

[8] See Carp and Stidham, p. 23.

[9] See Tarr, p. 32.

The Federalists, on the other hand, supporters of a strong central government, distrusted certain of the state court systems and advocated establishing a national network of trial and appellate courts.

After considerable debate and deadlock, the Founders drafted the U.S. Constitution that created the U.S. Supreme Court, outlined the judicial power of the United States, and left to Congress the job of establishing the remainder of the national court system.[10] In the First Congress another round of political struggle ensued. In the Judiciary Act of 1789, after lengthy arguments about the distinct needs and interests of the states and the country as a whole, the Congress did create a national judicial system featuring new federal courts.

However, the Federalists' victory was not as sweeping as they might have hoped. The Judiciary Act did not attempt to set the federal courts above their state counterparts. Rather, Congress curtailed the responsibilities of the federal courts and chose to distribute them about the country rather than concentrate them in the national capitol. American leaders ultimately selected a decentralized organizational scheme for the federal courts that underscored, rather than undercut, the continuing responsibilities of state courts.

Responsibilities of Federal and State Courts

Over time, the division of labor between federal and state courts crystallized. The U.S. Congress passes national laws, prohibiting certain acts and prescribing appropriate penalties. As a general rule, federal courts hear cases regarding disputes that arise under those laws, under treaties, and under the U.S. Constitution. State legislatures decide which acts will be illegal within each state, and how that unlawful conduct will be penalized. State courts decide most, but not all, questions of state law, whether concerning automobiles, contracts, corporations, property, debtor and creditor disputes, and family or **landlord** and **tenant** relations. Since state criminal law is far more extensive than federal criminal law, state prosecutors handle the vast majority of American criminal cases. Most lawsuits regarding personal injuries and commercial transactions are also heard in state courts.

The Framers might have chosen to have federal courts exercise authority over their state counterparts. In fact, Americans selected a different constitutional scheme. Each state court system is capped by its own court (or courts) of last resort. These ultimate state courts of appeals stand as the final arbiters of legal controversies arising under each state's laws. Even the U.S. Supreme Court cannot overrule a state court on a matter of state **jurisprudence,** including the interpretation of that state's constitution. The overwhelming majority of America's judicial business thus occurs in its state courts, and most of these cases will not be reviewed by any federal court, including the U.S. Supreme Court.

Rather than serving as an all-purpose court of last resort for all American cases, the U.S. Supreme Court has been granted the discretion to hear an appeal

[10] U.S. Constitution, Article III, Sections 1–2.

of a state court case only if a significant question of federal law[11] is involved and the state courts have handed down a final decision that leaves no other possible state remedy available to be pursued. Thus, even though U.S. citizens have rights under both state and national laws and constitutions, federal and state courts rule on the same case only under rather unusual circumstances. A state court decision might be appealed to the U.S. Supreme Court, for instance, if the state court had issued a controversial interpretation of an issue involving the U.S. Constitution. Such circumstances would be unlikely to arise in many ordinary cases.

Naturally, the jurisdiction of all state courts is limited geographically. A Maryland court will not hear and decide a case that involves only Virginians and Virginia state law. State judges, therefore, customarily follow precedents established by other judges from their state, rather than judicial interpretations of federal law or laws in other states. A judge in Alaska will be chiefly interested in precedents under Alaskan law, not the law of Ohio or North Carolina. Even judges in states like Hawaii, admitted to statehood relatively recently, have already compiled a considerable body of precedent to draw upon. Since state law covers so many areas of daily life, the courts in a single populous state may hear far more cases than in all the federal courts combined.

The dominance in numbers of state court cases is especially pronounced with regard to criminal matters. When criminal cases reach the federal court system, they normally deal with rights guaranteed to criminal defendants under the U.S. Constitution or with federal crimes, that is, crimes that violate laws passed by Congress, usually dealing with conduct that is somehow national in scope. The most obvious examples involve activities with effects that transcend state boundaries, such as illegal immigration, counterfeiting money, international terrorism, interstate auto theft, federal income tax evasion, trafficking in narcotics from abroad, and even illegal hunting of migrating birds. However, federal crimes also include various offenses that are less obviously national in character, but that fall under federal jurisdiction because the criminal has used some national instrument, such as the postal or telephone service, in the course of committing the crime. While this may seem like a broad criminal jurisdiction, criminal cases filed in federal court have been likened to "a spit in the ocean" compared with those filed in state courts.[12]

Federal courts also hear many **civil cases** that involve a question of federal law (that is, a *federal question*). As one Congress after another has busied itself with law-making and as presidents and their executive branches have issued volumes of executive orders and administrative regulations, the scope of federal law has grown exponentially. It now covers diverse matters ranging from an individual's entitle-

[11] In addition, the federal question must have been properly raised by one of the parties when the case was being litigated in state court or the Supreme Court will decline to hear the appeal.

[12] Lawrence M. Friedman, *Crime and Punishment in American History* (New York: Basic Books, 1993), p. 268, states that "Felony prosecutions in federal courts amount to less than 2 percent of the national total."

ment to Social Security and other federal welfare benefits to a corporation's responsibilities under national tax, labor, **antitrust,** and environmental policies. Federal law now encompasses matters concerning contracts, **bankruptcy,** civil rights, student loans, **criminal racketeering,** and a host of other topics.

A federal court will also hear a lawsuit between people who live in different states so long as the amount of money involved equals or exceeds $75,000.[13] So, if a citizen living in California has a dispute involving $80,000 with another citizen living in New York, the case could be heard in federal court by virtue of the **diversity of citizenship** of the parties. However, a citizen of Minnesota suing another Minnesotan for $100,000 would not amount to a diversity case, nor would a Minnesotan suing a citizen of Hawaii for $45,000. So long as no federal question were involved, those cases would be heard in Minnesota's state courts.

U.S. federal courts also hear a limited number of cases on account of the subject matter of the lawsuit. For instance, under their federal question jurisdiction, federal district courts automatically hear cases regarding bankruptcy, maritime matters, and many **intellectual property** issues regarding **copyrights, patents,** and **trademarks.** In fact, the federal courts hear all cases to which the U.S. government is a party, whether the government is a defendant or plaintiff in the action.

To assert that state courts concern themselves solely with state law and federal courts with federal law would overgeneralize.[14] In fact, federal courts regularly deal with state law issues in diversity cases. In addition, cases often arise that involve questions of both state and federal law and may be heard in either court system. In such cases, a state court may have to decide an issue of federal law, and a federal court may have to rule on state law. When issues of state law arise in federal court, the judge applies the law of the state in which the court is sitting.

The U.S. Constitution grants sufficient rights to criminal defendants that individuals convicted in state court often find federal court review possible. An enterprising defense attorney whose client has been convicted in state court may be able to raise an appeal in federal court regarding a constitutional question. Nevertheless, because of a lack of resources or a very slender chance of victory, not all possible avenues of appeal are pursued in every case. A case brought in state court is ordinarily settled or resolved in state court. A case brought in federal court is almost invariably settled or resolved in federal court.[15]

[13] In 1988, Congress raised the threshold amount-in-controversy requirement from $10,000 to $50,000, a sum that was further increased to $75,000 in 1996. While this change has reduced the number of cases filed in federal court, a party intent on going to federal court is often still able to do so since in various types of cases a potential plaintiff can calculate actual damages, then add on sufficient "psychological damages" to exceed the threshold. See Carp and Stidham, p. 128.

[14] Guam, the Northern Mariana Islands, and the Virgin Islands are American territories without established local or state court systems. In these territories, the federal district courts hear both federal cases and cases arising under local law. For an example of a federal district court deciding an interesting case that had arisen under local law see *Government of Virgin Islands v. Stull,* 280 F.Supp. 460 (D. V.I. 1968).

[15] It is possible for a case to be incorrectly brought in federal court and then removed to a state court.

The Benefits and Drawbacks of a Dual Court System

Is the dual court system a positive or negative feature of American justice? Although foreign students and commentators often focus on the costs and confusion inherent in having two sets of courts, Americans have never been eager to adopt a unitary court system. Given the federal division of responsibilities, most citizens seem to believe that the Founders correctly assessed the need for state and federal courts to decide questions of state and federal law.

With time, an additional possible advantage to a dual court system has become apparent. Although judges are expected to try to remain objective, neutral, and dispassionate, courts can be expected to reflect, to some degree, the social and political biases and legal philosophies of the dominant groups from which judges are selected. Since the United States has both state and federal courts, and since certain important cases could be brought before either court system, in appropriate circumstances a lawyer may weigh the predominant biases of the two courts and choose to bring a controversial case before the more favorable of the two.

Such **forum shopping** is an integral part of a dual court system in which courts have overlapping responsibilities. It is, of course, often simply one aspect of the competitive nature of an American trial, in which each attorney looks to gain whatever advantage might be available. Rather than locating an impartial court, a party might select one court over another for any number of reasons, ranging from the practical to the philosophical to the procedural.

Certainly, forum shopping can have positive, negative, or neutral consequences for the overall administration of justice. Yet, for the American people, who long have been especially intent on providing the injured with every opportunity to gain redress through law, a dual court system that offers the possibility of forum shopping may, on balance, be more attractive than a unitary one. In the 1960s, for instance, when many state judges in certain parts of the country might not have been receptive to their claims, African American and Hispanic victims could bring civil rights lawsuits in federal courts before judges selected in a different manner and often drawn from a pool of candidates with different characteristics than the state judges.[16]

As federal courts grew more conservative with the appointment of many judges by Republican presidents Ronald Reagan and George Bush, individuals with claims to which a conservative court might be hostile, such as those involving gay rights, might prefer to bypass the federal courts and instead bring their lawsuit before the courts in a politically liberal state.[17] Thus, while a dual court system that

[16] For the argument that state courts remain incapable of protecting important federal rights as vigorously as federal courts see Larry W. Yackle, *Reclaiming the Federal Courts* (Cambridge, MA: Harvard University Press, 1994).

[17] See Henry R. Glick, *Courts, Politics, and Justice,* 3d ed. rev. (New York: McGraw-Hill, 1993), p. 50.

permits forum shopping in certain cases complicates the administration of justice, those with a grievance that could be heard in either court system often welcome the opportunity to choose the court in which they would like their claim to be heard.

THE SCHEME OF STATE COURTS

Within a particular state, the organization of the courts, their names, numbers, hierarchy, and jurisdictions, is determined by that state's constitution or legislation. Hence, while all share certain features, state courts differ markedly in many other respects. States have different court procedures, enforce distinct bodies of state laws, and appoint their judges in varying manners.

Although all the states divide their court systems into some type of hierarchical scheme, the precise dimensions of that scheme vary from state to state. In all states appeals move up a ladder of courts. In all states the decisions of a higher court as to how a law should be interpreted must be followed by all lower courts. Yet, while many states have general trial courts, intermediate appellate courts, and courts of last resort, at least a dozen states have enacted systems that do not fall so neatly into such categories. Some states divide trial courts into criminal and civil divisions. Arkansas actually separates its general trial courts into three categories: chancery courts, circuit courts, and a hybrid known as chancery probate courts. Some states have separate courts of last resort: one for appeals in civil cases, the other for appeals in criminal cases. Thus, not only does terminology vary from state to state, but the superstructure of the court system may differ noticeably even in neighboring states.

The variegated shapes of the state court systems have been molded by changing needs and diverse historical traditions and experiences. The federalist system has permitted state courts in Louisiana to develop quite differently from those in Massachusetts. New York State has long had to contend with the many legal needs of an extraordinarily large city. New York legislators have thus created a court system markedly different from that which their counterparts in Wyoming have enacted. Similarly, Colorado politicians have seen a pressing need for a water court, a court that has not seemed at all necessary to Hawaiians.

To enable each state to tailor its legal system to suit its needs, Americans have sacrificed some simplicity and efficiency to accommodate diversity. The incremental addition, subtraction, and consolidation of courts has led to a bewildering lack of uniformity within each state court hierarchy as well as among the different state court systems. Not only do courts naturally differ from state to state in number, variety, and structure, but they are also likely to differ in quality from place to place, though this is, of course, quite difficult to measure.

To explain something of how this complicated system functions, we will turn next to examine several cases that have been heard by different types of state courts. Since much scholarship on the legal system focuses exclusively upon outstanding or unusual cases of historical or national significance decided in the U.S. Supreme Court, it may be useful to examine, instead, a handful of ordinary cases that help to illustrate how the various courts handle their daily business.

A Traffic Court Case

Several years ago I went to court after a traffic policeman gave me a speeding ticket. My wife and I had been driving along a major highway when a police car stopped us. The officer claimed that I had been driving at about 75 miles per hour in a 55 mile-per-hour zone, and he ordered me to pay a fine of $120. In fact, however, the policeman was mistaken: I had been driving at the speed limit. His error occurred when another car sped by at just the moment the policeman focused the radar in my direction. Consequently, the officer mistakenly concluded that I had been speeding when, in fact, the other driver was at fault.

In certain cultures a person treated unfairly by the authorities would be inclined to ignore the incident and avoid public attention. In other cultures unfairness might prompt a citizen to rebel in some manner against the government. Modern American society, however, is exceptionally litigious. When treated unfairly, an American frequently responds by placing the dispute before a court for a decision. Accordingly, I demanded a court hearing and soon appeared before a judge to protest that the policeman had unfairly penalized me with a speeding ticket that I did not deserve.

I first described for the judge the relevant circumstances. In particular, I recalled that another car had sped by just before the policeman had signaled me to stop. I pointed out that in fifteen years of driving, I had never before been penalized with a ticket for speeding in excess of the 55 mile-per-hour speed limit. I also told the judge that I had brought to court a witness, my wife, who had been in the car during the incident and was prepared to testify both that I had been driving at the speed limit and that I habitually drive at the speed limit. Finally, I argued that, unlike a new car with a large, powerful engine, my old diesel car, which had already been driven over 220,000 miles, could not speed without my realizing it. After the judge heard this argument and testimony from the police officer, she said: "Mr. Fowler, you have created a **reasonable doubt** in my mind as to whether you were speeding. Case dismissed."

All the courts in the United States are part of either the state or federal court systems; all are either trial or appellate courts. Although technically a traffic court is the lowest form of a state trial court, it may sensibly be analyzed as one in a separate category of courts, which might best be termed the local courts. Although local courts go by different names in different state court systems, a low-level judicial official presides over them. In some places he or she is called a **judge;** in others the title is **justice of the peace** or **magistrate.** The minor speeding dispute outlined above thus illustrates one of the lowest American courts in action.

A Municipal Court Case

Traffic courts are by no means the only type of local court. States have also created small claims courts, which hear cases involving modest amounts of money, usually less than $1,000. Other common local courts are **family courts,** also called **domestic relations courts** or **juvenile courts,** which deal with the problems of children who commit offenses, and probate courts, which determine issues of inheritance. When such local courts handle a particular set of problems for a metropolitan area, they are often called **municipal courts** or, less frequently, **metropolitan courts.** The next example of an American court in action involved just such a local municipal court.

Some years ago, I agreed to provide legal counsel to a quite poor and very elderly woman on a *pro bono publico* basis.[18] In other words, I volunteered to provide her legal services without charging her for my time. This is not uncommon. Many American lawyers feel a professional and ethical obligation to spend some days each year working for people with legal problems who cannot pay the fees a lawyer would customarily charge or for social causes such as promoting civil rights and liberties, consumer protection, or a healthy environment.

My client's problem was simple and sad. She and her adult son had been locked out of their house by her adult niece. The elderly woman, too sick to work, had no money other than welfare payments. Her only son suffered from a mental illness that had precluded his working for any extended period of time. As a result, for some time my client had been unable to make the monthly payments due on her property. To help to make those payments, the elderly woman had invited her niece to come to live with her. The two had agreed that the older woman would allow the niece to become a co-owner of the property, and that the niece would then be responsible for making the monthly payments.

This housing agreement might have proven beneficial to all, except that one day the mentally ill son tried to set fire to the curtains in his room in the house. The niece then waited until the old woman and her son had gone out, and she called a locksmith to change the locks on all the doors. She then refused to let the pair back into their home. So, at the time the old woman called for legal assistance, she and her son were living at a neighbor's house, without any of their possessions, without even a change of clothing. My client believed that she had been treated very unfairly, particularly since she still owned one-half of the property.

To assist the woman in her effort to regain access to her house, I decided to ask a judge in the city **housing court** to issue an **injunction** to compel the niece to permit the elderly woman back into her house. As noted in the preceding chapter, one important source of American law has been the traditional laws of England. An injunction, derived from an ancient practice of the English **Courts of Eq-**

[18] *Pro bono publico* is a Latin term best translated as "for the public good" or "for the welfare of the whole."

uity,[19] is designed to prevent a legal wrong from continuing. It is simply an order from a court telling someone to do something or to refrain from doing something.[20]

So, one morning the elderly woman and her son and I made our way through the crowds of people in housing court to discuss this dispute with the judge. I told the judge how the cruel niece had prohibited the elderly woman and her son from entering their own home. When I had fully explained what had occurred from my client's viewpoint, the judge asked the niece's lawyer to explain her version of the events. Her lawyer was a seasoned attorney quite experienced in housing matters, with a flair for showboating to the gallery. The flamboyant attorney, whose appearance contrasted sharply with the bow-tied **partner** supporting me at the plaintiff's table, argued that his client had changed the locks and refused entry to the other family members because she was afraid that the mentally ill son might injure or kill her.

After I argued with the other lawyer for several minutes about the content of the various state laws applicable to persons who jointly owned a house, the judge leaned down from the bench and declared: "Since both women own the house together, neither has the right to lock the other out. I will sign an injunction that says the niece must allow the elderly woman back into her home. However," the judge continued, "I will not order the niece to permit the adult son to enter the house until a court doctor has examined him and concluded that he poses no danger to the niece."

This case illustrates the work of a different type of local court: the housing court in a sizeable American city. Every day such a court decides scores of disputes between landlords and tenants[21] and among **joint tenants** and **joint owners.** While perhaps more prestigious than a mere traffic court, a city housing court typically shares many characteristics with it. In particular, both must deal with a high volume of cases in short order without much staff assistance.

The Nature of Local Courts

It bears emphasizing that, technically, local courts like those that resolved the cases involving the speeding ticket and the housing dispute are part of the state court system. Nevertheless, because of common characteristics, they may sensibly be grouped together for analytical purposes.

[19] In early English law, courts would act only if the facts supporting a legal claim fit some recognized **cause of action.** Otherwise, the plaintiff's claim would be dismissed even though he or she was clearly suffering a wrong. To provide legal recourse in such situations, the Courts of Equity (also called the **Courts of Chancery**) formed a parallel system of justice. Rather than relying upon the common law, equity courts administered justice without juries in the name of the King or Queen in accordance with general notions of fairness.

[20] Technically, I first asked the judge to grant an **interlocutory injunction.** This requests the court to issue a temporary order for some specified length of time in order to prevent irreparable injury before the court can reach a considered decision on whether a permanent order should be granted or denied. Interlocutory injunctions are divided into two categories: **temporary restraining orders** and **preliminary injunctions.** A single party, the **petitioner,** may request that a judge issue a temporary restraining order even though the other party, the **respondent,** has not been given notice of the hearing and has not appeared. However, both parties must be heard before the court will issue a preliminary injunction.

[21] A *landlord* or *landlady* is a person who owns land or lodgings and leases them to another person, called the *tenant.*

A local court is a **court of limited jurisdiction** that hears cases that involve small amounts of money, or property of limited value, or less serious offenses, than do the higher courts in the state system. The jurisdiction of local courts varies substantially from state to state and may be limited to a geographic area (a municipal or metropolitan court), a certain subject-matter (a traffic court), or a limited amount of money (a small claims court). Indeed, the jurisdiction of local courts is often limited by more than one of these factors, as in the Small Claims Court of Marion County, Indiana.

Local courts are designed to settle the many minor civil and criminal legal matters that arise in cities, towns, and rural areas. While from place to place in the United States these low-level courts are entrusted with enforcing somewhat different bodies of law, such courts of limited jurisdiction generally handle disputes regarding modest sums or relatively unimportant offenses. A local court is often strictly limited in the size of the fine or the duration of the prison time it can order. Such courts would not be empowered to hear a civil case in which a significant amount (such as $20,000 or more) is in dispute, or a **criminal case** in which the defendant faces a considerable penalty, such as several years in prison. However, in some states such courts of limited jurisdiction are permitted to handle certain preliminary proceedings, such as **arraignments** or **preliminary hearings,** in serious criminal cases, even though the legislature has deemed it beyond the competence of the court to preside over the trial that may ensue.

Despite the mundane nature of the local court business, or perhaps on account of it, many Americans find this aspect of the legal system to be especially fascinating. While few lay persons would have sufficient background to find a complicated antitrust case interesting, virtually all could identify with the many problems arising in local courts: a dog disturbing a neighborhood by barking incessantly or one running free without a leash, a business violating a city ordinance dealing with trash collection, a minor contractual dispute between a young couple and the housepainter they hired, or a homeowner who refuses to cut the grass in the front yard or rents a basement apartment in violation of neighborhood **zoning ordinances.** For many years, "People's Court," a popular television program, capitalized on this widespread interest by broadcasting as entertainment proceedings that resembled those in a California small claims courts. Through television, a retired judge presiding over that TV court, Judge Joseph Wopner, became one of the most widely recognized members of the American judiciary!

Local courts, like TV's "People's Court," typically confront a number of common problems. In some states the judge in a local court need not be an attorney: the vestige of an idea that legal training was unnecessary in these courts since anyone blessed with common sense could apply the law to minor disputes. Unlike the higher state courts and their federal counterparts, local courts do not normally employ large staffs of administrators and assistants. Along with keeping abreast of a formidable case load, a local court judge must often carry out administrative functions such as overseeing the court's budget and its personnel. He or she may also be charged with a variety of quasi-judicial tasks, ranging from performing civil marriages to serving as **notary public.**

The judges in a local court receive limited salaries and may not enjoy adequate resources and facilities. Moreover, local courts handle an enormous number of routine matters, and the judges may simply lack the time to consider carefully all relevant circumstances. For example, the judge who heard my speeding-ticket case may have had a hundred other hearings scheduled for that same afternoon. She could not spend much time trying to find out precisely what happened in every dispute before her.

The trend across the country has been for states to ease the pressure of heavy caseloads in the state trial courts by permitting local courts to hear cases involving ever larger amounts of money. Thus, in a state like Minnesota any claim for less than $7,500 may now be heard in small claims court. One can see why local courts have been referred to as "factories" in which judges dispose of cases as quickly as an assembly line worker might once have packed sausages at a meat-processing plant! Such courts do, however, perform the important function of freeing the county courts to devote their resources to more weighty and serious disputes.

The widespread problem of too many cases waiting to be heard and too few judges available to hear them contributes to the peculiar culture of local courtrooms. One observer described a Chicago municipal court in the following terms: "The clamor is nerve-racking. The section before the bench is jammed with policemen, lawyers, bondsmen, reporters, detectives, visitors. . . . During the entire session the bailiffs constantly rap for order and plead with the mob to move back from the bench. . . . The smoke is always thick, the noise deafening. People are whispering, laughing, talking, spitting."[22] A legal services attorney described another Chicago municipal court in the following terms:

> The judges were nasty and peremptory. They rushed through the cases without allowing the defendants to talk, and they ridiculed defendants for attempting to say a few words in their own behalves. The clerks and bailiffs were worse, refusing to answer questions or give explanations. . . . Every courtroom on the eleventh floor seemed to operate in continual bedlam. The plaintiffs' attorneys were always huddled and talking to each other. The clerks were always shouting orders to the ill-fated defendants. The judges were always barking out their judgments—seven days to move, thirty days to pay, add on the attorney's fees, and do not ask any questions.[23]

The lack of support personnel and overload of cases thus often result in chaotic courtrooms.

In such a litigious society as the United States, local courts seem necessary to resolve minor local disputes, yet the importance of the vast majority of local court decisions is strictly limited. They ordinarily affect only the people directly in-

[22] Friedman, p. 385, citing I. P. Callison, *Courts of Injustice* (1956), pp. 419–421.

[23] Mary Ann Glendon, *A Nation Under Lawyers: How the Crisis in the Legal Profession Is Transforming American Society* (New York: Farrar, Straus, & Giroux, 1994) p. 62, citing Stephen Lubet, "Professionalism Revisited," *Emory Law Journal* 42 (1993): 205.

volved in the case. To avoid paying legal fees, the parties often opt to present their arguments themselves without the assistance of an attorney. The court frequently announces its decision without producing an extensive supporting written record or **opinion.** The informality of local court proceedings explains why appeals bring about a new trial (***trial de novo***) in a higher court, rather than appellate scrutiny of the **record** of the case in the lower court.

Since local courts do not solve weighty, complicated legal problems and do not make law through establishing precedent, in many respects they are the least important tribunals in the American legal system.

A County Court Case

Moving up the scale of state courts, one finds state trial courts to be substantially more important than local courts.[24] Once again, since states have enacted different judicial schemes, the primary state trial court might be called a county court, circuit court, district court, superior court, or court of common pleas, depending on the state in which it is located. In New York, state trial courts are known as supreme courts—a matter of considerable confusion for those accustomed to thinking of supreme courts as courts of last resort!

Whatever the label that is employed, all state judicial systems contain **courts of unlimited jurisdiction** that hear cases arising in a certain judicial district or county. That is, some designated level of trial courts will be able to hear civil cases without any maximum limit on the amount of money or the value of the property in dispute. Such a level of court will also hear criminal cases without any maximum limit on the seriousness of the alleged criminal offense. Thus, while a local court known as a police court,[25] city court, or night court would be likely to deal with a **misdemeanor,** such as disorderly conduct or prostitution, the criminal trial for a **felony,** such as armed robbery or murder, would normally be heard in a state trial court.[26]

States organize their trial courts of unlimited jurisdiction by dividing their territory into judicial districts and assigning a court or courts to each district. Since each American state is already divided into the territorial subdivisions known as counties (in Louisiana, as **parishes**), some legislatures have chosen to create judicial districts that correspond with county lines. The state judicial system in Massachusetts, for instance, relies heavily on its county courts. State trial courts vary in

[24] For a description of the work of state trial courts see John Paul Ryan, et al., *American Trial Judges: Their Work Styles and Performance* (New York: The Free Press, 1980).

[25] In some cities, particularly in past eras, police prosecute defendants accused of minor crimes. See Glick, p. 215.

[26] A *misdemeanor* is a petty offense, such as disorderly conduct, prostitution, or writing graffiti on a public building. Under state (and federal) law, such criminal infractions are classified as a separate group of offenses, less important than a *felony,* such as armed robbery or murder. In some states, such as Minnesota, a felony is a crime punishable by more than one year in prison, a misdemeanor is punishable by less than one year in prison, and a petty misdemeanor is punishable by a fine, but not a prison sentence. Still other states have created *capital felonies,* a separate category for very serious felonies that may be punished by death.

size, caseload, and sophistication depending on the responsibilities accorded them under state law and the nature of the judicial district in which they function. Since much of the metropolitan area of Boston lies within Suffolk County, Massachusetts, the Suffolk County courthouse is a much busier place than is the courthouse serving Franklin County, a sparsely populated rural portion of western Massachusetts.

Some years ago I was involved in a curious case in the circuit court for Anne Arundel County, Maryland. The dispute involved two elderly neighbors, a lawyer and a writer, both of whom lived on an island in the Chesapeake Bay. When the writer planted four pine trees to screen her new swimming pool from the adjoining property, her neighbor, the lawyer, brought a lawsuit in circuit court, alleging that the trees interfered with the enjoyment of his property by blocking his view of the bay. The plaintiff[27] also claimed that the town, technically, a **municipal corporation,**[28] that supervised certain zoning matters on the island had failed to abide by its own procedures in approving construction of the pool and the adjacent planting.

Ultimately, after chiding both parties for not compromising outside of court, the judge ruled in favor of the woman who had planted the trees. The judge stated that ownership of land normally includes the right to landscape the property. He also observed that the plaintiff had wholly failed to show that the pine trees were, in fact, impeding his view of the bay or otherwise seriously impairing the enjoyment of his property.

Given the weakness of the complaint, one might term this case a **nuisance lawsuit**—an effort by someone to intimidate, harass, or annoy another individual. Since such lawsuits arise from time to time in such a litigious society, American judges have the power to punish a plaintiff who has brought a wholly frivolous case by forcing him or her to pay the defendant's court costs and attorneys' fees. In addition, bar associations[29] have the power to discipline lawyers who permit a client to waste the court's time with a nuisance lawsuit. One might wish that America's judges and bar associations used their authority in this regard more assertively!

The resolution of this neighborly dispute over planting pine trees shows a state trial court at work. Since most American legal disputes are brought in the state court systems, county courts and other such trial courts of unlimited jurisdiction are among the busiest tribunals in the country. Once again, however, although many important cases originate in a state trial court, the vast majority of disputes are significant only to the immediate parties involved. For instance, apart from the municipal corporation and the two neighbors involved in the pine-tree planting

[27] In a civil lawsuit, the *plaintiff* is the party who brings the dispute to court for resolution, whereas the *defendant* is the party against whom the recovery or relief is sought.

[28] When a given area contains a sufficient population density, the state will designate that area a *municipal corporation.* The state then grants to that municipal corporation local legislative and administrative powers sufficient to govern the territory. In this case, the municipal corporation covered the entire island and served as the local government for its several hundred inhabitants, providing for road repair, trash pickup, police protection, and other services.

[29] *Bar associations* are professional licensing and regulatory bodies, found in each state, which oversee the practice of law. They are described in more detail in Chapter 9.

dispute, and perhaps a few other property owners facing similar circumstances, the outcome of that case would be inconsequential for most Maryland citizens.

The Nature of State Trial Courts

In attempting to do justice, state trial courts of unlimited jurisdiction often share with the local courts the advantages of determining violations of law within the social, cultural, political, and economic context of a particular state, or even a particular judicial district or metropolitan area. Knowledge of the local style of life may aid a judge in wisely and fairly interpreting the law. Despite such similarities, however, a sizeable gulf separates much that transpires in these two categories of courts.

Cases at this state trial court level are customarily treated with a degree of professionalism uncharacteristic of many courts of limited jurisdiction. While the participants in a local court case may or may not be represented by attorneys, while they may or may not be appearing before a judge with formal legal training, and while observance of the rules of evidence and procedure may be rather lax, such is not true of courts of unlimited jurisdiction. The judges of the courts of unlimited jurisdiction are law school graduates with academic and practical legal training and experience.[30]

Each case in a state trial court of unlimited jurisdiction also occupies much more time than does a hearing in traffic court, housing court, or small claims court. The parties present their view of what happened in considerable detail. The rules of court procedure tend to be more formal and complicated—some would say too complex—and they are followed more strictly. Yet, while county courts and other state trial courts of unlimited jurisdiction differ from the local courts, they also differ from the federal courts. One legal scholar who gained experience practicing in Chicago described that city's state and federal courts as follows:

> There was scarcely any difference in atmosphere between my firm's sedate quarters in the Continental Bank building and the austere federal courthouse just around the corner from the bank. An aura of solemnity surrounded the federal judges in their courtrooms, as it did our senior partners in their spacious but simply furnished offices. Lawyers exchanged pleasantries and conversed genially in the hallways of both places.

She continued by describing the state courthouse as

> . . . filled with everything that made Chicago such an exhilarating and alarming city—jostling, shouting, joking, cajoling, backslapping, backstabbing, bargaining, dealing, favors granted, grudges paid with interest, intimidation, bribery, conciliation, grand gestures, obscene remarks, and the occasional spontaneous act of generosity.[31]

[30] For the experiences of two state trial judges see Judge Robert Satter, *Doing Justice: A Trial Judge At Work* (New York: Simon & Schuster, 1990) and Judge Harold Rothwax, *Guilty: The Collapse of Criminal Justice* (New York: Random House, 1996).

[31] Glendon, pp. 60–61.

For all the chaos that surrounds their proceedings, state trial courts enjoy clerical help that produces a complete written record of the case and decision. For this reason state trial courts of unlimited jurisdiction are known as **courts of record.**

An Appellate Court Case

Since the right to an appeal has always been ingrained in American law, all state and federal court systems include appellate courts to review the decisions of the trial courts. Although in most states a single court of appeals originally handled all appeals, over time most state legislatures have created intermediate appellate courts and a court or courts of last resort. On account of the hierarchical nature of the American legal system, no matter how convinced a judge may be of the wisdom of his or her decision, a trial court must always defer to an appellate court. In the many states that have more than one level of appellate court, an intermediate appeals court must in turn bow to the decision of a court of last resort. The following case illustrates not only how readily Americans go to court to settle their disputes, but how they sometimes persist through appeals to higher courts.

In 1952 John Fenton bought a house and some land next to a golf course owned by a country club in Massachusetts. At the time he bought the house, Mr. Fenton apparently knew very little about the game of golf. After moving in, he claimed to be very surprised to find that golfers frequently hit golf balls off the course by mistake. In fact, the golfers at this country club seem to have had particularly poor aim. Each year from 1952 to 1959 they hit about 250 golf balls onto Mr. Fenton's land. Then, matters worsened. In 1960 the count reached 320 balls. In 1961 the country club positioned a sand trap on the golf course, directly opposite John Fenton's house. That new hazard on the course caused golfers to aim away from the center of the fairway and toward Mr. Fenton's land. Thus, with the passage of time Mr. Fenton's problem got progressively worse.

One might well wonder: Why would this homeowner care if a few golf balls bounced onto his property each day? John Fenton later testified that, over the years, golf balls had broken sixteen windows in his house and had frightened one dog so badly that the family had to give him away. A golf ball actually struck his next dog, and Mr. Fenton often watched golfers shake their clubs at this pet to scare it away. Worse still, on one occasion a golfer hit a ball right under the grill, stopping the Fenton family's cookout. Another time, someone hit a ball into his yard that had "Hello, Johnnie!" written on it. Then, one night, someone stood on the golf course in front of the Fenton property and hit a ball right off the front wall of his house.

Angry at these repeated encroachments on his property, John Fenton complained to the country club. The club owners responded by building a 25-foot-high fence between the course and the house. Unfortunately, however, the Fenton family did not like the appearance of the fence, and substantial numbers of golf balls continued to come flying over the fence into the yard. In 1965, for instance, 81 golf balls landed on the Fentons' property. Mr. Fenton then hired a lawyer to take the case to county court. In claiming that the country club continued to violate his property rights, Mr. Fenton asked the judge for an injunction, ordering the club to stop playing golf on that part of the course that was in front of his house.

After successive appeals from the decisions of the trial court and the court of appeals, the case finally arrived at the state court of last resort. The Supreme Judicial Court of Massachusetts decided that the country club had violated the property rights of its neighbor. The judges ordered the club to pay John Fenton several thousand dollars for all the trouble it had caused him over the years. They also ordered the country club to try to stop golf balls from coming into the yard in the future. While the court did not order the golf course to be closed, the judges implied that perhaps the location of the sand trap should be changed. Were it moved over in front of Mr. Fenton's property, golfers would be inclined to aim away from his land.

The case regarding the bouncing golf balls started among the fascinating and frenetic state trial courts of unlimited jurisdiction. It could not be considered a particularly important case: Other than the parties involved, few citizens took an interest in what the court decided. Nevertheless, Mr. Fenton pursued appeals that eventually took his dispute all the way to the state supreme court. There, the **justices** who heard his case produced written opinions that could be used by others confronting similar future disputes.

The Nature of State Appellate Courts

The terminology and structure of appellate court systems, including the number of courts and number of judges, varies from state to state. The court of last resort is usually termed the **state supreme court,** but in some states it is called the **court of appeals,** the **supreme judicial court,** or the **supreme court of appeals.**[32] Connecticut once called its court of last resort the **court of error,** and New Jersey and New York each once capped their systems with a **court of errors and appeals.** In each case the state legislatures eventually decided to change the name, presumably because the label might imply that the court was making errors, not correcting them!

In general, the more heavily populated states have instituted more extensive systems of courts of appeals, and several of the larger states have regional appellate courts that hear appeals from certain judicial districts, but not others. In contrast, certain lightly populated states, such as South Dakota and Vermont, have enacted a judicial system without any intermediate appeals courts in which appeals ordinarily go to the court of last resort.

Rather than listening to the evidence all over again, an appeals court normally reviews a case primarily to decide whether or not the prior judge handled the legal issues correctly.[33] In examining a case on appeal, appellate judges try to avoid

[32] For a study of state courts of last resort, see G. Alan Tarr and Mary Cornelia Aldis Porter, *State Supreme Courts in State and Nation* (New Haven, CT: Yale University Press, 1988).

[33] An exception occurs when the decision of a court of limited jurisdiction is appealed, and a new trial in a court of unlimited jurisdiction is sought. For the experiences of state appellate judges, see Richard Neeley, *Why Courts Don't Work* (New York: McGraw-Hill, 1983) and Edward F. Hennessey, *Judges Making Law* (Boston: Flaschner Judicial Institute, 1994).

both undue deference to the trial record and irresponsible substitution of their judgment for that of the trial judge, who has had the advantage of actually watching the trial.

The higher state courts handle cases involving more money or more serious offenses than those resolved by local courts. A dispute over several hundred dollars might be disposed of in a local small claims court on the bottom rung of the state court ladder. A dispute over several million dollars is likely to come before an appeals court toward the top of the ladder. State judges in the court of last resort, which sits in the state's capital city, are more likely to spend their time hearing appeals regarding some noteworthy social issue, a large award in a civil suit, or a criminal conviction involving an allegation of murder or armed robbery.[34] A minor neighborhood dispute, or an offense such as shoplifting, graffiti-writing, or disturbing the peace, will likely be disposed of in a local court. Thus, although some state court cases are simple and of limited relevance, others are very complicated with high stakes and considerable significance for many people living or doing business in the state. In fact, the largest damages ever awarded—more than $10 billion—came in the state court case of *Texaco v. Pennzoil.*[35]

Unfortunately, the problem of an overload of cases appears to be getting worse, not better. According to the National Center for State Courts, fully 99 percent of all American cases are filed in state courts.[36] From 1984 to 1991 the number of civil cases in state courts rose 33 percent, while criminal cases in state courts increased 25 percent.[37] These overall increases did not, of course, affect every state in the same manner. Nevertheless, an increasingly litigious American society has asked all different levels of many state judicial systems to decide more cases than ever before.

Yet, despite their increased caseloads, states have not always allocated sufficient funds to their court systems. In fact, the amount of federal, state, and local budgets devoted to furthering the administration of justice—civil and criminal, police and judicial—stands at just over 3 percent.[38]

Not only have state legislators often been faced with other pressing needs, but many are well aware of the current unpopularity of the legal system. In addi-

[34] For a useful collection of essays, see Mary Cornelia Porter and G. Alan Tarr, *State Supreme Courts: Policymakers in the Federal System* (Westport, CT: Greenwood Press, 1982).

[35] Carp and Stidham, p. 133. See also *Texaco v. Pennzoil,* 729 S.W. 2d 768 (1987).

[36] Roger A. Hanstrom and Brian J. Ostrom, "Litigation and the Courts: Myths and Misconceptions," *Trial* 29 (April 1993): 40.

[37] Ibid., p. 43. The authors point out, however, that it was not *tort* cases that caused this substantial increase. In the 1986–1991 period tort cases rose only 1 percent, whereas the American population increased 5 percent.

[38] See Steven Keeva, "Demanding More Justice: Whether Americans Get What They Want from the Legal System Depends on its Ability to Stretch Limited Resources," *ABA Journal* 80 (Aug. 1994): 47. In 1990, of the approximately $74 million that American governments spent on administration of justice, only $9 million went to the courts as opposed to almost $32 million for police protection and $25 million for prisons. Kathleen Maguire and Ann L. Pastore, *Sourcebook of Criminal Justice Statistics—1993* (Washington, DC: U.S. Government Printing Office, 1994), p. 2. Also in 1990, $5.5 million went to prosecution and less than $1 million to public defenders.

tion, in those states in which a politician such as the governor appoints judges (and in the federal system, in which the president enjoys powers of appointment), a proposal to increase the size of the judiciary may be perceived as an effort to fill the courts with new judges who are philosophically compatible with whoever is appointing them. Consequently, partisan political considerations may also hamper efforts to improve judicial resources.

To dispose of heavier caseloads expeditiously, states may need to change court procedures.[39] For the time being, lack of resources and the inability to hire additional judges and staff and to modernize their facilities helps to explain why many state courts are characterized by inexperienced or overworked staff and by substantial delays, particularly on less important legal matters. For instance, by 1996 resolving even a routine criminal **assault** and **battery** case in the Superior Court in Washington, DC often occupied more than a year.[40]

To counter such problems, the courts increasingly press mediation and other alternative forms of dispute resolution on litigants. States also now often employ part-time "retired" senior judges and a host of quasi-judicial figures, known as referees, commissioners, and hearing officers, to dispose of minor legal problems or preliminary proceedings. Nevertheless, the timely performance of state court responsibilities has suffered in many parts of the country.

THE SCHEME OF FEDERAL COURTS

Federal courts in the United States fall into one of several categories. The U.S. Constitution distinguishes between two sets of federal courts, each inferior to the U.S. Supreme Court: the legislative courts, established under Article I of the Constitution, and the constitutional courts, established under Article III. While the constitutional courts have purely judicial responsibilities, legislative courts also have certain administrative and quasi-legislative functions. Since the legislative courts tend to be quite specialized, our primary focus will be on the constitutional courts.

A District Court Case

The most numerous of the constitutional courts are the trial courts known as **federal district courts.**[41] A trial in federal district court proceeds in much the same manner as one in state court. Experienced attorneys might note differences between the federal and state rules of evidence and procedure, but lay observers would find the trial processes to be remarkably similar. As is true of state trial

[39] This issue is taken up in more detail in Chapters 7 and 8.

[40] See "Three Guilty of Beating D.C. Teacher," *Washington Post,* March 20, 1996, p. C1.

[41] Federal district courts do have certain appellate functions. For instance, they may review the decisions of certain bankruptcy courts and federal administrative agencies. However, for the most part, district courts are trial courts. Similarly, general state trial courts often have limited appellate functions, hearing appeals from minor local courts and administrative agencies.

courts, a single judge presides over most federal district court trials,[42] and the court is obliged to hear any legal dispute properly brought before it.

The case of *Smith v. United States*,[43] arising out of a tragic accident on federal land, nicely illustrates the ordinary business of a federal district court. After the trial, the district court issued the following finding of facts: In August 1970 Cameron Smith, a Canadian boy, entered Yellowstone National Park with his family. Park rangers gave them a brochure that contained a map and a warning in bold type that stated: "Thin crusts overlie and conceal pools of boiling water. Each year, many careless visitors are burned. For your safety, stay on the trails or boardwalks at all times—watch your children carefully. Keep pets under physical restraint." The Smith family neglected to read the brochure.

While hiking in the Mammoth Hot Springs area, some members of the Smith family departed from the boardwalks. Another visitor immediately pointed to a warning sign, and the Smiths got back on the trail. Shortly thereafter, the family saw another warning sign, and the father again cautioned the children that the ground off the boardwalk could cave in. Despite these warnings, Cameron Smith got off the boardwalk and knelt to look down into a thermal pool. As he stood up, the ground gave way under his weight, and he suffered severe burns across much of his body. During six months in the hospital while his injuries healed and skin grafting took place, the boy suffered additional, indeed "immeasurable," pain and suffering.

Smith's father brought suit against the United States to recover for the injuries sustained. The suit alleged that the U.S. Park Service had not adequately warned visitors of the dangerous thermal pools, that it had never erected guardrails in the area in which the injury occurred, and that it had neglected to conduct inspections to discover, warn about, and make safe the dangerous conditions.

After considering the testimony of various witnesses, the district court declared: "The plaintiff, Cameron Smith, in proceeding as he did to the edge of the hot pool into which he fell failed to conform to the standards of conduct required for his own protection because he did not behave as a reasonable man of his age, learning, and experience, exercising those qualities of attention, knowledge, intelligence, and judgment which society requires of its members for the protection of their own interests and the interests of others." The Court reasoned: "Even if Cameron Smith were an invitee in Yellowstone National Park to whom the United States owed a duty to use ordinary and reasonable care to keep the premises reasonably safe for his visit and to warn him of any hidden danger, there was no breach of any such duty on the part of the defendant, the United States of America." And, the Court held: "[T]he United States . . . has no liability for the injuries of Cameron Smith."

[42] A three-judge panel is required to hear a few types of federal district court cases, such as those requesting an injunction to stop enforcement of a state or federal statute on constitutional grounds.

[43] 383 F.Supp. 1076 (D. Wyo. 1974).

The *Smith* case illustrates something of the activities on the ground floor of the federal court system. The federal district court served as a trial court and, with the help of the lawyers, determined the facts in the dispute. Federal judge Jerome Frank once observed: "Since the actual facts of a case do not walk into court, but happened outside the courtroom, and always in the past, the task of the trial court is to reconstruct the past from what are at best second-hand reports of the facts." He went on: "[I]t is most misleading to talk . . . of a trial court 'finding' the facts. The trial court's facts are not 'data,' not something that is 'given'; they are not waiting somewhere ready made, for the court to discover, to 'find.' More accurately, they are processed by the trial court—are, so to speak, 'made' by it, on the basis of its subjective reactions to the witnesses' stories."[44]

In the *Smith* case, the Court gave both parties the opportunity to present their sides of the dispute and to bring relevant facts and legal arguments to the Court's attention. After a full trial, the judge wrote an opinion applying both federal and Wyoming law to the case and justifying the judgment. Eventually, the plaintiff appealed, and the federal appellate court affirmed, writing: "It is true that as a boy of fourteen plaintiff was required only to exercise for his own protection that care that may fairly and reasonably be expected from children of his own age. We are satisfied, however, that the court applied that standard of care. Further, even as an invitee, the plaintiff owed a reciprocal duty to the invitor to exercise ordinary care to avoid injuring himself. . . . [P]laintiff's conduct did not conform to the standard required of him. . . . Since we cannot conclude that the **contributory negligence** ground supports the trial court's decision, the judgment is affirmed."[45]

The Nature of Federal District Courts

Although originally each state had a single federal district court, over time Congress granted additional federal district courts to those states that needed them. The thirteen original district courts have grown to more than ninety today. Each state now has at least one district, and the District of Columbia and certain American territories, such as Guam and Puerto Rico, contain a district as well. The largest and most populous states are divided into more than one district. The most federal judicial districts are found in California, New York, and Texas which each have four: eastern, southern, western, and northern districts.

The number of judges within each federal district also varies substantially: Several judges might handle a relatively inactive federal district, but more than two dozen are necessary in a very busy urban district, such as the Federal District Court for the Southern District of New York. Of course, since each trial occupies only one judge, different judges may be presiding simultaneously over different cases in the same judicial district. Although the number of district judges has steadily risen, it

[44] Jerome Frank, *Courts on Trial: Myth and Reality in American Justice* (Princeton, NJ: Princeton University Press, 1973), pp. 23–24.

[45] *Smith v. United States,* 546 F.2d 872 (10th Cir. 1976).

has rarely kept pace with the increased workload. Between 1960 and 1990 filings in federal court tripled.[46]

Although the total of civil cases filed in federal court actually declined during the late 1980s, this was partially offset by a rise in criminal cases, especially those dealing with narcotics.[47] Consequently, federal district judges remain overworked. Americans appearing in district court are often astonished at the long delays before their cases are heard. This has been especially true in recent years as stringent federal narcotics laws have caused federal courts to continue to move criminal cases to the front of the **trial docket** to ensure that prisoners are granted the speedy trials guaranteed them under the Constitution.

In addition to the approximately 650 district judges, the federal district courts are staffed by another several hundred bankruptcy judges. The bankruptcy courts, which may be envisioned as special courts under the federal district court umbrella, resolve legal issues regarding those who can no longer pay off their debts. These courts, very busy in times of economic hardship, decide how the assets of a bankrupt person or business are to be distributed to creditors and how a business might be reorganized. An appeal from a bankruptcy court goes first to a federal district court and then on up the federal appellate ladder.

The federal system also includes other supplementary lower courts of the legislative variety.[48] The **U.S. Claims Court** hears lawsuits against the U.S. government that involve the interpretation of a federal law, including the Constitution, a federal regulation, or a federal contract. Most cases involve disputes over taxes, contracts, salaries, and confiscated property.[49] The **U.S. Court of International Trade,** established by Congress in 1980,[50] hears cases involving the import and export of goods and especially how much **customs duties** must be paid to the United States. The **U.S. Tax Court** decides disputes regarding whether an individual or company must pay additional taxes assessed by the **Internal Revenue Service.**

The federal court system need not handle the sheer bulk of legal problems that find their way into the state courts. Despite the frequency with which they must dispose of prisoner appeals, only a small percentage of which are granted, federal judges confront frivolous claims less frequently than do their colleagues on the state bench. Certainly, disputes of negligible importance are more common in state than in federal court. However, the cases that do enter the national court system often require considerable resources to resolve since they tend to be serious matters dealing with problems involving major crimes or fairly substantial sums.

Although federal judges must also try to cope with rising numbers of

[46] Glendon, p. 53.

[47] See Glick, p. 32.

[48] Congress has changed the status of certain legislative courts to constitutional courts. The Court of Claims, for instance, was originally a legislative court, then became a constitutional court, then was disbanded and eventually reestablished as a legislative court. See Abraham, p. 143.

[49] Ibid., p. 37.

[50] The U.S. Claims Court and the U.S. Court of International Trade replace the now defunct U.S. Court of Claims and the U.S. Customs Court.

cases,[51] particularly as narcotics laws and their enforcement have become stricter over time, federal courts tend to be somewhat better prepared to handle an increased caseload. Since deciding federal cases is often viewed as more prestigious than resolving state disputes, and since the personnel that staff the federal courts tend to be better paid, the federal court system attracts especially well-qualified individuals. While lower state judges sometimes work without many assistants or with clerks who have not yet graduated from law school, federal judges can choose among dozens of young lawyers who compete vigorously to serve as their law clerks. For such reasons America's federal court system has long been characterized by a degree of pride and competence that is the envy of those who staff court systems in many other countries.

An Appellate Court Case

Although in most federal trials the **verdict** handed down by the jury[52] or the decision by the federal judge concludes the case, the federal courts of appeals are available for parties who believe that the district court acted in error and should be reversed.[53] The federal appellate courts also hear appeals from decisions in bankruptcy proceedings and before specialized tribunals like the U.S. Tax Court and federal administrative agencies.[54] Although in the American legal system federal prosecutors do not have the right to appeal a not-guilty verdict,[55] as they do in many other countries, a criminal defendant or a civil litigant who lost at the district court level does have the right to appeal. Given the considerable costs of an appeal, however, most district court decisions are not reviewed.

The *Leuro-Rosas* case illustrates the work of a federal court of appeals.[56] In September 1989, while patrolling international waters in the Caribbean Sea, U.S. Coast Guard officers overheard a suspicious radio conversation. Two nearby ships seemed to be trafficking narcotics from Colombia to the United States. When confronted by the Coast Guard ship, the Colombian captain Jorge Leuro-Rosas per-

[51] See Richard A. Posner, *The Federal Courts: Crisis and Reform* (Cambridge, MA: Harvard University Press, 1985), pp. 59–93. In contrast to this trend, the U.S. Supreme Court has made a conscious, and successful, effort to take on fewer and fewer cases. During the tenure of William Rehnquist as Chief Justice the Court's caseload has diminished considerably.

[52] For a discussion of when a jury decides a case and when a judge assumes responsibility for such a decision see Chapters 3 and 5.

[53] In a very limited number of instances an exceedingly important federal district court decision may be appealed directly to the U.S. Supreme Court, as occurred in *United States v. Nixon*, 417 U.S. 683 (1974). See Abraham, pp. 162–163.

[54] Federal administrative agencies are government departments, such as the Department of Agriculture, the Department of Labor, the Food and Drug Administration, or the Environmental Protection Agency. As explained in Chapter 8, each state also has its own network of administrative agencies.

[55] The government may appeal to clarify a legal principle that the prosecutor believes the judge misunderstood. However, the not guilty verdict as to the defendant will stand since under the **double jeopardy** clause in the U.S. Constitution no one may be prosecuted a second time for the same offense. See U.S. Constitution, Amendment V.

[56] *United States v. Leuro-Rosas*, 952 F.2d 616 (1st Cir. 1991).

mitted American officials on board to search his vessel, which was flying a Panamanian flag.

During the search Coast Guard officials came upon certain sealed metal containers in the ship's cargo hold. Captain Leuro-Rosas, without offering any convincing reason, refused to allow the officials to open those suspicious containers. The Coast Guard lieutenant in charge of the search called his superiors in Puerto Rico by radio, who in turn contacted the U.S. State Department. A U.S. diplomat then reported that Panamanian authorities did not object to the American authorities searching the containers in question. Shortly thereafter, the Coast Guard discovered that the metal containers contained 1,211 kilograms of cocaine. The U.S. District Court that heard the criminal trial convicted Captain Jorge Leuro-Rosas of the federal offense of possession with intent to distribute cocaine.

The defense attorney for Leuro-Rosas appealed the district court's decision to the First Circuit Court of Appeals. He claimed that the search had been illegal and that the district court had erred in stating that the Coast Guard had jurisdiction to board and search the Panamanian ship in international waters. In particular, Leuro-Rosas' attorney argued that no Panamanian official still holding a political office had authorized the search. Rather, the State Department had relied upon **blanket authorization** given by Eric Arturo Delvalle, a former elected president of Panama, who had been forced to flee from Panama to the United States by dictator Manuel Noriega. Leuro-Rosas' attorney argued that, since the search that uncovered the narcotics was illegal, the conviction must be reversed on appeal.

After considering the case, the court of appeals upheld the district court's conviction of Jorge Leuro-Rosas. The judges reasoned that under U.S. constitutional law the president has exclusive authority to decide **political questions,** such as when and whether to **recognize a government.** The Constitution thus entitled the U.S. government to determine that no legitimate government existed in Panama on the date the Coast Guard requested authorization, and the State Department could appropriately recognize Delvalle as the leader of the legitimate regime, even though he had fled Panama. Thus, the judges stated, the search of the Panamanian ship rested on legal authorization, and the conviction of Jorge Leuro-Rosas should be affirmed.

Both the *Leuro-Rosas* case and the *Smith* case show federal courts of appeals engaged in the task of reviewing a district court decision to decide whether to affirm or reverse. Rather than engaging in additional fact-finding, the reviewing appellate court scrutinizes how the trial court applied the law to the facts. Did the trial judge misunderstand the law and apply it wrongly to the case? If so, the appeals court may overturn the court's decision, and in certain cases a judge will call for a new trial, a *trial de novo.* If not, it will allow that decision to stand.

Appellate courts also try to ensure that the weight of the evidence really does support the verdict in the case, and the judges attempt to satisfy themselves that the "interests of justice" have been achieved. However, an appellate judge often acknowledges that the trial court enjoyed the critical advantage of inspecting the physical evidence and listening first-hand to all the witnesses, and that the trial court will thus normally have a much better sense of how justice will be served in a particular case than will an appeals court reviewing a **written record** many months later. Hence, most appeals judges try to defer to the trial court unless a clear error has occurred.

The Nature of Federal Appellate Courts

Although, by tradition, each U.S. Supreme Court justice heads one of the courts of appeals, for many years the business of the Supreme Court has fully occupied all the justices. Hence, the justices participate in their courts of appeals primarily as nominal figureheads, not as influential colleagues or supervisors. Nonetheless, long ago, each justice would ride on horseback from one appellate court to another actually sitting and hearing appeals.[57] The grueling horseback ride from court to court became known as a "circuit." Thus, these courts that make up the next level of the federal court system are often referred to as *circuit courts of appeals.*

Today, twelve of the circuits hear appeals from the federal district courts of a handful of states grouped in a particular region. For instance, the First Circuit Court of Appeals hears cases appealed from the federal district courts of Maine, Massachusetts, New Hampshire, and Rhode Island, and the territory of Puerto Rico. (Table 2.1 lists these federal Courts of Appeals and their responsibilities.) One additional circuit, called the U.S. Court of Appeals for the Federal Circuit, hears appeals in patent, tax, trade, and certain other specialized cases.[58] Although this amounts to a thirteenth circuit, it has never been formally labeled the Thirteenth Circuit.

In deciding a case on appeal, judges review the record of the case below and the briefs submitted by the attorneys on each side. Briefs are also sometimes written by one or more ***amicus curiae***—a person or organization with a strong interest in the subject matter of the dispute that is granted permission by the court to file a "friend of the court" brief in support of the legal position of a party to the suit.

In important cases appellate courts provide the attorneys on each side with an opportunity for a brief oral argument, sometimes consisting of as little as ten minutes for each side. Typically, lawyers in oral argument will start to emphasize the strengths of their legal case only to be cut off by judges probing the weaknesses and ambiguities in their briefs. Finally, appellate judges write opinions. A full opinion describes the facts of the case and explains the reasoning and decision regarding all substantial legal issues that arose on appeal. Often, however,

[57] Originally, the appellate court was composed of two Supreme Court justices and one federal district judge. For the evolution of this system over time see Carp and Stidham, pp. 36–37.

[58] Many matters before the U.S. Court of Appeals for the Federal Circuit were once the business of certain formerly legislative courts that Congress turned into constitutional courts in the 1950s, such as the U.S. Court of Claims and the U.S. Court of Customs.

TABLE 2.1 **The U.S. Courts of Appeals**

There follows a list of the states and territories that are covered by the Courts of Appeals in the federal judicial system. The Supreme Court, of course, is another federal court of appeals that stands above these circuit courts of appeals.

First Circuit	Maine, Massachusetts, New Hampshire, Puerto Rico, Rhode Island.
Second Circuit	Connecticut, New York, Vermont.
Third Circuit	Delaware, New Jersey, Pennsylvania, Virgin Islands.
Fourth Circuit	Maryland, North Carolina, South Carolina, Virginia, West Virginia.
Fifth Circuit	Louisiana, Mississippi, Texas.
Sixth Circuit	Kentucky, Michigan, Ohio, Tennessee.
Seventh Circuit	Illinois, Indiana, Wisconsin.
Eighth Circuit	Arkansas, Iowa, Minnesota, Missouri, Nebraska, North Dakota, South Dakota.
Ninth Circuit	Alaska, Arizona, California, Guam, Hawaii, Idaho, Montana, Nevada, Northern Mariana Islands, Oregon, Washington.
Tenth Circuit	Colorado, Kansas, New Mexico, Utah, Oklahoma, Wyoming.
Eleventh Circuit	Alabama, Florida, Georgia.
Twelfth Circuit	District of Columbia.

Also The Court of Appeals for the Federal Circuit.

judges decide that a brief announcement of how the case has been resolved will suffice.[59]

In reviewing the trial proceedings and decisions of the lower federal courts and certain administrative agencies, the 179 federal appellate judges normally sit in panels of three and decide a case by majority vote.[60] Although the chief judge used to determine the composition of the panels, these days that decision is made randomly, normally by computer. The composition of the panels also constantly shifts so that over time a judge will decide cases with all of his or her colleagues, not just two others. In very contentious cases, such as when different panels within the same circuit have been deciding similar cases differently, the court of appeals may choose to sit ***en banc,*** that is, with all the judges joining to hear and decide the case. Thus, a federal appeals court will often simultaneously have different panels of judges hearing different cases in different cities.

As with the district courts, Congress has added more judges to those circuits with the heaviest caseloads.[61] Thus, the First Circuit, primarily serving the northern New England states, has fewer than a quarter of the judges found in the

[59] Such a brief announcement is sometimes referred to as a ***per curiam*** opinion. However, technically, *per curiam* simply means "by the whole court." Thus, while *per curiam* opinions are ordinarily short, a chief justice or a presiding judge could write a *per curiam* opinion that was substantially longer than the more usual brief announcement of how a case was decided.

[60] The numbers of federal district and appellate judges changes with time. The totals cited in this and the prior paragraph are as of 1992. See Maguire and Pastore, p. 69.

[61] Although the number of federal judgeships has been increased repeatedly, all efforts to appoint additional federal judges become entangled in partisan politics, given the president's appointment prerogative discussed in Chapter 3.

Ninth Circuit,[62] which covers an area stretching from Alaska to Nevada and includes far and away the most populous state, California. The appellate judges within a circuit are continually rotated, so that the composition of the panels of three judges is never fixed over time.

The time and effort of state and federal appellate courts is largely focused upon correcting the errors of the lower courts in applying the relevant law. One may question, however, the extent to which all, or even the majority of errors that occur in a case are in fact corrected. Not all civil litigants and criminal defendants have the financial resources necessary to pursue an appeal. Moreover, appellate judges are not invariably more perceptive in their application and interpretation of the law than are their colleagues below. And, if errors have occurred in the assessment of facts undertaken at the trial court level, an appellate judge may find it difficult or impossible to rectify that type of problem. In this regard two legal scholars observed:

> American appellate judges receive a case in the form of a record shaped by the procedural rulings and findings of fact in the trial court. The litigation, like rough dough, has already been partly molded. When the record consists largely of documents, . . . appellate judges may feel at least as competent as the trial judge to weigh the evidence. But when the evidence consists mostly of oral testimony and the witnesses have contradicted each other . . . , appellate judges, because they themselves neither saw nor heard those witnesses, are loath to overturn a trial judge's findings.[63]

Although the problem of overworked judges is perhaps not quite so dire as in the state courts, or even as in the federal district courts, the federal courts of appeals remain quite busy with a workload approaching 50,000 cases each year.[64]

The U.S. Supreme Court

The United States Supreme Court occupies the leading position at the pinnacle of the federal court system. (Figure 2.1 shows the movement of cases through the federal court system.) The court of last resort in the federal system, the Supreme Court is also the ultimate court of appeals for cases finally decided in state courts that contain a question of federal law. The Supreme Court also has very limited **original jurisdiction,** that is, the power to hear a case the first time it is argued. For instance, the Supreme Court must hear lawsuits between states and those that involve an ambassador from a foreign country. However, the Supreme Court principally functions as the ultimate American court of review, the national court of last resort.

[62] See Tarr, p. 43.

[63] Walter F. Murphy and C. Herman Pritchett, *Courts, Judges, and Politics,* 3d ed. rev. (New York: Random House, 1979), p. 442. The term *upper court myth* is drawn from Frank, pp. 222–224. Judge Frank likewise noted: "An upper court can seldom do anything to correct a trial court's mistaken belief about the facts."

[64] See Abraham, p. 163.

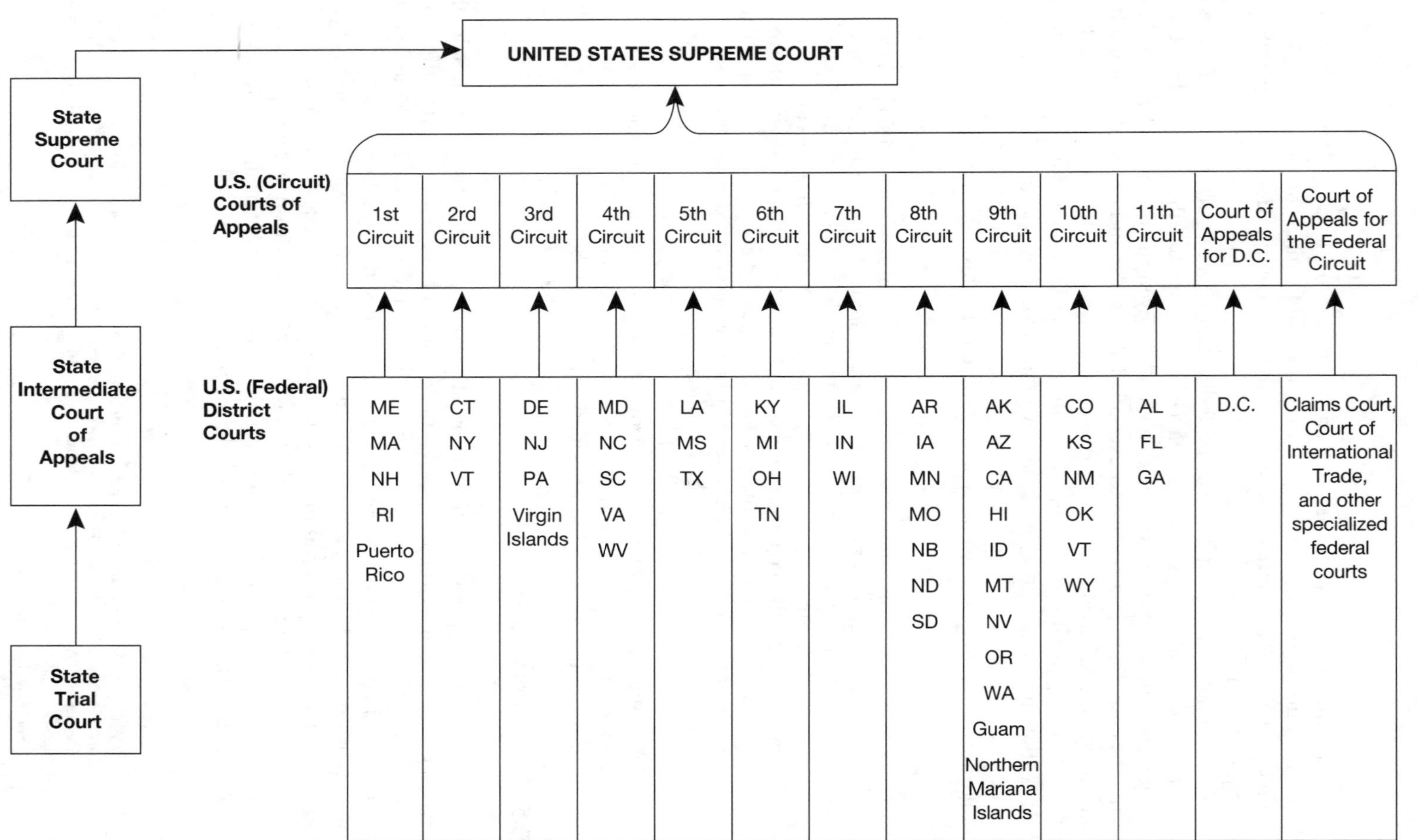

FIGURE 2.1 **Movement of a typical[1] case through the U.S. court system**

[1] In unusual cases, the U.S. Supreme Court may preside over a trial or hear appeals directly from a U.S. district court or a specialized federal court, such as those dealing with tax or military matters.

Since the state and federal appellate courts provide American litigants and criminal defendants with the single appeal guaranteed to them, the **Chief Justice** and the eight associate justices have substantial discretion to decide which appeals to review and which to ignore. This distinguishes the national Supreme Court from the state supreme courts, most of which are bound to hear appeals in various categories of cases.

The U.S. Supreme Court thus selects for review a small number of the many cases on appeal from the U.S. courts of appeals and the ultimate state courts. These cases invariably involve questions of federal law.[65] A party that has lost such a case in state court may appeal to the U.S. Supreme Court through a process known as ***certiorari,*** in which a party requests that the Supreme Court must review a particular lower court decision. The justices, usually through assistants known as **law clerks,** examine the many requests that are filed and select for Supreme Court review those of greatest significance. When the Court agrees to exercise its **appellate jurisdiction** and review a case, it issues a **writ of *certiorari,*** that is, an order to the lower court to forward to the Supreme Court the full case record for its review. Under the so-called **Rule of Four,** four justices must agree before a writ of *certiorari* will be granted. When a request for *certiorari* is denied, the decision of the lower court becomes final.

Of the thousands of Supreme Court appeals each year, the justices choose to hear only those cases with the greatest potential impact on the development of federal law. Rather than focusing on correcting the errors of lower courts, the justices customarily decide to hear a particular appeal if the case will raise a significant question of constitutional or federal statutory law that the Supreme Court has yet to confront, that the Court may have dealt with incorrectly in the past,[66] or that different appellate courts have resolved in conflicting manners. In the present era more than half of the cases selected for Supreme Court review involve constitutional interpretation, and in an average year the Court issues about 150 opinions.[67]

THE PURPOSES OF COURTS

A country that lacks a functioning court system is a frightening place in which to live. All modern societies need courts to interpret and enforce the law. Not long ago, my wife and I were living in Panama, a country that had long suffered from a grossly inefficient court system. During our visit about 90 percent of the prisoners in Panamanian jails had never been to court.[68] Crime levels, particularly in the

[65] One authority found that of over 4,000 cases appealed to the Supreme Court in one year, the Court accepted less than 5 percent. Tarr, p. 46.

[66] When two or more circuit courts of appeal have resolved similar cases differently, the Supreme Court is especially likely to hear the case.

[67] See Carp and Stidham, p. 32.

[68] See Americas Watch, *Human Rights in Post-Invasion Panama: Justice Delayed is Justice Denied* (New York: Americas Watch, 1991), p. 2, and "Hacinamiento y justicia tarde, drama de cárceles panameñas" ["Overcrowding and Slow Justice: The Drama of Panamanian Prisons"], *La Prensa* [Panama], July 3, 1990, p. 8A.

cities, were high and rising. People often carried guns to defend themselves from criminals, many of whom were likely never to be caught and punished. At the same time, civil cases were so terribly backlogged as to preclude many possible litigants from pursuing a judicial resolution of their dispute. Absent effective courts, people ignored serious differences or resolved them with naked force. That image of a society without a well-functioning court system raises important questions. Why have courts? What purposes do courts serve?

One cardinal function of courts is to punish those who violate the criminal law. Governments devote considerable resources to arresting, prosecuting, and penalizing criminals and maintaining a respect for law and order. Authorities aim to incarcerate dangerous individuals, so that they do not continue to commit crimes and injure innocent people. Strict punishment may also deter potential criminals. Harsh penalties may prevent people from committing crimes by showing them that violating the law generally leads to punishment.

Apart from the vital job of punishing criminals and curbing crime, courts also provide a means to resolve disputes fairly. Courts help to prevent anarchy by interpreting and formally upholding social rules. In analyzing a civil or criminal issue, a court should try to discover the truth and to act fairly in applying the law to the facts. However, courts do not and cannot always discover the truth and deliver correct decisions. Not only do judges naturally make occasional mistakes, but courts cannot spend unlimited resources doing everything possible to ensure that all relevant facts have been considered and all legal decisions have been rendered correctly. The available time and money must be distributed among all the cases that await final decision.[69] Nevertheless, courts can try, within reasonable limits, to fulfill these objectives.

In this regard one might consider again the two local court cases reviewed above. The judge in traffic court, who listens to 100 people in an afternoon, knows that she will make some mistakes. She will surely let some guilty people go free, and she will make some innocent people pay fines. What is important for the health of the legal system is that the judge attempts to act fairly and that citizens can see her trying. In fact, public scrutiny of trials has increased tremendously in recent years as television cameras have been allowed into more courtrooms for more types of trials, and television stations have broadcast ever-larger segments of both controversial and routine proceedings.

Certainly, a judge should allow each side in the dispute to tell its version of the events. He or she should treat each side with respect and give each person with a plausible claim a "day in court." Moreover, the more serious the legal issue, the more important it is that an opportunity should be granted to the parties and the court to delve deeply into what happened. While perhaps a murder case ought not carry on for such an extraordinary period as occurred in the O.J. Simpson criminal trial in 1995, the issue of murder should certainly be scrutinized more carefully than a breach of contract or a drunk driving issue.

[69] One might also note that "[e]ndless scrutiny does not necessarily make for a better judgment . . ." Philip K. Howard, *The Death of Common Sense: How Law Is Suffocating America* (New York: Warner Books, 1994), p. 87.

However, once the purpose of conscientiously attempting to be fair to the parties is served, then a busy judge in any court must reach a decision and move on to another case. Judges should conclude one case expeditiously in order to give themselves ample time to consider the next dispute. Few problems are so important that a court can consider them for extraordinarily long periods. Courts exist, not just to try to act fairly or to ponder legal philosophies, but actually to decide something—to determine, for instance, whether Mr. Fenton or the country club is right about the legal consequences of all those golf balls bouncing toward his house.

In fact, all involved in a case normally want the court to decide the matter, so that they can go on about their lives. The elderly woman locked out of her house and the niece concerned about the woman's mentally ill son need to have the court come to some decision, so they can put their dispute to rest. In the final analysis, courts must act to resolve legal issues one way or another. Courts bring closure to disputes so that people can move on to other matters. Perhaps that traditional impetus to move forward and come to a decision—while sometimes subverted by a lack of resources—counts as a real strength of American courts that distinguishes them from those government bureaucracies that prefer to study or ignore a problem in the hope that, over time, it will diminish in importance or vanish altogether. In the final analysis, courts are legal institutions that help society to order itself.

SELECTED ADDITIONAL READINGS

ABRAHAM, HENRY J. *The Judicial Process: An Introductory Analysis of the Courts of the United States, England, and France.* 6th ed. rev. New York: Oxford University Press, 1993.

BAUM, LAWRENCE. *American Courts: Process and Policy.* Boston: Houghton Mifflin, 1995.

CARP, ROBERT A., and STIDHAM, RONALD. *The Federal Courts.* 2d ed. rev. Washington, DC: Congressional Quarterly Press, 1990.

FRANK, JEROME. *Courts on Trial: Myth and Reality in American Justice.* Princeton, NJ: Princeton University Press, 1973.

GATES, JOHN P., and JOHNSON, CHARLES A. *The American Courts: A Critical Assessment.* Washington, DC: Congressional Quarterly Press, 1991.

GLICK, HENRY R. *Courts, Politics and Justice.* 3d ed. rev. New York: McGraw-Hill, 1993.

HOWARD, J. WOODFORD, JR. *Courts of Appeals in the Federal Judicial System.* Princeton, NJ: Princeton University Press, 1981.

POSNER, RICHARD A. *The Federal Courts: Crisis and Reform.* Cambridge, MA: Harvard University Press, 1985.

RICHARDSON, RICHARD J., and VINES, KENNETH N. *The Politics of Federal Courts.* Boston: Little, Brown, 1977.

STUMPF, HARRY P., and CULVER, JOHN H. *The Politics of State Courts.* New York: Longman, 1992.

TARR, ALAN G., and PORTER, MARY CORNELIA ALDIS. *State Supreme Courts in State and Nation.* New Haven, Conn.: Yale University Press, 1988.

3

The Judge

Just as three categories of American courts exist—the local,[1] state, and federal courts—so each of those courts has its own set of judges. Naturally, serving as a judge in **traffic court** or any other **local court** differs markedly from undertaking a judicial career at the highest federal court, the United States Supreme Court. This chapter focuses upon several questions regarding the extent to which the American judiciary serves the goal of providing justice for all: How are American judges selected? What role does the judge play within a common law legal system, such as that found in the United States? How does it differ from the judge's role in a civil law legal system such as that found in Japan and continental Europe? How do judges think about legal issues and formulate legal opinions? What is meant by judicial activism and restraint and judicial policymaking? Finally, what accounts for the status of American judges?

THE JUDICIAL PROFESSION

Selection of Judges[2]

The features of the federal system for selecting judges are designed to ensure that someone appointed to the federal judiciary can serve in an independent manner. All judges are supposed to decide cases on the legal merits without considering whether the public or any politician, including the president, will be pleased with the decisions. Thus, for the **constitutional courts,** the president nominates

[1] As noted in Chapter 2, local courts are technically part of the state court system; however, to clarify analysis, they are treated as a separate category of courts in this work.

[2] One thorough and readable introduction to the selection of federal and state judges is Robert A. Carp and Ronald Stidham, *Judicial Process in America,* 3d ed. rev. (Washington, DC: Congressional Quarterly, 1996), pp. 229–262.

people for federal judgeships who will, if confirmed, serve lifetime appointments.[3] After nomination, the U.S. Senate then votes to confirm or reject each nominee. Article III of the U.S. Constitution stipulates that the compensation of a federal judge on a constitutional court shall not be diminished during his or her time in office.[4] According to the Constitution, a federal judge is to serve during "good behavior."[5] Certain judges whose unlawful conduct has come to public attention have chosen to resign; others have been impeached and convicted[6] by the U.S. Congress.

State judges take office in different manners. Some are elected; others are appointed by governors, usually with the consent of the state senate, or in a few states by that state's legislature.[7] In various states judges are elected to lower courts and appointed to higher courts.[8] In some states candidates for judicial office make clear their party affiliations. Elsewhere elections are nonpartisan and party connections are not formally noted on the ballot, though they may be an open secret.[9] In states with judicial elections, such as Texas, a judge often resigns before his or her term in office expires.[10] The governor then appoints a replacement, who faces reelection as an incumbent and thus ordinarily gains a key advantage on potential rivals, many of whom may choose not to run against a sitting judge. Although occasionally ill health or other personal problems force an untimely resignation, judges in Texas frequently resign early simply because they want a politically friendly governor to appoint a like-minded successor.

About four out of every ten states have adopted a hybrid **merit selection system** in which judges are selected for particular courts by a combined appointment-and-election process. First, the governor appoints a state judge from a list of candidates nominated by a blue-ribbon panel. After a period has elapsed, the appointee must then gain voter approval in an uncontested **retention election.** This selection process is sometimes called the **Missouri plan** after the state in which it was first used. The American Judicature Society, a well-respected, private organization, has long lobbied for the selection of judges on merit, supporting the Missouri plan of selection and opposing the election of judges. Over the past decades it has

[3] Federal judges in legislative courts serve for a designated period of years.

[4] U.S. Constitution, Art. III, Sec. 1.

[5] Ibid.

[6] The term *impeachment,* when used properly, refers to the proceeding, not to its result. Hence, a public official can be impeached and found innocent.

[7] Among the states that still appoint judges by legislative vote are Rhode Island, South Carolina, and Virginia.

[8] For instance, Arizona, California, Florida, Indiana, New York, and South Dakota elect only trial court judges.

[9] Carp and Stidham, p. 256. The authors wrote: "[I]n [certain] . . . technically nonpartisan states, the political parties still endorse individual judicial candidates and contribute to their campaigns so that by the time of the election, only a dullard would fail to distinguish the 'nonpartisan' Republican from the 'nonpartisan' Democrat." Ibid., p. 258.

[10] See James V. Calvi and Susan Coleman, *American Law and Legal Systems* (Englewood Cliffs, NJ: Prentice Hall, 1992), p. 59; Carp and Stidham, p. 256; and Henry R. Glick, *Courts, Politics, and Justice,* 3d ed. rev. (New York: McGraw-Hill, 1993), pp. 118–119.

been instrumental in persuading several state legislatures to abolish judicial elections and establish merit selection processes.

Just as the mode of selecting judges differs from state to state, so the laws of the states also vary on the necessary qualifications for judges.[11] Rather than choosing judges from the graduates of a judicial school, as is common in many civil law countries, the American judiciary is drawn from the ranks of legal practitioners. Among the qualifications that certain states impose on candidates are a minimum or maximum age, U.S. citizenship, a minimum term of residence in that state, and membership in that state's bar.

Although most state court judges serve for six or eight years, the term of office differs from state to state and from one court to another. For instance, supreme court judges in Oklahoma serve for six years; in Massachusetts, New Hampshire, and Puerto Rico they serve to age 70, and in Rhode Island they are appointed for life. In North Dakota judges in the general trial courts known as district courts serve for six years and judges in the Supreme Court serve for ten. But in Maryland judges in the general trial courts known as the circuit courts serve for fifteen years, and judges in the intermediate appellate courts, known as courts of special appeals and in the court of last resort, known as the Court of Appeals, serve for just ten years.[12]

Identifying the best qualified individuals to serve in the judiciary is always a formidable task. Each of the American methods of selecting judges has advantages, yet each is far from perfect. On the federal level, appointment by the president with confirmation by the Senate can screen out undistinguished lawyers, sometimes derogatorily called *party hacks*, who might be able to gain appointment through political connections alone. In addition, the federal process, through scrutiny by the Senate and with background checks by the Federal Bureau of Investigation, disqualifies some candidates whose appointment might prove troublesome. Once the judge has taken the bench, however, the federal appointment process shields him or her from undue popular or political pressures by dispensing with reappointment or reelection.

But appointing judges also has clear drawbacks. It can lead to arbitrary behavior by individual judges who are not accountable to anyone. Lifetime appointment can be problematic when an elderly judge does not wish to resign, yet can no longer serve as competently as he or she once did.[13] The several state legislatures that appoint state judges are notorious for *cronyism*. They appoint to the bench a disproportionate number of former legislators.[14]

[11] Massachusetts alone has no special qualification requirements for judges.

[12] For additional information on state court judges, see Kathleen Maguire and Ann L. Pastore, eds., *Sourcebook of Criminal Justice Statistics—1993* (Washington, DC: U.S. Government Printing Office, 1994), p. 77.

[13] Some states alleviate this problem by designating a mandatory retirement age.

[14] One study of judges appointed by state legislatures showed that former legislators were selected to positions on trial courts 80 percent of the time; another revealed that more than three-quarters of state supreme court justices had served on the legislature. See Glick, p. 122, and Henry R. Glick and Craig F. Emmert, "Selection Systems and Judicial Characteristics: The Recruitment of State Supreme Court Justices," *Judicature* 70 (Dec./Jan. 1987): 232. See also Carp and Stidham, p. 260; Tarr, p. 68.

The federal mode of appointing judges can also embroil candidates in a highly partisan political process.[15] On average, about nine out of ten nominees for positions in the federal judiciary belong to the president's own political party.[16] Thus, should one party control the presidency for several terms, highly qualified individuals from the party that is out of power may be overlooked.[17] Moreover, under such circumstances the political biases and judicial philosophies of the party in the White House may come to be reflected on the federal bench as well.

Nominees to a federal district court are often selected with a view to pleasing a U.S. senator or senators from the state in which that court sits.[18] By virtue of the practice of **senatorial courtesy,** senators have been able to veto judicial candidates from their state whom they oppose.[19] As one authority noted: "[Senatorial courtesy means] . . . a senator of the President's party can ask . . . Senate colleagues not to approve a nominee from the senator's state that does not meet with the senator's approval. All other senators will support another senator's request, expecting similar treatment in return."[20] Since senators are naturally influenced by political considerations, one can question whether it is the most able candidates who emerge from the federal appointment process or merely the most politically palatable.

Although appointments to a federal district court are usually not exceptionally controversial, the Senate Judiciary Committee scrutinizes proposed judges on the U.S. courts of appeals much more closely than nominees to the federal trial courts. Prospective Supreme Court justices are often analyzed with painstaking care. Indeed, the Senate has rejected about one in five Supreme Court nominees, though that statistic might mislead the modern observer since many of the rejections occurred before 1900.[21]

While interest group participation in Senate hearings is considered a customary and healthy part of the public debate over the suitability of a judicial appointment, especially to the Supreme Court,[22] confirmation hearings have occa-

[15] See Stephen L. Carter, *The Confirmation Mess: Cleaning Up the Federal Appointments Process* (New York: Basic Books, 1995).

[16] Calvi and Coleman, p. 50. During the last century about 95 percent of federal district court judges have hailed from the same political party as the president nominating them. See David M. O'Brien, *Judicial Roulette: Report of the Twentieth Century Fund Task Force on Judicial Selection* (New York: Priority Press, 1988), p. 35.

[17] After two terms of President Reagan and one term of President Bush, the federal judiciary was 75 percent Republican.

[18] Calvi and Coleman, p. 52. Normally, to be influential with the president, the senator will be a member of the president's political party, though that is not always the case.

[19] The term *senatorial courtesy* is not customarily applied to appointments to the federal appeals courts. While federal district courts are contained within a single state, a federal appellate court covers several states. Although senators continue to play a substantial role in suggesting and reacting to candidates, one might more accurately refer to *senatorial clearance* rather than *senatorial courtesy.* See Glick, p. 145.

[20] Ibid., p. 144.

[21] Ibid., p. 136.

[22] See John Anthony Maltese, *The Selling of Supreme Court Nominees* (Baltimore, MD: Johns Hopkins University Press, 1995).

sionally turned into raw and ugly partisan contests. From time to time senators have primarily tried to score political points and curry favor with interest groups, and only secondarily analyzed seriously the training, qualifications, and professional competence of the nominee. The prospect of being at the center of such a battle has doubtless caused certain potential nominees to withdraw their names from consideration.

The federal appointment process is dignified to some extent by the voluntary,[23] yet common, practice of submitting a potential nominee's name to the **American Bar Association.** An independent and supposedly nonpartisan judicial screening panel, the ABA's Standing Committee on the Federal Judiciary, evaluates nominees for integrity and legal skills by reviewing their records and interviewing judges and lawyers who know them.[24] Eventually, it issues a finding as to whether the nominee or potential nominee is qualified in its opinion to serve as a federal judge. Although the ABA has occasionally endorsed judges of dubious competence and raised questions about others that seem driven by considerations other than professional ability,[25] the process of having a recognized body of lawyers submit their views on a nominee is often useful.

Selecting judges by election, as occurs in many states, operates on a different theory altogether.[26] It involves the public in the judicial process by giving voters the opportunity to show their approval or disapproval of judicial behavior. For better or for worse, judges under this system are unlikely to diverge markedly from local views of how the laws should be interpreted, and if they do contradict local opinion, they may not win reelection. Nevertheless, since many judges run for reelection, or even for election, unopposed or with negligible competition, crass efforts to win votes are unusual.

While this process seems well suited for a democratic government that values citizen participation, it also suffers from considerable drawbacks. If a judge is to win a party's nomination or is to run with a party affiliation, he or she may gain office primarily because of exceptional political skills or a history of campaign contributions or other party favors, rather than on account of outstanding legal experience or a brilliant legal mind.

[23] Among various exceptions, President Ronald Reagan chose not to submit Sandra Day O'Connor's name to the ABA panel. See Carp and Stidham, p. 252; Calvi and Coleman, p. 51.

[24] For an article reviewing the dispute over whether the ABA committee is truly nonpartisan, see Saundra Terry, "ABA's Judicial Panel Is a Favorite Bipartisan Target," *Washington Post,* April 29, 1996, Washington Business sec., p. 7. In fact, during the twelve years of Republican administrations under presidents Ronald Reagan and George Bush, the ABA found only one nominee unqualified. Of the 185 men and women nominated to the bench by President Bill Clinton between 1992 and early 1996, the panel found four to be unqualified. Ibid. See also Carp and Stidham, pp. 250–252, Glick, pp. 140–149.

[25] The ABA and sixteen of its former presidents testified in favor of Clement Haynesworth, nominated to the Supreme Court by President Richard Nixon, yet rejected decisively by the Senate. Seven former ABA presidents testified against Louis Brandeis, nominated by President Woodrow Wilson, confirmed by the Senate, and generally considered one of the finest legal minds to serve on the Supreme Court in the twentieth century. See Glick, pp. 141–142. One of the notable biographies of Brandeis is Philippa Strum, *Louis D. Brandeis: Justice for the People* (Cambridge, MA: Harvard University Press, 1984).

[26] For a work critically analyzing judicial elections see Philip L. Dubois, *From Ballot to Bench* (Austin: University of Texas Press, 1980).

Worse still, voters may be as uninterested or as unable to choose wisely from among judicial candidates, as they are from among candidates for state auditor, state treasurer, or other offices that do not ordinarily command much media attention.[27] Citizens may simply pick the incumbent or vote on ethnic or party lines regardless of the professional merits of the candidates. In addition, electing judges may adversely affect the composition of the judiciary should the majority of voters overlook the talents of candidates who belong to a different race or ethnic group from the one which predominates among eligible voters. One legal scholar wrote: "In judicial . . . elections, white voters vote overwhelmingly for white candidates, and blacks and others vote heavily for black or ethnic candidates. If blacks or Hispanics are in a minority in a judicial district, few or none of their number will be elected."[28] For all these reasons, one may question whether selecting the judiciary by election identifies the most highly qualified candidates.

The election process can also directly expose judges to pressures avoided by the federal judiciary. A judge likely to face a competitive contender and intent on winning reelection may shy away from taking unpopular political stances.[29] A judge may harbor ill feelings toward lawyers who supported an opposing candidate and may allow that bias to influence decisions. Equally disturbing, judges eyeing reelection may strive to retain their popularity with the lawyers who practice in front of them and, perhaps, contributed to their campaigns. A well-known American lawyer commented:

> The electorate as a whole does not know enough about the candidates or care enough about the issues to exercise discretion when voting for judges. It's the lawyers who care, who contribute to the judges' reelection campaigns, who influence the party leaders when they make the selection of candidates. And one of the oldest traditions of politics is that you get even with those who you feel have done you damage. A judge, like anyone else who runs for office, wants to be reelected. It's difficult to persuade him to police the lawyers who come before him when those lawyers are or easily can become active in political clubs.[30]

He concluded: "Any reform movement that relies on the cooperation of judges must start, then, in the federal courts, where judges are appointed for life and owe no favors to the lawyers who appear before them."[31]

In summary, although the judiciary is supposed to function in an apolitical

[27] One survey found that less than 5 percent of the voters in one Texas election could even name a single candidate for the trial court of general jurisdiction. See R. Neal McKnight, Roger Schaefer, and Charles A. Johnson, "Choosing Judges: Do the Voters Know What They're Doing?," *Judicature* 62 (August 1978): 94–99, cited in G. Alan Tarr, *Judicial Process and Judicial Policymaking* (St. Paul, MN: West, 1994), p. 71.

[28] Glick, p. 121.

[29] One study suggests that judges up for reelection stop writing controversial dissents. See Melinda Gann Hall, "Constituent Influence in State Supreme Courts: Conceptual Notes and a Case Study," *Journal of Politics* 49 (1987): 1117–1124, cited in Glick, p. 322.

[30] Sol Linowitz here paraphrases former ABA president Justin Stanley. See Sol M. Linowitz with Martin Mayer, *The Betrayed Profession: Lawyering at the End of the Twentieth Century* (New York: Charles Scribner's Sons, 1994), p. 168.

[31] Ibid.

manner, both the appointment and election of judges are highly politicized processes. Whether the president appoints judges, as in the federal system, or the governor or legislature does so, as in various states, or the people vote for judges, as in other states, the judicial selection process is rife with political considerations. Perhaps as a consequence, the American judiciary has never been an especially diverse body. For years the unrepresentative nature of the judiciary reflected the composition of the legal profession as a whole. Relatively few women and minorities had entered legal careers and fewer still had reached the top echelons of the profession. However, those circumstances have changed dramatically in the last several decades.

Since recent presidents, especially Jimmy Carter and Bill Clinton,[32] have found numerous qualified[33] women and members of minority groups to appoint to the federal bench, the problem of a judiciary that does not sufficiently draw upon the talents of all lawyers is now most pressing in the state courts. Two scholars recently noted: "As of the mid-1990s, only about 14 percent of state judges were women and 6 percent were either black, Hispanic, or Asian."[34] As candidates for the judiciary from these groups increase in number and their credentials steadily improve, the American judiciary may lose legitimacy if women and minorities continue to be overlooked in the state and federal selection processes.

The Judicial Staff

Once appointed, judges take charge of a large staff of assistants.[35] Federal judges and judges in the higher state courts are assisted by law clerks in researching, drafting, and editing opinions, in discussing legal issues, and occasionally in running errands and performing an array of less substantive professional tasks such as check-

[32] When President Carter was elected, women accounted for more than 50 percent of the population, yet less than 2 percent of the judiciary. More than 34 percent of Carter's appointees were women or minorities; 14 percent of Reagan's, 28 percent of Bush's, and more than half of Clinton's appointments have been women or minorities. Carp and Stidham, pp. 231, 234.

[33] Tarr observed: "The American Bar Association rated over 50 percent of [Carter's] . . . district court appointees and 75 percent of his appeals court appointees exceptionally well qualified or well qualified, ratings comparable to those received by the nominees of preceding presidents." Tarr, p. 84.

[34] Carp and Stidham, p. 261. See also Tarr, p. 80.

[35] National supervisory bodies give federal judges administrative support from above. The Judicial Conference, presided over by the chief justice, meets twice a year to discuss salaries, budgets, new judgeships, the revision of procedural rules, and other such administrative matters. The Administrative Office serves as an information clearinghouse and liaison between the federal judiciary and the public, the legal community, and the other branches. The Federal Judicial Center provides orientation and continuing education training programs for federal judges and magistrates, probation officers and public defenders, staff attorneys, clerks of the court, and other court personnel. Although the state courts tend to be less funded and less well organized, each state has an office of court administration that compiles statistics, issues reports, and conducts training sessions. Since 1977, the National Center for State Courts, located in Williamsburg, Virginia, and supported principally by state appropriations, has provided for state courts and judges much of the support services that the U.S. Judicial Conference, U.S. Administrative Office, and the Federal Judicial Center offers the federal judicial system. For more detailed descriptions see Carp and Stidham, especially pp. 72–77. See also Peter G. Fish, *The Politics of Federal Judicial Administration* (Princeton, NJ: Princeton University Press, 1973) and Russell R. Wheeler and Charles Nihan, *Administering the Federal Judicial Circuits: A Study of Chief Judges' Approaches and Procedures* (Washington, DC: Federal Judicial Center, 1982).

ing case citations.[36] Law clerks often can save time for overworked judges by carefully reviewing the record of a case and drawing the judge's attention to key facts and issues. One federal appellate judge remarked: "As a result of the preparatory work of the clerks, the judge's critical and judgmental faculties are released for action at a stage when the development of the opinion has ripened and the issues needing decision have been pinpointed."[37] Especially in recent years, many clerks in appellate courts have been given the added responsibility of preparing early drafts of written opinions and, in the Supreme Court, of sorting through all the *certiorari* petitions.

Each year in federal court systems, clerks are recruited, usually to one- or two-year positions, from among the very best students graduating from American law schools. Each federal district and bankruptcy judge is entitled to the services of two personal law clerks, while appeals court judges may use three, and Supreme Court justices can hire four.[38] In addition, courts often hire additional staff law clerks who work for all the judges or justices, rather than for particular members of the bench.

The judicial staff in state and federal courts also frequently includes **probation officers,** court reporters, bailiffs, marshals, legal assistants, interpreters, librarians, deputy clerks, secretaries, messengers, and sometimes staff attorneys and **special masters.**[39] In every courthouse the **clerk of the court** or the **court administrator** is accorded a very prominent position. Elected in most states, though appointed in some, the clerk through the court staff looks after important administrative responsibilities, such as recordkeeping, organizing the trial docket, and collecting filing fees and other court costs. A court administrator usually has fewer specific courtroom functions, but broader budgetary and management responsibilities.

The federal bench also enjoys the assistance of **federal magistrates,** technically **U.S. magistrate judges,** who attend to many routine legal matters over an eight-year term of office.[40] Magistrates issue **search-warrants** and **arrest warrants** and preside over **pre-trial conferences,** settlement conferences, and preliminary hearings, regarding such matters as appointing an attorney for an indigent defendant, overseeing a defendant's initial appearance and plea, and narrowing the evidence that may be considered at trial in accordance with settled rules of law. Mag-

[36] For analysis of the roles of law clerks, see Abraham, especially pp. 239–244 and John Bilyeu Oakley and Robert S. Thompson, *Law Clerks and the Judicial Process: Perceptions of the Qualities and Functions of Law Clerks in American Courts* (Berkeley: University of California Press, 1980).

[37] Frank M. Coffin, *The Ways of a Judge: Reflections From the Federal Appellate Bench* (Boston: Houghton Mifflin, 1980), p. 69, cited in Carp and Stidham, p. 87.

[38] Carp and Stidham, p. 85.

[39] A special master is an individual with expertise in a specialized field, such as prison reform, who is appointed by a court to help to prepare it for trial or to ensure that court orders are properly implemented. See Philip J. Cooper, *Hard Judicial Choices* (New York: Oxford University Press, 1988).

[40] In 1968 Congress established the Office of Federal Magistrates, which replaced the old office of the U.S. commissioners, who performed some of the same functions. In 1990 the official title of these individuals was changed to U.S. magistrate judges. Two notable works on magistrates are Christopher E. Smith, *United States Magistrates in the Federal Courts* (New York: Praeger, 1990) and Carroll Seron, *The Roles of Magistrates in Federal District Courts* (Washington, DC: Federal Judicial Center, 1983).

istrates also often determine when a case is ready for trial, and they may even preside over certain minor criminal trials involving misdemeanors and petty offenses. Since 1990, with the mutual consent of the parties, magistrates may decide a full spectrum of legal questions. Consequently, parties now frequently choose to hold their trial before a magistrate in order to gain a speedier resolution of the dispute.

In recent years the judicial staff has been subject to contradictory criticisms. Some have argued that courthouses are understaffed and that one reason for delay and inefficiency is that judges are trying to do too many tasks that ought to be delegated to others. In response to this argument, some courts have added personnel—more secretaries, staff clerks, and so-called elbow clerks, who are prepared to serve as all-purpose personal assistants. Judges have also responded to this criticism by delegating more responsibilities, for instance, by relying upon clerks to summarize the briefs submitted by lawyers and to write early drafts of opinions.

Others argue that the chief problem the American judiciary faces is too many assistants and too much bureaucracy.[41] Clerks and magistrates "become . . . the eyes and ears of the judiciary, the sense organs by which the facts of the case are conveyed to the judges who decide them . . ."[42] Delegating opinion-drafting to clerks, according to one critic, "is the equivalent of replacing an experienced surgeon with a resident or intern after the patient is anesthetized."[43] She concluded: "In all too many cases, litigants get no more from the judge than supervision—sometimes very light—of the work of a twenty-four-year-old."[44]

When a judge relies too heavily on clerks, magistrates, and other members of the judicial staff, a fresh adversarial clash in court can easily turn into a stale review of an opinion formed by a subordinate. One critic concluded: "In the process, an important spur to the imagination is lost and deliberation replaced by the deference on which every system of tiered review depends."[45] The shortcut of having Supreme Court clerks examine *certiorari* requests has also been criticized as an example of "the transfer of judicial work to nonjudges."[46] One commentator has pointed to the immature interests of the clerks in explaining why so many "important but unglamorous business-related issues," such as conflicting interpretations of trademark law, have not recently received Supreme Court review, yet the Court did agree "to determine whether 2 Live Crew's raunchy parody of 'Oh Pretty Woman' infringed Roy Orbison's lyrics."[47]

[41] See, for instance, Anthony T. Kronman, *The Lost Lawyer: Failing Ideals of the Legal Profession* (Cambridge, MA: Harvard University Press, 1993); Judith Resnick, "Failing Faith: Adjudicatory Procedure in Decline," *University of Chicago Law Review* 53 (1986): 494–560; and Owen Fiss, "The Bureaucratization of the Judiciary," *Yale Law Journal* 92 (1983): 1442–1468.

[42] Kronman, p. 328, paraphrasing Fiss, pp. 1454–1455.

[43] Mary Ann Glendon, *A Nation Under Lawyers: How the Crisis in the Legal Profession Is Transforming American Society* (New York: Farrar, Straus, & Giroux, 1994), p. 145.

[44] Ibid.

[45] Kronman, p. 328.

[46] Glendon, p. 145.

[47] Ibid., p. 147, citing Kenneth W. Starr, "Supreme Court Needs a Management Revolt," *Wall Street Journal,* October 12, 1993, p. A23.

These conflicting arguments suggest that it is easier to locate the flaws in the functioning of the American judiciary than to create a consensus on what has caused the problems and how they might best be rectified.

Judicial Behavior

When asked whether an individual changed upon putting on the judicial robes and assuming a place on the bench, Justice Felix Frankfurter is said to have replied: "By God, he'd better!"[48] Not only must a new judge set aside the mindset, nurtured from law school on, of zealous advocacy for clients, but also he or she must strive to reach the extremely high standards of judicial behavior set forth in the *Canons of Judicial Ethics* found within the *Code of Judicial Conduct.*[49] This special code of professional rules calls upon judges to avoid even appearing to do something that the public might believe would result in unfair or biased judgments.

To uphold the integrity and independence of their office, judges in the United States are forbidden from engaging in politics. While sitting on the bench, judges do not belong to political parties or campaign for politicians. In those states that elect judges, judicial campaigning is rarely as open, aggressive, and expensive as in legislative contests. Open criticism of a judicial opponent is most uncommon. American judges do not ordinarily hold press conferences or publicize their political views in any manner. Even on legal matters, a judge customarily lets his or her written opinion speak for itself. And, a judge does not run for a purely political office without resigning from the bench.[50]

The judicial code also prohibits judges from acting in a manner that the public might view as undignified or unrespectable. Trips to nightclubs, race tracks, massage parlors, casinos, and other establishments that the public might view as seedy or unbecoming would be frowned upon,[51] as would membership in discriminatory private clubs.

Typically, judges try to manage their finances carefully to avoid embarrassment or obvious conflicts of interest. Federal judges have been explicitly prohibited from serving as officers or directors of all corporations except those considered nonprofit.[52] Especially scrupulous judges are often concerned that the business dealings and the personal behavior of their spouses not embarrass their office or cast doubt upon their impartiality. For this reason Judge Lance Ito **recused** himself from hearing arguments concerning a particular motion in the

[48] Linowitz, p. 178.

[49] See American Bar Association, *Model Rules of Professional Conduct* (Washington, DC: American Bar Association, 1983), pp. 135–149.

[50] The fact that controversial Ohio Chief Justice Frank Celebrezze "actively explored" a campaign for governor while sitting on the bench contributed to his defeat at the polls. Tarr, pp. 71–72. See also G. Alan Tarr and Mary Cornelia Aldis Porter, *State Supreme Courts in Nation and State* (New Haven: Yale University Press, 1988), chapter 5.

[51] See Glick, p. 115.

[52] Henry J. Abraham, *The Judicial Process: An Introductory Analysis of the Courts of the United States, England, and France,* 6th ed. rev. (New York: Oxford University Press, 1993), p. 167.

O. J. Simpson murder trial, since part of the evidence concerned opinions a Los Angeles police detective held regarding Judge Ito's wife, a high-ranking policewoman.

Lobbying a judge to influence his or her decision is not permitted on the part of politicians, the media, parties to the case, or other interested observers.[53] Before accepting so much as a social invitation, many judges will give some thought to the circumstances of the function: who will attend, what will occur, what should be said and left unsaid, and how guarded ought their behavior and conversation be. When an American judge is presiding over a case, he or she normally refrains from speaking with the lawyers in that case outside of the courtroom. If the judge does call a meeting in chambers, he or she ordinarily makes certain that lawyers representing both sides will be present.[54]

Such private meetings are held for various reasons. Sometimes a judge will suggest the possibility of a settlement that might be found mutually agreeable. At other times a judge will seize the opportunity to scold or threaten with sanctions lawyers who are misbehaving in court, without embarrassing them in public or influencing the jury against their client. Occasionally, a judge will use a meeting in chambers to speak to the lawyers more informally or, even, to make a substantive point about the law or the case. I recall one such meeting in the early stages of a contested divorce suit in which the judge in a nonjury trial made it clear to the opposing lawyer that he found the lawyer's view of how state law ought to be applied to the facts to be farfetched. In effect, the judge indicated to the lawyer that he might want to reconsider his decision not to agree to an **out-of-court settlement,** since the judge was not going to award a disproportionate sum to the lawyer's client on the basis of that particular legal argument.

Of course, not every one of the thousands of American judges lives strictly by the rules set forth in the judicial code.[55] Judges are human and are not always as open-minded, impartial, and attentive as they should be. Since 1980 federal judges who are alleged to have acted wrongfully by engaging in conduct that somehow prejudices judicial business have appeared before **regional judicial councils.** Council members investigate the complaint and have the power to discipline the judge. However, a judicial council cannot remove a judge from office, no matter how egregious the behavior and how strong the evidence. Rather, the council can merely advise the U.S. Congress that in its opinion **impeachment** is warranted. The Congress must then act to impeach the judge, if he or she has not already resigned from office in disgrace.

Federal impeachment proceedings are quite cumbersome and time-

[53] As with any ideal, this principle has, on occasion, been ignored. See, for instance, Jack Peltason, *Fifty-Eight Lonely Men* (New York: Harcourt, Brace, 1961).

[54] A judicial proceeding, such as a hearing, that is carried out on the application of, or for the benefit of, only one party to the case is called *ex parte,* meaning "on one side only." Holding *ex parte* hearings is discouraged in the American legal system.

[55] For the intriguing story of how two of the most prominent Supreme Court justices in American history secretly engaged in politics, see Bruce Allen Murphy, *The Brandeis/Frankfurter Connection: The Secret Political Activities of Two Supreme Court Justices* (New York: Oxford University Press, 1982).

consuming,[56] and Thomas Jefferson dismissed them as a "mere scarecrow" under most circumstances.[57] Federal impeachment entails a majority vote of the House of Representatives as to whether the judge should be impeached and removed from office followed by a full trial before the Senate, to be concluded by a vote of guilty or not guilty. One might characterize the House's actions as similar to a grand jury and the Senate's as similar to a trial jury. Though various federal judges have resigned after charges of wrongdoing, and more than a dozen have resigned just before the onset of impeachment proceedings, only thirteen have been subjected to federal impeachment and only seven of those have been convicted.[58]

Judicial conduct organizations, broadly similar to the federal **regional judicial councils,** investigate complaints against state judges. The Maryland Commission on Judicial Disabilities, for instance, investigates allegations of judicial misconduct or disability. In appropriate cases it then asks the state's highest court, the Maryland Court of Appeals, to reprimand, remove, or censure the judge. Many states have instituted formal impeachment procedures to investigate and, when appropriate, remove judges accused of criminal acts. In addition, many states rely upon **legislative address** proceedings, in which the legislature may vote to remove a judge not for criminal behavior, but for bias, senility, or incompetence. Some also rely on **recall petitions,** in which, if a sufficient number of citizens sign a petition, a special election is held in which voters choose whether or not to remove the judge from office.

Although oversight can be used to intimidate or silence unpopular or outspoken judges, this ethical supervision of the judiciary, absent in many countries, probably contributes to the good behavior and positive reputation of American judges. In fact, although investigations still occasionally uncover a corrupt judge or even a court dominated by corrupt judges, as occurred in the celebrated Operation Greylord investigation in Chicago's municipal courts, judicial scandals in the United States are exceptional, not commonplace, and judicial conduct organizations are not usually overwhelmed with business. In fact, corruption was more common years ago at the local and state court levels[59] than it is today or ever has been in the federal courts.[60]

Even criminals seem to have been affected to some degree by the esteem for the judge in American society—a fact that may be seen most clearly in comparative perspective: In Colombia hundreds of judges have been assassinated during the last decades. Powerful drug-trafficking organizations have ordered, fi-

[56] For two recent works on impeachment, see Michael J. Gerhardt, *The Federal Impeachment Process: A Constitutional and Historical Analysis* (Princeton, NJ: Princeton University Press, 1996) and Mary L. Volcansek, *Judicial Impeachment: None Called It Justice* (Urbana: University of Illinois Press, 1993).

[57] O'Brien, p. 16.

[58] Carp and Stidham, p. 279.

[59] See Charles R. Ashman, *The Finest Judges Money Can Buy* (Los Angeles: Nash, 1973).

[60] One scholar wrote that the federal judiciary has been relatively independent of political influence, intimidation, and bribery: "From the mid-1930s to the mid-1980s, few federal judges were prosecuted for corruption, only one was impeached, and only one was killed by criminals. These numbers increased during the late 1980s but still totaled barely 1 percent of the federal judiciary." Ethan A. Nadelmann, *Cops Across Borders: The Internationalization of U.S. Criminal Law Enforcement* (University Park: Pennsylvania State University Press, 1993), p. 265.

nanced, and carried out most of these killings. In contrast, American criminals rarely attack judges. The occasional assault or threat is treated as an extremely serious offense, to be investigated by the Federal Bureau of Investigation if it is directed against an individual serving on the federal bench.

Given that judges are human and often work under considerable pressure, no judiciary can boast a flawless record of judicial behavior. However, a sufficiently high percentage of American judges do act correctly that the judicial profession has gained, and maintained, a reputation for integrity not usually found in other countries.

THE ROLES OF THE AMERICAN JUDGE

Since a judge in a common law accusatorial system, such as that found in the United States, does not control the investigation or question witnesses at trial, observers who are more familiar with civil law systems often wonder just what American judges do. How do American judges gain the admiration of the people? What roles does the American judge assume?

In fact, American judges perform a myriad of tasks, from handling mundane administrative chores to reasoning through abstruse legal footnotes. Judges hire court personnel and establish the working hours of the court. They ensure that courthouses are kept in reasonable order and that amenities are provided for jurors, witnesses, and attorneys. They testify before state and federal legislatures on the needs and budgets of their courts. They promulgate court rules. They make speeches before bar associations, Law Day audiences, groups of law students, and other such forums. Some hold swearing-in ceremonies to welcome new citizens into the United States. Some conduct training classes for law-enforcement personnel. Yet, to determine why American judges are generally held in such high esteem, particular attention might be focused on six more lofty responsibilities that American judges fulfill: acting as referee in court; making decisions in bench trials; making decisions in jury trials; sentencing; deciding appeals; and acting as legal historians and philosophers.

Acting as a Referee in Court

First, judges in the United States act as referees, in some respects similar to the officials who supervise a game of basketball or volleyball. The legal system in the United States is premised on the belief that the judge or jury will be able to rule most justly if that decisionmaker watches a contest in which both sides have the opportunity to review all relevant circumstances and facts, raise appropriate points of law, and argue about how the law should be applied to the circumstances and facts. Since the American adversarial system sets one party against the other in this manner and encourages zealous advocacy by the lawyers on both sides, some neutral figure must supervise the trial to ensure that each side abides by the rules of courtroom procedure and evidence.

For example, Judge William Hoeveler, the federal judge who presided over the 1992 trial of Panamanian dictator Manuel Noriega, acted several times to force the government and the defense to abide by American legal rules. Judge Hoeveler strongly criticized the government for secretly tape-recording certain telephone conversations from Noriega's prison cell to persons outside the jail. He barred an American television station from revealing the contents of those tape recordings for fear that the jury might be influenced by Noriega's private conversations. At a different stage in the proceedings Judge Hoeveler is said to have privately chided the lawyers for raising irrelevant facts that might wrongly influence the jury. In all these instances, Judge Hoeveler was acting as a referee in the courtroom contest that would decide Noriega's fate.

While it may be impossible for human beings to be entirely impartial—in the sense of having no opinion as to which side they would like to win a hotly disputed contest—the American legal system at least asks its judges to leave behind at the courthouse door whatever partiality they may feel. Judges are to act in a way that is true to the rules of court procedure and the finest traditions of conduct on the bench, and they are not to tilt the playing field to give an advantage to one side or the other.

A good judge is also an active referee in the sense that he or she focuses the attention of the lawyers on relevant issues. One well-known federal judge, J. Skelly Wright, once observed: "The lawyers are likely, in their advocacy, to run off in different directions; it's the judge who brings them back to the issues, it's the judge who shows them where the point of the case is, where the issues are."[61]

Decision Making in Bench Trials

American judges are vital decisionmakers as well as referees. Chapter 5 examines in detail the role of the American jury in deciding whether a person is innocent or guilty in a criminal case and in determining which party prevails in a civil lawsuit. In many U.S. cases, however, a judge, rather than a jury, finds the facts and determines the outcome of the trial.[62] Such **bench trials** commonly occur in several noteworthy situations.

Under American constitutional law a person accused of an insignificant offense is not entitled to a jury trial. In the states, the extent to which a jury will be used in minor cases is a matter of state law. Someone arrested for the minor offense of **shoplifting,** for instance, will not likely succeed in arguing that state law requires a jury to decide the case.

Although Americans do have a right to a jury trial in important criminal matters and in noncriminal disputes that exceed a designated sum, this does not mean that a jury is mandatory in such cases. Often, a party will choose as a matter of strategy to waive the right to a jury trial. The lawyers on both sides may prefer to

[61] J. Skelly Wright, "The Pre-trial Conference," in Sheldon Goldman and Austin Sarat, eds. *American Court Systems: Readings in Judicial Process and Behavior* (San Francisco: W. H. Freeman, 1978), p. 119.

[62] Judges, not juries, decide over half of all federal trials. Tarr, p. 42.

have a judge decide the case, rather than a jury. Often in these cases, the lawyers believe that a judge would better understand complicated matters of law and fact, or that a judge would be more sympathetic to their particular circumstances, or that a jury might react irrationally or emotionally in situations in which a judge would not. So, one leading decision-making role for the American judiciary occurs in nonjury trials in which the judge actually determines who prevails.

Decision Making in Jury Trials

Even in those trials in which a jury will ultimately decide who wins the case, judges retain substantial decision-making responsibilities. In jury trials the judge will permit the jurors to decide all factual issues. However, the judge will still rule on all technical legal issues that arise before and during the court proceedings. Before the trial begins, the judge will have to decide motions raised by the parties concerning the exclusion of evidence and other such legal matters.[63] Once the trial is under way, the judge must decide whether to allow or overrule objections, often "on the spur of the moment, without the luxury of lengthy reflection or discussion with staff or colleagues."[64]

Although the line between a legal and a factual issue is not often so clear in practice as in theory, a simple example may help to clarify the distinction. Imagine that a defense lawyer is arguing a case to a jury in which he or she represents a man whom the police caught emerging from his brother's house late one night carrying his murdered brother's blood-stained knife in his pocket. Since the police found the man's brother murdered inside the house, the prosecution has now charged that several different crimes occurred, including **murder** and **burglary.**

Suppose that state law defines the crime of burglary as "entering a house at night with the intent of stealing some object from that house." Suppose that the prosecution concludes its case at trial without directly addressing the man's intent to steal something from his brother's house. Rather, the prosecution has focused upon the evidence that might show that the man entered the house intending to murder his brother. He simply left his brother's house carrying one of his brother's knives.

Along with the factual issue to be decided by the jury concerning whether the brother committed murder, this scenario might also raise a technical legal issue that ought to be decided by the judge. The defense lawyer might argue that the jury should not even be permitted to consider the matter of burglary since the prosecution never introduced any evidence that the man entered that house intending to steal something. The defense could argue that, whether his or her client is or is not found guilty of murder, he is surely not guilty of the crime of burglary as defined under state law. Therefore, the lawyer will call on the judge to eliminate the charge of burglary from the prosecution's case.

[63] See Carp and Stidham, p. 292.

[64] Ibid. The authors reported one trial judge as saying: "We're where the action is. We often have to 'shoot from the hip' and hope you're [sic] doing the right thing. You can't ruminate forever every time you have to make a ruling."

If the prosecutor wished to pursue the burglary charge, the government might respond that the alleged assailant intended to steal the knife in order to conceal evidence of the crime of murder. The prosecutor might argue that the jury should be allowed to consider both the burglary and murder charges since state law defines burglary in terms of stealing something from within a residence at night. Whether the object of the burglary was personal profit or concealing evidence of a crime is irrelevant.

Since this issue involves deciding a legal matter, not a factual one, the judge should take responsibility for deciding it, not the jury. Out of earshot of the jury the judge would listen to arguments by both sides, read the documents, perhaps conduct a bit of additional research into relevant precedents, and decide whether or not the charge of burglary should be eliminated from the prosecution's case under these circumstances.

Thus, under the American legal system judges in jury trials are supposed to decide legal issues and determine what the law means. In determining who wins and loses a case, juries are supposed to decide only factual issues.[65]

Sentencing

In all but five states American judges also decide how someone convicted of a crime should be penalized. This contrasts with judgments in civil trials before a jury, in which the presiding judge has only limited authority in the determination of the civil judgment entered against a losing party.

In all but one of the states in which juries, not judges, prescribe sentences, the trial judge has the power to alter that sentence. Thus, whereas juries often decide whether an accused person is guilty or not guilty of a crime, American judges usually determine the final **sentence**—that is, the official judgment imposing a punishment upon a criminal defendant after conviction. Sentencing alternatives range from **community service** to **probation,** from **work release** to **house arrest** to **electronic monitoring,** from a fine to imprisonment for a term of years, and for very serious offenses either life imprisonment without the possibility of **parole** or, in some states, the death penalty (known as **capital punishment**).[66]

[65] In practice, of course, legal and factual issues are not always easily distinguished. One lawyer wrote: "When we ask jurors to decide, as a matter of fact, whether the defendant acted with malice, we are asking them to make a complicated assessment of the nature of the defendant's mental state —an inquiry far different from finding facts in the who did what, when, and where sense. To label the defendant's behavior malicious is partly to find the historical facts, but it is also to render a judgment about its blameworthiness. Juries are constantly presented with these mixed questions that jump the artificial law/fact boundary. This is true in negligence cases, where juries decide the fact of whether a defendant's behavior fell below the behavior expected of a reasonable person. It is true in obscenity cases, where juries apply 'contemporary community standards' to decide the fact of whether the work in question is pornographic." Jeffrey Abramson, *We, the Jury: The Jury System and the Ideal of Democracy* (New York: Basic Books, 1994), pp. 91–92.

[66] For a notable recent addition to the voluminous literature on capital punishment, see Welsh S. White, *The Death Penalty in the Nineties: An Examination of the Modern System of Capital Punishment* (Ann Arbor: University of Michigan Press, 1991).

Legislatures in some states have passed **mandatory minimum sentences** for particularly serious crimes, usually felonies involving use of a deadly weapon. In a mandatory sentence, the law dictates the minimum amount of time a convicted person should serve in prison. In other instances, the law that defines the crime grants the judge a range of different sentences to impose on a guilty person. For instance, a state law might designate the penalty for **armed robbery** at between five and ten years in prison. To determine how long to sentence a convicted felon within such a range, the judge considers all the circumstances of the crime. For a sense of how a judge might take into account diverse aspects of the crime of armed robbery, consider the following: "A bank robber with (or without) a gun, which the robber kept hidden (or brandished), might have frightened (or merely warned), injured seriously (or less seriously), tied up (or simply pushed) a guard, a teller, or a customer, at night (or at noon), for a bad (or arguably less bad) motive, in an effort to obtain money for other crimes (or for other purposes), in the company of a few (or many) other robbers, for the first (or fourth) time that day, while sober (or under the influence of drugs or alcohol) . . ."[67]

The judge may also take into account various personal factors, such as the criminal's age, whether the individual has a past **criminal record** of committing other offenses, and whether a spouse or family depends upon the criminal for support. Judges often rely heavily on the presentencing investigative report submitted by a probation officer—the official charged with supervising prisoners released under various specified conditions. Then, after considering all the factors proposed by the prosecutor and the defense counsel—and in four states after considering the recommendation of the jury as well—the judge decides on a sentence.

Plainly, a cross section of judges is apt to weigh these many factors quite differently at sentencing. To take one of many possible examples, reasonable judicial minds could certainly differ on whether a defendant's drunkenness while committing a crime should be considered a mitigating factor or an exacerbating one. Judges will also disagree on more fundamental theoretical matters, such as whether the sentence should fit the criminal or fit the crime. That is, should it primarily aim to punish the defendant to the extent of his or her culpability, or to deter other criminals and thus control crime? One judge might carefully tailor two sentences so that a less blameworthy armed robber would receive a lesser penalty than a more blameworthy one. Another might impose a severe penalty on both armed robbers. Such an action would keep both criminals in prison and stop them, during their years behind bars, from harming the public by engaging in more criminal activity. It might also deter potential armed robbers who might otherwise commit similar crimes.[68]

While the discretion given to judges in sentencing decisions permits penalties to be tailored to particular circumstances, it has also led judges in the same state to prescribe very different sentences for the same crime. In 1967, a presiden-

[67] See U.S. Sentencing Commission, *Federal Sentencing Guideline Manual* (St. Paul, MN: West, 1987), p. 2.

[68] Ibid., p. 3.

tial task force reported of a Detroit criminal court: "Over a 20-month period in which the sample cases were about equally distributed among the ten judges, one judge imposed prison terms upon 75 to 90 percent of the defendants whom he sentenced, while another judge imposed prison sentences in about 35 percent of the cases. One judge consistently imposed prison sentences twice as long as those of the most lenient judge. The study also showed that judges who imposed the most severe sentences for certain crimes also exhibited the most liberal sentencing policy for other offenses."[69] Since penalties under state laws for the same crime may differ markedly, the discrepancies from one state to another are often even more notable than the differences from court to court within a single state.

Some state legislatures have responded to the dramatically different penalties handed down by various state judges by narrowing the range of permissible sentences for various offenses and imposing either mandatory or voluntary **sentencing guidelines** for judges to follow. Sentencing discrepancies also prompted the U.S. Congress in 1984 to authorize sentencing guidelines for all federal court cases. In order to influence federal judges to hand down similar sentences for similar crimes, a politically appointed commission determines a range of standard sentences for each federal crime. Judges then consult a grid with hundreds of boxes that is designed to take into account a range of possible offenses and the defendant's criminal history. A federal judge who wishes to issue a penalty that does not fall within the sentencing guidelines may do so, but the judge is required to write an explanation, and the criminal can appeal such an unusual sentence to a higher court.

In the relatively short time that the system of federal sentencing guidelines has been in place, it has become ever more apparent that some of the same inequities that the reforms were designed to overcome have arisen in different guise. Since sentencing by the judges is controlled by the crime or crimes prosecuted, a substantial measure of sentencing power has been placed in the hands of the politically appointed federal prosecutors who determine which crimes are to be presented to the court. The sentencing process is then further manipulated by the prevailing system of **plea bargaining,** discussed in detail in Chapters 7 and 10. Thus, despite the efforts of Congress, the goal of equal treatment for defendants who committed the same crimes remains elusive.

Deciding Appeals

While acting as referee, determining who wins a nonjury trial, issuing rulings on legal issues, and determining sentences are each largely the province of trial judges, judges in America's higher courts decide all appeals. Since appeals are important both to correct errors in individual cases and to determine definitively what the law means, judges on the state appeals courts, the state supreme courts, the federal circuit courts of appeals, and the U.S. Supreme Court often command much attention.

[69] Sanford H. Kadish and Monrad G. Paulsen, *Criminal Law and Its Processes: Cases and Materials,* 3rd ed. rev. (Boston: Little, Brown, 1975), p. 1508.

In interpreting the law, judges make especially significant decisions when they engage in **judicial review**—that is, the review of laws and other public acts to determine if they violate the U.S. Constitution or a state constitution and hence must be declared void.[70] This judicial power to annul legislative and executive acts serves as a check or balance against the power of the other branches of government to make laws. It may be worth noting that in the process of judicial review, American appellate courts act in a markedly different manner than do common law courts in Great Britain, since the U.S. Constitution, as opposed to a body of common law precedent, is the controlling guide in such review.

Although American judges are generally reluctant to decide that a law is unconstitutional, occasionally they do so. Between 1789 and 1992 the national and state legislatures in the United States passed over 95,000 laws. The U.S. Supreme Court decided that 142 federal laws and 1,200 state laws violated the U.S. Constitution.[71] While this is a far more assertive use of judicial review than is common in Japan and many other countries, it amounts to a relatively small percentage of all the laws whose constitutionality has been challenged in the American courts.

While judicial review is now a firmly established feature of American government, it has evident benefits and drawbacks. The very fact that judicial review is available to overturn a law keeps the attention of legislators on crafting legislation that will pass constitutional muster.[72] Judicial review thus elevates the constitutional principles upon which the United States was founded and which many Americans still revere. Through judicial review interpretations of constitutional principles take on exceptional importance, and legislative majorities are kept from imposing laws on the people that violate traditional and fundamental American values.

On the other hand, aggressive judicial review diminishes direct democracy. Social questions come increasingly to be decided by the courts on constitutional grounds, rather than within the state and federal legislatures on political grounds. One legal scholar wrote:

> [L]egislators cannot talk back when the courts speak in their constitutional voice. It is never easy to marshal a legislative majority to modify or override a court decision, but if legislators deem the matter important enough, they can

[70] A good introductory overview of judicial review is found in Abraham, pp. 270–346. More theoretical works include John Hart Ely, *Democracy and Distrust: A Theory of Judicial Review* (Cambridge, MA: Harvard University Press, 1980); Christopher Wolfe, *The Rise of Modern Judicial Review* (New York: Basic Books, 1986); and Sylvia Snowiss, *Judicial Review and the Law of the Constitution* (New Haven, CT: Yale University Press, 1990).

[71] Abraham, p. 272. Of the more than 1,300 state and federal laws declared to be unconstitutional since 1870, the Supreme Court has struck down the vast majority (850). Ibid., p. 272.

[72] Justice Cardozo wrote of judicial review as follows: "By conscious or subconscious influence, the presence of this restraining power aloof in the background, but none the less always in reserve, tends to stabilize and rationalize the legislative judgment, to infuse it with the glow of principle, to hold the standard aloft and visible. . . . The restraining power of the judiciary does not manifest its chief worth in the few cases in which the legislature has gone beyond the lines that mark the limits of discretion. Rather shall we find its chief worth in making vocal and audible the ideals that might otherwise be silenced, in giving them continuity of life and expression, in guiding and directing choice within the limits where choice ranges." Benjamin N. Cardozo, *The Nature of the Judicial Process* (New Haven, CT: Yale University Press, 1949), pp. 93–94, also cited in Abraham, pp. 314–315.

> do so. When the courts hang their rulings on constitutional pegs, however, the "dialogue" is over and the ordinary political process comes to a halt. The broader the court's ruling, the less room is left for future exchanges. The matter is off the table—unless the Constitution is amended or the court changes its mind. Political energy, lacking its normal outlets, flows into litigation and the judicial selection process.[73]

While reasonable minds can differ on how broadly or narrowly judicial review ought to be applied, no one will doubt that it constitutes a vitally important power of the American judiciary.

Acting as Legal Historian and Philosopher

American judges, especially appellate judges, also act as legal historians and philosophers. One scholar wrote: "Judges, more than any other officials, are expected not only to listen but to show that they have listened; not only to reason their way through to the decisions they reach but to expose their reasoning processes to the parties and the public."[74] American judges must also preserve their legal reasoning so that future generations of lawyers, judges, and students of law may consider it.

In common law legal systems, including that in the United States, much emphasis is placed on interpreting legal principles and on the development of precedent. In adhering to precedent, judges make legal decisions today by considering how other judges decided similar issues in the past and by following that reasoning whenever practicable. To help to provide useful precedents for future cases, judges write detailed opinions, to be published for future reference, that explain their legal reasoning in arriving at particular decisions. In advising clients and preparing trial strategy, lawyers rely upon such opinions, and when judges are confronted by similar issues, they are to take such precedents into account in coming to a decision on how to resolve that issue.

Appellate courts are normally composed of several **appellate judges,** and in the case of the U.S. Supreme Court of nine justices. Often, all the judges on a court disagree with one another on how the law should be applied to the case at hand, and the court splits into majority and minority factions, each supporting a different side in the case. An opinion written for the controlling majority is known as a **majority opinion.** From time to time a judge will agree with the conclusion reached in the majority opinion, but disagree with the reasoning. He or she may then write a **concurring opinion** that arrives at the same conclusion as the majority, but through different reasoning.

Americans and their judiciary highly value independence of thought. Consequently, judges who disagree with the majority view of which party should prevail and how the law should be interpreted are free to express their own views in a **dis-**

[73] Glendon, p. 138.

[74] Ibid., p. 146, citing Joseph Vining, "Justice, Bureaucracy, and Legal Method," *Michigan Law Review* 80 (1981): 248–253. See also Joseph Vining, *The Authoritarian and the Authoritative* (Chicago: University of Chicago Press, 1986).

senting opinion.[75] Dissents usually aim to be adopted in the future as the true expression of the law. Since a dissent undermines to some degree the persuasiveness of the majority opinion, although not its immediate legal authority, judges on an appellate court normally promote compromise and split into majority and minority factions only when consensus is impossible to attain.

The degree to which consensus is pursued varies from court to court and from one era to another. In recent years the U.S. Supreme Court has issued a unanimous ruling in less than a third of its cases, with dissents just a bit less frequent in other federal and state appellate courts.[76] During his tenure in the early years of the Supreme Court, Chief Justice John Marshall reversed the initial practice of having each justice write a separate opinion in every case. To ensure that Americans could confidently state what the Supreme Court had ruled the law was, Marshall encouraged justices to band together in majority opinions, and he discouraged the writing of dissents.

Over time, however, as the Supreme Court's authority became well established and as legal issues increased in number and perhaps in complexity, thoughtful dissenting opinions came to be valued highly. Charles Evans Hughes, U.S. chief justice from 1930 to 1941, observed: "A dissent . . . is an appeal to the brooding spirit of the law, to the intelligence of a future day, when a later decision may possibly correct the error into which the dissenting judge believes the court to have been betrayed."[77] A well-known state court judge once remarked: "I welcome dissents because they test the soundness of my own opinions. . . . The dissenting opinion is . . . a forecast of things to come. The writers of dissents are usually men who look forward—not back, nor to the immediate present. . . ."[78]

Whether a judge writes a majority, dissenting, or concurring opinion, the practice of trying to articulate in a logical, powerful, legal argument precisely how the judge views the case compels close attention from the bench, sharpens court decisions, and increases judicial legitimacy. One authority noted: "It is one thing to reach a tentative conclusion in a case, but something very different to write an opinion defending it. The search for the right words to support a judgment one has provisionally formed often stirs up new objections and compels the reexamination of earlier beliefs."[79] Another legal scholar argued: "The discipline of writing out the reasons for a decision and responding to the main arguments of the losing

[75] This feature of the American system contrasts sharply with that found in many civil law countries in which courts issue majority decisions only.

[76] See Tarr, p. 281.

[77] Charles Evans Hughes, *The Supreme Court of the United States* (New York: Columbia University Press, 1928), p. 68, cited in Abraham, p. 213.

[78] Abraham, p. 213.

[79] Kronman, p. 330. Kronman continued: "A judge may feel that he has decided a case and is finished with it. But when he attempts to justify his decision in writing, he will be forced to reenact the drama of the original conflict in his imagination, taking first one side and then the other in an effort to anticipate the strongest arguments that might be made against his own earlier position and the best responses to them. Writing judicial opinions imposes on the writer a duty of responsiveness that can be met only by giving each side to a dispute its due, by entertaining every claim in its most attractive light, and that in turn demands a special effort of imagination." Ibid.

side has proved to be one of the most effective curbs on arbitrary judicial power ever devised."[80] This is especially the case since American judges are expected to use an opinion to describe fully all the material facts and relevant legal principles on which the decision is based and "to follow those principles consistently in future cases."[81]

Perhaps the most famous author of opinions among American judges was Oliver Wendell Holmes, first an influential professor at Harvard Law School, then chief justice of the Supreme Judicial Court in Massachusetts, and finally a U.S. Supreme Court justice for thirty-four years.[82] Opinions authored by Justice Holmes tended to express his keen sense of history and consistently emphasized the importance of precedent. "A page of history," the Justice once observed, "is worth a volume of logic."[83] In 1880 Justice Holmes made perhaps his best known observation, writing: "The life of law has not been logic; it has been experience. The felt necessities of the time, the prevalent moral and political theories, the institutions of public policy, . . . even the prejudices which judges share with their fellow-men, have a good deal more to do than logic in determining the rules by which men shall be governed."[84]

At the center of Justice Holmes' political philosophy were the principles of the common law. Holmes believed that judges should draw on the wisdom of past generations in forming their own legal reasoning. Accordingly, when Holmes wrote the most influential nineteenth-century American book on law, he titled it *The Common Law.* At the end of his long career Justice Holmes noted that he was most proud of his written opinions. Just before his death at ninety-three in 1935, three years after retiring as a judge, Oliver Wendell Holmes remarked that he had left his judicial decisions and other writings scattered behind like "little fragments of my fleece that I have left upon the hedges of life."[85]

FORMULATING LEGAL OPINIONS

Since judges have a well-earned status in the American legal system because of their functions as impartial referees, key decisionmakers under various circumstances, and as historians and legal philosophers,[86] one might wonder how judges think about legal issues and formulate their legal opinions.

[80] Glendon, pp. 147–148.

[81] Ibid., p. 166.

[82] See Alfred Lief, ed., *The Dissenting Opinions of Mr. Justice Holmes* (New York: Vanguard Press, 1929). For recent biographies of Holmes, see G. Edward White, *Justice Oliver Wendell Holmes: Law and the Inner Self* (New York: Oxford University Press, 1993) and Sheldon M. Novick, *Honorable Justice: The Life of Oliver Wendell Holmes* (New York: Dell, 1989).

[83] Charles Haar, Lance Liebman, *Property and the Law* (Boston: Little, Brown, 1977), p. 135.

[84] Oliver Wendell Holmes, Jr., *The Common Law* (Boston: Little, Brown, 1881), pp. 1–2.

[85] William O. Douglas, *Go East, Young Man* (New York: Random House, 1975), p. xii.

[86] In particular states, judges serving on the court of last resort are also given the important responsibility of determining procedure in the state—civil, criminal, and appellate; however, in other states the legislatures handle such matters.

As renowned Supreme Court Justice Benjamin Cardozo pointed out, judicial philosophizing is an exceedingly murky subject:

> The work of deciding cases goes on every day in hundreds of courts throughout the land. Any judge, one might suppose, would find it easy to describe the process which he had followed a thousand times and more. Nothing could be farther from the truth. . . . What is it that I do when I decide a case? To what sources of information do I appeal for guidance? In what proportions do I permit them to contribute to the result? In what proportions ought they to contribute? If a precedent is applicable, when do I refuse to follow it? If no precedent is applicable, how do I reach the rule that will make a precedent for the future? If I am seeking logical consistency, the symmetry of the legal structure, how far shall I seek it? At what point shall the quest be halted by some discrepant custom, by some consideration of the social welfare, by my own or the common standards of justice and morals? Into that strange compound which is brewed daily in the cauldron of the courts, all these ingredients enter in varying proportions.[87]

Of course, legal issues sometimes are relatively simple. On surprisingly rare occasions a judge can simply find a legal text, such as a statute or administrative regulation with a provision that is nicely tailored to resolve the issue at hand. Sometimes the meaning of a statute may be clarified by the *legislative history* of the act, that is, the recorded discussions and debates by legislators when the legislature considered and passed the statute. Though the U.S. Constitution is drafted quite broadly, a judge may even come across a straightforward constitutional issue, particularly when other courts have repeatedly interpreted the meaning of the constitutional provision at hand.

However, most decisions a judge must make are not at all simple or straightforward. In such cases, one scholar hypothesized: "Judges' decisions are a function of what they prefer to do, tempered by what they think they ought to do, but constrained by what they perceive is feasible to do."[88] Such ambiguous factors help to explain why judicial philosophies are so difficult to pin down.

Often, legislatures write laws that consist of general principles, leaving to the judges the task of interpreting those principles to decide particular legal issues. Even the more detailed state and federal laws usually contain unclear passages and large gaps or loopholes that the legislature never anticipated when it drafted, debated, and voted on the law.[89] As one legal scholar observed years ago, "difficulties of . . . interpretation arise when the legislature has had no meaning at all; when the question which is raised on the statute never occurred to it; when what judges

[87] Cardozo, pp. 9–10.

[88] James L. Gibson, "From Simplicity to Complexity: The Development of Theory in the Study of Judicial Behavior," *Political Behavior* 5 (1983): 9, as cited in Tarr, p. 281.

[89] Philip Howard argued that the *more* detailed the law is, the *more* loopholes it is likely to contain. See Philip K. Howard, *The Death of Common Sense: How Law is Suffocating America* (New York: Warner Books, 1994), especially pp. 1–54.

have to do is, not to determine what the legislature did mean on a point which was present to its mind, but to guess what it would have intended on a point not present to its mind, if the point had been present."[90]

By longstanding tradition an American judge presented with a dispute to settle does not refer it to the legislature for clarification. Not only is the legislature busy with its own business, but its composition has likely changed since the law passed. Instead, the judge fills in whatever gaps exist in the law through *statutory interpretation,* that is, through reference to the probable intent of the legislature or to firmly established legal principles relevant to the problem at hand.[91]

An example of the U.S. Supreme Court attempting to interpret an ambiguously phrased law arose in 1983 in *Bob Jones University v. United States.*[92] The case involved a ruling by the Internal Revenue Service (IRS) that revoked the university's tax-exempt status because it practiced racial discrimination by refusing admission to black students who had married white men or women. The IRS declared that Bob Jones University was not tax exempt since it was not a charitable institution. Rather, the IRS contended, through its discriminatory racial policies the university pursued activities contrary to public policy, not supportive of charity.

Vital to the arguments in the case was the language found in Section 501 (C)(3) of the **Internal Revenue Code** which granted **tax-exempt status** only to those organizations that operated exclusively for "religious, charitable, scientific, . . . or educational purposes." Attorneys for the university argued that while their institution might not qualify as "charitable," it was certainly "educational" and therefore fell within the language of the statute that stated "charitable *or* educational," not "charitable *and* educational."

In ultimately supporting the IRS, however, the Supreme Court ruled that the intent of Congress had been to exempt charitable organizations. In a footnote to the opinion Chief Justice Warren Burger argued that if 501 (C)(3) were interpreted to mean that either charitable or educational purposes would suffice, then a training school for terrorists would qualify for tax-exempt status.[93] While the provision certainly could have been worded more clearly, the Court concluded that the intent of Congress seems to have been to confine tax-exempt status to charitable organizations. Regardless of whether one agrees with the Court's rationale or not, the *Bob Jones University* case plainly shows a court attempting to guess what the legislature "would have intended on a point not present to its mind, if the point had been present."

[90] Justice Cardozo attributes these words to Gray in his lectures on the "Nature and Sources of Law." Cardozo, p. 15.

[91] See Felix Frankfurter, "Some Reflections on the Reading of Statutes," in Mark W. Cannon and David M. O'Brien, eds. *Views From the Bench: The Judiciary and Constitutional Politics* (Chatham, NJ: Chatham House, 1985), pp. 181–189; Edward F. Hennessey, *Judges Making Law* (Boston: Flaschner Judicial Institute, 1994), especially pp. 19–42; and Lief H. Carter, *Reason in Law,* 4th ed. rev. (New York: HarperCollins College, 1994), pp. 54–115.

[92] *Bob Jones University v. United States,* 461 U.S. 574 (1983). For a more comprehensive account of this case see Calvi and Coleman, pp. 14–17.

[93] One might, of course, dispute Chief Justice Burger's reasoning by claiming that a training school for terrorists would not be "educational" in the sense meant by Congress.

More frequently than one might at first think, neither statutes nor the Constitution definitively determine the answer to many legal issues. In such cases, the judge in a common law system must delve into precedent, attempting to discover how similar issues have been disposed of in prior opinions. In this task, judges commonly rely upon the lawyers on both sides—reading their legal briefs and then challenging the lawyers to defend different propositions in oral argument. Often, judges will also call upon their clerks to undertake further legal research, filling out or amplifying the points raised by the attorneys.

However, consulting past cases raises difficult issues.[94] How recent must the precedent be? How closely must the facts of a prior case resemble those at hand? Is precedent still valid if it comes from cases in other states or other federal circuits? Which precedents should be followed and which should be ignored or distinguished from the present case? How is the controlling reasoning of the court in a similar case to be differentiated from mere ***dicta,*** that is, the incidental statements not logically necessary to resolve any legal issue in the case and, hence, not binding as precedent? Again, reasonable judges often differ in assessing how to use precedent in deciding a case.

Since no two judges are likely to take exactly the same steps in thinking through a legal issue, and since judges vary markedly in their legal experience and their judicial, political, and personal philosophies, even two experienced and conscientious judges will likely arrive at somewhat differing conclusions on any particular legal issue. Some differences are simply small matters of degree, and the judges can align their views by discussion. In such a case, one or more judges will opt to join the majority opinion or the dissent, rather than write separate views. In other cases, however, the legal reasoning varies so dramatically that each judge will want to write separately to ensure that his or her views are fully articulated.

Judicial Philosophies

At first glance, it may seem presumptuous for one who has never served as a judge to theorize about how judges think about their work. **Solicitor General**[95] John W. Davis once observed that no one would read fishing manuals if one could ask the fish directly how best to catch it![96] And, many of the most well-known American justices, including Holmes, Cardozo, Felix Frankfurter, and William Douglas, have written extensively on their work.

[94] Glick, p. 9.

[95] The duties of the solicitor general include deciding which cases the executive branch of the U.S. government should ask the Supreme Court to review, determining which cases the U.S. government should appeal, and conducting oral arguments for the government before the Court.

[96] William O. Douglas, *The Court Years (1939–1975): The Autobiography of William O. Douglas* (New York: Random House, 1980), p. 177. For an interesting biography of Davis, see William Henry Harbaugh, *Lawyers' Lawyer: The Life of John W. Davis* (New York: Oxford University Press, 1973).

Nevertheless, it is also true that American lawyers and legal scholars devote a considerable portion of their professional lives to analyzing how judges think.[97] Law school professors customarily spend the vast majority of class time evaluating judicial opinions. In advising clients, conducting legal research, and plotting trial strategy, American lawyers constantly focus attention on how particular judges once thought, or now think, or are likely to think in the future. A few thoughts on judicial philosophies may thus be in order, if only to introduce and supplement what the judges themselves have to say.

The Judicial Role

Many philosophical matters divide the American judiciary. Some judges tend to interpret the words of the U.S. Constitution narrowly; others quite broadly. Some value the original intent of the Founding Fathers; others emphasize the nature of the Constitution as a flexible living document designed to be adapted to changing circumstances. For all those differences, however, judges of different temperaments, ideologies, and philosophies share certain broad principles regarding what a judge should and should not do when presented with a dispute.[98]

For instance, federal judges in constitutional courts[99] and most state judges[100] will not rule on hypothetical situations or issue advisory opinions. Instead, a true dispute—an actual "case or controversy"—must have arisen between real parties.[101] Judges will also decline to rule on cases that have become moot: that is, cases that, because of a major change of circumstances, have become no longer controversial or that no longer exist. American judges also require that all possible remedies in lower courts be exhausted before a higher court will hear the case.

While judges may occasionally differ on the proper application of such principles to particular circumstances, each is essentially noncontroversial, a matter of longstanding American legal custom or judicial interpretation. Whether a judge is liberal or conservative, innovative or traditional, he or she is very likely to view such principles as binding. Beyond these well-settled principles defining the judicial role, however, American judges differ markedly in their willingness to use judicial power to pursue notions of justice.

[97] Two useful works are Carter, *Reason in Law,* and Steven J. Burton, *An Introduction to Law and Legal Reasoning* (Boston: Little, Brown, 1985).

[98] The ensuing discussion draws on, but is organized differently from, the analysis of Henry Abraham, followed by Carp and Stidham among others. For a general overview, see Abraham, pp. 348–370, Carp and Stidham, pp. 137–154.

[99] Federal judges in legislative courts may issue advisory opinions.

[100] See Carp and Stidham, p. 141. Under seven state constitutions, the court of last resort may issue advisory opinions. Several other states permit judicial advisory opinions even though a constitutional provision expressly authorizing them is absent. Ibid., pp. 152–153, n. 17.

[101] American judges do issue declaratory judgments. But, these concern actual, not hypothetical, cases or controversies in which the court defines the rights and status of the parties although it does not order *damages* or other relief.

Activism versus Restraint

One common way to analyze this more controversial issue is to divide judges into those bent on **judicial activism**[102] and those intent on **judicial restraint.**[103]

Activist judges tend to perceive their role as using the law to see that the legal system accomplishes justice. They are less concerned with precedent and with honoring the prerogatives of other branches of government. Often, though not always, activist judges believe that the independence of the judiciary confers a special responsibility to safeguard the rights of unpopular people. Because the judiciary is considerably more divorced from popular pressures than are politicians, activist judges sometimes feel a special duty to apply and interpret the law so that all are treated fairly and to aid those who might otherwise find themselves victims of tyrannical majorities. This is especially the case when the other branches are stalemated, causing injustice, or when political processes are functioning abnormally, denying adequate representation to particular groups.

In contrast, judges practicing judicial restraint perceive their role in the American political system less majestically. Restrained judges define the judicial role cautiously: limiting the circumstances the court takes into account in issuing its ruling, finding the narrowest possible legal grounds for every decision, emphasizing the usefulness of *stare decisis,* overruling prior decisions as infrequently as possible, and defining the judicial role as modestly as possible. Judges attentive to the principle of judicial restraint may be more concerned with applying the letter of the law to the facts of the case than with trying to divine the spirit of the law and to determine how the law might be applied most equitably to the persons involved in the dispute.

Keenly aware of the constitutional separation of powers, judges practicing judicial restraint defer to the legislature and the executive so long as the government action fails to violate a constitutional provision, a longstanding tradition of interpretation, or some fundamental principle of law.[104] Consequently, they are less likely to uphold constitutional challenges to state and federal legislation. Above all else, judicial restraint implies that a judge should keep personal views on social and political matters from influencing the application of existing laws to the legal dispute at hand.

An activist judge recognizes the human element involved in serving on the bench. Chief Justice Earl Warren wrote: "Our judges are not monks or scientists,

[102] For activist views see Lawrence H. Tribe, *Constitutional Choices* (Cambridge, MA: Harvard University Press, 1985); Michael J. Perry, *The Constitution, the Courts, and Human Rights* (New Haven, CT: Yale University Press, 1983); Michael J. Perry, *Morality, Politics, and Law* (New York: Oxford University Press, 1989); and Arthur S. Miller, *Toward Increased Judicial Activism* (New York: Greenwood Press, 1982).

[103] See, for instance, Robert H. Bork, *The Tempting of America: The Political Seduction of the Law* (New York: Simon & Schuster, 1990); and Gary L. McDowell, *Curbing the Courts: The Constitution and the Limits of Judicial Power* (Baton Rouge: Lousiana State University Press, 1988). To compare contending views see Stephen C. Halpern and Charles M. Lamb, eds., *Supreme Court Activism and Restraint* (Lexington, MA: Lexington Books, 1982) and Mark W. Cannon and David M. O'Brien, *Views From the Bench: The Judiciary and Constitutional Politics* (Chatham, NJ: Chatham House, 1985), pp. 253–302.

[104] For an interesting overview of the debate on political questions see Abraham, pp. 358–362.

but participants in the living stream of our national life, steering the law between the dangers of rigidity on the one hand and formlessness on the other."[105] A judge who practices judicial restraint believes that the widespread respect for the judiciary among the American people depends upon judges applying the law, not substituting their political views for those of the legislature. In this vein Justice Holmes once colorfully remarked: "Young man, about 75 years ago I learned that I was not God. And so, when the people . . . want to do something I can't find anything in the Constitution expressly forbidding them to do, I say, whether I like it or not, 'Goddamit, let'em do it.' "[106]

The notion that American judges can be evaluated as activist or restrained ought to be qualified and supplemented. In fact, few judges are entirely active or wholly restrained. Most feel compelled to some extent by both sets of principles. When the principles collide in a particular case, most judges feel the tension between the two interpretations of their roles. Indeed, the vast majority of judges have been so moved by particular sets of circumstances as to write opinions that could be viewed as contradicting their own customary approach.

Furthermore, while today politically conservative judges tend to focus on judicial restraint and politically liberal judges tend to be more activist, such correlations are not necessary ones. In an era marked by progressive legislation, parties may call upon the courts to declare statutes unconstitutional; liberal judges may then find notions of judicial restraint to be appealing. In such an era conservative judges may find a more active role to be called for in upholding constitutional challenges and striking down liberal laws. For instance, a conservative, though activist, Supreme Court majority originally struck down laws creating a federal income tax[107] and a minimum wage for women[108] in the face of liberal arguments that the principle of judicial restraint called on the Supreme Court to permit the legislation to stand and not to substitute its political views for those of the people's elected representatives.

Despite the predominant current trends, there have been, and still are, activist conservative judges and rather restrained liberal judges. For instance, Justice Hugo Black, while a political liberal in many regards, saw his role on the bench in narrow terms on many occasions. Black's record may be contrasted with that of various conservative judges who have actively sought to overturn liberal precedents or to advance a conservative vision of the Constitution. For instance, Justices Anthony Kennedy, David Souter, and Sandra Day O'Connor, all conservatives appointed by Republican presidents, joined in an opinion that stated that the Supreme Court's

[105] Earl Warren, "The Law and the Future," *Fortune* 52 (November 1955), p 106, cited in Abraham, p. 317. Justice Frankfurter likewise observed: "Judges are men, not disembodied spirits, as men they respond to human situations." Abraham, p. 317.

[106] Abraham, p. 368, citing Charles P. Curtis, *Lions Under the Throne* (Boston: Houghton Mifflin, 1947), p. 281. In a letter to Harold Laski, Holmes likewise wrote: "If my fellow citizens want to go to Hell I will help them. It's my job." Abraham, p. 368, n. 114, citing Mark De Wolfe Howe, ed., *The Holmes-Laski Letters, 1916–1935* (New York: Atheneum, 1968), p. 249.

[107] *Pollock v. Farmer's Loan and Trust Co.,* 157 U.S. 429 (1895). See also Glendon, p. 120.

[108] *Adkins v. Children's Hospital,* 261 U.S. 238 (1936).

role was to tell the American people what their constitutional values should be.[109] Those who truly value judicial restraint would be unlikely to cast their vision of the proper role for the Supreme Court in such grandiose terms.

Two of the most conservative justices in recent years, Chief Justice William Rehnquist and Justice Antonin Scalia, have authored opinions that dramatically narrow *stare decisis* in constitutional cases. Rather, they favor actively reinterpreting the Constitution to endorse a more conservative political viewpoint.[110] Similarly, one scholar noted that William Brennan, one of the most liberal justices to serve on the Court, "deferred as humbly as any classical judge" when legislators had been motivated to pass a challenged law by concern for the individual in American society.[111] It seems fair to conclude that while today liberal judges tend to be more activist and conservative judges tend to be more restrained, both groups are tempted to rely on the judicial restraint argument when it suits their political purposes.

Judges also tend to be more or less active on different legal issues and at varying stages in their careers. Justice Holmes, for instance, believed that judges ought to restrain themselves strictly in considering economic legislation, but interpret broadly the personal liberties safeguarded in the Constitution. Various judges who seemed rather restrained when serving on lower courts have become more active when appointed to the U.S. Supreme Court. Hence, rather than attempting to characterize every judge as either active or restrained, one might more accurately view judicial activism and restraint as two poles on a philosophical spectrum and acknowledge that a judge's position on that spectrum is likely to vary with different issues and over time.

Students of American law should also realize that the contrast between activism and restraint is but one of the many conceivable modes of analysis that might be applied to American judicial philosophies. One might construct an alternative typology, for instance, that divides judges on the basis of their concern for the individual and his or her rights or for the community and its interests.

Finally, what is most interesting about analyzing judicial philosophies is the marked unpredictability of many American judges. Certainly, the study of American law would be much less fascinating if judges acted in a thoroughly consistent or transparently political manner. In fact, while one can speculate as to how particular judges will react to particular legal disputes, only a very rash observer would claim to be able to state with confidence how each judge or justice will vote on a series of cases covering different legal subjects. And, while predicting the views of

[109] *Planned Parenthood of Southeastern Pennsylvania v. Casey,* 505 U.S. 833 (1992). One commentator observed: "Americans do hold the Court in relatively high esteem. But it's quite a leap from John Marshall's emphatic insistence on the Court's power and duty 'to say what the law is' to the notion that the Court should tell us what our constitutional values should be. Ultimately (or so the Framers repeatedly insisted) the voice that is privileged 'before all others' in our system of government is the voice of the people, expressed in a variety of republican ways." Glendon, p. 114.

[110] See *Payne v. Tennessee,* 501 U.S. 808 (1991); *Webster v. Reproductive Health Services,* 492 U.S. 490 (1989). See also John F. Decker, *Revolution to the Right: Criminal Jurisprudence during the Burger—Rehnquist Court Era* (New York: Garland, 1992), pp. 112–114, and Tarr, p. 290.

[111] Glendon, p. 160.

the more politically extreme judges can be tricky at times, trying to figure out how more mainstream judges will respond can be exceptionally challenging.

For these reasons the ability of a lawyer to present a case in a persuasive and convincing manner—to narrow the legal issues to ones on which victory is possible for his or her client and to argue the case with spirit and intelligence—is a matter of cardinal importance in many appellate cases. To represent the client in the best possible manner, an expert litigator must often be aware of the judicial philosophies of the judges or justices in question. He or she will try to gain a sense for the trends that characterize relevant judicial decisions. In oral and written argument the attorney will attempt to emphasize those aspects of the facts or the law which benefit his or her client and which might appeal to the judge or judges hearing the case. That continuing interplay, or dialogue, between judge and lawyer concerning particular points of law in particular cases frames the subject of judicial philosophy. Focusing upon the subtleties of that dialogue will reveal much about how American judges think.

Judicial Innovation

American judges also differ from certain of their counterparts in other countries since they are not shy about deciding novel legal disputes. The judiciary does not customarily sidestep a case simply because the circumstances are significantly different from those faced by a court before or because the legislature has yet to pass a law that specifically addresses those circumstances.[112] Instead, the American judiciary has usually opted to apply well-established legal principles to new circumstances and in that way to broaden the law.[113]

For instance, imagine that a couple unable to conceive a child decides that the husband will contract with another woman to have his child, which he and his wife will then adopt. After the birth of the child, the surrogate mother decides she would like to keep the child and contests its custody in court. When such a case arose in New Jersey, the judge conceded that neither state law nor any prior case clearly resolved the issue of who was to gain custody. Rather than avoiding any decision, the judge extended established principles of law to these new circumstances and awarded the father custody instead of the surrogate mother.[114] Such a decision, refined by appellate court proceedings, broadened family law in New Jersey to cover new circumstances.

With the technological revolutions of the twentieth century, hitherto unheard of disputes—involving automobiles, condominiums, pollution, mass-

[112] See ibid., p. 132.

[113] In part, this reflects the fact that legislatures in common law systems operate in incremental, piecemeal fashions. They do not aim to create comprehensive codes of law applicable to all situations, as is the case in civil law systems.

[114] For the Superior Court decision, see *In the Matter of BABY M,* 217 N.J. 313, 525 A.2d 1128 (1987). After the New Jersey Supreme Court affirmed in part and reversed in part, 106 N.J. 396, 537 A.2d 1227 (1988), the Superior Court considered visitation rights in 225 N.J. Super. 267, 542 A.2d 52 (1988). See also Glick, p. 356.

produced manufactured products, medical innovations like *in vitro* fertilization, and a host of other modern developments—challenged American judges to innovate in resolving disputes.[115] From principles of property law that developed in Anglo-American agrarian societies, judges developed precepts of landlord-tenant law and, eventually, environmental law. Judges extended legal principles derived from ancient tort concepts to form early **product liability** and medical **malpractice** law. Over time, such judge-made law influenced, merged with, and sometimes was superseded by legislative enactments.

With judges focusing primarily on defining the rights and duties of the parties before them, rather than on forming consistent philosophical positions, no clear consensus has ever emerged as to which types of changes in American law ought to be made by a legislature and which ought to be made by a court.[116] Often, judges acted to resolve the legal dispute before them by innovative extensions of legal principles—until the legislatures provided more concrete guidance. One scholar wrote:

> [E]very twentieth-century judge has been obliged to handle novel and complex problems with uncertain guidance. It was mainly out of necessity, rather than through lust for power, that judges at all levels moved increasingly into areas where their legitimacy was weakest and their traditional skills of least use. They found themselves doing things that legislatures are better equipped to do, such as making judgments about broad social and economic facts rather than just finding the facts at issue in the case before them. In weighing and balancing competing social interests (as distinct from merely resolving the concrete dispute at hand), they began making the types of decisions that a republic ordinarily entrusts to elected representatives.[117]

Judicial Policymaking

These days judges are often criticized for no longer simply declaring what the law is and choosing the party that has a superior legal claim. Rather, the critics contend, judges have moved into the amorphous realm of judicial policymaking. Some critics imply that in judicial policymaking the judge is stepping beyond the rightful bounds of the office, which is that of interpreting legislation and the Constitution and resolving concrete disputes, and is encroaching upon the duties of legislators. Other observers contend that policymaking is an inherent part of judging: A host of individual decisions, in the aggregate, form a policy.

Given the importance of this debate, one might expect that legal scholars would agree on just what constitutes policymaking. In fact, however, the flavor of the conclusions drawn concerning the appropriateness of policymaking often directly relates to the breadth of the definition offered. Moreover, the term *policy* has slippery and elusive qualities that make its meaning difficult to pin down absent a

[115] The following examples are drawn largely from Glendon. See ibid. See also Carp and Stidham, p. 70.

[116] This echoes a point made by Glendon, p. 309, n. 14.

[117] Ibid., p. 137.

careful definition.[118] In ordinary discourse, *policy* is sometimes used to mean a set of broad, general principles designed to guide a government institution. For instance, one might say: "The president-elect is meeting with his closest advisers in order to determine the outlines of the new administration's social, financial, and foreign policies." Two legal scholars used *policy* in this sense when they wrote: "The Judicial Conference of the United States remains the policymaker for the federal judiciary . . ."[119]

In other circumstances *policy* is used to refer to a discretionary decision to do something in order to advance toward an objective. For instance, one might say: "I pay taxes as a matter of law; I make charitable contributions as a matter of policy." One academic used *policy* in this sense when he wrote: "[T]he highest appellate courts often are described as *policymaking courts* because they can be selective in deciding the more significant disputes."[120] In this view, selecting which cases ought to be decided amounts to making policy because the judge exercises discretion to reach a goal.

At still other times people refer to *policy* as a loose synonym for *law*. For instance, a lawyer might tell a client: "Unfortunately, the Internal Revenue Service will not allow that deduction as it clearly violates the administration's tax policy." Another legal scholar seemed to use *policy* in this sense when he wrote:

> Courts in any political system participate to some degree in the policymaking process because it is their job. Any judge faced with a choice between two or more interpretations and applications of a legislative act, executive order, or constitutional provision must choose among them because the controversy must be decided. And when the judge chooses, his or her interpretation becomes policy for the specific litigants. If the interpretation is accepted by the other judges, the judge has made policy for all jurisdictions in which that view prevails.[121]

Here one might substitute the word *law* for *policy* at every point without gravely distorting the meaning of the passage.

For the student of American law who sets out to determine when judicial policymaking is and is not appropriate, the multiple meanings of *policy* are confusing and unfortunate since "[A] word that means everything means virtually nothing, a conceptual tool used indiscriminately has its analytical edge irreparably dulled."[122] It may thus be instructive to compare ideas of *domestic policymaking* with ideas of judicial policymaking and in that way arrive at a useful understanding of the term.

[118] The following discussion draws heavily on an April 1, 1996 letter written to the author by Inis L. Claude, Jr., Professor Emeritus of Government and Foreign Affairs at the University of Virginia.

[119] Carp and Stidham, p. 93.

[120] Glick, p. 27.

[121] Robert H. Birkby, *The Court and Public Policy* (Washington, DC: Congressional Quarterly Press, 1983), p. 1, cited in Carp and Stidham, pp. 31–32.

[122] Inis L. Claude, Jr., "The Peace-Keeping Role of the United Nations," in E. Berkeley Tompkins, ed., *The United Nations in Perspective* (Stanford, CA: Hoover Institution Press, 1972), p. 49. For similar analysis of the term *sovereignty*, see Michael Ross Fowler and Julie Marie Bunck, *Law, Power, and the Sovereign State: The Evolution and Application of the Concept of Sovereignty* (University Park: Pennsylvania State University Press, 1995), especially pp. 4–8.

In domestic policymaking, an administration might first perceive an *interest,* for instance, the development and maintenance of an efficient road transport system. From this interest might be derived the *goal* of keeping gasoline supplies plentiful and prices stable. The *strategy* to achieve that goal might include steps to encourage domestic oil production. The *policy* aimed at putting that strategy into effect might involve a reduction of the tax burden on oil companies that explore for new oil fields. Finally, the government might enact a *law* that provides a tax break for companies engaged in oil exploration.

The purpose of describing domestic policymaking in these terms is not to suggest that leaders actually make political decisions in this type of formalized, step-by-step reasoning. Nor is it to suggest that law constitutes the only means by which policy may be put into action. Policy may also be effectuated by the making of speeches, the acts of bureaucracies, the movement of troops, and various other government initiatives. Rather, the description of policymaking is meant to advance the idea that, while the three are related ideas, *policy* can be distinguished from *strategy,* on the one hand, and *law,* on the other. Indeed, whether the context is judicial or domestic affairs, *policy,* properly defined, ought to fall between *strategy*—that is, a plan or method for obtaining a specific result—and *law*—that is, a rule or rules established or confirmed by the government and enforceable by the state. When speaking of judicial policymaking, one might most sensibly refer to policy not as a broad set of general principles, not simply as a discretionary decision, and not merely as a synonym for law. Rather, policymaking entails setting a course of specific government action with three principal characteristics. It carries out a strategy. It is usually aimed at resolving or ameliorating social, economic, political, or national-security problems. And, it is primarily derived not from legal principles but from political or philosophical considerations as to how a government should operate.

If the term is used in this relatively narrow manner, one might next ask when judges engage in it. An administrative group like the Judicial Conference that decides to ask Congress to create fifty new federal judgeships has arrived at a plan to reach a particular goal. Hence, by the above definition, it has engaged in judicial strategizing, not judicial policymaking. A judge who applies settled contract law principles to a vague, disputed provision and concludes that it should be interpreted according to the plaintiff's reading, not the defendant's, is not primarily concerned with political or philosophical considerations about how a government should operate. Rather, he or she is applying legal reasoning to a particular dispute.[123]

[123] Here, of course, a member of the Critical Legal Scholar (CLS) school of thought would likely argue that legal reasoning merely masks underlying political considerations. In my view, however, the CLS perspective fails to account adequately for the historical momentum of rulemaking via common law dialectical reasoning, a subject taken up in more detail in Chapter 9. I would agree with Mary Ann Glendon who wrote: "It is a big step . . . from observing . . . that there are certain leeways inherent in fact finding and rule application to asserting that there is no such thing as a fact and that all rules are radically indeterminate and manipulable. It is another major leap from being realistic about the difficulties of fair and impartial decision making to a condemnation of the entire legal system as fatally corrupted by racism, sexism, and exploitation." Glendon, p. 214.

During the course of the twentieth century, however, the American legal community has become increasingly interested in considering the social, economic, and political ramifications of different possible legal decisions. Consequently, American lawyers have come to include policy considerations in their briefs and oral arguments. A *Brandeis brief* refers to a written argument to an appellate court that includes economic and social data along with legal principles and citations. (The term is named for Supreme Court Justice Louis Brandeis, who crafted innovative and persuasive arguments of this sort while in private practice.) Moreover, law professors and scholars in related fields, such as political science, economics, criminal justice, and sociology, have focused ever more critical attention on the policy consequences of court decisions. Consequently, American judges have increasingly tempered purely legal reasoning with policy considerations.

Judges now sometimes frankly identify policy considerations in their reasoning. To take one of many possible examples, one judge cited "that general and well-settled public opinion relating to man's plain, palpable duty to his fellowmen . . ."[124] In such cases a judge might rule that public policy considerations dissuade the court from interpreting a contractual or statutory provision in a certain way. With the increased sophistication of economic and social science data during the twentieth century, courts considered such social welfare arguments with increasing seriousness and frequency.

Alongside the direct influence of policy considerations on the outcome of legal disputes, cases before the courts will inevitably help to shape policy in indirect ways. Sometimes a legal case will focus the spotlight of public attention on a particular issue. On occasion, judicial decisions will bring about a reaction by the legislature or executive, a change in policy direction, a statute clarifying or overriding a judicial precedent, even a constitutional amendment. Indeed, sometimes cases that are not before the courts will also shape policy, as when police and prosecutors choose not to pursue particular types of offenses. A variety of judicial activity and inactivity thus has significant policymaking ramifications. Most controversially, however, in a range of politicized legal disputes the term *judicial policymaking* could be appropriate, depending on whether the government action ordered by the court is derived principally from political or philosophical, rather than legal, grounds. For instance, the judge in the child custody case described previously might decide in favor of the surrogate mother or the contracting father by extrapolating from legal principles in cases that bore some resemblance to that at hand or by interjecting personal or majority political or philosophical views of how society ought to function.

In addition, when other branches of government have failed to carry out judicial orders, judges have come to be intimately involved in the administration of prisons, schools, public housing projects, mental health hospitals, and other institutions. By 1992, federal and state judges had issued court orders supervising the

[124] *Hammonds v. Aetna Cas. & Sur. Co.,* 243 F.Supp. 793, 796 (N.D. Ohio, 1965).

operation of more than 500 school districts as well as prisons in nearly forty states."[125] Such judicial actions would also fall within the ambit of judicial policymaking.

The extent to which American judges should engage in these types of judicial policymaking is a controversial issue that raises again the benefits and drawbacks of activist versus restrained judging. One might conclude that trying to wholly eradicate judicial policymaking would be neither feasible nor wise. Considering the social implications of legal decisions helps courts to do justice. However, judicial policymaking run amok has dangerous implications for the legitimacy of the judiciary and its separation from other branches of government.

THE STATUS OF AMERICAN JUDGES

As in other countries, the American judiciary has been tarnished by occasional scandals and periodically excoriated after controversial decisions. From time to time, the unpleasant odor of political patronage has mixed with the sharper smell of bribery and other forms of corruption. In recent years, partisan political attacks have once again increased in number and venom, especially as judges have exercised their powers of judicial review more rigorously and have ventured more often into activist interpretations and assertive policymaking to correct perceived inequities. Nevertheless, over the years American judges have belonged to one of the most influential judiciaries in the world, and judges remain by far the most respected individuals in the American legal system.[126]

The position occupied by American judges can be brought into focus by comparing the judiciary in the United States with that in other countries. Many countries today enjoy neither strong judicial traditions nor widespread public trust in the judiciary. In economically poor developing countries that are making the difficult transition from authoritarian pasts to democratic futures, judges are often not at all highly respected. Under such circumstances, one sees how Americans often take for granted the valuable asset of their own judiciary.

For instance, in Honduras many judges are young and inexperienced.[127] Their salaries are often quite low, and many have entered the judicial profession because of political ties. Traditionally, when a new political party takes power, many judges are dismissed and replaced, or at least moved to a different court. Some observers argue that Honduran judges also tend to be less educated and to come

[125] Glendon, p. 142, citing David O. Steuart, "No Exit," *ABA Journal* (June 1992): 49.

[126] One might note that while wags in the media and late-night television often criticize and ridicule lawyers, they more rarely poke fun at the judiciary.

[127] Interviews with Dagoberto Mejia Pineda, Director, Public Defenders Service of Honduras (former Professor of Criminal Procedure at the National Autonomous University of Honduras), and Manuel Antonio Fortin Aguilar, Sub-Director of the Judicial School of Honduras (former Professor of Legal History and Theory, National Autonomous University of Honduras), Dec. 19, 1991, Tegucigalpa, Honduras. See also Nadelmann, p. 266.

from a lower social class than do the most sophisticated lawyers in the country. Frequently, Honduran law students decide that, after graduation, they would like to be a judge for a while in order to learn how to be a lawyer.[128] Both the Honduran people and knowledgeable law-enforcement officers widely believe that many judges accept bribes to decide a case in favor of the party that gives them the most money.[129]

The role of the judiciary in Honduras, of course, contrasts sharply with its role in the United States. This is largely a result of cardinal differences in procedure and in judicial culture and tradition. However, it also partly reflects the fact that Honduran judges are so poorly compensated for their work that corruption is ingrained in the system through bribery. By contrast, U.S. federal judges earn adequate salaries. Although their pay by no means approximates the high salaries those judges might earn as lawyers in private practice, this may well enhance the prestige of the judiciary, not detract from it. "[J]udging is not a vehicle for making money . . . ,"[130] and the public seems to appreciate that judges primarily work to bring order to society, not to become exceptionally rich.

State court judges tend to earn less than their federal counterparts, though the exact salaries differ substantially from state to state. As of 1993, on average, state trial judges earned $83,048, intermediate appellate judges earned $91,491, and judges at the highest appellate court earned $92,806.[131] Tables 3.1 and 3.2 show annual salaries for federal and state judges as of January 1, 1994.

Though its learning, independence, and rectitude contribute to the traditional public faith in the American judiciary, judges in the United States also enjoy considerable status because of the particular powers they exercise. Most judicial hierarchies are capped by a tribunal whose sole function is to resolve constitutional disputes.[132] In most legal systems, a constitutional issue is not handled by just any court; rather, it is directed to the constitutional court or courts. However, in the United States and a few other countries, including Japan, no separate constitutional court exists. Rather, any judge may rule on a constitutional issue. In particular, the power of judicial review may be exercised by any judge in any court, subject, of course, to appeals to higher courts and ultimately to the U.S. Supreme Court. In Japan, for example, the same power of judicial review is tempered by the

[128] Mejia Pineda interview.

[129] See "En Honduras ha aumentado el trafico y uso de drogas" ["In Honduras the Traffic and Use of Drugs Has Increased"], *La Prensa* [Honduras], April 15, 1988, p. 56; and "El Narcotrafico en Honduras y la opinion publica nacional" ["National Public Opinion Concerning the Narcotics Traffic in Honduras"], *La Prensa,* [Honduras], Sept. 9, 1988, p. 80. My information is based on confidential interviews with law-enforcement sources in Honduras. One reliable source told me that government officials in the country pay as much as $250,000 to be appointed to a particular government position and thus to be positioned to reap the benefits of bribes while in office. See also Nadelmann, p. 252.

[130] Kronman, p. 319.

[131] Maguire and Pastore, p. 81.

[132] The following discussion draws on Glendon, pp. 130–131.

TABLE 3.1 **Annual Salaries of Federal Judges**

Chief justice of the U.S. Supreme Court	$171,500
Associate justices of the U.S. Supreme Court	$164,100
U.S. Circuit Court of Appeals judges	$141,700
U.S. District Court judges	$133,600
U.S. International Court of Trade judges	$133,600
U.S. Court of Federal Claims judges	$133,600
U.S. bankruptcy judges	$122,912
U.S. magistrate judges (full-time)	$122,912

Source: Kathleen Maguire and Ann L. Pastore, eds., *Sourcebook of Criminal Justice Statistics—1993* (Washington, DC: U.S. Government Printing Office, 1994), p. 77.

judiciary's deep-seated reluctance to use it. Japanese courts very rarely declare legislative acts to be unconstitutional. In the United States, by contrast, "judges have spread their constitutional wings"[133] throughout the twentieth century and "exercised their powers of constitutional review with much greater frequency and boldness than judges elsewhere."[134]

Moreover, American judges inherited from their English forebears the substantial powers once lodged in the English courts of equity. Not only can vestiges of the courts of equity still be identified in a few state court systems, but American judges have always been authorized to issue certain forms of equitable relief, such as the *injunction* described in the prior chapter.

Just as important, the U.S. judiciary has long been empowered to hear, consider, and decide ***habeas corpus*** issues. A **writ** of *habeas corpus* is an order issued by a judge to bring a prisoner before the bench to determine whether he or she has been illegally imprisoned. A *habeas corpus* proceeding does not determine a prisoner's guilt; rather, it inquires as to whether the authorities properly granted that prisoner due process before imprisoning the individual.

In a global comparative perspective, all such judicial powers are quite unusual. In these regards American judges enjoy broader authority than do their colleagues in most other countries. In considering judicial review and the other powers of the U.S. judiciary, one legal scholar observed: "[T]he toolbox of every American judge has always contained some highly potent instruments."[135] If the judiciary were stripped of such powers, its status in American society would also likely diminish.

In the minds of many Americans, however, the judiciary can retain its prestige only if it restricts the use of the potent tools at its disposal. To some degree the judicial innovations required by the technological changes of the twentieth century coupled with increased policymaking and judicial review have eroded public

[133] Ibid., p. 130.

[134] Ibid., p. 131.

[135] Ibid.

TABLE 3.2 **Sample of Annual Salaries of State Judges**

State	Court of Last Resort	Intermediate Appellate Court	General Trial Court
Alabama	$107,125	$106,125	$ 72,500
California	$127,267	$119,314	$104,262
Colorado	$ 84,000	$ 79,500	$ 75,000
Georgia	$ 96,118	$ 95,509	$ 73,344
Idaho	$ 79,183	$ 78,183	$ 74,214
Louisiana	$ 94,000	$ 89,000	$ 84,000
Michigan	$111,941	$107,463	$ 98,844
New Mexico	$ 77,250	$ 73,388	$ 69,719
New Jersey	$115,000	$108,000	$100,000
Pennsylvania	$108,045	$104,444	$ 92,610

Source: Kathleen Maguire and Ann L. Pastore, eds., *Sourcebook of Criminal Justice Statistics—1993* (Washington, DC: U.S. Government Printing Office, 1994), p. 77.

approval and trust in the courts.[136] While the judiciary remains a healthy feature of the American legal system, warning signs have begun to appear. This may help to explain why judges in the United States, like so many other American authority figures, have lost a measure of status in recent years. Growing public cynicism and other deep-seated cultural changes have led the American public and American lawyers to criticize the judiciary more freely, to regard it, perhaps accurately, as more politicized. In recent years, these trends have curbed the respect traditionally shown for the judiciary by all Americans.

One particularly worrisome consequence of lower status, higher caseloads, modest pay, less time for deliberation, and increased critical scrutiny in the selection of judges is that fewer top lawyers now show special interest in judicial positions. One observer noted: "Today, many capable lawyers no longer regard appointment or election to the bench as the capstone of a distinguished career. It is not uncommon, when a judgeship is being filled, to hear that prominent attorneys have declined to have their names placed in nomination—or that a firm is angling to relieve itself of an unproductive partner by touting him or her for a judicial appointment. Sitting judges, meanwhile, are resigning in record numbers, often after a relatively short tenure."[137] Since the status of the American judiciary depends in the first instance on the personal characteristics of its judges, such trends bear careful watching.

[136] According to a Gallup poll in 1949, 83.4 percent of Americans expressed trust and approval in the Supreme Court; by 1973 that figure had dropped to 32.6 percent; by 1993 it had rebounded to 44 percent. Linowitz, p. 182.

[137] Glendon, p. 148.

SELECTED ADDITIONAL READINGS

ABRAHAM, HENRY J. *Justices and Presidents: A Political History of Appointments to the Supreme Court.* 3d ed. rev. New York: Oxford University Press, 1992.

CARDOZO, BENJAMIN N. *The Nature of the Judicial Process.* New Haven, CT: Yale University Press, 1949.

CARTER, LIEF H. *Reason in Law.* 4th ed. rev. New York: HarperCollins College, 1994.

DOUGLAS, WILLIAM O. *"Stare Decisis,"* in Walter F. Murphy and C. Herman Pritchett, eds., *Courts, Judges, and Politics,* 3d ed. rev. New York: Random House, 1979, pp. 521–526.

FULLER, LON L. "The Forms and Limits of Adjudication," in Sheldon Goldman and Austin Sarat, eds., *American Court Systems: Readings in Judicial Process and Behavior.* San Francisco: W. H. Freeman, 1987.

HUGHES, JOHN C. *The Federal Courts, Politics, and the Rule of Law.* New York: HarperCollins College, 1995.

KEETON, ROBERT E. *Judging.* St. Paul, MN: West, 1990.

MURPHY, WALTER F. *Elements of Judicial Strategy.* Chicago: University of Chicago Press, 1964.

PERRY, BARBARA A. *A "Representative" Supreme Court?* Westport, CT: Greenwood Press, 1991.

WATSON, GEORGE C. and STOOKEY, JOHN ALAN. *Shaping America: The Politics of Supreme Court Appointments.* New York: HarperCollins College, 1995.

WHITE, EDWARD G. *The American Judicial Tradition.* New York: Oxford University Press, 1988.

WICE, PAUL. *Judges and Lawyers.* New York: HarperCollins College, 1991.

4

The Lawyer

Speaking a language that the layperson often finds impenetrable, practicing a profession that is essential to American society, yet contains singularly unattractive features, American lawyers are alternately reviled and respected. Yet they are absolutely critical to the functioning of the American legal system. How do Americans view the legal profession? What types of lawyers exist? What does the practice of law entail? Why is law considered a profession, and what professional obligations do lawyers assume? What is distinctive about legal thinking and legal education? How and why do lawyers supervise their profession?

PUBLIC PERCEPTIONS OF THE LEGAL PROFESSION

Dr. Samuel Johnson once observed: "As it rarely happens that a man is fit to plead his own cause, lawyers are a class of the community, who by study and experience, have acquired the art and power of arranging evidence, and of applying to the points at issue what the law has settled."[1] The United States is approaching the day when 1 million Americans will earn their livings practicing law. Why do so many clients pay American lawyers so handsomely to apply "to the points at issue what the law has settled"? What accounts for this tremendous boom in the American legal profession?

Long ago, Americans laid the foundation for their current mammoth legal industry. Even before the birth of the republic, attorneys acquired a prominent role in American society, and they have succeeded in advancing that position over time. British economist John Maynard Keynes once wryly observed that the *Mayflower*, the ship that carried early settlers to colonial Plymouth, must have ar-

[1] Dr. Samuel Johnson, cited in Lloyd Paul Stryker, *The Art of Advocacy: A Plea for the Renaissance of the Trial Lawyer* (New York: Simon & Schuster, 1954), p. 111.

rived packed full of lawyers! In 1862 distinguished British novelist Anthony Trollope noted: "[L]awyers are the leading men in the [United] States. . . . [T]he governance of that country has been almost entirely in their hands ever since the political life of the nation became full strong."[2] In recent years the age-old prominence of American lawyers has seemed to some to be metamorphosing into an unhealthy dominance—or, as one legal scholar titled her recent book, *A Nation Under Lawyers.*[3]

As law has permeated more aspects of American life, American lawyers have been in greater demand. Today, legal skills are more necessary than ever to determine what citizens may and may not do and how they should best do it. A business deal that might once have been closed on a handshake and a so-called *gentleman's agreement* is now often subject to lengthy negotiations aimed at producing a contract that comprehensively states the rights and obligations of the parties. A corporation, facing stiff domestic and international competition in a high technology field, may now find it imperative to supplement its standard employment contract with a **confidentiality agreement** aimed at keeping employees from shopping secret information to competitors. Personal and family relations that might once have been carefully screened from public scrutiny have now been pervaded by *prenuptial agreements, divorce decrees,* and *spouse-abuse* and *child-abuse proceedings.* Although reasonable minds can differ on the extent to which such social changes are positive, few Americans will doubt that these changes mean that they are more likely to visit a lawyer than were their parents or grandparents.[4]

Accompanying the growth of the legal profession has been a popular backlash against lawyers, their ethics, fees, and mindsets. The Watergate scandal of the 1970s, the savings and loan scandal of the 1980s, even the Whitewater scandal of the 1990s showed lawyers, among others, at their worst.[5] If ever the American public imagined its attorneys to be distinguished, principled professionals, that image has succumbed to a stereotype of lawyers as scheming, money-grubbing, "connoisseurs of conflict"[6] and as shrewd manipulators of the American systems of law, politics, and criminal justice.

Scorn for lawyers is, of course, nothing new. As long ago as 1770 Dr. Johnson quipped to a group of friends: "I do not care to speak ill of any man behind his

[2] Anthony Trollope, *North America,* vol. II (Gloucester, Gloucestershire: Alan Sutton, 1987), p. 329. Trollope continued: "Lawyers form the ruling class in America as the landowners do with us." (p. 330)

[3] Mary Ann Glendon, *A Nation Under Lawyers: How the Crisis in the Legal Profession Is Transforming American Society* (New York: Farrar, Straus & Giroux, 1994).

[4] A 1989 survey found that almost 75 percent of adult Americans had consulted a lawyer. Ibid., p. 322, n. 29, citing Barbara A. Curran, "1989 Survey of the Public's Use of Legal Services," in *Two National Surveys: 1989 Pilot Assessments of the Unmet Legal Needs of the Poor and the Public Generally* (Chicago: American Bar Association, 1989), p. 57. According to a 1993 *National Law Journal* survey, 68 percent of Americans had contacted a lawyer for professional advice in the prior five years. Sol M. Linowitz, with Martin Mayer, *The Betrayed Profession: Lawyering at the End of the Twentieth Century* (New York: Charles Scribner's Sons, 1994), p. 147.

[5] See Glendon, p. 7.

[6] Ibid., p. 40.

back, but I believe the gentleman was an attorney."[7] Nevertheless, the vehemence of recent attacks on the American legal profession warrants notice. For instance, for years a beer company ran a television advertisement showing a rodeo in which a cowboy on horseback chases and catches a tax lawyer in a corral surrounded by cheering fans! The front of a long-popular T-shirt belligerently expresses frustration with America's lawyers, quoting William Shakespeare's play *King Henry VI:* "The first thing we do, let's kill all the lawyers!"[8]

Yet, many who hurry to criticize the legal profession in the United States conveniently forget the positive feats accomplished by several centuries of American lawyers. The vast majority of the widely respected Founding Fathers, for example, were not doctors or professors, soldiers or farmers. They were lawyers. More than any other group in society, American lawyers wrote the Declaration of Independence and the Constitution.[9] Then, over the next 200 years, the many lawyer-legislators serving in Congress played critical roles in amending the Constitution and drafting other laws that have enjoyed considerable popular support.[10]

Indeed, while many rue the vast reaches of American law, tourists, retirees, executives, and many others often find the prospect of living or doing business in more informal and less legalistic countries to be quite daunting. While American corporate leaders often rail against the high costs of legal services, few would be comfortable entering a business transaction of any complexity without the services of an able attorney or law firm. While American politicians have periodically capitalized on negative views of laws and lawyers, few have aggressively promoted sweeping reforms. While ordinary citizens complain of the shortcomings of the American legal system, few would be inclined to trade for a different system. Fewer still would wish to be put on trial in a foreign country rather than in the United States or even to bring suit in another country's courts.

Moreover, although the public nowadays routinely denounces the legal profession, voters still regularly turn to lawyers to represent them at the city, state, and national levels of government. To date, fully two out of every three American presidents has had training in law, and more than half the members of most American congresses and legislatures have been lawyers. With the election of Bill Clinton in 1992, thirteen of the eighteen members of his cabinet held law degrees.[11] In the 1996 presidential election, even the spouses of the two leading presidential candidates were lawyers.

[7] Stryker, p. 255.

[8] Before one hastens to place Shakespeare in the camp of those who loathe lawyers, it may be worth remembering that Shakespeare put those words "in the mouth of a self-interested and disreputable revolutionary." Linowitz, p. 5; *King Henry VI,* Act IV, ii, 86.

[9] Twenty-five of the 56 men who signed the Declaration of Independence were lawyers, as were 31 of the 55 delegates to the Constitutional Convention. Robert A. Carp and Ronald Stidham, *Judicial Process in America,* 3d ed. rev. (Washington, DC: Congressional Quarterly Press, 1996), p. 107.

[10] This is not meant to imply that lawyers form a cohesive interest group on many issues. To the contrary, a corporate lawyer from a large firm is likely to have few common political views with a solo practitioner in the personal injury field. See Henry R. Glick, *Courts, Politics, and Justice,* 3d ed. rev. (New York: McGraw-Hill, 1993), pp. 81–83.

[11] Glendon, p. 12.

Thus, although the legal profession certainly merits constructive criticism, the evenhanded critic might also acknowledge the essential contributions that attorneys have made and are making to American society. In the very unlikely event that the legal profession in the United States were to be dramatically scaled back, numerous aspects of American society would be radically transformed.

One reason that American lawyers have been so maligned is that, apart from the occasional American Bar Association (ABA) promotional campaign,[12] the legal profession has done an exceptionally poor job in explaining just what it does and just how it proceeds.[13] Particularly in recent years lawyers have focused virtually all their attention on handling ever-greater workloads, and, for those in private practice, pursuing earnings in an ever more single-minded fashion. Public relations, in the most positive sense of the term, have been all but ignored.

As has been true from the dawn of legal systems, the dense and unfamiliar vocabulary of law continues to render the legal profession uncomfortable and difficult to understand for many who are not lawyers or long-time students of the courts. Indeed, lawyers themselves may have felt an incentive, conscious or subconscious, to cloak their activities with a degree of mystery to enhance their own self-importance and to contribute to the mystique of the profession. Under these circumstances, it is especially important that a work introducing the American legal system dissect the role of the lawyer.

VARIETIES OF AMERICAN LAWYERS

One can learn much about any lawyer by discovering for whom he or she works, that is, who the lawyer's clients are. Although certain attorneys work for a single client, perhaps a large corporation or government agency, most are employed by various clients. A first step in trying to understand what all those lawyers do for all their clients is to divide the legal profession into categories.

In selecting a job, lawyers typically choose to become public interest or government lawyers, solo practitioners, in-house counsels, or attorneys in law firms. These categories are by no means mutually exclusive. During a lengthy legal career many lawyers move from one category to another and from one part of the country to another. It is not at all unusual to meet a Boston corporate lawyer who started practicing law as a public interest attorney in California, an in-house counsel in New York who once prosecuted securities cases in Washington, DC, or a solo practitioner in Ohio who served on the legal staff of a congressional committee. Many lawyers in Washington, DC, make a career out of hopping back and forth between jobs in government and private practice.

[12] The ABA spent $1 million on one public relations campaign designed to improve the image of the legal profession. Linowitz, p. 144.

[13] See Walter T. Fisher, *What Every Lawyer Knows* (Boston: Nimrod Press, 1974), p. 15, and Jerome Frank, *Courts on Trial: Myth and Reality in American Justice* (Princeton, NJ: Princeton University Press, 1973), p. 1.

Yet, while lawyers may have a taste of different types of legal work during their careers, attorneys also tend to become more specialized as they gain experience. It used to be that specialization particularly marked the careers of attorneys who worked in certain very narrow subfields: bonds, for example, or intellectual property, or admiralty and maritime law. (A cynic might still observe that once a lawyer has done patent work for ten years he or she is not fit for anything else!) These days, however, generalists are scarce in all job categories.

In a law firm a young lawyer might start in business law, move into the subfield of mergers and acquisitions, and finally specialize in the acquisitions of factories that turn trash into energy. Although individuals practicing law alone often undertake legal work that deals with different fields of law, even these solo practitioners tend to specialize over time. For instance, a lawyer might open a law office intending a general litigation practice. With time he or she might begin to accept only personal injury cases and, eventually, only cases dealing with injuries resulting from medical malpractice. And, even a lawyer who moves from government service to private practice may work on the same specialized issues in both settings.

Understanding the lawyer's role in America presumes some familiarity with the principal types of American lawyers, five categories of which are briefly outlined below.

Public Interest and Government Lawyers

Some American lawyers join an organization of attorneys all working for a charitable cause. Such **public interest lawyers** typically specialize in one of many fields of law.[14] Attorneys for the American Civil Liberties Union (ACLU)[15] and the Legal Defense Fund of the National Association for the Advancement of Colored People (NAACP)[16] use their expertise in civil rights and liberties issues. The Sierra Club, Environmental Defense Fund, and World Wildlife Fund employ legal staffs expert in environmental and natural resources issues. Lawyers at the Children's Defense Fund focus upon family and juvenile law. Lawyers in these public interest organizations either lobby the government or bring or participate in lawsuits, often by filing *amicus curiae* briefs.

Most attorneys working in criminal law do not work for charitable organizations. Rather, these **public defenders** are appointed to their posts and employed by the county, state, or federal government to defend the more than two out of every three criminal defendants who do not have the financial resources necessary

[14] See Nan Aron, *Liberty and Justice For All: Public Interest Law in the 1980s and Beyond* (Boulder, CO: Westview Press, 1989).

[15] See Samuel E. Walker, *In Defense of American Liberties: A History of the ACLU* (New York: Oxford University Press, 1991).

[16] For works on the NAACP see Jack Greenberg, *Crusaders in the Courts: How a Dedicated Band of Lawyers Fought for the Civil Rights Revolution* (New York: Basic Books, 1994), and Clement E. Vose, *Caucasians Only: The Supreme Court, the NAACP, and the Restrictive Covenant Cases* (Berkeley: University of California Press, 1959).

to hire a private attorney.[17] Since landmark Supreme Court cases in 1938 and 1963, the federal government and the states have been constitutionally required to provide an attorney to an impoverished defendant charged with a felony.[18] If a public defender is not available,[19] a private attorney may voluntarily accept the case on a *pro bono* basis, or a judge may assign a lawyer from a list of those who have agreed to represent indigent defendants for a set fee to be paid by the state.

Some attorneys employed by the government to further public interests are engaged in civil, not criminal, work. For instance, the civil division of the New York Legal Aid Society aims to help the poor with legal problems other than allegations of criminal behavior. In 1974 Congress founded the **Legal Services Corporation** to ensure that poor Americans received equal access to justice in noncriminal legal matters. The Corporation currently funds more than 300 programs, employs 11,000 people, and operates over 1,000 neighborhood law offices that annually serve 1.7 million clients.[20] Although various politicians have periodically attempted to curtail the corporation's functions or to slash its budget, it has strong support from the **American Bar Association** and both political parties. Thus, federal funds continue to be used to ensure that poor Americans are also able to use the court system to enforce rights, recover for injuries, and settle personal matters such as landlord-tenant disputes, divorce and child custody problems, the denial of welfare benefits, and a range of other legal issues.

While their careers are socially useful and can be intellectually stimulating, life as a public defender or other public interest lawyer has drawbacks. Public defenders are not directly rewarded for winning cases in the same way that a private lawyer gains clientele, reputation, and the ability to charge higher fees through trial successes.[21] Instead, public defenders please their outside supervisory agency by running an efficient, low-cost office that provides some counsel to the many defendants who are very likely to be ultimately convicted. Some lawyers find themselves fascinated, year after year, by the challenges of such work; others eventually wish to move on.

Public interest lawyers also normally earn quite low salaries. Approximately half of all American lawyers earn $35,000 or less.[22] Many of these are public interest attorneys. An entry-level lawyer in this field might make as little as

[17] The federal government finances federal public defender organizations and community defender organizations. In addition, most states finance their own public defender programs. For works focusing on legal services to the poor, see Susan Lawrence, *The Poor in Court* (Princeton, NJ: Princeton University Press, 1990) and Aron, *Liberty and Justice for All.*

[18] *Johnson v. Zerbst,* 304 U.S. 458 (1938) and *Gideon v. Wainwright,* 372 U.S. 335 (1963). See also Anthony Lewis, *Gideon's Trumpet* (New York: Vintage Books, 1964).

[19] Sometimes a public defender's office is overloaded with work and lacks the resources necessary to assist all impoverished defendants. Alternatively, in some states the offices of public defenders serve urban populations but not rural ones.

[20] Sarah Neville, "Legal Services Faces Cuts in Funds, Authority," *Washington Post,* Sept. 14, 1995, p. A21.

[21] Glick, p. 233.

[22] Jonathan D. Glater, "Loansome Law Students: Why Payback is Tough," *Washington Post,* Aug. 21, 1995, Washington Business section, p. 7.

$25,000 a year;[23] a midcareer public interest lawyer might earn an additional $8,000 or $10,000. Such low salaries serve as disincentives for lawyers working in large cities where the cost of living is high, and for lawyers who have accumulated large debts from paying expensive tuition bills in law school.[24] As a result of the low pay scale, many public interest lawyers are young, unmarried men and women, who gain valuable experience, but then eventually move on to another kind of law practice that enables them to support themselves and their families more easily.

Apart from the public defenders and the other public interest lawyers, whose activities may or may not be supported by state or federal funds, many other American lawyers work for the government directly. Today, more than 65,000 attorneys, amounting to more than 8 percent of America's lawyers, work for the state or federal government, many of them as prosecutors representing the government in criminal trials. Another 20,000 or so, about 3 percent of the total, work in the state or federal judiciary.[25]

The most prominent non-judicial legal position in the federal government is that of the **attorney general.** The U.S. attorney general heads the Department of Justice, represents the U.S. government in various substantial legal matters, and provides counsel on legal issues to the cabinet and the president. (The president also is advised by the **White House counsel,** an attorney who offers legal advice to the president on personal and political matters as well as on governmental issues.)

Another highly influential federal legal post is that occupied by the **solicitor general,** who with help from various deputies and assistants within the Justice Department[26] represents the U.S. government in the vast majority of cases before the U.S. Supreme Court.[27] The Office of Solicitor General also decides which cases the U.S. government should appeal to the Supreme Court. While the Supreme Court justices need not hear every such appeal, the fact that the solicitor general would like a hearing usually carries substantial weight with the Court.

The **U.S. attorneys** hold the most prestigious and powerful prosecutorial offices in the United States.[28] Although the Office of U.S. Attorney has various courtroom responsibilities, its most important duties are to prosecute all offenses against the United States and to represent the U.S. government in all civil actions

[23] The average, annual starting salary for lawyers at the Legal Services Corporation is $25,337. Neville, p. A21.

[24] The Access Group, which administers about 70 percent of all loans to law students, reported that half of all the graduating law students in 1994 owed $38,000 or more. Glater, p. 7.

[25] *Statistical Abstract of the United States* (Washington, DC: U.S. Government Printing Office, 1994), p. 210.

[26] For a critical view of recent Justice Department cases, see David Burnham, *Above The Law: Secret Deals, Political Fixes and Other Misadventures of the U.S. Department of Justice* (New York: Charles Scribner's Sons, 1996).

[27] See Rebecca Mae Salokar, *The Solicitor General: The Politics of Law* (Philadelphia: Temple University Press, 1992). For the reminiscences of a solicitor general see Charles Fried, *Order and Law: Arguing the Reagan Revolution—A Firsthand Account* (New York: Simon & Schuster, 1991).

[28] See James Eisenstein, *Counsel for the United States: U.S. Attorneys in the Political and Legal Systems* (Baltimore, MD: Johns Hopkins University Press, 1978).

in which it becomes involved. Thus, the office determines which criminal cases to prosecute and which civil cases to bring to court, to defend, or to try to settle.

In each federal judicial district the president appoints a U.S. attorney, who must then be confirmed by the Senate and who serves a four-year term unless removed or reappointed by the president. Thus, one U.S. attorney will serve in the Central District of Florida, another in the Eastern District of Virginia, and so on. Each U.S. attorney then appoints staff attorneys known as *assistant U.S. attorneys.* The busiest federal district, the Southern District of New York, has over 100 assistant U.S. attorneys.

Each state also has an *attorney general,* usually elected, who fulfills parallel responsibilities for the state government and its governor. State attorneys general have staffs of lawyers known as *assistant attorneys general.* They are normally grouped by the subject matter of their cases into divisions, such as the civil, consumer protection, or environmental divisions of the state attorney general's office. Along with their courtroom responsibilities, state attorneys general also issue **advisory opinions,** often to state agencies that request clarification on some legal issue.

While the public focuses on highly adversarial courtroom clashes between the state and private parties, assistant attorneys general also sometimes give informal guidance to private practitioners by clarifying how the state interprets an ambiguous provision and even by stating whether the state feels strongly enough about its interpretation to take a particular type of case to court. For example, on various occasions, in trying to decide whether my client was complying with state environmental law in an ambiguous and untested area, I first called the Massachusetts Department of Environmental Quality Engineering (now called the Department of Environmental Protection) for guidance on how that state agency interpreted a particular regulation or statutory provision. In very important cases, if that discussion failed to clarify the issue, I sometimes found it useful to contact the environmental division of the Massachusetts Attorney General's office to try to determine how likely the state would be to enforce the agency's interpretation of the statute.

Such discussions are sometimes called **blind calls,** since the private attorney poses to the government lawyer a hypothetical question, rather than revealing the client's identity. A similar, though more formal, process occurs in the field of tax law. Private tax attorneys often request lawyers with the Internal Revenue Service (IRS) to issue a *letter ruling,* that is, a written opinion interpreting an ambiguous provision of the tax code and often stating whether or not the IRS would allow a deduction under a particular set of circumstances.

Since the state Attorney General's Office does not often bring routine criminal cases, the busiest prosecutors' offices are those of the district attorneys (or "DAs"), sometimes called **state's attorneys** or **county attorneys.** Usually elected to a two-to-four–year term, district attorneys and their staffs of assistant DAs decide which cases to prosecute and which to dismiss. They also determine whether to press for a plea-bargain or take a particular case to trial. In a large city a district attorney's office may include hundreds of assistant prosecutors and may oversee special programs aimed at preventing juvenile or other crime, enforcing child-support orders, curbing domestic violence, and handling other special problems. Some offices of district attorney are organized so that ordinarily, a single prosecutor will be in charge of a case from its inception to its resolution. In others, however, particular DAs handle different steps of the trial process.[29] For instance, one DA might specialize in screening cases to decide whether to prosecute or dismiss; another might routinely handle preliminary hearings, but not actual trial work.

During the O. J. Simpson trial, an international spotlight of attention shone on one of the largest district attorney's offices in the United States: that in Los Angeles County, California. From 1992 to 1996 the Los Angeles District Attorney's Office, which includes a staff of more than 900 prosecutors located in thirty offices, handled almost 400,000 felony cases and achieved a 92 percent conviction rate.[30] Despite the loss of the Simpson case and several other celebrity cases, the office's overall success in prosecuting violent crime helps to explain why forty-five of the country's largest fifty cities have violent crime rates higher than that found in Los Angeles County.[31]

It bears emphasizing that, like their counterparts at the national level, many **government lawyers** who work for states, counties, or localities have civil, not criminal, practices. A government attorney might as easily specialize in tax matters, zoning issues, cable television regulation, or highway construction, as in the prosecution of criminal cases. While their roles may be less glamorous and less frequently newsworthy than that of the prosecutor, the government lawyer dealing with noncriminal matters is a vital cog in the machinery of national, state, and local governance.

As with public interest lawyers, government lawyers often derive satisfaction from working for the people, and thus serving a necessary function in American society. Some ambitious government lawyers hope that their devotion to public service will lead to a state or federal judicial position or to political careers in the state legislature or the U.S. Congress. Thus, while not especially rewarding financially, having worked as a government lawyer may provide a valuable credential for career advancement.

Although their salaries differ substantially from state to state, government lawyers tend to be paid more than public interest lawyers. Compensation for a junior government prosecutor might start at $28,000. A mid-career government lawyer might earn $35,000, and the head of an office of government attorneys might make $45,000.

Solo Practitioners

Today, more than 260,000 American attorneys classify themselves as individual lawyers in private practice.[32] Attorneys who go into the business of law alone are called **individual** or **solo practitioners,** and a lawyer who opens his or her own law office is often said to **hang out a shingle.** This phrase refers to the practice, still

[29] For a more detailed analysis see Carp and Stidham, p. 107.

[30] "L.A. District Attorney Garcetti Haunted by Case That Won't Go Away," *Washington Post,* April 4, 1996, p. A3.

[31] Ibid.

[32] *Statistical Abstract,* p. 210.

common in small towns and cities, of attracting legal business by hanging a sign above the front door of a law office stating one's name and occupation, perhaps, "John P. Smith, Attorney-At-Law." Many years ago, it is said, lawyers embarking on a solo practice would sometimes use a shingle off their roof to make the sign announcing the presence of their new law firm!

More lawyers enter solo practice than join small, medium, or large law firms,[33] and both the benefits and drawbacks of practicing law alone are considerable. Having one's own law office permits an attorney to make all sorts of professional and financial decisions alone. Successes bring feelings of personal accomplishment; failures need not be justified to senior lawyers or colleagues. Just as important, the solo practitioner may keep all the profits as income, rather than dividing them up among partners and associates in a law firm.

Another benefit solo practitioners enjoy is the ability to choose to represent particular clients, especially those whose causes closely parallel the lawyer's own interests and beliefs. In theory, solo practitioners can simply turn away or refer on to another lawyer all those cases that appear distasteful or uninteresting. In reality, however, financial considerations often tightly bind solo practitioners. Month by month, a lawyer practicing alone must maintain the law office, pay for supplies and staff, and keep equipment functioning and reasonably up-to-date. A solo practitioner is thus often constrained to accept a less-than-ideal client in order to pay monthly bills.

Certain fields of law are more conducive to solo work than others; hence, one finds many solo practitioners working on cases involving automobiles, contracts, crimes, debt collections, divorces, real estate, the organization of businesses, personal bankruptcies, and personal injuries. Much of this work serves individuals or small enterprises, not major corporations. Wealthy clients in the corporate world ordinarily have their own top-flight legal departments and take specialized business to prestigious law firms of national renown. Consequently, solo practitioners do not normally rely on the same several clients year in and year out. Rather, an individual practicing alone normally uses advertising and referrals from other lawyers and satisfied clients to bring about a steady stream of new business. However, solo practitioners must contend with the possibility that their legal business may dry up, and no partners will be ready to ease them through slow periods.

All these circumstances imply that a rather special kind of person is likely to succeed practicing law alone. Good solo practitioners need exceptional self-confidence. A strong reputation in a particular city or town, most preferably, the county seat, is an invaluable asset. An exceptionally broad knowledge of law, particularly in legal fields that generate problems for ordinary people, is also a considerable advantage. Thus, a lawyer who specializes in handling legal matters regarding wills, divorce, and real estate, and who would like to return to the town in which he or she grew up, might be a successful solo practitioner.

[33] It is, however, true that more lawyers join small, medium, *and* large law firms than enter solo practice. See Barbara A. Curran, "American Lawyers in the 1980s," *Law and Society Review* 20 (1986): 29.

While some solo practitioners work in large cities, they also commonly set up shop in small cities and towns. Here, the costs of doing business are substantially less, the work force does not flee to the suburbs every evening, and the individual lawyer can more easily build a reputation through residents, social contacts, small businesses, and advertising in the local media. The character of a law practice thus differs markedly depending on its location. A courthouse in a large city may hold scores of courtrooms, judges, and lawyers. Rather than squaring off against each other time after time, lawyers tend not to know one another well. Lawyers may not even argue cases before the same judge very frequently. With such characteristics in mind, one judge commented that if young lawyers wish "to practice law as it should be practiced, they should go . . . to small cities, where the members of the bar know each other and the judge knows all of them and a lawyer's reputation and ability to function are to no small degree a function of his character."[34]

Individuals practicing law alone do not ordinarily earn as high salaries as senior lawyers in large law firms. Yet, while some struggle to earn a living, many live quite comfortably, and the most successful earn enough money to do very well financially. I know of one young, but accomplished, solo practitioner in the personal injury field who has earned $250,000 in a single good year. Another, older lawyer, with whom I am acquainted, earns closer to $100,000 each year practicing labor law. Another friend in solo practice on a part-time basis earns about $15,000 a year while spending much of her time raising a family.

In-house Counsels

Another substantial group of American lawyers enters business and works as lawyers in company management, as so-called **in-house counsels.**[35] Since many corporations have come to discover that hiring their own lawyers can be much more economical than retaining a major law firm, more than 70,000 attorneys, or 9 percent of the total, now work on a salaried basis for private industry.

Rather than hire outside lawyers to do their legal work, many American corporations have a **general counsel** and a staff of junior attorneys who review all the legal matters that arise in the business. These attorneys will try to ensure that the company complies with labor, environmental, worker safety, and other laws and regulations. They will negotiate contracts with suppliers and buyers, reach collective bargaining agreements with labor unions, advise on potential mergers and acquisitions, and handle various personnel matters relating to pensions, workplace accidents, hiring and firing, and so on. Although exceptions do exist, especially among insurance companies with large, expert legal staffs, an in-house corporate counsel will not normally litigate cases on behalf of the corporation or undertake sophisticated, specialized legal tasks. Rather, the corporate lawyers will call upon attorneys in private practice to handle such matters.

[34] Judge Edward Lumbard's advice to his clerks as paraphrased in Linowitz, p. 173.

[35] Ibid.

Although corporations often face many similar problems year in and year out and the practice of law in these organizations may not be as varied as in other corners of private practice, many lawyers find a career as an in-house counsel to be an attractive option. One need not worry about attracting clients. Job security is better than in a large firm, and the hours tend to be more reasonable. In addition, corporations usually pay their in-house counsels quite well. A lawyer at a medium-sized, publicly traded company might earn between $75,000 and $100,000 annually. A senior lawyer at a major American corporation, like Shell Oil or Pepsi-Cola, might earn more than $200,000 a year.

Law Firm Associates and Partners

Today, about two-thirds of all lawyers work in private practice. Although many opt for solo practice, the majority work in a law firm. Firms, of course, vary in size from two or three attorneys to many hundreds of lawyers. Small law firms of fewer than ten attorneys greatly outnumber the medium-sized firms of eleven to fifty, which themselves outnumber the large firms of more than fifty attorneys. Although exceptions exist, smaller firms tend to be less well known than larger ones and tend to focus their practice on a particular field of law, such as litigation, real estate, or business.[36]

Large law firms with regional, national, or international practices generally enjoy the wealthiest corporate clients. As recently as 1975 fewer than four dozen law firms employed more than 100 attorneys, but by 1993 more than 250 firms had 100 or more; 66,700 lawyers worked in these large firms,[37] and scores of firms were approaching the 100-lawyer mark. At the head of the list of largest U.S. law firms, Baker and McKenzie now employs about 700 attorneys, scattered all over the world.

Since a problem of hundreds of millions of dollars seems to concentrate the mind more readily than one involving tens of thousands of dollars, attorneys may be especially attracted to large law firms by the prospect of the hefty sums hanging in the balance for their clients. Although corporate law firms do pride themselves on particular specialties, the largest firms are able to offer their clients what has been called "one-stop shopping" or "soup-to-nuts representation." That is, they boast well-stocked tax, labor, pension, environmental, general business, and litigation divisions, as well as smaller, more specialized divisions dealing with subjects like antitrust, bonds, securities, criminal law, and trusts and estates.

For many years, joining a reputable law firm in a large city has been the most prestigious and lucrative option available to a a neophyte lawyer. The top firms in New York, Washington, DC, and other large cities now pay their first-year

[36] Very elite, reputable, and high-priced small firms are sometimes said to have "boutique" practices. That term implies that the firm is very narrowly specialized in a prestigious field of law. An example might be a firm that takes on cases that deal only with constitutional or civil rights litigation.

[37] See Linowitz, pp. 27–28.

lawyers salaries of $85,000 a year.[38] Since an in-house counsel will often handle routine corporate legal matters, the legal business handled by a large law firm tends to be challenging and relatively varied. Law students thus compete fiercely for high-paying slots in top firms, which usually can choose from good students at law schools with national reputations and the very top students at regional law schools. Attorneys working in major firms have long been assumed to form an elite group in terms of expertise, income, and—more arguably perhaps—professionalism.[39]

After a lawyer works for a law firm as an **associate** for between approximately seven and ten years, the senior lawyers in the firm, known as the *partners,* customarily decide whether to invite that associate to join their partnership or to release the associate from the law firm to find employment elsewhere. This process of trying to become (or "make") partner in a law firm is extremely competitive. At certain top New York firms less than 10 percent of the associates will eventually be made partner. Even at less prestigious large firms, the percentage of associates who will never make partner ranges from 40 to 75 percent.[40]

Although a lawyer who was made a partner was once considered very likely to remain with that firm, partners now often leave law firms either of their own accord or after a push by unhappy colleagues. The ABA reported that of 105 large firms surveyed in 1991, fully 59 percent had fired partners in the preceding eighteen months.[41] Those lawyers who fail to make partner or are pushed out of a partnership position often reconsider their career options. Many join a smaller or less prestigious law firm or find a firm that needs their particular expertise and, hence, will offer them partnership at once or after a year or two of additional work. Other attorneys who have failed to make partner become in-house counsels, government lawyers, or solo practitioners.

The decision whether to accept an associate as a partner is determined by the associate's ability to impress the senior attorneys in the firm.[42] Those impressions largely depend on how much legal work that lawyer can be expected to bring to the firm or supervise for the firm.[43] Certainly, most partners covet associates who already have large rosters of clients or have the potential to draw clients to the firm.

[38] See Saundra Terry, "Law Firm Ups the Ante to $85,000 for First-Year Associates," *Washington Post,* July 22, 1996, Washington Business section, p. 7.

[39] See Marc Galanter and Thomas Palay, "The Transformation of the Big Law Firm," in Robert L. Nelson, David M. Trubek, and Raymond L. Solomon, eds. *Lawyers' Ideals/Lawyers' Practices: Transformations in the American Legal Profession* (Ithaca, NY: Cornell University Press, 1992). For an article on overbilling in law firms see Saundra Terry, "Decision Exposes the Pitfalls of Padding Legal Bills," *Washington Post,* Sept. 11, 1995, Washington Business section, p. 7. For a zealous attack on corporate lawyers see Ralph Nader and Wesley J. Smith, *No Contest: Corporate Lawyers and the Perversion of Justice in America* (New York: Random House, 1996).

[40] See Sheila V. Malkani and Michael Walsh, eds., *The Insiders' Guide to Law Firms 1993–94* (Washington, DC: Mobius Press, 1993).

[41] Glendon, pp. 25–26, citing Don J. DeBenedictus, "Firings to Continue," *ABA Journal* (March 1992): 24.

[42] For an interesting comparison of how life in a large firm has changed over time, see Linowitz, especially pp. 27–30.

[43] At Chicago-based Winston & Strawn, to be made a full partner a lawyer must bring in at least $750,000 in business or supervise $1 million of legal work each year. See "Economics Pushes Some Firms, Associates to Tiers," *Washington Post,* Mar. 4, 1996, Washington Business section, p. 7.

However, associates expert in a particular subfield of law or especially gifted in attending to client's needs are also attractive candidates for partnership.

Making partner is far and away the most important milestone in the career of an attorney at a law firm. Not only does it signify acceptance among the more prestigious ranks of the senior attorneys, but it can be quite financially rewarding. While a senior associate at a large firm might earn $125,000 a year, a new partner might take home $150,000 annually, and an average midcareer partner might be compensated at two or three times that rate. At the wealthiest firms, such as Skadden, Arps, Slate, Meagher & Flom, headquartered in New York City, the median annual income for partners has exceeded $1,000,000. In extremely profitable years the most highly compensated Skadden partners have received seven-figure bonuses in addition to their seven-figure earnings.[44]

While associates draw salaries from their law firms, the partners split the profits from all the legal work that all the attorneys in the firm have undertaken. In order to divide the firm's earnings fairly, partners today typically rely upon a complicated mathematical formula, one that varies from one law firm to the next.[45] It usually provides differing credit for bringing legal business to the firm, actually doing work for a client, and attending to the legal needs of a client that another lawyer brought to the firm. The formula may also take into account seniority, recruiting responsibilities, administrative supervision, and other such factors.

Incidentally, slang terms are often used in law firms to pigeonhole the lawyers working there. Those who spend much of their time bringing legal business to the firm are known as **rainmakers**[46] or **finders;** those who ensure that the clients' affairs are attended to properly are called **minders;** and those who do the legal work for a client that another lawyer brought to the firm are labeled **grinders!** Most firms operate in a manner that might be likened to an upside-down pyramid with a few rainmakers supporting a somewhat larger level of minders and a considerably larger quantity of grinders. As might be expected, the most prestigious and lucrative of these categories is that occupied by the rainmakers who are said, mixing metaphors a bit, to "eat what they kill"—that is, to devour the bulk of the profits from the clients they bring to the firm.[47]

In recent years rainmaking partners have been jumping from one large law firm to another at an increasingly frenetic pace, often taking their substantial rosters of clients with them.[48] To ensure that such important attorneys are not lost

[44] Glendon, p. 25. See also Lincoln Caplan, *Skadden: Power, Money and the Rise of a Legal Empire* (New York: Farrar, Straus & Giroux, 1993).

[45] For an interesting account of how large firms moved away from seniority pay scales, see Linowitz, pp. 102–104.

[46] This usage, of course, inspired the title for John Grisham's novel, *The Rainmaker* (New York: Doubleday, 1995).

[47] See Glendon, p. 24.

[48] The president of a legal consulting firm recently estimated that "about 40 percent of the partners in the 2,000 largest firms . . . are lateral hires." Bradford Hildebrandt paraphrased by David Segal, "When Legal Eagles Fly the Coop: Job-Hopping Soars as Less-Loyal Lawyers Auction Themselves to the Highest Bidder," *Washington Post,* July 1, 1996, Washington Business section, p. 10.

to competitors, major firms need to keep them happy with a large slice of all the profits earned. At the same time, corporate clients have been clamoring for cost-cutting and for lower legal bills. Many corporations have instituted so-called beauty contests in which law firms bid against one another for legal work. And many partners and associates are working such long hours that little time remains for the social and community activities through which lawyers have long cultivated corporate clients. Thus, the methods that large firms traditionally used to win clients are being transformed.

Consequently, many large law firms face a problem with several different faces. Operating expenses continue to soar into the millions or tens of millions or, occasionally, hundreds of millions of dollars.[49] Clients threaten to take their business to firms that charge less. Rainmaking partners insist on obtaining a larger slice of the financial pie. Able associates come up for partnership, yet lack large rosters of their own clients.[50] To earn the substantial profits that the partners wish to divide among themselves, any firm must keep associates sufficiently content that they work exceedingly long hours. However, keeping associates content requires very high salaries or reasonable prospects of making partner or both.[51] To add partners implies adding supporting associates and, especially, adding clients to pay the bills.

Large firms that do not handle such complicated problems adeptly soon find themselves in quite a bind: partners quarreling, clients leaving, associates jumping to other firms or being fired, and sometimes the firm spiraling downwards and perhaps going out of business. Among the notable major firms that proved unable to compete in the ultracompetitive legal marketplace of the 1980s and 1990s and that eventually collapsed altogether were the New York firms Shea & Gould, Finley & Kumble, and Mudge, Rose, Guthrie, Alexander & Ferdon; and the Boston firms Herrick & Smith, and Gaston Snow and Ely Bartlett.[52]

Within this exceptionally competitive environment, attorneys in law firms have become perhaps the most transient of American professionals, often leaving one firm for another, at which they hope to be happier or to be better compensated or to make partner more quickly or easily. Such **lateral movement** within the legal profession is often aided by regional or national **legal headhunters**—professional employment experts who find out what law firms need and which lawyers might be available to join those firms in order to meet those needs.[53]

Large firms have responded to this dangerous new era with various strate-

[49] Linowitz, p. 110.

[50] The *managing partner* of a Washington, DC law firm recently observed: "What do you do with good lawyers eight to twelve years out of school who don't command their own business?" "Economics Pushes Some Firms," p. 7. One legal consultant observed: "[F]irms trying to find a way to keep people on board without having to further slice the pie and dilute profits [find a tiered partnership attractive]."

[51] See Linowitz, p. 108.

[52] Without worrying unduly about accuracy, wags in Boston legal circles once referred to that last firm as "Ghastly Slow and Easily Beaten"!

[53] The new climate within which law is practiced has resulted in a boom for the headhunters. The National Association of Legal Search Consultants now includes approximately 300 members. In 1996 the head of one such firm remarked: "Our revenue has increased about 20 percent each year since 1991." Segal, "When Legal Eagles Fly the Coop," p. 11.

gies. Virtually all have grown ever larger, some exponentially so. Unfortunately, larger firms tend to enjoy less collegial atmospheres and they confront more diverse interests among their attorneys. Some become top heavy with too many partners unable to generate sufficient work for the associates. Others become revolving doors as lawyers at all levels come and go, entering and leaving the firm's employment, sometimes taking clients with them and often shaking the confidence of long-time clients in the stability and quality of the firm.

One common response by large firms has been to complicate their hierarchy and adopt a **two-track partnership** in which senior attorneys are divided into two groups. While the **junior partners**[54] spend another few years attempting to impress their senior colleagues in order to be made **full partners,** they continue to draw a salary from the firm. Under such a system only the senior partners split the profits, whereas the junior partners simply enjoy a substantial pay raise, larger office space, a vote on various management issues, and the additional prestige of having become a nominal partner of the firm.

To help attorneys to woo corporate clients and compete for legal business, a large corporate law office is typically furnished quite lavishly and fully equipped with a law library, staffed by specially trained librarians. A sizeable firm will be well equipped with computers in the libraries and on the desks of all lawyers, paralegals, and secretaries. All the attorneys enjoy first-rate secretarial help, often twenty-four hours a day. In addition, large firms normally employ staffs of administrators, computer experts, and legal assistants known as **paralegals.**

While solo practitioners and attorneys at small law firms may have to travel to public law libraries for research, lawyers in large firms can rely on considerable legal materials close at hand. The library will contain various collections of **case reports,** that is, judicial decisions in numbered and bound volumes, including relevant state reporters and the federal reporter and federal supplement series, that contain all major federal district and appellate court opinions. Such a law library would also normally include all three Supreme Court reporters and numerous law reviews, legal digests, dictionaries, encyclopedias, and scholarly treatises (sometimes called **hornbooks**). Lawyers would also find sets of state and federal law; the Federal Register,[55] listing regulations passed by the executive branch; and *Shepherd's Case Citations,* a series that indicates whether a particular precedent in state or federal court remains "good law" or has been overturned on appeal or reversed in a later decision. Many of these sources are kept reasonably up to date by **pocket parts,** that is, inserts sent from the publisher to be retained for reference in a pocket on the inside back cover of the volume.

[54] Law firms use different terms for the attorneys who have moved beyond the associate stage but have not been made full partner: Along with "junior partner," other common labels are "non-equity partner," "non-share partner," "guaranteed-share partner," and "special partner." See ibid.

[55] Sol Linowitz noted: "The government began publishing a Federal Register only after it was embarrassed by a 1935 Supreme Court decision pointing out that the parties, prosecuting authorities, and lower courts had all mistakenly relied on a section of the Petroleum Code that had been eliminated by an unpublicized Executive Order." Linowitz, p. 81, citing *Panama Refining Co. v. American Petroleum Corp.,* 293 U.S. 388 (1935).

With the coming of the computer age, lawyers rely increasingly on computerized data bases, especially the LEXIS-NEXIS and Westlaw services. Through their computers lawyers can quickly and easily search for recent precedents that might not yet have appeared in the printed reporters. They can also search much more extensively and comprehensively than was possible in past eras. A computerized search by key word or phrase might well turn up material missing from a traditional index. Perhaps most important, a single lawyer skilled at computer research can complete in a fraction of the time what would once have been extraordinarily time-consuming legal research projects. Of course, the computerized services charge for every search a lawyer performs. Since computer research is expensive for clients of modest means, solo practitioners and small law firms do not rely on computerized services to the same extent as the large firms that do much of their work for wealthy corporate clients.

Law firms use all these resources to compete with one another, often quite aggressively, for high-paying clients. Large American and multinational corporations and partnerships will pay very high rates in order to obtain the services of attorneys who can help to negotiate agreements, win cases in court, and provide expertise and guidance on the legal consequences of various business decisions. The repeated opportunities to outsmart and "outlawyer" other firms and government attorneys adds zest to the life of the **hired gun** lawyer in a major firm.

Miscellaneous Employment

If about two-thirds of all American lawyers work in law firms or as solo practitioners, and if about 10 percent are public interest and other government lawyers and judges, and if another 10 percent work as in-house counsels, how are all the other individuals who hold law degrees employed?

The remaining 14 percent, or so, of law school graduates work somewhere outside the professional practice of law. Some are politicians or consultants. Many are employed in businesses that indirectly use their legal skills, in such areas as accounting, lobbying, or investment advising. Others teach or serve as administrators in schools, colleges, and universities. Still others have retired or moved far from the legal profession. Various former lawyers have become well-known mystery writers and novelists: Louis Auchincloss, John Grisham, and Scott Turow among them. During a year in Japan I became well acquainted with a man from Wisconsin who quit practicing law shortly after World War II and is now an elderly Catholic priest in Naha, Okinawa!

THE PRACTICE OF LAW IN THE UNITED STATES

In moving next to the issue of what the practice of law in the United States entails, one might start with the observation that justice in America is administered according to perhaps the most markedly **adversarial system** in the world. Individuals or companies that are involved in a problem with legal dimensions—whether a business agreement, civil dispute, or criminal allegation—customarily hire a lawyer. The lawyer's job is to represent that client as zealously as possible within the limits of certain professional ethical principles. If the dispute goes to trial, a court then hears from the lawyers representing both sides and ultimately decides the case.

This legal system calls on American lawyers to perform two chief functions: to act as **counsel,** advising a client, and to act as a **trial attorney,** representing a party in court. Moreover, trial attorneys may themselves be divided into several groups. A *prosecutor* represents the government at those trials that deal with allegations that a criminal offense has been committed. A *defense counsel* defends clients accused of having committed a criminal offense.

In a civil lawsuit the attorneys on both sides are known as **litigators.** Litigators represent their clients in court in cases usually aimed at enforcing a right or seeking a **remedy** under state or federal law. Since litigators work under the pressure of filing deadlines and the public glare of courtroom appearances, they tend to have among the most stressful legal careers. However, litigation can also be exceptionally stimulating. The constant competition stirs adrenalin and the march of different cases often requires the litigator to study and master new subfields of law, one after another. (The distinguished judge Learned Hand once referred to litigators as lawyers with "bathtub minds": They fill their minds with the facts and law pertinent to one case, then drain it, only to refill it with the facts and law of the next.)[56]

Nonlawyers often imagine that the bulk of every attorney's time is spent consulting with injured clients, examining relevant laws and decisions, investigating the facts of the injury, interviewing potential witnesses, deciding whether a case should go to trial, and then actually arguing the case in court. Although rarely the subject of media attention and infrequently depicted in the movies, on television, or in novels, most American lawyers actually spend substantially more time in the role of counsel than in the role of trial attorney. They provide expert advice and up-to-date information. They negotiate agreements, evaluate legal issues, and help to settle disagreements. They help parties to cooperate and get things done. They do not necessarily run off to court every day.

One reason for this is that allowing a court to resolve a dispute may not be the most effective method of solving a problem. For instance, when the parties expect to have a continuing relationship, as in disputes involving neighbors, family members, buyers and sellers, and labor and management, a lawsuit may resolve a short-term problem at considerable long-term costs. As Abraham Lincoln, perhaps America's most beloved lawyer-politician, once advised fellow attorneys: "Persuade your neighbors to compromise whenever you can. Point out to them how the nominal winner is often a real loser—in fees, expenses, and waste of time. As a peacemaker the lawyer has a superior opportunity of being a good man. There will still be business enough."[57]

[56] Linowitz, p. 94.

[57] Glendon, p. 55, citing Abraham Lincoln, "Notes for a Law Lecture," in T. Harry Williams, ed., *Selected Speeches, Messages, and Letters* (New York: Holt, Rinehart, 1957), p. 33.

Indeed, a client may employ a lawyer to try to keep a dispute from becoming a lawsuit. For example, a business executive might tell a lawyer the company does not want to get bogged down in multiple lawsuits with the government, neighbors, employees, suppliers and distributors, and other potential litigants. How should the company reduce its exposure to future litigation? How is the company doing in complying with state and federal laws and regulations regarding contracts, personnel, pensions, the environment, product liability, health and safety, and other legal matters? From this perspective one distinguished attorney remarked: "[A]n actual lawsuit is a defeat for the lawyers, as war is a defeat for the diplomats."[58]

In a country so full of laws and expensive lawyers as the United States, few persons or organizations have the requisite financial resources to litigate even a small proportion of the legal issues that arise in daily life. Consequently, not only do lawyers spend more time advising clients on how to handle particular legal problems than in actually litigating those problems, but many American lawyers never step into a courtroom to argue a case in their entire careers. Such lawyers leave litigation to trial specialists and spend their time advising clients on how to comply with the law or how to solve particular business, financial, or personal problems.

The Role of Counsel

Many legal matters call primarily on cooperative skills, albeit often with an eye cocked to future potential adversarial conflicts. The fact that so many lawyers spend so much time planning for and counselling clients raises the question of how lawyers go about the task of providing advice.[59] Although virtually all people who hire a lawyer expect a discreet attorney who is able to keep confidential all those matters discussed within the professional relationship, many clients do not understand just how faithfully an attorney is supposed to serve his or her clients. An upstanding American lawyer will take seriously the role of **fiduciary,**[60] that is, someone who has a supreme duty of loyalty to another. In return, lawyers expect that their clients will trust them and will rely upon their good faith, judgment, and advice.

In acting as counsel, a lawyer is not unlike a doctor who persuades a pa-

[58] Linowitz, p. 172.

[59] Thoughtful works on this topic are nowhere near so readily available as one might presume. The best work I know of is that by Fisher cited above. Fisher's work examines, in substantially more detail, many of the issues analyzed in this subsection. One might also usefully consult Douglas E. Rosenthal, *Lawyers and Clients: Who's in Charge?* (New York: Russell Sage, 1974) and Susan M. Olson, *Clients and Lawyers* (Westport, CT: Greenwood Press, 1984).

[60] The term *fiduciary* has two common connotations in American law. In matters involving **trusts** and *estates,* a fiduciary is an individual who acts as a **trustee** by managing money or property for another. The term may also be employed more broadly, as I use it in this context, to mean an individual who transacts business for the benefit of another within a formal relationship that requires the benefactor's confidence and trust and the fiduciary's good faith and expert judgment. Attorneys, guardians, corporate directors, and others would qualify as fiduciaries in this latter sense.

tient to report all relevant symptoms so that the illness can be accurately diagnosed and properly treated. Furthermore, as in the medical profession, a lawyer counselling a client may decide that the attention of a specialist is called for. For example, an attorney specializing in family relations may refer a client with a medical malpractice claim to a trial lawyer with a personal injury practice. It is not unusual in such circumstances for the lawyers to have an agreement in which part of the fees or eventual settlement or award is passed back to the attorney who referred the client to the specialist.[61]

In hiring an attorney, a client may hope to pursue various common purposes. A small proportion of clients face criminal charges and need the assistance of an attorney to prepare a defense for trial or to negotiate a plea-bargain agreement[62] with the authorities. Rather more common are the clients who want to buy, sell, will, or protect property of some kind—money or securities, real estate or personal possessions, licenses or business franchises, or even such unusual forms of assets as livestock, inventions, and literary compositions.

One might also observe that clients often hire an attorney to resolve a problem of human relations, that is, to help the client to deal with other people with whom some legal issue has arisen—whether that other person is a government official, a family member, or prospective spouse; an architect, a doctor, or other professional; even perhaps a business competitor, a partner, or supplier.[63] In handling all the legal problems such relationships entail, a lawyer's chief responsibility is to serve the client loyally, to use his or her professional expertise in law to advance or protect the client's best interests.

Inexperienced clients also often fail to understand all the ways in which an attorney might help them. Lawyers are often called upon to draft documents, perhaps to turn a skeletal business agreement into a legal contract. While this may sound like drudgery, it can be a most challenging and difficult assignment. Americans rightly hail the Founding Fathers for drafting a constitution that provided a unifying legal structure for the country without unduly binding future generations to an outdated document. Yet few see similar elements, writ small, in ordinary legal agreements. How is one to provide necessary order without unnecessarily sacrificing flexibility? The parties to a contract will often want to provide explicitly for certain possible circumstances, yet leave others open to creative problem solving. Guiding their clients toward the best possible balance of such competing objectives can tax the abilities of the most experienced attorneys.

Moreover, clients often discover that legal skills can be useful not just for drafting letters and contracts, but for identifying, preventing, and solving a wide range of problems, for discovering important facts and keeping the client's atten-

[61] In 1984, all but four states prohibited such fee splitting. However, 40 percent of 600 lawyers polled in the jurisdictions in which fee splitting was illegal mistakenly thought the practice was legal and 27 percent did not know if it were legal or not. Of the one-third who recognized fee splitting as illegal, half felt that it was legitimate so long as the referral fee was reasonable. Richard L. Abel, *American Lawyers* (New York: Oxford University Press, 1989), p. 143, cited in Linowitz, p. 141.

[62] For information on plea bargains see Chapters 6 and 8.

[63] See Fisher, p. 2.

tion focused on them, for clarifying contrasting approaches to a legal issue, and for advising as to the legal repercussions of different options. Clients often discover that a lawyer is more valuable to them as counselor, consultant, or negotiator, than as drafter or litigator. While legal expertise is necessary to solve purely legal problems, it may also be useful in solving problems that merely contain some legal dimension.

For example, a small business that I represented for several years sold its services through a standard contract patched together from numerous negotiations that had taken place during the prior decade. One day I received a call from the head of the company's marketing division. He explained that the lawyer for a customer had asked him to add certain provisions to the standard contract. The marketing chief came to me to ensure that the new contractual language would not cause any unforeseen legal problems, or, at a minimum, that all of his colleagues would fully understand whatever legal risks they might be assuming if they agreed to sign the revised contract. After familiarizing myself fully with the business and the relevant state and federal statutes and caselaw, I gained the attention of the company's chief executive officer and explained how various critical provisions in the contract might be reworded and what legal and business advantages and disadvantages might flow from each of the most sensible variations.

Over the course of the next several weeks the management decided, first, that the standard contract should be wholly redone. Next, the company officials determined that various "second-best" provisions should be available to be inserted into contracts at the discretion of the chief marketing representative if the buyer proved sufficiently important and insistent. If the buyer demanded any further deviations, the marketing representative would turn the contract over to me to negotiate directly with the opposing lawyer. Thus, over time, my services to the company had expanded from assessing the wording of a single document to reworking a standard contract, to negotiating dozens of contracts with its most significant customers.

To provide such legal counsel to a client can be one of the most rewarding aspects of practicing law. Many people think of American law as a fixed set of rules. They then conceive of the practice of law as knowing or learning the appropriate rule and then applying it to a particular set of circumstances. In this view a lawyer, not so different from a car mechanic, searches through the appropriate manual to find the solution to a problem. However, this view fails to account for the fact that the law is both constantly evolving and quite fragmentary. No manual exists to supply the answers to many of the questions that arise in the daily business of practicing law.

In trying to come to an informed opinion on a legal issue, an American lawyer must regularly consult state statutes, federal statutes, even administrative regulations. Even so, the law often remains silent or ambiguous on the particular question being considered. Moreover, the law may change, sometimes rather dramatically, in the immediate future. Administrative regulations, in particular, can have exceedingly fleeting lives. Indeed, many whole fields of law, from criminal procedure to environmental law, to intellectual property, are developing at an unusually rapid pace, as new problems arise, as new technologies are created, and as legislatures write and rewrite statutes. Hence, while researching the law may prove to be a formidable task, it often marks only the beginning of the lawyer's inquiry. Frequently, different courts will interpret rules quite differently, as judges consider a spectrum of shades of circumstance.

Thus, to provide expert legal advice, an attorney must combine persistence in research with strong analytical skills and good judgment. Since developing those talents almost invariably takes years of experience, senior lawyers can usually command substantially higher rates for their legal counsel than can their junior associates. Indeed, even lawyers richly blessed with experience, skills, and judgment can often do no more than offer an educated guess as to the answer to a question posed by a client. As Judge Jerome Frank declared: "Only a soothsayer, a prophet, or a person gifted with clairvoyance can tell a man what are his enforceable rights arising out of a particular transaction, or against any other person, before a lawsuit with respect to that transaction or that person has arisen. For only a clairvoyant can foretell what evidence will be introduced and will be believed, and can foresee what will be the reaction of the trial judge or the jurors to such testimony as he or they may believe."[64] This correctly suggests that inexperienced clients often fail to understand not only all the different ways in which an attorney might help them, but also the limits to a lawyer's prescience.

Professional Dilemmas

Although lawyers have become increasingly specialized in the last several decades, it remains true that in the course of a single day lawyers often counsel clients with quite distinct problems. In attempting to carry out responsibly the many tasks that different clients set forth, lawyers routinely confront professional dilemmas, that is, situations that raise questions as to the proper manner in which to pursue the professional practice of law. Since nonlawyers are usually well aware of the potential conflict between a client's interests and the good of society, it may be useful to focus instead on two other common professional problems.

To illustrate the first of these dilemmas, consider just how much decision making a lawyer should share with a client.[65] Most clients will rightly expect to be consulted on "critical" or "ultimate" decisions, such as whether to bring a lawsuit and on what terms to settle it. Yet, many have neither the time nor the interest to learn about and participate in less important decisions relating to their problem. Few clients would expect to be updated on every step in a lawyer's preparation for trial, consulted about the meaning of every clause in a lengthy legal document, or kept abreast of all the questions a lawyer plans to ask a witness. Few clients would insist on reviewing all, or even any, of the legal precedents that support their lawyer's recommendation that they pursue a particular course of action. Most at-

[64] Frank, p. 25.

[65] This issue is explored in Douglas E. Rosenthal, *Lawyer and Client: Who's in Charge?* (New York: Russell Sage, 1974).

torneys and most clients would agree that such details are best left to the discretion of the professional.

However, it is more difficult to decide the extent to which an attorney should invite a business executive to participate in the many technical decisions that arise when the client corporation is engaged in the process of acquiring a smaller company. To what extent should a lawyer discuss alternative trial strategies in civil and criminal cases? Is the decision to opt for a jury trial or a *bench trial* properly made by the lawyer, the client, or the two in collaboration? The issues of just how to work with a client can become even more tangled in what might be termed **political litigation**—that is, a lawsuit brought on behalf of an individual or individuals but designed to establish a legal principle in a politically controversial area that will benefit a group of people.[66]

Competent lawyers are likely to share decision making in all such matters rather differently. The degree of decision making shared by the attorney with the client may depend upon the type of legal matter under consideration, the significance of the particular legal issue, the professional style of the lawyer, and the degree of interest and soundness of judgment shown by the client. In each professional encounter, a lawyer must evaluate the degree to which a client should be invited, or even encouraged, to participate in a range of large and small legal decisions.

A second, sometimes related, dilemma that regularly arises in the private practice of law is the degree of deference that the lawyer should accord the client who pays the bills.[67] The client may want the lawyer to do something that the lawyer may view as against the client's best interests. As a fiduciary, the lawyer is obligated to be independent and give the client his or her best advice, whether or not it reflects what the client would like to hear. At the same time, however, the lawyer must recognize that practicing law is not a license to become an all-purpose decision maker. Certain business issues, for example, are ultimately the responsibility of a corporation's board of directors or chief executive officer, and not of its outside counsel or even its in-house legal adviser. A good lawyer does not pretend to omniscience, particularly in matters well removed from purely legal considerations.

To illustrate this conflict, consider the example of an experienced corporate attorney who was approached by the chief executive officer from one of that lawyer's best corporate clients. The executive asked the lawyer to assist in a tremendous, nationwide expansion of the business—a plan that, if carried out, would have brought the lawyer many thousands of dollars in legal fees. The lawyer listened intently to the proposal, raised various questions about its wisdom, and ultimately advised strongly against it. When the enraged client threatened to take his legal busi-

[66] For an overview of the problem of political litigation, especially in the context of school desegregation cases, see G. Alan Tarr, *Judicial Process and Judicial Policymaking* (St. Paul, MN: West, 1994), pp. 136–137. The issue is explored in the context of the disabled rights movement in Susan M. Olson, *Clients and Lawyers: Securing the Rights of Disabled Persons* (Westport, CT: Greenwood Press, 1984).

[67] For a more extended discussion of this point see Fisher, pp. 5–13.

ness elsewhere, the lawyer predicted that the scheme would lead the company to financial ruin.

The company fired the lawyer immediately and went ahead with the plan. As the lawyer predicted, the corporation filed for bankruptcy a short time later. Though he had lost a client, the lawyer could at least feel that his unwelcome advice on a matter that had contained both legal and business dimensions had ultimately been vindicated. Another lawyer, however, might have viewed his or her role more narrowly and carried out the necessary legal maneuvers, dismissing the issue of whether the expansion was wise or not as a business decision, not a legal one.

This dilemma arises in other circumstances as well. Most lawyers will spend some portion of their time on a case educating the client about various options and estimating what might happen if one tactical approach to a problem were favored over another. A lawyer will commonly ask a client who has been informed of the alternatives to select the approach he or she would like the lawyer to adopt. If the lawyer feels uncomfortable with the approach favored by the client, the lawyer can always withdraw from the case and help the client to find another attorney.

Nevertheless, between the extreme of a perfect meeting of the minds, in which lawyer and client think in unison, and the extreme of substantial disagreement, in which lawyer and client agree to end their relationship, a range of discord often exists, ranging from minor matters to much more major ones. Here, the attorney must consider how many hours and how much energy should be put into trying to change the client's mind, rather than simply deferring to the client's wishes.

For instance, what ought a defense attorney do when a client insists on a line of argument at trial that the attorney views as wholly unpersuasive, if not actually counterproductive? Should an argument be advanced merely to placate the client or might that be viewed as wasting the time of the court? Should the answers to the preceding questions differ in civil and criminal proceedings? Should the amount of money at issue or the seriousness of the offence or the maximum penalty that may be imposed affect the lawyer's decision? In resolving all such matters different lawyers may choose to proceed in varying manners.

The practice of law in the United States, always highly adversarial in the courtroom, has become an increasingly cutthroat business with billable hours steadily rising and firms raiding one another for coveted clients and rainmakers. The more single-minded lawyers are in pursuing their fees, the more they lose their professional independence and become malleable in the hands of their clients. This is especially true when senior associates are invited to join the partnership largely on the basis of their ability to bring in and retain clients.[68] It may take fortitude for an established partner to tell an important client in frank or disapproving terms something he or she will not want to hear, but it may approach downright foolhardiness for a senior associate to do likewise.

Early this century Elihu Root, a distinguished attorney and government official, declared: "About half the practice of a decent lawyer consists in telling

[68] Linowitz, p. 109.

would-be clients that they are damned fools and should stop."[69] However, by the 1980s, Harvard Law Professor Emeritus Archibald Cox observed that few lawyers were willing to say to clients: "Yes, the law lets you do that, but don't do it. It's a rotten thing to do."[70] Unfortunately, in many firms struggling to increase profits in an ultracompetitive environment, the ideal of client loyalty has all but overwhelmed the ideal of independent professionalism.[71] In 1986, 68 percent of corporate officials polled by the American Bar Association's Commission on Professional Responsibility thought that professionalism among lawyers was decreasing; a mere 7 percent felt it was increasing.[72]

The tension between the professional independence a lawyer should maintain and the deference a lawyer should show to the client who is paying the bills can also arise when a client reacts emotionally or angrily. I recall a conference phone call some years ago that turned into a lengthy harangue, laced with obscenities, by a client angry about a particularly unfortunate set of circumstances. Although the client had been expostulating about the situation he faced, rather than the actions of his attorneys, I remember wondering how the senior lawyer on the phone call would respond.

As it turned out, she handled the situation wisely and tactfully. After waiting until the client had paused to catch his breath, the lawyer simply asked: "Bob, are you through?" That question, asked in a familiar, even, and unemotional tone of voice, served to remind the client that he had been behaving poorly, but it did so without causing lasting damage to the professional relationship between the lawyer and the business paying her bills.

Once again, no simple formula can resolve the many issues that arise concerning this dilemma between independence and deference. Lawyers have diverse styles, distinct concerns, and different levels of tolerance. I know of a senior partner who heard that his very junior associate had been bullied, harassed, and unfairly criticized by a wealthy client. The partner did not hesitate to call up the client and protect his associate by threatening to withdraw as counsel unless the client behaved more civilly to all the lawyers working on his case. I know of another attorney, attending a victory party after a successful negotiation, who chose to ignore an ethnic slur directed at him by the drunken president of a client corporation.

Again, the delicate professional choice between autonomy and servility is one that arises repeatedly as lawyers handle the affairs of clients. Fortunately, many

[69] Ibid., p. 4.

[70] Glendon, p. 35, citing Rita H. Jensen, "Where were the Lincoln Lawyers?" *National Law Journal* (May 6, 1991): 26. One study found that three out of four attorneys in large law firms could not remember one time they had disagreed with a client. Glendon, p. 75, citing Robert L. Nelson, *Partners with Power: The Social Transformation of the Large Law Firm* (Berkeley: University of California Press, 1988), p. 282.

[71] See ibid., p. 58.

[72] ". . . In the Spirit of Public Service: A Blueprint for the Rekindling of Lawyer Professionalism," Report of the Commission on Professionalism to the Board of Governors and the House of Delegates of the American Bar Association, August 1986, in 112 *Federal Rules Decisions,* p. 243, cited in Linowitz, p. 24.

clients do not value a lawyer who is a "yes man," that is, a sycophant, who simply tells the client what he thinks the client would like to hear. Instead, many expect a skilled practitioner who will pair loyalty with independence of thought. That should mean that most clients will want to hear an expert opinion on the legal matter at issue, even if it differs markedly from their own views.[73]

Legal Fees

The bill a client receives from a lawyer is typically calculated by one of various possible formulas. Although certain lawyers will bill by the day (a **per diem basis**) or by the project (a **per project basis**), most law firms customarily charge their clients on an hourly basis. While rates naturally differ substantially from one law firm to another and from region to region, a big firm in a large city might charge $125 per hour for the services of a junior associate, and two or three times that much for the services of a full partner. A very respected senior lawyer might command a fee as high as $500 an hour.

Under such an arrangement the lawyer keeps track of his or her **billable hours.** To provide a precise accounting of the time spent on each client, lawyers customarily divide each hour into ten six-minute intervals and carefully count how much time is spent on each client. Thus, if an associate at a major law firm solves a relatively simple legal problem, the client might be charged 2.3 billable hours at $150 per hour. The partner in charge of that client's account periodically issues a bill listing the hours worked by different attorneys and all the out-of-pocket expenses for travel, photocopying, mail, phone calls, work by paralegals and messengers, and even dinners in the office for attorneys working late on the client's matters.

In other cases, especially those dealing with personal injuries, lawyers proceed on a **contingency fee** basis in which the lawyer collects a percentage of the **damages.** For instance, the client might agree to compensate the lawyer with one-third of any money awarded after the trial. If the client receives no damages, the lawyer receives no fee and thus bears all the risk of losing the case. In still other cases, lawyers and clients agree to a mixed arrangement that combines hourly billing with a contingency fee arrangement. For example, a lawyer might agree to evaluate the strength of a potential legal claim on an hourly basis, then move forward with the case on a contingency fee basis if the chances for a substantial recovery look sufficiently promising.

The Lifestyle of a Lawyer

While a lawyer who takes a case on a contingency fee basis risks doing hours of legal work for no compensation, the potential payoff in a high-stakes lawsuit can be extraordinarily high. With **jury awards** and out-of-court settlements reaching mul-

[73] See Fisher, pp. 9–13.

timillion dollar levels and with few cases occupying more than several hundred hours of legal work, an attorney would reap far greater profits in winning a substantial personal injury case taken on a contingency fee basis than in billing the client for every hour spent on the case.

All the money that these lawyers earn, however, requires a tremendous amount of work. While billable-hour requirements vary from firm to firm, young lawyers at established corporate law firms are usually required to bill clients for at least forty hours of work each week. Although some high-powered firms now require as many as 2,200 to 2,500 billable hours a year, at most large firms billing forty hours every week will probably attest that the attorney is working hard enough to retain his or her position. Whether it testifies as to sufficient good work to warrant making partner is another issue altogether.

To average forty hours per week, a lawyer might have to be at the law firm fifty hours on a normal work week and as many as seventy or more hours on a very difficult week. This is so for several reasons. A lawyer meeting a billable hours target must compensate for weeks of vacation or sickness or slow business. A conscientious lawyer will turn off the "billable hour meter" whenever he or she is not actually doing work for the client. Indeed, inexperienced lawyers, concerned about incurring the wrath of clients and senior partners, often turn the meter off when they feel as though they are not working efficiently for the client. And, of course, chatting with office mates, telephoning family or friends, participating in firm meetings, exchanging pleasantries with senior attorneys, attending bar association or continuing legal education functions, interviewing prospective colleagues, and overseeing the administration of the firm (including the work of the lawyer's secretary) should not be included as billable hours.

Even such prosaic tasks as eating, visiting the doctor or dentist, cleaning the desk, organizing the office, and running to the bank, or attending to some other errand will not count toward that challenging average of eight billable hours per day. Firms differ as to whether *pro bono* work will count as billable hours; thus, work for the poor may have to be done on the lawyer's personal time. It is no wonder that attorneys in law firms, with lives fraught with imminent deadlines and ticking clocks, often gain a well-deserved reputation for brushing off unwanted intrusions in order to enable them to return to the business at hand.[74]

All this correctly suggests that the quality of life for lawyers in large firms can be a good deal lower than their high pay and glamorous business addresses might suggest. One ABA study concluded that the number of lawyers working more than 200 hours a month rose from 35 percent in 1984 to 50 percent in 1990. That same year half the lawyers in private practice who responded to the ABA survey complained of lacking adequate time for themselves and their families and almost three out of four reported feeling "fatigued or worn out by the end of the workday." One-quarter to one-third of the lawyers polled in various states predicted

[74] In 1991 a special committee formed by the Seventh Circuit Court of Appeals surveyed 1,400 lawyers and judges and concluded that "lawyers have become more rude, belligerent, manipulative, and even dishonest in dealing with each other, both in and out of court." Glick, p. 96.

that they would leave the practice of law before retirement or declared that they would not become lawyers if the choice were presented to them again.[75] In a 1990 speech to the American College of Trial Lawyers, a Canadian attorney remarked wistfully: "Not very long ago a lawyer was a lot more than a human punch clock churning out billable time units. . . . I suppose those days are gone forever."[76]

Attorneys engaged in such high-stress, yet high-paying, careers put their mental and physical health at risk by working so hard for so many years. Many suffer through serious personal problems, ranging from feelings of guilt over lack of time with their families to divorce, and health problems, ranging from obesity to heart attacks. One recent study estimated that one lawyer in six is a problem drinker. Depression brought on by "putting one's time in to put money in other people's pockets," as Felix Frankfurter once put it,[77] is also common. One Johns Hopkins University survey concluded that triple the number of lawyers suffer from depression as compared with the general population.[78] I am reminded of the story, perhaps apocryphal, of the New York law firm that used to brag that it had no elderly attorneys—for years no one had lived past their fifties!

Why, then, do so many intelligent Americans persist in practicing law? In most law practices the comfortable standard of living, the steady progression of fresh issues, and the challenge of stimulating problem solving prove to be quite alluring. Clients stream to lawyers with problems that might benefit from legal counsel and with potential cases that need to be thoughtfully assessed. Is this worthy of a lawsuit? Might it be settled? Should it be watched but otherwise ignored?

While some portion of routine, even dull, legal work sits atop most lawyers' desks, many attorneys find the spice of their life in the opportunity to be paid well to use their smarts to solve diverse, intellectually challenging problems for others. Justice Oliver Wendell Holmes once asked: "In what other [profession] does one plunge so deeply into the stream of life—so share its passions, its battles, its despair, its triumphs, both as witness and actor?"[79]

Moreover, just as a leather worker might find satisfaction in crafting a handsome handbag or saddle, so an attorney might feel a glow of accomplishment in reviewing a brief, contract, or settlement drafted soundly, carefully, and thoughtfully. An eminent legal scholar once observed:

> [T]he essence of [legal] craftsmanship lies in . . . practical, effective, persuasive, inventive skills for getting things done, any kind of thing in any field;

[75] The studies in this paragraph are cited by Nancy D. Holt, "Are Longer Hours Here to Stay?: Quality Time Losing Out," *ABA Journal* 79 (Feb. 1993), pp. 62–63. In a 1992 California Bar Association survey, 70 percent reported that they would choose another career if the opportunity arose and 75 percent would not want their children to become lawyers.

[76] Linowitz, p. 19.

[77] Ibid., p. 25.

[78] Glendon, pp. 15, 87.

[79] Ibid., p. 92, citing Oliver Wendell Holmes, "The Law," in Mark DeWolfe Howe, ed., *The Occasional Speeches of Justice Oliver Wendell Holmes* (Cambridge, MA: Belknap Press, 1962), pp. 20–21.

> in wisdom and judgment in selecting the things to get done; in skills for moving men into desired action . . . ; and then in skills for *regularizing* the results. . . . [Lawyers] concentrate on the areas of conflict, tension, friction, trouble, doubt—and in those areas we have the skills for working out results. We are the troubleshooters. We find the way out and set up the method of the way, and get men persuaded to accept it. . . .[80]

Steadily accumulating professional experience is itself fulfilling. Problems that might thoroughly confound the attorney one year are handled smoothly and effectively the next. As is doubtless true of other professions, lawyers take special pride in their sudden inspirations: the novel legal argument, the witty rejoinder in court, the brilliant solution to a festering dispute.

In a law firm such problem solving occurs in an environment that can be supportive and collegial with all the lawyers intent on boosting the prestige, reputation, and competitiveness of the firm. One distinguished attorney recalled: "Partners consulted with each other all the time; doors were usually open, and it was the most natural thing in the world for a lawyer who had just learned of a problem from a client to wander down the hall and talk it over with his partner. Some of the happiest memories of law practice . . . are the recollections of impromptu conferences in a senior partner's office, talking over some odd problem the firm had just been handed, engaging in discussions that challenged one's intellect, knowledge, and judgment."[81] The twin satisfactions of solving new problems and gaining professional expertise and craftsmanship help to explain why so many make a career of practicing law, for all of its drawbacks.

Nevertheless, the disadvantages of practicing law already loom large and appear to loom larger on the horizon. If ever there really was an era in which a young lawyer might settle into a firm, enjoy a genteel, comfortable, rewarding, and intellectually stimulating career, with a reasonably contented spouse at home minding the children and housework, that age has long since vanished. One distinguished attorney wrote: "The associates in large firms cannot play the piano or paint a picture or act in a church play because they simply don't have the time. The tragedy is that, in the end, the single-minded drive toward winning the competitions at the firm will make these young lawyers not only less useful citizens, less interesting human beings, and less successful parents but also less good as lawyers, less sympathetic to other people's troubles, and less valuable to their clients."[82] While the satisfied lawyer is by no means an extinct species, many can identify with the views of Charles Colson, former Nixon White House aide convicted of a felony in the Watergate scandal, who, after his release from prison in 1993, observed: "I really thank God for Watergate. If it weren't for that, I might be back practicing law."

[80] Karl Llewellyn, "The Crafts of Law Re-Valued," *ABA Journal* 28 (1942), p. 801, cited in Linowitz, pp. 2–3.

[81] Linowitz, pp. 96–97.

[82] Ibid., p. 108.

SELECTED ADDITIONAL READINGS

ABEL, RICHARD L. *American Lawyers.* New York: Oxford University Press, 1989.

BONSIGNORE, JOHN J., et al., eds., "The Legal Profession," in *Before the Law: An Introduction to the Legal Process.* Boston: Houghton Mifflin, 1994.

CLAYTON, CORNELL W., ed. *Government Lawyers: The Federal Legal Bureaucracy and Presidential Politics.* Lawrence: University of Kansas Press, 1995.

CURRAN, BARBARA A. "American Lawyers in the 1980s." *Law and Society Review* 20 (1986): 19–52.

FISHER, WALTER T. *What Every Lawyer Knows.* Boston: Nimrod Press, 1974.

GLENDON, MARY ANN. *A Nation Under Lawyers: How the Crisis in the Legal Profession Is Transforming American Society.* New York: Farrar, Straus & Giroux, 1994.

HEINZ, JOHN P., and LAUMANN, EDWARD O. *Chicago Lawyers.* New York: Russell Sage Foundation, 1982.

JACOB, HERBERT. *Justice in America: Courts, Lawyers, and the Judicial Process.* 4th ed. rev. Boston: Little, Brown, 1984.

KRONMAN, ANTHONY. *The Lost Lawyer: Failing Ideals of the Legal Profession.* Cambridge, MA: Harvard University Press, 1993.

LINOWITZ, SOL M., with MAYER, MARTIN. *The Betrayed Profession: Lawyering at the End of the Twentieth Century.* New York: Charles Scribner's Sons, 1994.

LUBAN, DAVID. *Lawyers and Justice.* Princeton, NJ: Princeton University Press, 1988.

WRIGHTSMAN, LAWRENCE S. *Psychology and the Legal System.* 2d ed. rev. Pacific Grove, CA: Brooks/Cole, 1991.

5

The Jury

Foreign observers and Americans alike typically find the jury to be the most fascinating dimension of the American legal system. Indeed, one might more accurately say the most fascinating dimension*s* since two principal types of jury exist in the United States: the **trial jury** (or **petit jury**) and the **grand jury**.[1] Each has its own distinctive characteristics and may be critically analyzed on its own terms. How have these institutions developed over the ages? What does jury service entail? What differentiates grand juries from trial juries? What are the leading criticisms of juries, and how do their defenders respond? Should American juries be retained, reformed, or eliminated? What particular measures might improve the performance of juries? This chapter explores each of these central issues.

HISTORICAL DEVELOPMENT

While American juries have unique aspects, the concept of a jury is common to many peoples. In various countries in different historical periods, a government official has brought together a special group to determine how a particular legal issue should be resolved—often to decide whether someone was innocent or guilty of a crime.

In western civilization the jury idea has especially ancient roots.[2] The Greeks employed juries 2,500 years ago. A thousand years later the Roman judicial

[1] The *grand jury* received its name from the fact that at common law its numbers were greater (or in archaic English "grander") than the number of citizens assembled for a *trial jury,* which is also called a *petit jury,* meaning "small jury."

[2] For a more detailed discussion, see Henry J. Abraham, *The Judicial Process: An Introductory Analysis of the Courts of the United States, England, and France,* 6th ed. rev. (New York: Oxford University Press, 1993), pp. 100–101. See also Stephen J. Adler, *The Jury: Trial and Error in the American Courtroom* (New York: Times Books, 1994), especially pp. 244–246.

system also used juries on occasion. Starting about 800 years ago, England came to rely on juries. Then, along with so many other aspects of the English legal system, the jury made its way across the Atlantic Ocean to colonial America. Since independent juries could act contrary to the British authorities, nullify unpopular laws,[3] and even free their imprisoned countrymen, Americans soon warmly embraced the jury system.[4] Today, juries are found in many countries: in other English-speaking states, like Australia and New Zealand; in various European states, like Austria, Belgium, Greece, Denmark, and Norway; even in some Latin American countries, like Panama and Belize.

While many view the jury as a familiar legal institution, students of law typically associate it with Americans. The reason is that the powers of juries elsewhere have gradually declined, yet in the United States the jury has remained firmly entrenched. In the early twentieth century, Germany and France dramatically limited the use of juries, and Scotland and certain Swiss cantons abolished them altogether.[5] Juries in England are now used in fewer than 5 percent of cases involving criminal allegations and in just 1 percent of cases involving alleged civil wrongs.[6] In the United States, by contrast, about 3 million Americans serve each year on a jury, and approximately 85 percent of all criminal jury trials in the world occur within the United States and its possessions.[7] So, while juries are not uniquely American, the U.S. legal system relies on juries more than any other country does.

JURY DUTY

Summoning Jurors

In the United States, any citizen of voting age who has not been convicted of a crime and is not mentally disabled may be eligible for jury duty. Certain states have passed laws that spell out age, literacy, and residency requirements, and that specify how much time must have passed since a person's last jury duty before he or she is eligible to serve again. Nevertheless, all the American states require the vast majority of citizens who are summoned to appear in court for jury duty unless a court official approves their absence.

With minor variations from one court to the next, a clerk—once with the help of a **jury wheel** and now, more commonly, with the assistance of a computer—randomly selects citizens who live in the area. The most common source used to locate citizens eligible for jury duty is voter registration lists. That source is often sup-

[3] For the benefits of having juries occasionally nullify laws, see Jeffrey Abramson, *We, the Jury: The Jury System and the Ideal of Democracy* (New York: Basic Books, 1994), especially pp. 67–68.

[4] Jerome Frank, *Courts on Trial: Myth and Reality in American Justice* (Princeton, NJ: Princeton University Press, 1973), p. 109.

[5] Ibid., p. 109.

[6] Abraham, p. 100. Juries are used in all "grave" criminal cases, about 4 percent of the total.

[7] Ibid., p. 109.

plemented, however, with information drawn from utility companies, tax and welfare agencies, motor vehicle divisions, and even telephone books.[8] From the resulting master list, a supposed cross section of the community is then summoned to appear for jury duty. Although the numbers differ from place to place, courts have come to expect that less than half of those who are sent jury summons will actually appear at the courthouse at the scheduled time.[9]

Since a jury trial might occupy up to 6 hours a day for periods ranging from a single day to several days, to a week or even a month or more, people serving society in vital positions are often excused from jury duty. For instance, the courts usually exempt doctors and dentists, soldiers and police, teachers and legislators, religious leaders, government workers, and others, including lawyers. In about half the states, virtually anyone employed professionally or with childcare or eldercare responsibilities can claim undue hardship, extreme inconvenience, or public necessity and can expect to be excused from jury service. However, recent changes in New Jersey, New York, and Texas law may signal a trend toward curtailing such automatic exemptions.

Jury Duty: Burdens and Benefits

The founders of the American legal system considered serving on a jury to be a civic duty for normal citizens, but a privilege to be withheld from persons convicted of serious crimes. Since not all share such a strong sense of community service, people react differently to the prospect of sitting on a jury. While a jury system retains popular support as a theoretical matter, most Americans are not especially happy about interrupting their lives for jury duty. Sitting in a **jury room** for lengthy periods, waiting to be called for trial, can certainly be frustrating, particularly for the self-employed, who will lose income on account of the time they devote to jury service.

Since jury duty is typically viewed as a burden, jury dodgers sometimes concoct stories to try to persuade the court to excuse them. In fact, across the country jury **scofflaws,** persons who entirely ignore laws that require jury service, are becoming an increasingly serious problem.[10] Although all but the most absurd excuses are still regularly accepted, judges have become increasingly inclined to discipline those who repeatedly avoid jury duty. Some state judges have ordered individuals who ignored a jury summons to spend a night in jail; others have resorted to fines of several hundred dollars as well as community service penalties. In one

[8] See Robert A. Carp and Ronald Stidham, *Judicial Process in America,* 3d ed. rev. (Washington, DC: Congressional Quarterly Press, 1996), p. 180; Abramson, pp. 129–130.

[9] According to studies cited by the National Center for State Courts, the national average is about 45 percent. Adler, p. 243, n. 1. Adler noted: "In big cities the yield is generally much lower. In Los Angeles, for example, about 25 percent of the notices can't be delivered; another 25 percent are ignored by the recipients; and an additional 35 to 40 percent of potential jurors get themselves excused."

[10] See Andrea Gerlin, "Jury-Duty Scofflaws Try Patience of Courts," *Wall Street Journal,* Aug. 9, 1995, p. B1.

unusual case in early 1995, a judge in New York discovered that a Wall Street executive had sent an imposter to court in his place. The judge punished the scofflaw with 500 hours of community-service work.[11]

Others, however, react more philosophically when called upon for jury duty. After serving on a jury, many conclude that the experience, though time-consuming, formed an interesting part of their responsibilities as American citizens.[12] However, few, if any, find jury service to be a delightful or financially rewarding pasttime.[13] One lawyer wrote: "[Jurors] wait in shabby, crowded assembly rooms, frequently staffed by hostile or condescending clerks. They are supposed to follow directions, ask no questions, make no demands. When they move from room to room, they go as a group, escorted by men in uniform."[14]

Most important, despite being unfamiliar with many formal and informal courtroom procedures, jurors must cope with the responsibility and pressure of serving as decisionmakers in what may be hotly contested and high-stake courtroom battles. A juror in one celebrated case later recalled:

> We were never consulted about the hours we were to report, or whether dismissal at a certain time was convenient. . . . We were never given any reason for delays or early dismissals, other than . . . vague statements that court business needed to be taken care of.
>
> We were told just where to sit and when to come and what we must not read and who we must not talk to. . . . Most importantly, we were not informed as to what actions on our parts would lead to our dismissal from the jury, or cause a mistrial. Not knowing the limits put a lot of pressure on us. Everyone else in the courtroom knew his or her job . . . everyone except us. We were overwhelmed.[15]

For their efforts, jurors in federal court receive $40 a day, a sum that can be raised to $50 a day at the discretion of the judge after 30 days of service. In the states the rates for jury duty vary from place to place, though no state is especially generous. Among the highest **jury fees** are those in Wyoming, where jurors are paid $30 a day with the possibility that the judge might raise that figure to $50 a day after four days of service. Massachusetts and Colorado require jurors to serve for free for the first three days, then at a $50 rate for every day thereafter. Hawaii, Vermont, and Virginia compensate jurors at a flat $30 a day, a rate matched under certain circumstances by Texas, Florida, North Carolina, and the District of Columbia.

[11] Ibid.

[12] See, for instance, Adler, p. 36.

[13] The statistics that follow are drawn from Kathleen Maguire and Ann L. Pastore, eds., *Bureau of Justice Statistics Sourcebook of Criminal Justice Statistics—1993* (Washington, DC: U.S. Government Printing Office, 1993), p. 89.

[14] Adler, p. 225.

[15] Ibid., pp. 225–226, quoting Mary Timothy, the forewoman in the 1972 trial of black activist Angela Davis, in her book *Jury Woman* (Palo Alto, CA: Glide Publications/Emty Press, 1974), pp. 127–128.

Among the lowest jury fees are those in New Jersey and in certain counties of Georgia, Idaho, and Illinois, which in 1994 compensated jurors at $5 or less a day. To increase the incentive to serve on a jury, New York state courts increased jury compensation from $15 a day in 1995 to $27.50 a day in 1996 and $40 a day in 1997.[16] This, of course, still amounts to a fraction of the daily wages of many New York citizens.

Since so many are happy to avoid jury service, whether or not they have a serviceable excuse, and since courts are reluctant to force people to abandon their daily routines if that would cause hardship, the composition of the millions of American jurors each year tends to differ markedly from the composition of the population as a whole.[17] The percentage of students, retired persons, and part-time employees is substantially higher on juries than is found in the general population. Since these categories of citizens may well have attitudes concerning crime and law that differ from the remainder of society, the fact that jurors are so often drawn from these particular groups probably affects the outcome of certain cases.[18]

THE *VOIR DIRE*

Before the trial commences, much of the delay that frustrates those called for jury duty is caused by the process of selecting a jury, known by the French phrase ***voir dire*** ("to tell the truth"). Jury selection proceeds a bit differently in the various state and federal courts. However, the constant objective is to allow each side to question potential jurors and then to disqualify a certain number of them.

At the beginning of a trial, the clerk of the court brings into the courtroom a group, sometimes called an **array,** of prospective jurors technically termed **venire members,** or veniremen.[19] Then, depending on the state, either the judge, or the lawyers, or most commonly the judge and the lawyers ask the venire members questions in an effort that, in theory, is aimed at choosing an unbiased jury.[20] In a routine case fifteen or twenty prospective jurors may be questioned; questioning thirty would not be thought exceptional; and in very special cases, such as those involving the death penalty, several hundred might be examined.

In the many states in which lawyers dominate the *voir dire,* each side has the opportunity to reject jurors who might be prejudiced in assessing the case. For example, imagine a case in which two men who emigrated from Portugal have been accused of assault and battery upon an off-duty policeman. A lawyer might ask a potential juror such questions as: "Are you an American citizen?" "Do you know the accused?" "Do you have any opinion about whether or not the accused is

[16] Gerlin, p. B1.

[17] Lloyd L. Weinreb, *Denial of Justice: Criminal Process in the United States* (New York: The Free Press, 1977), pp. 88–89.

[18] Ibid.

[19] The older term *veniremen* was long meant to include women; "venire member" is beginning to replace it as a more accurate term.

[20] Laws relating to the *voir dire* differ from state to state.

guilty of the crime that has been charged?" "Do you have any negative feelings toward Portuguese people?"[21] "Do you have relatives who are policemen?" "Have you or any member of your family recently been the victim of a violent crime?" "Have you or any member of your family ever been accused of committing a criminal offense?" Eventually, the lawyers meet with the judge, and each side is permitted to eliminate certain venire members from the array.

Lawyers are customarily permitted to disqualify some potential jurors without furnishing any reason for doing so, a process known as making **peremptory challenges.**[22] In most states the number of peremptory challenges permitted to each lawyer is greater in criminal than in civil trials. Indeed, the number often differs depending upon the seriousness of the alleged offense, with more challenges permitted a defendant facing a felony charge than one confronting a misdemeanor accusation. Often, a defense attorney is permitted more peremptory challenges than a prosecutor.

A lawyer is also always allowed to eliminate a prospective juror if he or she can convince the judge of a compelling reason to do so, such as bias or prior knowledge of the case. The judge determines whether such **for cause challenges** should be upheld. Since in well-publicized trials many potential jurors will know something about the case, some have criticized the *voir dire* for producing ignorant juries. One federal district judge, presiding over a controversial trial involving a well-known religious figure, critically evaluated the impaneling of the jury by observing: "The choice is being narrowed to those who don't read much, don't talk much, and don't know much."[23]

While the number of jurors challenged during the *voir dire* varies from court to court and case to case, it is unusual for an attorney to fail to challenge any venire members. From 1977 to 1986 lawyers in U.S. district courts challenged between 15.2 and 16.9 percent of the available pool of jurors; from 1987 to 1993 the percentages rose steadily from 17.3 to 18.9 percent. In both 1992 and 1993 more than 160,000 jurors were challenged in federal court.[24] Eventually, the lawyers exhaust their peremptory challenges; no additional for cause challenges seem necessary; and the pool is reduced to the correct number for a jury trial in that court. At that point, the jury is impaneled, the clerk of the court requires each juror to swear to carry out his or her duties responsibly, and the trial is ready to begin.

[21] A clever lawyer might elicit more revealing responses by phrasing such a question in an open-ended manner: "When I say 'Portugal,' what are the first things that come to your mind?" See Abramson, p. 151.

[22] The use of peremptory challenges, which were originally derived from English common law, is governed by statutory law not by constitutional provisions. However, the U.S. Supreme Court has ruled that using peremptory challenges to keep individuals off juries because of their race or sex is unconstitutional. See *Batson v. Kentucky*, 476 U.S. 79 (1986), *Edmondson v. Leesville Concrete Co.*, 500 U.S. 614 (1991), and *Georgia v. McCollum*, 505 U.S. 42 (1992).

[23] Abraham, p. 118, citing U.S. District Judge Gerard L. Goettel, who presided over the Reverend Sun Myung Moon tax evasion case in 1986. For an example of jurors who might bear out Goettel's views, see Stephen Adler's characterization of the jury in the Imelda Marcos corruption trial. Adler, pp. 59–60.

[24] The statistics in this paragraph are drawn from Maguire and Pastore, p. 88.

Problems and Criticisms

Unfortunately, the adversarial spirit of American trials often changes the *voir dire* from an effort to select an unbiased jury to an effort by each lawyer to select jurors who are likely to look favorably on his or her arguments.[25] Some attorneys in criminal and civil cases employ psychologists or professional *jury consultants* to help them to choose supportive jurors.[26] Thus, while the rhetoric often concerns finding a neutral or unbiased jury, defense lawyers actually try to find and pick jurors who will be sympathetic to their client, and prosecutors will attempt to choose those likely to favor the state.

Since only a limited number of questions are permitted, lawyers often rely ultimately upon intuition or stereotypes to select jurors. Some want to avoid people of a certain socioeconomic class; others hope to find some reason that would justify disqualifying people of a certain racial background. A few otherwise intelligent lawyers even analyze the body type of a juror, taking a large, heavy individual to be jovial or easygoing, and a thin person with sharp features to be shrewd and difficult to convince.[27]

While particular attorneys may view the *voir dire* as tactically useful, since they can establish a relationship with jurors or even get a headstart on trying the case by posing revealing questions, critics claim that the process largely wastes time. While the *voir dire* is designed to weed out biased citizens, unsuited for jury service, prospective jurors can often figure out how they should answer a lawyer's question. If they wish to avoid being challenged, they will answer one way; if they would like to be challenged, they will answer it another. Clever and unscrupulous venire members sometimes do give an answer that is bound to be considered prejudicial precisely in order to be eliminated from the jury pool.

THE GRAND JURY

The Function of a Grand Jury

Grand juries are less vital decisionmakers than trial juries, and they perform a very different function. A grand jury meets to determine whether government authorities have gathered sufficient evidence to justify formally accusing a person of a crime and then putting that person on trial. If, after hearing a prosecutor outline the government's allegations and its preliminary evidence against a particular per-

[25] Prosecutors, however, often avoid "law and order zealots" for fear that the defense might use a bias argument as grounds for appeal. See Adler, p. 12.

[26] See Abramson, pp. 143–176.

[27] Weinreb, p. 94. See also Abramson, pp. 146–147 and Adler, pp. 53–55, quoting Clarence Darrow, who liked to challenge the "cold as a grave" Presbyterians, the "almost always sure to convict" Scandinavians, and the "solemn" Christian Scientists; and Gerry Spence, who "liked fat people more than thin ones because he believed that fat people lacked self-control and wouldn't demand as much law-abiding discipline from others." Ibid., p. 55.

son, the grand jurors believe that the government's case is very weak, they will refuse to allow a criminal trial to occur. If the evidence is sufficient, the grand jury will authorize the government to bring formal charges. It makes certain "that the [district attorney] has done some homework and has in fact secured enough evidence to warrant the trouble and expense—for both the state and the accused—of a full-fledged trial."[28]

A grand jury that supports the prosecutor issues a **true bill.** This document states that sufficient evidence exists to justify holding a criminal trial. A grand jury that fails to support the government returns a **no bill.** The grand jury's decision to support the government and to call for a criminal trial is known as an **indictment.**[29] When a prosecutor has gone to a grand jury and has received that body's approval that a criminal trial should be held against "John Smith," then "John Smith" has been indicted for a crime. The prosecutor then initiates a criminal trial. If the suspect is already in **jail,** as is often the case, the criminal trial occurs as a matter of course. If the suspect has not yet been caught, a judge or magistrate will issue an arrest warrant (technically a **bench warrant**), and the police will try to track the suspect down and arrest him or her so that the criminal trial can begin.

A grand jury, then, is an accusing body only: It does not attempt to determine guilt or innocence. Technically, a grand jury may issue an indictment only after finding that **probable cause**[30] exists to believe that a crime has been committed by the accused. Thus, while conclusively proving guilt is not necessary, a prosecutor must present facts to the grand jury that indicate the guilt of the accused person.[31] Since an indictment merely amounts to an accusation, unanimity among the grand jurors is not a requirement. Rather, customarily, a majority vote of grand jurors suffices to bring the indictment.[32]

Serving as a Grand Juror

The government may require any mentally competent adult American citizen who has not been convicted of a serious crime to serve as a member of a grand jury. In convening, or **impaneling,** a grand jury, the clerk of the court orders certain citizens to as-

[28] Carp and Stidham, p. 171.

[29] An *indictment* may be defined as a formal, written accusation drawn up by the prosecutor and issued by the grand jury, which identifies the offense or offenses the defendant is alleged to have committed.

[30] *Probable cause* is a technical legal term that arises at various stages of the American legal process. Before making an arrest, police must have probable cause to believe that person was committing, had committed, or was about to commit a crime. In order to bring an individual to trial, a grand juror or judge must find that probable cause exists. While the exact meaning of the term has been the subject of voluminous litigation in all state and federal courts, probable cause basically means that sufficient circumstances exist to lead a reasonably prudent individual to believe in the guilt of the accused person. Some courts have described the standard in terms of more evidence for than against; others have framed the inquiry in terms of whether "reasonable grounds" exist to support the charge that a suspect committed a particular crime.

[31] For a similar formulation, see Walter F. Murphy and C. Herman Pritchett, *Courts, Judges, and Politics,* 3d ed. rev. (New York: Random House, 1979), p. 444.

[32] Exceptions to this rule occur in certain states. For instance, twelve-member grand juries in Texas require a vote of nine to indict, not a vote of seven. See Carp and Stidham, p. 199, n. 13.

semble at a particular courthouse on a specified day. The clerk then has each potential grand juror swear to carry out his or her duties faithfully, truthfully, and secretly.[33]

The size of the grand jury to be selected varies depending on the type of court. Grand juries in U.S. federal district courts consist of no less than sixteen and no more than twenty-three members. Grand juries in state courts range from five to seven people in Virginia up to twenty-three in Maryland and Massachusetts. A handful of other states employ twenty-three grand jurors only on certain occasions. For less important proceedings a smaller number is impaneled.

The length of time a grand jury is in session varies from state to state. Although most grand juries do not serve their full term, and many do not meet for a full day's work every day of the week, the different maximum terms do suggest the considerable investment of time, energy, and other resources represented by grand jury members. In the District of Columbia the maximum term is a mere twenty-five working days, in Alabama the maximum term is four months, in Illinois, Oklahoma, and South Dakota it is eighteen months, and in Vermont it is two years.[34] Although federal grand juries can serve for eighteen months, and in special cases for up to thirty-six months, they normally are in session several days a week for about four or five weeks. During that time the prosecutor's office brings a series of cases to the grand jury asking for indictments.

A Grand Jury in Session

Once a grand jury is assembled and the members are sworn in, a prosecutor outlines the evidence against the person suspected of committing a crime. For instance, the state prosecutor might say: "The State of Maryland intends to charge Mr. John Smith with the crime of armed robbery." Then, the prosecutor might bring before the grand jury three people ready to serve as witnesses. The witnesses might **testify** that they saw John Smith enter a supermarket, draw out a gun, and demand money from a store employee.

The grand jury stage is the least adversarial part of the American trial process. In sharp contrast to America's public trials, all grand jury proceedings are held secretly. Spectators are not admitted to a grand jury room, and records are not released to the public. The accused may not even realize that a grand jury is considering his or her case. Invariably, the prosecutor dominates the proceedings. Neither the judge nor the defense lawyers are even allowed to enter the grand jury room. The prosecutor brings before the grand jury any witnesses he or she feels are necessary to show that a criminal trial is called for. Often, but not always, the witnesses include the person suspected of having committed the crime.

In the grand jury proceeding, contrary to the rules that prevail at the criminal trial itself, the **suspect**[35] has no right to question the government's witnesses or

[33] The term *jury* is derived from the Latin term *jurati,* meaning "sworn."

[34] See David Rottman, Carol Flango, and R. Shedine Lockley, eds., *State Court Organization* (Washington, DC: U.S. Government Printing Office, 1995), pp. 281–282.

[35] By *suspect* I mean the person who may be brought to trial—the person who the authorities suspect may have committed a crime.

to present defense witnesses for the jurors to consider. All matters relating to the suspect's defense are reserved for the criminal trial that will take place if the grand jury decides that such a step is appropriate. The grand jury's job is simply to hear the government outline its case and to decide whether or not a criminal trial should occur. In the meantime the police may decide to arrest the suspect, especially if authorities fear the suspect may flee during grand jury deliberations.

The Information

Students of American law are often surprised to learn that more than half the states never use grand juries. The U.S. Constitution guarantees that a grand jury will consider all criminal charges that the federal government wishes to pursue in federal court; however, it permits each state to set up its own system for bringing people to trial in state courts. In fact, only fourteen states require a grand jury indictment in order for the authorities to begin proceedings in a felony case.

Although some state courts have retained grand jury procedures similar to those found in federal courts, other states merely allow for the option of using a grand jury or restrict its use to particular cases, such as those concerning wrongdoing by government officials. Various states rely instead on an **information** proceeding. In this alternative system the prosecutor brings the evidence before a judge, rather than a group of jurors. The judge then holds a preliminary hearing, attended also by the defense, to decide whether the government has mustered sufficient evidence to justify holding a criminal trial. Many of the rules of evidence and procedure applicable to trials do not apply to the preliminary information hearing.[36] Nevertheless, the defense may attend, cross-examine witnesses, and place favorable evidence before the court.

In a state like California that uses both grand juries and preliminary information hearings, lawyers face an initial strategic decision as to whether their side of the case would benefit from using one procedure instead of the other. In the O. J. Simpson murder trial, for instance, the defense concluded that, all told, an information hearing would put the state at a disadvantage. Hence, the defense team filed a motion designed to remove the grand jury in favor of a preliminary information hearing.

The defense team reasoned that the prosecutors could probably present considerable evidence that Simpson had committed the murders. Revelations in a public preliminary information hearing would likely cause public opinion to turn sharply against Simpson. Negative media reports might even influence prospective jurors. All this would be avoided in a secret grand jury proceeding. However, the defense thought, forcing the prosecution to commit itself publicly to a half-baked case that the defense could analyze carefully and attack vigorously at trial would ultimately serve the defendant's interests. For this reason Alan Dershowitz, a member of Simpson's so-called Dream Team of defense attorneys, later wrote that the

[36] See Weinreb, p. 56.

use of a preliminary information proceeding, rather than a grand jury, was an early turning point in Simpson's successful defense.[37]

Grand Jury Decisions

After the prosecution has reviewed all the evidence, the grand jury meets briefly and almost always decides that sufficient evidence of criminal wrongdoing exists to justify holding a criminal trial to determine whether the suspect committed the crime in question. In fact, about 95 percent of grand juries agree with government prosecutors that a criminal trial should occur,[38] a statistic that should surprise no one who reflects on the powerful position of prosecutors and the one-sided nature of normal proceedings before a grand jury.

Although American grand juries primarily hand down indictments, they also sometimes conduct investigations leading to public findings that some illegal action may have occurred. This public accusation is called a **presentment.** Grand juries have made presentments after conducting significant investigations of criminal behavior ranging from narcotics dealing to juvenile delinquency, from political corruption to police brutality.

THE TRIAL JURY

The trial or petit jury has always been a principal decisionmaker in the American legal system. In reflecting the distrust of authority long ingrained in American culture, the trial jury is supposed to safeguard individuals against arbitrary enforcement of the law by resting decision making in the hands of fellow citizens. In a criminal case[39] an American trial jury normally meets to make the single most important decision in the trial: whether the accused person is innocent or guilty of the crime that has been charged. In some civil cases—that is, in disputes in court concerning an issue that does not involve the prosecution of a crime, but instead is typically focused on whether a party legally injured or otherwise wronged another and hence owes damages—a trial jury decides who wins the case.

These introductory observations correctly imply that jurors do not decide every case that comes before the American legal system. Some cases—indeed, many civil cases—are bench trials, nonjury trials in which a judge serves as the *trier of fact* who decides the case. As is normally the case under American federalism, however, each state court system has developed a bit differently from the federal system with

[37] See Alan Dershowitz, *Reasonable Doubts: The O.J. Simpson Case and the Criminal Justice System* (New York: Simon & Schuster, 1996), p. 29.

[38] Abraham, p. 105. See also Herbert Jacob, *Justice in America: Courts, Lawyers, and the Judicial Process,* 4th ed. rev. (Boston: Little, Brown, 1984), p. 188. On occasion, a prosecutor may be pressured to bring a case before a grand jury and may imply or even state to the grand jurors that in his or her opinion a *no bill* is in order. See Carp and Stidham, p. 171.

[39] By *criminal case* I simply mean a case in which the state has formally accused an individual of committing a crime.

respect to matters that are not controlled by the U.S. Constitution. Hence, the frequency of jury trials varies widely depending on the type of case and type of court.

The Sixth Amendment to the U.S. Constitution declares that a criminal defendant is entitled to a "public trial, by an impartial jury of the State and district wherein the crime occurred."[40] This provision has been interpreted to mean that an adult defendant has a constitutional right to a jury trial for all criminal cases that could result in more than 6 months in prison.[41] Every state thus provides for trial by jury for all substantial criminal offenses. However, a criminal defendant may prefer to have a judge hear the case and, hence, he or she may agree to waive the right to a jury.

The Seventh Amendment grants a right to a jury trial in all civil cases in federal court exceeding a minimal threshold amount of money.[42] In civil cases heard in state courts, trial juries are used much less frequently than in criminal cases. Although all civil cases are decided by judges in a few states, most states give **litigants** the option of a jury, at least in cases that involve significant sums. Nevertheless, since much civil litigation is sufficiently complex that the parties prefer to have a judge render the decision, in most state courts juries decide only a very small percentage of civil cases, usually fewer than 1 percent.[43]

In the federal courts, trial juries in criminal cases are composed of twelve American citizens, while trial juries in civil cases are made up of six.[44] In state courts the number of jurors varies from a minimum of five[45] to a maximum of twelve, depending on the state and on the type of case, with juries in criminal cases generally being larger than those in civil cases. In the federal courts jury verdicts must be unanimous;[46] however, the U.S. Supreme Court has permitted the states to allow non-unanimous jury decisions to stand.[47]

A Jury Trial in Theory and Practice

At trial, the jurors listen to the arguments of both sides, while sitting together in the jury-box. Alternate jurors are included in their midst, ready to be pressed into service in case illness or some other intervening factor causes a juror to be excused

[40] U.S. Constitution, Amendment VI.

[41] *Baldwin v. New York,* 399 U.S. 66 (1970). Juveniles do not have the same constitutional rights to jury trials as adults.

[42] U.S. Constitution, Amendment VII.

[43] In fact, since most of the civil cases that are brought to court eventually settle, the percentage of cases heard by a jury is an even smaller proportion of all the civil cases filed.

[44] Under the rules of civil procedure the parties in federal court, and parties in many state courts as well, may stipulate that the jury shall consist of less than twelve.

[45] The Supreme Court ruled that five-member juries in criminal cases violated the constitutional fair trial guarantee. *Ballew v. Georgia,* 435 U.S. 223 (1978).

[46] For a discussion of the benefits of unanimity see Abramson, pp. 179–205.

[47] Such non-unanimous decisions are not allowed in trials concerning *capital offenses* or those rendered by six-member juries. See *Apodaca v. Oregon,* 406 U.S. 404 (1972), *Johnson v. Louisiana,* 406 U.S. 356 (1972), and *Williams v. Florida,* 399 U.S. 78 (1970).

from the remainder of the trial. During the trial the jurors are directed not to discuss the case with anyone or consider any media accounts of the proceedings. A judge, present throughout the proceedings, referees the contest between the lawyers.

At the close of the evidence, the judge gives formal **instructions** to the jury, sometimes referred to as the **charge to the jury.** This defines and explains the laws and the **burden** or **standard of proof** that the jurors should apply. In their instructions judges often concentrate the jury's attention on the **evidence,** that is, on the **testimony** of witnesses and on the exhibits introduced at trial, rather than on the statements by the lawyers, which are not considered evidence.[48] The judge may also summarize the case, list the different sorts of verdict the jury could bring, and specify what the jury must find to rule in favor of one party or the other. The jury then retreats into isolation as a group for deliberations. The jury members assess the evidence, discuss it with one another, and render a verdict.

Of course, such a sterile description misses not just the color and pageantry, but the subterfuge and human frailties that regularly stretch, perhaps even distort, actual jury trials. In practice, jurors often do read or listen to accounts of their trial and discuss the proceedings with their spouses and others. And, subconsciously or consciously, on occasion judges do draft jury instructions that favor one of the parties.[49] While jurors are supposed to apply the law whether they agree with it or not, in fact, jurors do sometimes ignore or interpret a law to suit their view of how a case should be justly decided. Although judges are not supposed to pressure disagreeing jurors to reach a verdict, they are usually intent on avoiding a retrial and, hence, indicate their displeasure with a deadlocked jury.

In the *voir dire,* although lawyers are not supposed to select jurors on the basis of race, sex, or ethnicity, some have become expert at masking their underlying motives by pointing to seemingly neutral rationales for disqualifying certain venire members.[50] During the trial, although lawyers are not supposed to influence jurors with references to inadmissible matters, they do sometimes inject highly prejudicial material into the proceedings. Moreover, lawyers do—many would say lawyers *must*—try to shade or mold the truth to suit their client's purposes, perhaps by clouding over or hurrying past awkward matters. One scholar observed:

> Both prosecution and defense generally conduct what is to all intents and purposes a legal sporting combat, with each side following evidence by counterevidence, examination by cross-examination, witness by counter-witness, each one sworn to tell the truth, the whole truth, and nothing but the truth.

[48] Adler, p. 229.

[49] Carp and Stidham wrote: "[I]f someone were accused of embezzlement and the judge favored acquittal, it might be possible to give the jury such a narrow legal definition of the word *embezzlement* that it would be difficult to bring in a guilty verdict. Likewise, if the judge were disposed toward conviction, a broader discussion of the laws on embezzlement might facilitate a conviction." Carp and Stidham, p. 189. Of course, jury instructions may be, and often are, appealed for review by a higher court.

[50] See Adler, p. 223.

> Not infrequently, this alleged search for the truth results in statements in open court that are clearly out of order. But even if the judge . . . asks the jury to disregard the statement at issue . . . it is conjectural at best whether or not it can be wiped from the jurors' minds. To arrive at the truth behind . . . "the curtain of flimflam and obfuscation" the jury may well have to decide which side, in its judgment, seemed to tell fewer lies, and in that way reach a verdict.[51]

By the time the various formal steps of a jury trial have occurred,[52] even a very simple trial may occupy a full day. Although criminal trials usually take longer than civil trials, either type ordinarily occupies several days or even a week or more of the court's time. Unusual trials with complicated issues, such as the O. J. Simpson murder trial, may demand month after month of attention. When sensational matters of substantial public interest come to trial, the judge may order the jurors to be **sequestered** during the proceedings. That is, they will have to live in a hotel and be isolated from contact with the public and media until their responsibilities are fulfilled.[53]

In most cases a jury **deliberates** for some time and agrees on a verdict the same day that the trial concluded. However, in complex or highly controversial cases jury deliberations may extend over several days, during which period the jurors are often sequestered. If jurors disagree, even after long discussions, and simply cannot compromise, the result is called a **hung jury.** Should the prosecutor wish to pursue the case, the state will bring a new trial, or *trial de novo,* in front of different jurors but concerning the same or lesser charges.[54]

The Dynamics of Jury Deliberations

Since a jury at work may not be videotaped for fear of influencing the decision, much of the information about jury deliberations is drawn from subsequent interviews with jurors. Hence, this information suffers from faded memories and inaccuracies. Moreover, only a relatively small sampling of juries has been studied in this way. Nonetheless, certain tentative conclusions may be drawn.

Plainly, no two juries are likely to deliberate in quite the same manner. The personalities and the experiences of jurors differ, as do the trials themselves in length, complexity, and character. The *foreman* or *forewoman,* that is, the juror who has been designated to lead and represent the jury, may take a relatively active or relatively passive role. Disagreements may be discussed calmly and intelligently, mediated quietly, or hashed out vigorously, loudly, and even abusively. In one tense deliberation regarding a notorious murder trial, the *New York Times* reported, "a near fight broke out. At the height of one heated debate, a male juror threatened to

[51] Abraham, p. 130.

[52] The steps of a criminal trial are reviewed in Chapter 7 and of a civil trial in Chapter 8.

[53] When the court sequesters jurors for an extended period, it often permits conjugal visits by their spouses.

[54] A new trial on more or different charges would violate the double jeopardy clause. See U.S. Constitution, Amendment V.

throw another [female juror] out of a window and turned over the jury table—he used to be a boxer—before she ran to the door. She was hysterical and pounded on the door for the bailiff."[55]

While such extraordinary passions occasionally erupt, jurors more commonly act in a serious, businesslike manner or adopt a bored demeanor that seems to favor disposing of the proceedings as rapidly as possible. Two authorities observed: "Almost all juries take a vote soon after they retire to their chambers—'just a nonbinding straw vote to see where we are.' In 30 percent of the cases it takes only one vote to reach a unanimous decision. In 90 percent of the remainder, the majority on the first ballot eventually wins out."[56] They continued: "Studies have shown . . . that men talk more than women in the jury deliberation process and have more influence on the final outcome. . . . [W]ell-educated people play a more significant role than those with weak educational backgrounds. There is also some evidence that ethnic or racial minorities carry some of their underdog values into the jury deliberation rooms, being more likely to favor the accused than are jurors with higher social status."[57]

In several interesting cases the American Bar Association persuaded particular judges to seat extra alternate jurors at selected trials. Since those jurors were not really deciding the case, their deliberations could be taped and analyzed. An ABA study concluded: "many jurors were confused, misunderstood their instructions, failed to recall evidence, and suffered enormously from boredom and frustration."[58] While the degree of comprehension and common sense displayed by juries may be debated, the effectiveness of jury deliberations as a procedure for coming to a decision is remarkable: Somehow only about 5 percent of American juries do not reach a unanimous verdict.[59] In the federal system, and in those states that share a unanimity requirement, hung juries are thus quite unusual. In those states that permit non-unanimous jury decisions hung juries are, of course, even less frequent.

When the jury concludes its deliberations, the foreman or forewoman notifies the bailiff who informs the judge. The court is then reassembled and the verdict is announced in open court. Thereafter, the judge customarily *polls* the jury; that is, the judge asks each juror in turn if he or she supports the verdict. If the polling reveals unacceptable disagreement, the judge may either order the jury to resume deliberations, or he or she may declare a mistrial, and order that the case be tried again before different jurors.[60] At that point, the jury is dismissed and the trial is over.

[55] *New York Times,* Mar. 13, 1960, p. 42, reporting on the Finch-Tregoff case, cited in Abraham, pp. 128–129.

[56] Carp and Stidham, p. 191.

[57] Ibid., p. 192.

[58] Adler, p. 46, citing Daniel H. Margolis, *Jury Comprehension in Complex Cases* (Chicago: American Bar Association, 1989).

[59] Abramson, p. 104, citing Harry Kalven, Jr., and Hans Zeisel, *The American Jury* (Chicago: University of Chicago Press, 1970), p. 456.

[60] Carp and Stidham, p. 192.

THE USEFULNESS OF AMERICAN JURIES

While grand juries and trial juries are entrenched in American legal tradition, their usefulness is open to question. How do critics attack grand juries, and how do defenders support them? In particular, if grand juries support the government's view in overwhelming numbers, then why does the American legal system retain such an apparently extraneous procedure?[61]

The American trial jury might be perceived as an equally enigmatic phenomenon.[62] Court authorities bring together a group of randomly selected citizens to serve at a single trial. Even at the most complicated trials, note taking is usually discouraged for fear that the notes will be inaccurate or that important points will be missed while the jurors write. Jurors are thus given the responsibility of deciding the most critical matter in the trial without consulting anything other than their memories and common sense.

American juries are never called upon to defend their decision by formally explaining their reasoning. Rather, jurors carry out their deliberations secretly, without much, if any, supervision,[63] and announce their verdict in the simplest terms. Once the jury does render its verdict, it is disbanded. That set of jurors, whether it did a good or bad job, will never be brought together again.

Equally surprising, the judge informs the jurors as to precisely what the law requires only after the lawyers have fully presented their cases and just before deliberations begin. One federal judge likened this practice to "telling jurors to watch a baseball game and decide who won without telling them what the rules are until the end of the game."[64] Another judge wrote: "[T]his order of procedure makes much of the trial of a lawsuit mere mumbo jumbo. It sounds all right to the professional technicians who are the judge and the lawyers. It reads all right to . . . the court of appeals. But to the laymen sitting in the box, restricted to listening, the whole thing is a fog."[65] While deferring instructions to the end of the trial is convenient for the lawyers, who can assess how the jury reacts before committing to a particular legal theory, and for judges, who can watch the trial and ponder the law, it tends to confuse the jurors,[66] particularly if the lawyers have not made clear the contours of the case during the opening and closing statements and the meaning of key terms during the testimony of witnesses.

[61] See Weinreb, pp. 55–59.

[62] The following passage echoes a point made by Hans Zeisel and Harry Kalven, Jr., "The American Experiment," in Murphy and Pritchett, p. 462.

[63] If a jury is deadlocked, the judge will occasionally tell the jury foreman to reconvene for some additional period to try to come to a definitive decision. And, in a few states a prosecutor may appeal a jury's judgment acquitting a defendant.

[64] Adler, p. 129, citing William W. Schwarzer, "Reforming Jury Trials," *University of Chicago Legal Forum* (1990): 130. Adler concluded: "[This] . . . process . . . virtually guarantees that in any complicated matter the jury will fail to comprehend the significance of various pieces of testimony until the end of the case, if at all." Ibid., pp. 129–130.

[65] Adler, p. 228, quoting E. Barrett Prettyman, "Jury Instructions—First or Last?," *ABA Journal* 46 (1960): 1066.

[66] Ibid., p. 227.

The foolishness and bumbling characteristic of various trial juries raises the issue of whether justice might better be administered by judges. Is the strange custom of a jury trial a laudable or lamentable feature of the American legal system? Could trial jury reforms make the institution more defensible?

A Defense of the Grand Jury

The supporters of the grand jury argue that putting someone on trial accused of committing a crime is a very serious matter. The accused will often pay substantial amounts to defend against the charges, and the suspect's reputation in the community may never fully recover, whatever happens in court.

From this perspective, then, the grand jury acts as a safeguard. The grand jurors, acting secretly, can discard meritless cases. If the government has presented little evidence that the accused committed a crime, the people can short-circuit the prosecution process. Supporters of the grand jury also claim that the public should be given the opportunity to investigate wrongdoing. If some important subject, such as organized crime, police misconduct, or official corruption, is not receiving sufficient public attention, grand jury proceedings can be used to publicize the problem.

For the defenders of the grand jury the institution underscores the democratic nature of American government. Ordinary people share responsibility with elected officials in determining which cases of alleged criminal conduct ought to be brought to court. A cross section of the community directly participates in deciding where the government should devote the resources at its disposal for further investigating crime and trying alleged offenders. While grand juries may not often resist prosecutorial wishes, they occasionally throw out a sloppy, ill-prepared, or biased case. Moreover, the very fact that prosecutors know that grand juries have the power to issue no bills forces the government to marshal its evidence with some care before attempting to gain an indictment.

A Critique of the Grand Jury

Critics respond that the grand jury is an outdated idea that has become costly and unnecessary. Years ago, when the United States was a largely rural country dotted with small villages and towns, asking a group of ordinary citizens to investigate crime may have made sense.[67] In those days, serious crimes were unusual events and directly threatened the peace of a community in which all the inhabitants had a direct stake. Moreover, the authorities investigated crime using nontechnical and, often, haphazard methods. Consequently, the common sense and local knowledge of community representatives were of valuable assistance in determining who committed crimes. They also might serve to check mistaken, and overly zealous, authorities.

[67] See, for instance, the parallel discussion in ibid., p. 55.

Today, however, most Americans live in a very different environment—not in small villages, but in large cities—or, at least, in urban areas with characteristics unlike those of eighteenth-century American towns and farms. Clearly, twentieth-century Americans are not usually interested in taking the time to participate in investigating all the serious crimes that occur in their community. Nor do they have the technical knowledge of criminal investigation or of legal process necessary to come to a critical, independent judgment of the government's case.

The critics claim that Americans today want their police to take care of investigations, and they are quite willing to allow the government to hold a criminal trial against practically anyone the authorities feel compelled to arrest. Since in the overwhelming majority of cases the grand jury does exactly what the prosecutor wants it to do, the critics believe that in practice the grand jury does not really amount to much of a safeguard for innocent citizens wrongfully accused of crime by the authorities. In fact, a judge in a preliminary information hearing will be more experienced and, hence, may be more skeptical about substandard prosecutorial preparation than inexperienced and easily duped grand jurors. Why occupy the time of as many as twenty-three grand jurors to do a job that a single judge could accomplish more effectively?

How about the grand jury's role in investigating crime? Although the supporters point to some important grand jury investigations in American history, such as the grand jury that inquired into the Watergate scandal, some critics claim that the grand jury system can be abused by governments out to cause trouble for some particular group in American society. For example, some have accused the Nixon administration of forming grand juries to investigate people who held radical political ideas or who simply threatened Nixon's political position.[68]

The grand jury's critics balance costs against benefits and find the institution unworthy of support. Many Americans are dissatisfied with jury service and never fulfill their civic obligations. This, in turn, leads to juries that do not fully represent the talents and experiences of all sectors of the population. The American legal system might draw back to trial jury service some of the many scofflaws and jury duty dodgers if civic obligations were less time-consuming and onerous. Eliminating lengthy and often superfluous grand jury duties would be a positive first step in revitalizing the trial jury.

A Critique of the Trial Jury

The American trial jury has also been roundly denounced. Certain critics have long argued that the average American is not sufficiently intelligent to decide a legal case correctly. Philosopher Herbert Spencer called a jury: "[A] group of twelve people of average ignorance."[69] Novelist Honoré de Balzac dismissed the work of

[68] See Lawrence S. Wrightsman, *Psychology and the Legal System* (Pacific Grove, CA: Brooks/Cole, 1987), pp. 194–195.

[69] Abraham, p. 134.

the jury as "twelve people trying to decide who hired the better lawyer."[70] Critics point out how various American juries have acted childishly, irrationally, even downright stupidly in trying to come to a decision.[71] One notorious example is the $10.5 billion jury award to Pennzoil against Texaco in a 1986 case. Jurors in this case later explained "that they had added $1 billion to the award for each of the Texaco witnesses they had most despised"![72]

In theory, the jury sets out to find the facts in a trial, and the judge resolves issues of law and instructs the jury as to the relevant law. The jury is then to issue its verdict on the basis of its interpretation of the factual record and its understanding of the relevant legal obligation. In fact, however, jurors may be lost, inattentive, or confused. They may not understand the judge's instructions on the law, or they may choose to ignore them. One close observer of juries recently concluded: "I repeatedly encountered . . . lots of sincere, serious people who—for a variety of reasons—were missing key points, focusing on irrelevant issues, succumbing to barely recognized prejudices, failing to see through the cheapest appeals to sympathy or hate, and generally botching the job."[73]

Longtime federal judge Jerome Frank argued: "To comprehend the meaning of many a legal rule requires special training. It is inconceivable that a body of twelve ordinary men, casually gathered together for a few days, could, merely from listening to the instructions of the judge, gain the knowledge necessary to grasp the true import of the judge's words. For these words have often acquired their meaning as the result of hundreds of years of professional disputation in the courts. The jurors usually are as unlikely to get the meaning of those words as if they were spoken in Chinese, Sanskrit, or Choctaw."[74] Frank further maintained: "[Jurors] are . . . brutally direct. They determine that they want Jones to collect $5,000 from the railroad company, or that they don't want pretty Nellie Brown to go to jail for killing her husband; and they bring in their general verdict accordingly. Often, to all practical intents and purposes, the judge's statement of the legal rules might just as well never have been expressed."[75]

In this view, the fact that juries need not explain their verdicts has helped to save the institution since the reasoning is thoroughly illogical, nonlegal, or even nonexistent. Years ago, a legal scholar declared: "Nor can we cut away the mantle of mystery in which the general verdict is enveloped to see how the principal facts were determined, and whether the law was applied under the judge's instruc-

[70] Frank, p. 122.

[71] For a series of such cases see Abraham, p. 129.

[72] Adler, p. 45. After Texaco appealed, the parties settled for $3 billion, and Texaco soon faced bankruptcy court proceedings, from which it eventually recovered. See Thomas Petzinger, Jr., *Oil & Honor: The Texaco-Pennzoil Wars* (New York: G.P. Putnam's Sons, 1987) and *Texaco v. Pennzoil,* 729 S.W.2d. 768 (1987).

[73] Adler, p. xiv. Adler continued: "[S]ome jurors succumb all too easily to emotional appeals. Some are stymied by the least bit of complexity. Many filter facts through such a thick mesh of prejudice that the facts become unrecognizable. Common sense mutates into mutual delusion." Ibid., p. 50.

[74] Frank, p. 116.

[75] Ibid., p. 111.

tions. . . . It is a matter of common knowledge that the general verdict may be the result of anything but the calm deliberation, exchange of impressions and opinions, resolution of doubts, and final intelligent concurrence which, theoretically, produced it. It comes into court unexplained and impenetrable."[76]

A critic might suggest that if juries were to be required to explain their reasoning in arriving at a verdict, the spectacle would be so absurd that Americans would follow so many other countries and greatly curb the role of juries or rid the legal system of them altogether. As Mark Twain wrote in *Roughing It,* "The jury system puts a ban upon intelligence and honesty, and a premium upon ignorance, stupidity, and perjury. It is a shame that we must continue to use a worthless system because it *was* good a thousand years ago."[77]

Other critics emphasize how much better equipped are judges, than juries, to decide legal cases justly. Is it not foolish to eliminate the wisest and most experienced authority in the courtroom from making the ultimate decision of guilt and innocence? These critics would prefer to have a judge try to lead a dispassionate, unbiased inquiry into what actually occurred. While it may in fact be true that judges and juries would come to the same decision in eight out of ten cases,[78] the American legal system might profit by having judges bring their more impressive experience and intelligence to bear on the two out of ten cases that are truly controversial.

One lawyer wrote: "Whatever criticisms might be leveled at the intellectual qualifications of the average federal judge, each of them has such minimal intellectual equipment as to have passed a bar examination, and presumably to have completed college and law school. This alone creates a probability that the powers of comprehension of a federal judge will exceed those of the average juror."[79] The idea that a lawyer can more easily dupe jurors than a judge leads to the conventional wisdom that "juries tend to acquit criminal defendants more often than judges [do]."[80]

In an era when law and order is a principal concern of Americans, substituting the wisdom of a judge for the folly of a jury seems a recipe for stricter enforcement of the law. Moreover, in an era marked by grave budget concerns the sums paid jurors, while hardly extravagant, amount to a cost that might usefully be avoided.[81]

[76] George B. Clementson, *Special Verdicts and Special Findings by Juries* (1905), cited in ibid.

[77] Adler, p. 43, citing Mark Twain, *Roughing It,* vol. II (New York: Harper and Brothers, 1913), pp. 55–58. (Italics in original.)

[78] The Ford Foundation's University of Chicago Jury Project found that judges agreed with juries in more than 80 percent of the thousands of cases analyzed. Many of the cases that judges felt that juries had wrongly decided involved rape, drunk driving, and various other laws that many jurors at that time considered to be unduly harsh. Many of the findings of the report are presented in Harry Kalven, Jr. and Hans Zeisel, *The American Jury* (Boston: Little, Brown, 1966). See also Abramson, pp. 65, 196–197; Abraham, pp. 131–132; Carp and Stidham, p. 191.

[79] Adler, p. 44, citing Patrick Lynch, "The Case for Striking Jury Demands in Complex Antitrust Litigation," *The Review of Litigation* 1 (1980): 3.

[80] Henry R. Glick, *Courts, Politics, and Justice,* 3d ed. rev. (New York: McGraw-Hill, 1993), p. 267.

[81] The administrative arm of the federal courts ordered federal district courts not to start new civil jury trials during a period from May 1993 until the next budget came into effect in October, since no money was available to pay jurors. Linowitz, p. 183.

Finally, as civil litigation has become more complex, the advantages to having a judge sort through the facts and law in such disputes have become ever more evident. Certain critics thus favor a constitutional amendment to eliminate juries in civil cases in federal court. The constitutional requirement of juries, they argue, arose in a less technical era when juries were expected to resolve simpler legal issues.[82] With technological advances and ever more complicated bodies of law, civil disputes might better be resolved by judges. This would eliminate such cases as the 1978 California mistrial of IBM, when after nearly half a year of testimony and deliberations the jury still could not define such key terms as "software," "interface," or "barriers to entry."[83]

One distinguished attorney argued: "The costs to litigants from the loss of a right to demand trial by jury are probably overbalanced by the costs to society at large from the lost working days of jurors, the less efficient trial procedures in situations where evidence must be evaluated by amateurs, and injustice from the weight juries may give to extraneous arguments cleverly presented."[84] In this vein Chief Justice Warren Burger once remarked: "[E]ven [Thomas] Jefferson would be appalled at the prospect of a dozen of his stout yeomen and artisans trying to cope with some of today's complex litigation."[85]

A Defense of the Trial Jury

While serious doubts about juries have long been expressed, often in scalding terms, defenders still associate the jury with substantial benefits. One supporter responded: "[T]here would be little point to a jury system if we expected jurors always to decide cases exactly as judges would decide them. The whole point is to subject law to a democratic interpretation, to achieve a justice that resonates with the values and common sense of the people in whose name the law was written."[86] The jury system in the United States may be worthy of support precisely because it requires the public to continue to participate in enforcing American laws. Alexis de Tocqueville observed: "By obliging men to turn their attention to other affairs than their own, [jury service] rubs off that private selfishness which is the rust of society."[87]

In many other legal systems ordinary people have very little contact with their courts. Such isolation sometimes leads to high levels of judicial corruption and to a preference for settling disputes by extralegal means. In Guatemala, for in-

[82] See Tocqueville, 1969, p. 271.

[83] Adler, p. 119.

[84] Sol M. Linowitz, with Martin Mayer, *The Betrayed Profession: Lawyering at the End of the Twentieth Century* (New York: Charles Scribner's Sons, 1994), p. 172.

[85] Ibid., p. 119, citing Burger's speech on November 10, 1989, at Loyola University, New Orleans, LA.

[86] Abramson, p. 6.

[87] Adler, p. 4, citing Alexis de Tocqueville, *Democracy in America* (New York: Vintage Books, 1990), pp. 280–287.

stance, almost all trials take place in secret, with no public audience and absolutely no public participation. This has helped to produce such a grossly malfunctioning judicial system that a sitting president of the Guatemalan Supreme Court characterized the administration of justice in the country as "bureaucratic, secretive, depersonalized, . . . slow, . . . lacking in the general confidence of the citizens, costly, divorced from social life, uncontrollable [and] . . . acting with impunity."[88] Around the world, legal systems in which judges are deeply suspected and mistrusted may well outnumber those in which the average person respects the judiciary as a largely uncorrupted institution that takes seriously the rule of law and the ideal of judicial impartiality.

From this perspective the jury serves as a vital element of American democracy. Though some jurors doubtless find their jury experience to be disheartening or disillusioning, nevertheless, to a greater extent than in any other large developed country, ordinary Americans directly participate in applying a highly sophisticated set of laws. Serving on a jury may thus benefit the juror and, through the juror, society at large. As Tocqueville commented: "I do not know whether a jury is useful to the litigants, but I am sure it is very good for those who have to decide the case." He continued: "The jury is both the most effective way of establishing the people's rule and the most efficient way to teach them how to rule."[89]

It may also be the case that, as compared with various other nationalities, Americans are peculiarly well-suited to serving on juries. For all their witticisms at the expense of American jurors, one might doubt that French novelists like Balzac and English philosophers like Spencer are well qualified to determine whether the average American is or is not sufficiently intelligent to serve as a capable juror. As a practical matter, virtually all Americans called to jury service will have had primary and secondary education. Many will have attended college, and a few, graduate school as well. Certainly, as the number of college-educated Americans nears 50 million, the pool of prospective jurors is better educated than that found in most other countries.

Equally important, the antiauthoritarian streak in American culture provides a measure of independence from the state and its prosecutors that one would likely not find in more deferential societies, such as Japan, with cultures based in part on communitarian or authoritarian principles. Such an educated, independent-minded population is a critical advantage for a country attempting to make a jury system function effectively.

It may be that American critics of the trial jury take for granted the benefits that juries bring to the legal system and exaggerate the advantages of having judges always find the facts and rule on the law. Would an American judge auto-

[88] See Michael Ross Fowler and Julie M. Bunck, "Legal Imperialism or Disinterested Assistance?: American Legal Aid in the Caribbean Basin," *Albany Law Review* 55 (1992): 819.

[89] Alexis de Tocqueville, *Democracy in America*, ed. J. P. Mayer, trans. George Lawrence (Garden City, NY: Anchor Books, 1969), pp. 275–276. He further observed: "Juries . . . instill some of the habits of the judicial mind into every citizen, and just those habits are the very best way of preparing people to be free." Ibid., p. 274.

matically do a much better job than American juries at determining who is telling the truth and who is lying and how to weigh the evidence on both sides of a case? Judges certainly are not immune from crowded schedules, human biases, and short attention spans.

Moreover, many Americans have long felt that a decision by a jury of one's peers is a legitimate method to determine guilt or liability. Two scholars have written:"[T]he jury serves as the conscience of the community. Although the jurors are not personally concerned with the outcome of the case, they are interested in seeing that the case is resolved in a peaceful, fair manner."[90] After all but the most nonsensical jury verdicts, criminal defendants and their friends and family may be more inclined to accept an adverse decision by twelve jurors than one by a judge whom they might hurry to criticize as biased or even corrupt. Whether or not twelve heads are really better than one, the theory that they probably are retains popular appeal. This is especially important since the conventional wisdom that juries are more lenient than judges on criminal defendants has recently been questioned: In 1990, juries in federal courts convicted 84 percent of defendants, while judges convicted 63 percent.[91] As for the issue of juries in civil trials, the parties to most cases already have the option of waiving their right to a jury trial in favor of having a judge hear the evidence, decide the facts, and apply the law to the facts.

Jury supporters also point out that since jurors meet for only a single trial, they may be more inclined to take a fresh look at a case than a judge who oversees many hundreds of cases in the course of a few months' work. In this vein British novelist G. K. Chesterton wrote that the principal problem with judges, "is not that they are wicked (some of them are good), not that they are stupid (several of them are quite intelligent), it is simply that they have got used to it. . . . They do not see the awful court of judgment; they see only their own workshop."[92] One experienced attorney observed: "Many lawyers fear that judges may be biased by their own social status or political connections. Or they may just have quirky views about some element of expert testimony one side of a case wishes to introduce. There is not much that can be done about a biased or quirky judge, while the biases of the members of a jury can be tested in the process of jury selection and in any event tend to cancel out."[93]

Another lawyer remarked: "Judges have heard every phony alibi dozens of times; they are certainly correct in assuming that it's usually not true that . . . the murder defendant was with his parents the entire night, or that the deadly mix of chemicals was intended to create a miracle drug rather than a bomb. But sometimes the excuse is true. And a judge may miss the clues because he has heard it all

[90] James V. Calvi and Susan Coleman, American Law and Legal Systems, 2d ed. rev. (Englewood Cliffs, N.J.: Prentice Hall, 1992), p. 72.

[91] Abramson, p. 253. This is especially surprising when one recalls that by 1990 the composition of the federal judiciary had become markedly more conservative after two terms of Ronald Reagan and half a term of George Bush. Of course, as Adler pointed out, the statistics may be distorted if "defendants with particularly strong legal defenses choose bench trials in disproportionate numbers."

[92] Adler, p. 9, citing Shirley S. Abrahamson, "A View from the Other Side of the Bench," *Marquette Law Review* 69 (Summer 1986): 463.

[93] Linowitz, p.172.

before and has lost sight of the awful court of judgment, something a jury, for all its faults, almost never does."[94] Thus, a jury verdict, representing the perspectives and often the compromises of a group of citizens of differing backgrounds and experiences, may be preferable to the decision of a single judge.

Furthermore, while either a judge or a jury may be influenced by public pressure, members of a jury at least have the option of retiring into anonymity immediately after the trial.[95] Notwithstanding the powerful ideal of judicial independence, judges, concerned with their reputations and careers, may be more directly affected than jurors in issuing unpopular decisions.[96]

The American trial jury also keeps legal proceedings from becoming quite as stale and dominated by technicalities as might otherwise be the case. All legal systems aim to do justice: to ensure that criminals are punished and innocent people are not, and that the litigant with the better legal position prevails. Toward this end, lawyers, judges, and legislators create elaborate networks of rules aimed at having the system do justice in as many cases as possible. What may sometimes be lost among all the technicalities is flexibility and common sense applied via the ordinary person's considered view of who is truthful and what is right and wrong for society.

While acknowledging recent psychological studies that cast doubt on the ordinary person's ability to distinguish truth from falsehood, one authority nonetheless commented: "[J]urors do bring a lifetime of experience to judging whether other people's words square with their deeds. In their daily lives jurors make hundreds of such calculations: whether the used-car dealer is telling the truth about the mileage; whether the job applicant is lying about his experience; whether the child is concocting a tall tale about the missing homework; whether the spouse is working late or playing around. A knack for knowing whom to trust, whom to believe, whom to shun is the essence of common sense."[97]

Whether or not the average juror is really able to apply common sense to the issue at hand, the institution of the jury appeals to the independent, populist, antigovernment strains in the American psyche. One trial lawyer declared: "[T]he glory of the jury is its beautiful lawlessness . . . [It represents] the yeasty independence of the average man over officialdom."[98] Another observer of juries commented: "I found myself delighting in the spectacle of entrusting whatever was at issue to a random slice of the community, rather than to a single judge. In New York City a ragtag, multiethnic jury had the proud task of deciding whether two world figures, Imelda Marcos and Adnan Kashoggi, had violated U.S. criminal laws.

[94] Adler, p. 207.

[95] In certain celebrated cases, of course, jurors choose to reap financial gain from their jury service by writing books, participating in television interviews, and cooperating with the media in other respects. Yet, they need not do so.

[96] Tocqueville, 1969, p. 272, n. 4.

[97] Adler, p. 177. He continued: "Collectively twelve jurors would seem likely to have a great deal more of [common sense] than any single judge, no matter how well versed in law or experienced in life."

[98] Abraham, p. 131, citing Thomas Lambert, *Time,* July 26, 1968, p. 80.

I imagined the jurors as hastily assembled minutemen aiming their muskets over stone walls: They were there to enforce our laws."[99]

In fact, the Anglo-American jury system developed hand in hand with the common law "which glorifies the particular situation and invites common sense."[100] Such a system is well-suited for having "a group of peers, not an expert in law, . . . decide right and wrong in each case."[101] Some years ago two professors at the University of Chicago questioned 550 American judges and drew on their experience in watching tens of thousands of jury trials. These judges concluded that the freedom of the jury to rely on its own sense of justice was one of the greatest strengths of the American legal system.[102]

A THIRD PERSPECTIVE

If one were to consult the founders of a new political regime on how best to construct their legal system, one would not want to be overly enthusiastic about relying on grand jurors or trial jurors, given their evident shortcomings. Nonetheless, one would want to be sure that the founders clearly understood the considerable benefits of each institution before they committed to a different decision making scheme. The United States, of course, faces no such new beginning. The issue is whether to reform or eliminate age-old institutions or to muddle along, cognizant of their drawbacks. Under such circumstances, after weighing the costs against the benefits, I favor eliminating grand juries yet reforming and retaining trial juries, at least in criminal cases.

Eliminating Grand Juries

The fact that states have increasingly opted to replace the traditional grand jury with the information proceeding suggests that the grand jury has largely outlived its usefulness. Eliminating the grand jury altogether, as the English did more than sixty years ago, would save considerable time and expense. This is especially significant in the federal system with its sixteen to twenty-three grand jurors and in those states that require twenty-three grand jurors. While grand juries do occasionally perform a useful function in actively investigating crime, American police and prosecutors, and even the American media, usually have ample motives—professional, personal, and sometimes political—to investigate virtually all criminal behavior.

However, whether the critics or the supporters are right, the institution of the grand jury is likely to remain a prominent feature of the federal legal system

[99] Adler, p. xiv.

[100] Philip K. Howard, *The Death of Common Sense: How Law Is Suffocating America* (New York: Warner Books, 1994), p. 23.

[101] Ibid.

[102] Abraham, p. 132.

for many years. To date, no political campaign has arisen challenging the grand jury. Indeed, while public complaints about the American legal system abound, no politician has advanced a detailed formula designed to cure the multiple ills of American justice.[103] In the case of the grand jury, constitutional obstacles will make reform especially difficult in the federal legal system. Since the Fifth Amendment guarantees grand juries in federal criminal cases, the Constitution must be amended again before the federal grand jury system can be eliminated. Although altering state grand juries might prove to be somewhat easier, the compromise of retaining the option of a grand jury may well continue to be the favored alternative. Thus, although easily criticized, the American grand jury, unfortunately, is in no immediate danger of extinction.

Reforming Trial Juries

American juries are being asked to come to an important decision in a very peculiar manner.[104] Jurors listen to the trial in public, often without much opportunity for private reflection, in surroundings that are often intimidating, or at least uncomfortably formal. They arrive at their decision in private under time pressure without assistance or advice or even the ability to ask questions of the participants. In civil cases jurors often must assess damages without the benefit of guidelines or information about verdicts in other similar cases. Despite these difficulties, jury decisions must be made either by unanimous vote or at least by the vote of an overwhelming majority.

As Judge Frank conceded: "Even twelve experienced judges, deliberating together, would not function well under the conditions we impose on the twelve inexperienced laymen."[105] Viewed from this perspective, what seems remarkable is not that the system functions poorly from time to time, but that it functions well at all! Under such difficult circumstances, rather than rushing to eliminate the trial jury, Americans might search for ways to reform the jury system to make the juror's task easier to carry out thoughtfully and conscientiously. If Americans put so much stock in the common sense of the jury and so much weight on the jury verdict, it seems only logical to redesign the jury system so that it can function as effectively as possible.

First, to promote jury deliberations that draw on different perspectives and that reduce prejudice to a bare minimum, the American legal system ought to strive to select juries that reflect the whole community: blue collar and white collar, working and retired, young adults and old, male and female, well-informed and detached, and of differing ethnic backgrounds. One authority noted: "Jurors are not disembodied angels; each hears the evidence from perspectives rooted in per-

[103] It is true that the Republican Party's "Contract with America," discussed in the elections of 1994, dealt with one aspect of legal reform: changes in **tort law** to cap the amount of money a plaintiff might receive in **punitive damages.**

[104] This discussion elaborates on that found in Frank, pp. 119–120.

[105] Ibid., p. 120.

sonal experience as well as in the experiences of others on the jury. This is why democratic deliberation requires that jurors be recruited from a cross section of the community. Whenever any group is intentionally excluded from the jury, the fullness and richness of jury debates are compromised. Lost is the distinctive knowledge and perspective that persons from the excluded group may have contributed to the collective effort. Let loose into the deliberations are the prejudices that people more freely express about a group in its absence."[106]

Voir dire sessions not only distort the cross section of the community chosen to sit on juries, they also waste judicial resources and further alienate citizens sincerely trying to carry out their civic duty. One observer noted: "Through the deceptive, frequently cynical process of jury selection, lawyers can and often do steer some of the least capable and least fair-minded people on to some of the most important cases."[107] A legal scholar concluded: "[In fact,] the most that lawyers can do at the *voir dire* stage is to rely on their rational or irrational hunches about persons concerning whom, even after extensive questioning, they know almost nothing. There is little reason to believe that in most cases a jury selected after intensive questioning is 'better' in any regard than a group of twelve jurors selected at random."[108]

"[I]n England," it has been said, "the trial starts when jury selection is over; in the United States, the trial is already over."[109] In fact, the English have already extensively reformed their method of choosing a jury.[110] One British commentator observed: "Picking the jury here requires about as much time as it takes twelve people to swear an oath."[111] Another declared: "The whole principle of the jury in England is that, as far as possible, it should be a random selection and just luck of the draw."[112] In the name of promoting impartiality,[113] the American legal system has turned jury selection into another facet of a sporting event. Yet, having psychologists and other jury consultants advise the lawyers on how to pick the most sympathetic jurors does not seem an especially thoughtful or effective method of ensuring that a jury does justice.

As has already occurred in certain states, the American system could be im-

[106] Adler, p. 10. See also ibid., p. 104: "[W]hen jurors of different ethnic groups deliberate together, they are better able to overcome their individual biases," citing "Out of the Frying Pan or into the Fire? Race and Choice of Venue After Rodney King," *Harvard Law Review* 106 (1993): 709, and "Developments: Race and the Criminal Process," *Harvard Law Review* 101 (1988): 1559.

[107] Adler, p. 50.

[108] Weinreb, p. 94.

[109] Abramson, p. 143.

[110] Adler wrote that in England "Potential jurors are picked at random from voter lists. As few as twenty prospects are called to court to be considered for a routine case. A clerk shuffles the index cards on which their names and addresses are written. The first twelve take their seats. . . . The process takes a matter of minutes or hours, instead of the days or weeks that are consumed by *voir dire* in many American trials." Adler, p. 224.

[111] Abraham, pp. 118–119, citing *Los Angeles Times,* Dec. 20, 1985, p. 1.

[112] Adler, p. 224.

[113] For an argument that impartiality has been overly emphasized as a goal in jury selection see Abramson, especially pp. 17–95.

proved and streamlined by having the judge take primary responsibility at the *voir dire* stage for briefly questioning jurors. If the lawyers took any part in the reformed *voir dire,* they certainly would not be permitted peremptory challenges. The task would be to disqualify only those jurors with clear conflicts of interest or who exhibit some definite bias that would be likely to affect their judgment in the case. A system of jury selection would work better if it firmly discouraged jury dodgers and scofflaws, yet invited compliance with respectful and efficient treatment of jurors. In particular, the actors in the American legal system ought to treat the time that jurors spend at the courthouse as a valuable resource, not a drop of which ought to be wasted by hyperadversarial questioning, disorganized and arrogant administration, and largely superfluous tasks, such as rubber-stamping indictments for prosecutors.

Once the trial begins, American juries are customarily silent and passive throughout the proceedings before them. Although no constitutional provision dictates their inactivity, jurors do not usually take notes or ask questions to clarify points that they do not understand. In many courts judges and clerks have long discouraged more active behavior. The guiding principle has been that jurors should, in the words of the Indiana Supreme Court, "register the evidence, as it is given, on the tablets of [their] memory, and not otherwise."[114] In accordance with this rationale, juries have traditionally been banned even from taking copies of the judge's instructions into the jury room.[115]

Somehow Americans have reached the extraordinary practice of having lawyers roaming all about the terrain of their case, all the while trying to figure out what the jurors are thinking without asking them. In the meantime, the jurors—trying to keep all the facts about the case in their heads without taking notes—are frequently wondering why the lawyers are being so redundant about less relevant matters when the most important ambiguities they find in the case are being ignored.

Those who argue that competent judges are regularly unable to explain the law in ordinary cases in terms that are comprehensible to the average juror may be exaggerating. Jurors are not brought together in a casual forum, nor do they listen to the instructions of the judge in a vacuum. Rather, they are brought together in a highly formal and serious setting, and they listen to the judge's instructions in the factual context of the trial they have been attending. Thus, although drafting clear jury instructions, especially in complicated civil trials, is often a challenging undertaking, the suggestion that jurors "might just as well listen to jury instructions in Chinese" goes too far.

Rather than eliminating all trial juries because laws are so complicated, reformers might focus on retaining juries in criminal cases and abolishing their use in civil cases. In any event, judges should exert themselves to instruct juries in the clearest possible language, and to clarify technical instructions should the jury ask

[114] *Dudley v. State,* 255 Ind. 176, 180, 263 N.E.2d 161 (1970). See also Abramson, p. 121, citing L. L. Bromberger, "Jurors Should Not Be Allowed to Take Notes," *Journal of the American Judicature Society* (1948): 57–58.

[115] Abraham, p. 123.

for additional assistance.[116] One federal judge pointed out: "[T]he object of a charge to a jury is not to satisfy an appellate court that you have repeated the right rigamarole of words, but to try to make jurors who are laymen understand what you are talking about."[117]

Appellate judges might also curb the desire to reverse trial judges who draft jury instructions that stray from the precise, technical language of appellate opinions. As one authority noted: "To enable all jury instructions to be made understandable to nearly all jurors, . . . [a]ppellate judges will have to cease demanding that the precise wording of court decisions and statutes be parroted by a trial judge's instructions. The new question will have to be merely whether the instructions were faithful to the law in spirit and meaning and whether they made sense to the jury."[118]

Judges might also encourage jury members to take notes, particularly during lengthy and complex trials.[119] In appropriate circumstances jurors might be given copies of documents to assist them in their deliberations. To help the jury through complicated cases, lawyers might be permitted to provide short summaries of their cases at appropriate moments in the trial.[120]

Judges might even ask that jurors submit written questions throughout the trial. To avoid disrupting the rhythm of the legal presentations and to keep lawyers from having to object to inadmissible questions and, hence, risk alienating jurors, the questions might be passed to and screened by the judge. When such questions relate to testimony, the judge might ask them of a witness,[121] or they might be distributed to the lawyers before each side rests or at least before closing arguments.

If the focus were shifted toward doing everything possible to help juries to make wise decisions, the jury might even be allowed to interrupt its deliberations to ask the judge to have the lawyers reargue a particular point. In this technologically advanced era court personnel might at least replay a television recording of a critically important part of a trial if jurors so requested during their deliberations.[122] No constitutional provision bars any of these common-sense reforms. In-

[116] One study found that three of every four jurors did not understand the highly technical instructions given in death-penalty cases in Cook County, Illinois. Carp and Stidham, p. 189.

[117] Adler, p. 130, quoting Judge Charles Wyzanski in *Cape Cod Food Products v. National Cranberry Association,* 119 F. Supp. 900, 907 (D. Mass. 1954).

[118] Adler, pp. 231–232.

[119] See Victor E. Flango, "Would Jurors Do a Better Job If They Could Take Notes?," *Judicature* 63 (April 1980): 436–443.

[120] For more extended discussions of this point see Weinreb, pp. 112–113; Larry Heuer and Steven Penrod, "Juror Notetaking and Question Asking During Trials," *Law and Human Behavior* 18 (1994): 121–150; and Larry Heuer, *Toward More Active Juries: Taking Notes and Asking Questions* (Chicago: American Judicature Society, 1991). In certain courts, under the direction of certain judges, questions by the jury have been raised at trial; however, this is by no means an established practice in either the state or federal courts. The idea of "mini-summations" is explored in Adler. See, for instance, Adler, p. 174.

[121] For an example of a major case in which this procedure seemed to work well, see ibid., pp. 237–238.

[122] If instant replay is to be used to help officials in sporting events, the same device ought to be made available to help jurors to decide far more serious matters.

stead, the chief reason that practical reforms have been resisted is simply hidebound tradition: "In the United States we have never done it that way."[123]

ASSESSING JURIES

Certainly, many of the criticisms of American juries are well founded. Dozens of countries, including Germany, Israel, and Costa Rica, have administered justice equitably without using this ancient legal institution. Various states, such as India, France,[124] and Japan, have experimented with juries and eventually dropped them as ill-suited for their cultures. While in the current era the benefits of the *grand jury* do not appear to outweigh its drawbacks, the critical problems with the *trial jury* might be ameliorated with reforms so that the legal system can continue to take advantage of the institution's considerable strengths.

Criticisms of the jury may mask a more fundamental concern with a system of laws that in various areas of life has become so detailed, abstruse, or arcane that the positive virtues of the jury are not as easily drawn upon as they once were. That raises the further issue of whether Americans should aim to reform their legal system, not by eliminating the jury, but by crafting laws that are more flexible and dependent on common sense and circumstance.[125] A different approach to law and a reformed jury system might buttress the institution's strengths and curb its weaknesses.

On balance, I am persuaded that the American people are better off for participating actively in their legal system. While eliminating the jury from civil litigation might prove to be useful, assembling groups of citizens to take a fresh look at a case against a person accused of a crime remains a positive feature of American administration of justice.

SELECTED ADDITIONAL READINGS

ABRAHAM, HENRY J. *The Judicial Process: An Introductory Analysis of the Courts of the United States, England, and France.* 6th ed. rev. New York: Oxford University Press, 1993.

ABRAMSON, JEFFREY. *We, The Jury: The Jury System and the Ideal of Democracy.* New York: Basic Books, 1994.

ADLER, STEPHEN J. *The Jury: Trial and Error in the American Courtroom.* New York: Times Books, 1995.

CLARK, L. D. *The Grand Jury: The Use and Abuse of Political Power.* Chicago: Quadrangle Books, 1975.

HANS, VALERIE P., and VIDMAR, NEIL. *Judging the Jury.* New York: Plenum Press, 1986.

HASTIE, REID, PENROD, STEVEN D., and PENNINGTON, NANCY. *Inside the Jury.* Cambridge, MA: Harvard University Press, 1983.

KASSIN, SAUL M., and WRIGHTSMAN, LAWRENCE S. *The American Jury on Trial.* New York: Hemisphere, 1988.

LITAN, ROBERT E., ed. *Verdict: Assessing the Civil Jury System.* Washington, DC: Brookings Institution, 1993.

[123] Arizona is leading the rest of the states in jury reform measures, including some of those suggested above.

[124] See Abraham, p. 108.

[125] The Howard volume explores this issue in detail.

6

The Police

Alongside the courtroom actors—judges, lawyers, and jurors—the police also play a critically important role in administering justice in the United States. What accounts for American crime rates? What types of police forces exist in the United States? How do their responsibilities differ? How has police work changed? What is the role of the police within the U.S. legal system? What constitutes illegitimate police behavior, and how serious are the problems? How might the legal system be reformed to improve the law enforcement record?

CRIME IN AMERICA[1]

The United States imprisons a higher percentage of people than any other developed country. While not all of the prison population committed violent crimes—in fact, many committed property, immigration, and possession of narcotics offenses instead—curbing violence is the single most challenging task for American law enforcement authorities. One scholar wrote: "American violence is still a historical puzzle. Other societies, as they modernized, lost much of their violent edge. . . . Economic growth, no doubt, helped. People who voted and had a bit of money and security were less prone to violent crime. This may have been the case in the United States as well. There is some evidence that serious crime did decline in the nineteenth century. But the level of crime remained higher than in other countries."[2] One study of crime in western societies over a recent 40-year period

[1] Two notable recent works with differing perspectives on crime are James Q. Wilson, *Crime* (San Francisco: ICS Press, 1995) and Kathlyn Taylor Gaubatz, *Crime in the Public Mind* (Ann Arbor: University of Michigan Press, 1995).

[2] Lawrence M. Friedman, *Crime and Punishment in American History* (New York: Basic Books, 1993), p. 175. See also Charles E. Silberman, *Criminal Violence, Criminal Justice* (New York: Random House, 1975), p. 19.

concluded: "[R]ates for all categories of crime are approximately three times higher [in America] than in other developed nations and the differences have been growing."[3] Indeed, the number of homicides and rapes reported in New York City in a single day sometimes exceeds the number reported in a year in major cities like Tokyo and Helsinki.[4]

Several factors help to explain the puzzle of American violence, though they by no means entirely resolve it. Perhaps most important, American culture has never distinguished itself as especially law-abiding. The Boston Strangler, Billy the Kid, Bonnie and Clyde, Ma Barker, John Dillinger, Al Capone, and many other outlaws and criminals have cast long shadows across American society. To some extent the violence that Hollywood, network television, and the writers of mysteries and novels capitalize upon reflects American culture. To some extent it shapes that culture. Whichever is the hen and whichever the egg, popular culture is likely to have played a substantial role in encouraging American violence.

In 1787 Thomas Jefferson remarked, "A little rebellion now and then is a good thing,"[5] and mob violence of varying severity may be traced from American colonial history to the present day. A half a century later Abraham Lincoln declared that violence was America's chief problem, and he lamented "the increasing disregard for law that pervades the country."[6] While American lawlessness is nothing new, different historical periods are closely associated with different forms of violent behavior. Lynchings repressed freed slaves in the south; robbers repeatedly struck frontier banks and **vigilantes** chased some of them down; underworld figures exerted authority with execution-style killings and other gangland violence; and urban rioters looted and burned private property to protest various events. Today, warring drug traffickers and urban gangs defend their turf with "rumbles" and driveby shootings.

Deeply rooted American values may actually encourage violence. Unlike people in more repressed, traditional, or aristocratic societies, Americans have always valued individualism, self-fulfillment, economic success, and social climbing.[7] The idea that one should try to improve one's lot in life is far more deeply ingrained in American culture than is the competing idea that one should know one's place and act in an appropriate and lawful manner. A noted sociologist and political scientist concluded:

> Since the emphasis is on success in the United States, those individuals or groups who feel themselves handicapped . . . are under strong pressure to "innovate," to use whatever means they can find to gain recognition or money. This pressure to be creative may be reflected in . . . the development of new and risky industries by those of recent immigrant background . . . or low

[3] Louise I. Shelley, "American Crime: An International Anomaly?" *Comparative Social Research* 8 (1985), cited in Seymour Martin Lipset, *American Exceptionalism: A Double-Edged Sword* (New York: W. W. Norton, 1996), p. 46.

[4] Friedman, p. xiv.

[5] Thomas Jefferson, from a 1787 letter to James Madison.

[6] Silberman, p. 21.

[7] See Lipset, pp. 47–48.

> status who are prevented by lack of education, skill, economic resources, and by social discrimination from advancing up economic ladders. The pressure to succeed may also lead individuals and groups to serve social needs through employment *outside* the law. . . . The comparatively high crime rate in America, both in the form of lower-class rackets, robbery and theft, and white-collar and business [offenses] . . . may, therefore, be perceived as a consequence of the stress laid on success.[8]

As the American population has become increasingly larger and more developed, modern, urban, and antiauthoritarian, crime has risen among youth, and many jurisdictions have had to contend with more violent crime spread more evenly through society. Unpredictable violence has induced special fear. Rare is the state that has yet to experience the terror of a psychotic serial killer or the shock of a domestic or international terrorist incident. Dire inner-city problems, including the proliferation of gangs and high levels of narcotics consumption, have plagued major metropolitan areas. Violent social ills such as child abuse and domestic violence have surfaced throughout society.

Responding to this violence and simultaneously feeding on it is the popular view that the U.S. Constitution protects the right of the individual, as opposed to the right of a local militia, to bear arms.[9] In stark contrast to popular attitudes in Britain, Japan, and many other countries, the idea that individual gun ownership is legitimate, and perhaps even sensible, remains entrenched in American culture. With the strong support of police chiefs and police associations, various **gun control laws** have been passed regulating the sale and use of guns by requiring licenses, prohibiting concealed weapons, and imposing other such restrictions. Nevertheless, in comparison to most other advanced countries, guns abound in the United States. Indeed, perhaps no other country can point to mainstream political groups that vigorously defend the right of individuals to own military assault rifles or bullets that fragment upon impact.

Further exacerbating the problem of violence in American society is the towering problem of illegal narcotic use. The effort to pass stricter laws prohibiting narcotics trafficking and possession has swollen the ranks of prisoners and diverted law enforcement resources away from other crime-control tasks. The widespread use of narcotics has also kept the price of narcotics artificially high[10] and

[8] Ibid., p. 48. Sociologist Robert Merton likewise observed: "[V]ice and crime constitute a 'normal' response to a situation where the cultural emphasis upon pecuniary success has been absorbed, but where there is little access to conventional and legitimate means for becoming successful. . . . In this setting, a cardinal American virtue, 'ambition,' produces a cardinal American vice, 'deviant behavior.'" Charles Silberman, *Criminal Violence, Criminal Justice* (New York: Random House, 1975), p. 87.

[9] The Constitution reads: "A well regulated Militia, being necessary to the security of a free State, the right of the people to keep and bear Arms, shall not be infringed." U.S. Constitution, Amendment II.

[10] For analysis of this issue, see the following articles by Ethan A. Nadelmann, "Drug Prohibition in the United States: Costs, Consequences, and Alternatives," *Science* 245 (Sept. 1, 1989): 939–47; "U.S. Drug Policy: A Bad Export," *Foreign Policy* 70 (1988): 1–39; and "The Case for Legalization," *Public Interest* 92 (1988): 3–31.

stimulated crime as addicts desperate for drugs prostitute themselves, steal, rob, and even kill for money.

On a more positive note, the high crime rates may also be the result of police and prosecutors carrying out more vigorous and sophisticated crime investigation than do authorities in various other countries. Exposing criminal activity is rewarded in the United States with plaudits and promotions, not just among law enforcement personnel but also among prosecutors and among journalists engaged in investigative reporting. Criminal activity that might remain undisturbed elsewhere is often rooted out in the United States.

By the same token, however, the American criminal justice system seems to have failed to capture, try, and punish enough wrongdoers with sufficient severity to deter criminals and to lower crime rates substantially. Those considering criminal activity often correctly believe that, although they may ultimately be caught in the act,[11] the odds suggest that they will not be caught immediately. Moreover, the penal system's record of rehabilitating criminals to curb **recidivism,** or backsliding into crime, is also uneven at best.

Each of these factors helps to explain why American crime rates are substantially higher than those in France, Canada, and Britain, Japan, Australia, and Singapore, Germany, Taiwan, and Costa Rica, or many other advanced states. The differences between crime rates in the United States and crime rates in other countries are so great, however, that one is left wondering whether all these factors taken together adequately account for the ugly streak of violent crime that runs through American society.

TYPES OF POLICE FORCES

The Local Police

To help to counter high crime rates, American politicians have long turned to hiring police. American governments currently employ more than half a million police officers.[12] The first order of business for local city and county "cops" is to maintain law and order and restore peace in the community when necessary. Carrying out these tasks within communities that include unruly, disrespectful, and violent individuals can be a most challenging and stressful task. One authority noted:

> [T]he patrol officer, working alone or with one partner, must impose authority on people who are unpredictable, apprehensive, and often hostile. Most of the time when an officer on patrol is summoned, by radio call or passing citizen, he or she can expect to encounter a situation in which great discretion must be exercised over matters of the utmost importance (life and death,

[11] See Silberman, pp. 75–78.

[12] Robert A. Carp and Ronald Stidham, *Judicial Process in America,* 3d ed. rev. (Washington, DC: Congressional Quarterly Press, 1996), p. 164.

> honor and dishonor) involving frightened, drunk, quarrelsome, confused, angry, injured, evasive, or violent people. The officer in this situation must "take charge." At least in large American cities . . . the uniform and badge do not automatically signify authority to which people will defer. The officer's behavior must supplement and extend such authority as the law may confer.[13]

In contrast to civil law societies which usually rely on a judicial police force to investigate crime, American communities also call upon the local police to act as detectives. When a crime is discovered, whether murder, robbery, or theft, the police tend to be called immediately to the scene. Police then secure the crime scene, calm onlookers, find and preserve evidence, identify and question witnesses, provide comfort to victims, and occasionally apprehend suspects.

Apart from taking control of volatile situations and investigating crime, local police perform various other tasks. Often, they act as "catch-all" authorities whom citizens call when assistance is needed and no one else comes to mind.[14] In the course of a typical week, a suburban policeman might be called upon to investigate a ringing car alarm, release a small child from a locked bathroom, help bring down a kitten stuck in the branches of a tree, and urge quarreling family members to resolve their dispute amicably. Where people of another culture might rely on a neighbor, a community elder, a religious leader, or some other private or public figure to solve or assist problems that no other official may be qualified to perform, Americans habitually pick up the phone, dial 911, and expect a prompt response from the police.[15]

In calling upon their local police so frequently, Americans need skilled officers who, if pressed, can quiet rowdy partygoers, subdue a robbery suspect high on drugs, mediate between neighbors, identify and arrest drunk drivers, negotiate in a hostage situation, determine who is committing neighborhood burglaries, and prepare evidence for trial. To do all this within the bounds of an increasingly complicated, and perhaps less and less logical, set of criminal procedure rules is indeed a tall order! Unduly high expectations may explain why so many Americans grow frustrated with their police, and so many police with their jobs.

To prepare officers to handle such varied tasks, both instructors in police academies and experienced officers engaged in on-the-job training have to sup-

[13] James Q. Wilson, *Bureaucracy: What Government Agencies Do and Why They Do It* (New York: Basic Books, 1989), p. 37.

[14] One study found: "Two thirds or more of the average police officer's time is spent in duties other than law enforcement." Lawrence S. Wrightsman, *Psychology and the Legal System* (Pacific Grove, CA: Brooks/Cole, 1987), p. 91, citing James Q. Wilson, *Varieties of Police Behavior: The Management of Law and Order in Eight Counties* (Cambridge, MA: Harvard University Press, 1978). See also Lloyd L. Weinreb, *Denial of Justice: Criminal Process in the United States* (New York: The Free Press, 1977), p. 15.

[15] One authority wrote: "[C]ars, radios, stationhouses . . . are deployed to allow the police to perform all their regular assignments, including peacekeeping patrols, and still to respond swiftly whenever and wherever they are needed within their jurisdiction. Large items in the police budget . . . increase their readiness to respond: fleets of cruising police cars connected by a sophisticated communications system, 'call boxes,' strategically located sub-stations. The amount of time it takes the police to appear after they are summoned, what they call 'response time' is regarded as a critical indicator of effectiveness . . ." Weinreb, pp. 15–16.

plement such subjects as ballistics, target practice, crowd and traffic control, and hand-to-hand combat with information about human behavior. Rather than simply focusing on dexterity with a nightstick or close familiarity with back alleys, types of weapons, or suspicious hangouts, able police officers sometimes draw on knowledge of different languages and cultures, of laws of evidence and procedure, of psychology, penology, criminology, and sociology. Knowledge in these areas will help inexperienced cops to become streetwise as quickly as possible.

Supervising the local police is an official who in cities is customarily appointed by the mayor and is called the **chief of police,** and who in counties is customarily elected and is called the **sheriff.** The ranks of police leadership also ordinarily include **deputies,** and, in large police forces, intermediate commanders and sergeants. Substantial police forces are also usually divided into different specialties. A typical sheriff's department for a county might be split into traffic, civil, and criminal divisions. These might be supported by an administrative division in charge of recordkeeping and identification, and a corrections division that supervises the jail.

Major urban police forces are even more specialized. A police officer in Boston, for instance, might be part of a traffic unit or part of a **vice** group suppressing narcotics, prostitution, and gambling. He or she might be on patrol with a **beat** covering a particular city neighborhood, or on detective work investigating crimes that have already been committed. Detectives may themselves be divided by specialty: a **homicide** detective, for instance, would investigate only murder cases. A Boston police officer might even be a member of the elite Strategic Weapons and Assault Team (SWAT), used most commonly when terrorists or criminals have taken hostages inside a building or airplane.

To succeed at each of these tasks requires diverse skills and different temperaments. A successful patrol officer is able to establish a long-term rapport with people in a neighborhood who will come forward with information necessary to help to maintain law and order. An experienced officer on patrol will know who are the troublemakers and what are the most common types of disputes in the neighborhood. He or she will have the interpersonal skills necessary to nurture positive community relations, yet also to resolve situations of considerable tension, such as the often dangerous **domestic disputes.**[16] When violence does occur, the officer must be able to do more than merely show the badge: He or she must also be capable of restoring order forcibly and effectively.

Detective work calls upon some of these same talents and characteristics. In order to solve crimes, a detective must be able to elicit immediate support, even from strangers. The best crime solvers are also experienced in handling and assessing evidence, analyzing fingerprinting and **ballistics** evidence, and understanding **forensic medicine,** that is, medical knowledge as it is applied to legal ends and the solution of crimes. Increasingly, even local detectives must be familiar with **DNA fin-**

[16] One study found that 20 percent of police deaths and 40 percent of police injuries occurred when officers intervened in family disputes. Wrightsman, p. 87, citing M. Bard, *Training Police as Specialists in Family Crisis Intervention* (Washington, DC: U.S. Government Printing Office, 1970).

gerprinting, that is, the linking of physical evidence found at a crime scene, such as blood, semen, or hair, bone or skin fragments, with a particular suspect.

As important as such technical knowledge may be, detective work also requires a knack for analytical reasoning. Some years ago, detectives in a small town in Connecticut asked a retired policeman named Al Seedman, former chief of detectives in New York City, to help with a particularly difficult case. A skeleton had been discovered in the woods close by the town, and the **coroner** determined that the man had been dead for about three months. The police initially assumed that the man's family would eventually report him missing, but after another three months passed the body remained unclaimed. Here is the detective's account of what happened:

> Once I got the answer to one question I was able to give [the detectives] . . . a method. I asked whether this skeleton showed signs of any dental work, which can usually be identified by a dentist. But, according to the local cops, they said no, although the skeleton had crummy teeth. No dental work at all. Now, if he'd been wealthy, he could have afforded to have his teeth fixed. If he'd been poor, welfare would have paid. If he was a union member, their medical plan would have covered it. So this fellow was probably working at a low-paying, non-unionized job, but making enough to keep off of public assistance. Also, since he didn't match up to any family's missing-person report, he was probably single, living alone in an apartment or hotel. His landlord had never reported him missing, either, so most likely he was also behind on his rent and the landlord probably figured he had just skipped. But even if he had escaped his landlord, he would never have escaped the tax man.
>
> The rest was simple. I told these cops to wait until the year is up. Then they can go to the tax authorities and get a printout of all single males making less than $10,000 a year but more than the welfare ceiling who paid withholding tax in the first three quarters but not in the fourth. Chances are the name of their skeleton will be on that printout.[17]

Alongside the local police, states customarily employ either highway patrols or state police, often referred to as state troopers. These police often cruise state roads on the lookout for traffic violations. However, the work of state police need not be confined to patrolling highways and often varies markedly from one jurisdiction to another. Thus, state police often use their superior resources to investigate serious crimes that occur within a state.

The Federal Police

Americans traditionally have considered law enforcement to be a local and certainly a domestic process. To this day, much crime remains local—the shoplifter, burglar, car thief, or murderer may well live relatively near the crime scene. However, throughout the twentieth century more and more crime has crossed state

[17] Wrightsman, p. 86, citing A. A. Seedman and P. Hellman, *Chief!* (New York: Arthur Fields, 1974), pp. 4–5.

lines. To explore the new nationalization of law enforcement,[18] one might consider how markedly police work has changed in the course of American history.

From the Revolutionary War through the end of the nineteenth century, police in cities and towns investigated the vast bulk of American crime. Occasionally, authorities might send the celebrated Pinkerton detectives[19] to chase down some notorious fugitive who had fled to another state or abroad. More normally, however, a criminal who had vanished was thought to be someone else's problem. Indeed, when an individual entered the country, immigration authorities were usually ignorant of their past criminal acts.[20] For much of the period, Americans firmly resisted secret police, national police, and undercover operations of all kinds. All were associated with tyrannical rule and were considered to be thoroughly un-American. None were seen as vital to combating the types of crime that most concerned the average American.

Over the years, however, this traditional view changed. Criminals became more sophisticated; the local police became more professional;[21] and new attitudes and institutions developed. For instance, the use of **informants** and **confidential sources** came to be viewed as a legitimate[22] and vital weapon in the law-enforcement arsenal.[23] When the victim can identify no suspects, when no witnesses are available, when the criminal leaves no incriminating evidence at the scene, and when the authorities do not catch the criminal **fencing**[24] the stolen goods or bragging about the crime, the police may be helpless without additional information supplied by informants.[25]

[18] For an extended discussion of the following points see Ethan A. Nadelmann, *Cops Across Borders: The Internationalization of U.S. Criminal Law Enforcement* (University Park: Pennsylvania State University Press, 1993).

[19] The Pinkertons, of course, also operated within the United States, often hired by private companies. See generally ibid., pp. 49, 55–60, and 99–100, and James D. Horan, *The Pinkertons: The Detective Dynasty That Made History* (New York: Crown, 1967). One example of the Pinkertons at work abroad came when American authorities sent them to track down the notorious outlaws, Robert LeRoy Parker and Harry Longbaugh, better known as Butch Cassidy and the Sundance Kid, who were probably killed in Bolivia by that country's army, not by Pinkerton agents. Nadelmann, *Cops Across Borders,* p. 60, n. 141.

[20] When serving as secretary of state in 1793, Thomas Jefferson remarked: "The laws of this country take no notice of crimes committed out of their jurisdiction. The most atrocious offender coming within their pale is received by them as an innocent man, and they have authorized no one to seize and deliver him." Nadelmann, *Cops Across Borders,* p. viii. One might note that, while the U.S. Constitution authorizes the extradition of an alleged criminal from one state to another (Article IV, sec. 2), extradition treaties between the U.S. and other countries had not yet come into vogue.

[21] See Samuel Walker, *A Critical History of Police Reform: The Emergence of Professionalism* (Lexington, MA.: Lexington Books, 1977); Robert Fogelson, *Big-City Police* (Cambridge, MA: Harvard University Press, 1977); and Craig D. Uchida, "The Development of the American Police: An Historical Overview," in Roger G. Dunham and Geoffrey P. Albert, eds., *Critical Issues in Policing: Contemporary Readings* (Prospect Heights, IL: Waveland Press, 1989), pp. 14–30.

[22] In a series of cases in the 1950s and 1960s the Supreme Court authorized the use of informants or their information in different circumstances. See *Lee v. United States,* 343 U.S. 747 (1952), *Rovario v. United States,* 353 U.S. 53 (1957), *Lopez v. United States,* 373 U.S. 427 (1963), and *Hoffa v. United States,* 385 U.S. 293 (1966).

[23] See James Q. Wilson, *The Investigators: Managing FBI and Narcotics Agents* (New York: Basic Books, 1978), pp. 61–88, and Nadelmann, *Cops Across Borders,* especially pp. 208–221.

[24] A fence is a dealer in stolen goods. See generally Darrell J. Steffensmeier, *The Fence: In the Shadow of Two Worlds* (Lanham, MD: Rowan & Littlefield, 1986).

[25] Wilson, *Investigators,* p. 61.

Disgruntled co-conspirators or hangers-on, known by the slang terms "snitches" or "stool pigeons," are usually the most valuable informants. Some lesser member of a criminal gang may be able to provide critical evidence against much higher figures or introduce undercover cops to kingpins. A source inside a criminal gang who feeds information to authorities can disrupt the entire organization, leading to multiple arrests and the discovery of valuable evidence. Even individuals who merely travel in the same circles as criminals may be able to give the police valuable leads. Moreover, confidential sources, such as doormen, bartenders, taxi drivers, flight attendants, maids and custodians, and others who can unobtrusively listen in on conversations or keep watch for suspicious activity can also help the police to combat crime.

Police recruit informants in various ways. Many potential informants are threatened with arrest and prosecution[26] if they fail to cooperate. If they go to work for the authorities, many are coaxed with promises of money, dropped charges, lesser sentences, or even places in the **witness protection program.** One scholar observed of recruiting informants:

> Money is usually a factor, although not necessarily the initial incentive. That may come from the fear of a participant in a drug deal who decides he wants out, the vengeance of a jilted lover, the self-interest of a business competitor or political opponent, the need for self-esteem, a sense of identity with police agents, or simply a sense of friendship with a law enforcement agent. Sometimes the motive is nothing more than a citizen's sense of obligation to report a crime he or she has witnessed.[27]

As technology improved, the pace of change in police work picked up greater momentum. In large part, advances in police work responded to more sophisticated crime. As the means of travel multiplied and quickened, criminals could become more mobile. As communications developed, criminals could better organize their activities and networks. Yet, police could also use phones and jets to track down suspects and exchange information.[28] Informants and undercover officers could be wired to record conversations, and hidden cameras and two-way mirrors could be used to monitor criminal activity. "Computers," as one scholar wrote, ". . . presented new opportunities for criminals, both in defrauding legitimate actors and in setting up their own operations, but they also provided police with more efficient means of keeping track of criminals, exchanging intelligence . . . , and creating data bases on criminals and criminal activities."[29]

Thus, much more American police work has come to involve "plain clothes" officers (who wear ordinary clothes, not uniforms), secret operations, and

[26] Arrest or the threat of arrest is "the principal means of informant recruitment in the United States." Nadelmann, *Cops Across Borders,* p. 209. See also Wilson, *Investigators,* p. 66.

[27] Nadelmann, *Cops Across Borders,* pp. 210–211. Although Nadelmann was referring specifically to the recruitment of informants abroad, his analysis applies equally in the domestic context.

[28] See ibid., p. 105.

[29] Ibid., p. 105.

surveillance by video, wiretap, and even satellite.[30] Hypnosis, lie detectors, and electronic "bugs" and other wire-tapping devices[31] have become commonplace tools, and American cops pride themselves on being the world's most artful at trapping criminals in undercover operations, sometimes called "stings." Even the **controlled delivery,** once considered an especially risky technique, is now standard practice, particularly in countering narcotics trafficking. In a controlled delivery the authorities "let the drugs walk"—that is, rather than seizing a shipment of narcotics, they permit it to go forward under tight surveillance. In that way they hope to arrest more of the criminals involved and find out more information about the gang and its operations.[32] Police work in the United States today thus contrasts starkly with that at the turn of the century, and the public has come to accept, and even applaud the use of many new crime-fighting tools.[33]

In the midst of these changes, both stimulating and responding to them, were new ideas as to the worth and appropriate responsibilities of federal police units. In the latter half of the nineteenth century the first step toward a national, or federal, police force came in response to the problems of counterfeit money and then of assassinations—a form of political violence new to American politics. The administration of Abraham Lincoln established the Secret Service to curb and investigate criminals counterfeiting currency.[34] The assassinations of Lincoln in 1865, President James Garfield in 1881, and President William McKinley in 1901, brought the Secret Service new responsibilities, but also a larger budget and more agents. In the twentieth century, the Secret Service has devoted substantial resources to protecting American politicians, and diplomats and other official visitors to the United States. And, since the assassination of President John Kennedy in 1963, the Secret Service has prevented the assassination[35] of subsequent presidents—a difficult task since politicians customarily mix with crowds of people at political rallies, parades, and other functions.

The next major development in the nationalization of American law enforcement occurred between 1908 and 1935[36] when in one step after another the

[30] For information on surveillance laws and techniques, see Gary T. Marx, *Undercover: Police Surveillance in America* (Berkeley: University of California Press, 1988) and James G. Carr, *The Law of Electronic Surveillance,* 2d ed. rev. (New York: Clark, Boardman, 1985). U.S. wiretapping law may be found in Title III of the Omnibus Crime Control and Safe Streets Act of 1970 at 18 U.S.C. 2510–2520 and in the Foreign Intelligence Surveillance Act of 1978 at 50 U.S.C. 1801–1811.

[31] The leading case authorizing wiretapping, but requiring a court order upon a showing of probable cause, is *Katz v. United States,* 389 U.S. 347 (1967).

[32] P. D. Cutting, "The Technique of Controlled Delivery as a Weapon in Dealing with Illicit Traffic in Narcotic Drugs and Psychotropic Substances," *Bulletin on Narcotics* 35 (Oct.–Dec. 1983), pp. 15–22, cited in Nadelmann, *Cops Across Borders,* pp. 235–236.

[33] See Nadelmann, *Cops Across Borders,* p. 469.

[34] For information on investigating counterfeit dollars, see ibid., p. 166, n. 130.

[35] Among the near misses have been the assault on President Gerald Ford and the shooting of President Ronald Reagan in Washington, DC.

[36] The Justice Department procured funding for its agents in 1908; in 1909 the unit became known as the Bureau of Investigation, and twenty-six years later as the Federal Bureau of Investigation; by 1934 these national police agents had gained the authority to carry arms and conduct searches and seizures. See Nadelmann, pp. 52–53.

Department of Justice created a police force to assist state and local police and to investigate crimes that were somehow national in scope. Eventually, under the guidance of its director, J. Edgar Hoover,[37] this Federal Bureau of Investigation (FBI) became more widely recognized and more highly professional than any other American police unit.

Although certain municipal police units maintained impressive reputations, comparable with and occasionally superior to their national counterparts in certain fields of policework, the FBI soon differed from the average local police force in size, methods, resources, and hiring standards. FBI agents scorned haphazard or intuitive methods of investigation and emphasized instead the "scientific" solution to crimes. While photo and fingerprint identification certainly predated the FBI, the local police could not compete with the breadth of information in FBI files on criminals, including extensive personal data on each one. The FBI also favored wiretaps and other methods of electronic surveillance to try to stop criminal activity before it occurred.

Over the years FBI agents, initially known as "G-men" or "Government men," succeeded in breaking up various bands of notorious criminals. Capitalizing on its successes, on the publicity and propaganda that flowed from the director's office, and on the lobbying skills of Director Hoover, the FBI came to occupy a large building in Washington, DC, with thousands of agents creating elaborate, and eventually computerized, systems for identifying criminals.

The FBI now fights crime by investigating all violations of federal laws that have not been specifically assigned to other agencies. FBI agents thus have jurisdiction over a wide spectrum of criminal activity, including kidnapping, bank robbery, **extortion,** civil rights violations, espionage, and assaults upon federal officials, including federal judges. Even interstate transportation of stolen property falls within the FBI's bailiwick. Moreover, the FBI cooperates with local, state, and national law enforcement authorities in helping to train officers, analyze laboratory samples, identify fingerprints, and exchange information on criminal activity.

As the FBI grew swiftly in middle of the twentieth century, some of the stories about the prowess of its agents and their amazing crime-solving feats were propaganda efforts,[38] designed to deter criminals, increase public respect for the bureau and its director, and maintain the flow of funding from Congress. Moreover, on occasion, the FBI abused its authority by collecting embarrassing information on American academics, and political, religious, and civil rights leaders, rather than on criminals. Nonetheless, the FBI was a new kind of national police force with generally higher professional standards than found in other police forces. In comparison with city, county, and state police, FBI agents tended to be better trained and educated, more intelligent, and more adept at using technological advances, especially in forensic medicine and science, to fight crime. The overall suc-

[37] Among the scholarly works on Hoover are Richard Gil Powers, *Secrecy and Power: The Life of J. Edgar Hoover* (New York: The Free Press, 1987) and Athan G. Theoharis and John Stuart Cox, *The Boss: J. Edgar Hoover and the Great American Inquisition* (Philadelphia: Temple University Press, 1988).

[38] See Friedman, p. 271.

cess of the FBI thus contributed directly to the creation of various other national police forces designed to deal with particular violations of U.S. law.

Alongside the Secret Service and FBI, a host of other, smaller U.S. police forces came to be charged with particular duties that were somehow national in scope. The U.S. Customs Service, for instance, tries to ensure that those entering the United States properly pay custom duties and that contraband, including illegal drugs, is duly seized.[39] From its roots in the old Bureau of Prohibition and the Federal Bureau of Narcotics, the Drug Enforcement Administration (DEA), now with agents in more than five dozen countries, curbs the flow of illegal narcotics across American borders. The U.S. Border Patrol has responsibility for stopping illegal immigration, a particular problem on the long land border between the United States and Mexico. The U.S. Marshals Service tracks down fugitives who have fled abroad and controls prisoners in federal custody who are en route to court appearances or to prison.[40]

Twentieth-century American governments not only promoted the growth of national police forces, they also criminalized an increasingly wide range of behavior.[41] Much human activity has been declared illegal that in previous times, in 1950 or 1900 or 1800, would have been considered legal, if perhaps unethical or immoral. Indeed, under the pressure of technological advances, criminal law is growing so swiftly that various present-day crimes would have been legal in 1960.

Money laundering, income tax evasion, and the sale and possession of once-legal narcotics are all examples of activities that American legislatures criminalized during the twentieth century. American governmental bodies are now policing securities and commodities markets and attempting to protect citizens by regulating foods, prescription drugs, and other consumer goods. Criminal penalties now attach to activities ranging from passing bad checks to computer fraud, from environmental degradation to portraying child pornography on the Internet. If all American police had to do was to enforce the relatively simple and traditional laws against murder, robbery, and theft, there would be no urgent motive to nationalize law enforcement. Instead, in order to combat the many new types of crimes, especially **organized crime** and **white-collar crime,**[42] authorities have had to broaden the scope of their endeavors.

Although the existence of national police forces seems perfectly natural to twentieth-century Americans, suspicious early critics of the Secret Service argued

[39] See U.S. Customs Service, *A History of Enforcement in the United States Customs Service, 1789–1875* (Washington, DC: Treasury Department, 1986).

[40] U.S. marshals also carry out judicial orders issued by the U.S. federal courts, determine in which prisons convicted offenders should serve their time, and undertake various other responsibilities. See Henry J. Abraham, *The Judicial Process: An Introductory Analysis of the Courts of the United States, England, and France,* 6th ed. rev. (New York: Oxford University Press, 1993), pp. 161–162. For a more general view, see Frederick S. Calhoun, *The Lawmen: United States Marshals and Their Deputies, 1789–1989* (Washington, DC: Smithsonian Institution Press, 1990).

[41] See Nadelmann, *Cops Across Borders,* pp. 1–2. See also Ethan A. Nadelmann, *Criminalization and Crime Control in International Society* (New York: Oxford University Press, 1995).

[42] White-collar crimes are nonviolent economic crimes that involve fraud, collusion, or deception. See Friedman, *Crime and Punishment,* p. 290, citing sociologist Edwin Sutherland.

that this un-American institution would surely develop into an oppressive, European-style national police unit. In fact, unlike the FBI, the Secret Service has not been known for serious misconduct. However, if one takes "un-American" to mean that which is uncharacteristic of traditional American culture, the early critics of this nationalized police force were certainly correct. The Secret Service was a harbinger of a wholly new and quite foreign development in American police work. Yet, given the steady growth in the powers of the federal government over so many aspects of national life, and with the extraordinary technological changes in American society in the last century, nationalized police forces may have been destined to become an integral feature of American law enforcement, working alongside state and local law enforcement agents.

From National to International Police Work

Since World War II, and especially since about 1970, much crime has come to have international dimensions. As the world has become more interdependent and as transportation and communication have become far swifter and more reliable, international criminals—that is, criminals whose illicit enterprises cross national boundaries—have become more sophisticated and their objectives more sweeping. In the second half of the twentieth century, police forces have had to break up networks of organized criminals with far more international connections than ever before. Federal and, occasionally, local law enforcement agents have had to try to cope with hostage-taking and other forms of terrorist violence, and national and corporate espionage as well. National police forces must contend with the illicit trade in certain weapons and in high-level technology. Illicit trade in these goods might have dangerous national security consequences.[43] In less than a century, the challenge of controlling crime has moved from an almost wholly local context to an increasingly national setting, and now on to an even more challenging international domain.

Today many criminals commit a crime in one country and flee to another. Even more important, under international and domestic laws someone need not step outside the borders of one country to commit a crime under the laws of another. For instance, most of the world's drug kingpins have conspired to import narcotics into their largest market—the United States. They may never have set foot outside Colombia or Bolivia or the Golden Triangle of Southeast Asia, but they still have been committing crimes under American law by conspiring to import narcotics into the United States.

American criminal organizations have long tentacles reaching abroad, and many criminal networks operating in the United States actually have central headquarters in other countries. The Colombian cocaine cartels and their Mexican middlemen, the Chinese **triads,** the Japanese **yakuza,** and the Jamaican **posses** all undertake illicit business in the United States. International crime also includes

[43] See August Bequai, *Technocrimes* (Lexington, MA: Lexington Books, 1987) and Linda Melvern, David Hebditch, and Nick Anning, *Techno-Bandits* (Boston: Houghton Mifflin, 1984).

the complicated networks of money launderers and other white-collar criminals who hide assets derived from American criminal activity in countries with a reputation for keeping financial matters secret, such as Switzerland, Liechtenstein, Panama, and the Cayman Islands. For all such individuals, one scholar observed, "[F]oreign territories and alien systems offer safe havens, lucrative smuggling opportunities, and legal shields and thickets to disguise their criminal enterprises."[44]

All this international criminal activity has brought about an international response in law enforcement circles. Authorities in the United States and many other countries have had to extend their police efforts out beyond their borders: "The challenge [police officers] . . . confront is to nullify the advantages that criminals derive from operating across borders and to reduce, circumvent, or transcend the frictions that hamper international law enforcement."[45]

Although various transnational organizations have been created to multiply links among police from different countries—most notably, perhaps, the International Association of Chiefs of Police and Interpol[46]—most of the cooperation has come through ad hoc problem solving as low- and medium-level officials in different countries contact one another requesting assistance in dealing with specific criminal activities. Cooperation is often effective since police tend to share crime-fighting values and can identify with one another's problems and concerns. "[P]olice," one authority observed, "tend to place a higher priority than most politicians on going after criminals, and a lower priority on political considerations and sensitivities of national sovereignty. The common sentiment that a cop is a cop no matter whose badge he or she wears, and that a criminal is a criminal no matter what his or her citizenship is or where the crime was committed, serves as a kind of transgovernmental value system overriding political conflicts between governments. It provides, in many ways, the oil and glue of international law enforcement."[47]

One of the most potent tools that American police and prosecutors wield

[44] Nadelmann, *Cops Across Borders,* p. 6. Nadelmann later observed: "As transnational securities transactions, banking exchanges, commercial ventures, and credit card charges increased dramatically, so too did the number of frauds associated with them. One need only assume that the criminal proportion of overall transnational economic activity has remained constant to conclude that the overall magnitude of transnational criminal activity must have increased dramatically." Ibid., p. 104.

[45] Ibid.

[46] See Malcolm Anderson, *Policing the World: Interpol and the Politics of International Police Co-operation* (New York: Oxford University Press, 1989); Michael Fooner, *Interpol: Issues in World Crime and International Criminal Justice* (New York: Plenum Press, 1989); and Trevor Meldal-Johnson and Vaughn Young, *The Interpol Connection: An Inquiry into the International Criminal Police Organization* (New York: Dial Press, 1979).

[47] Nadelmann, *Cops Across Borders,* p. 201. Julie Bunck and I observed: "[A]n official who wishes to gain custody of a suspect who has fled abroad will soon contend with the sovereignty of that foreign country. The police officer who wishes to investigate criminal activity that extends abroad, or who would like to hire informants or carry out undercover operations abroad, must confront the implications of sovereignty. So, too, is sovereignty uppermost in the mind of the prosecutor who needs evidence to be collected abroad for use in a domestic court." Michael Ross Fowler and Julie Marie Bunck, *Law, Power, and the Sovereign State: The Evolution and Application of the Concept of Sovereignty* (University Park: Pennsylvania State University Press, 1995), p. 158.

against organized international criminals is the charge of **conspiracy.** (A wag once called conspiracy the "darling of the prosecutor's nursery"!) Under American law[48] a person is guilty of conspiracy to commit a crime if, to further a criminal enterprise, that individual agrees with others that they will engage in criminal conduct or he or she agrees to aid them in planning or committing a crime.

Under American law a conspiracy can continue over time. Conspirators can drop in and out of the planning, and they remain guilty of the crime of conspiracy. Moreover, a conspirator need not know all the details of the plan. To be a conspirator, one need not know the part that all the others are playing or even their names. All that the authorities must prove is that the conspirator knew the unlawful purpose of the conspiracy and that he or she agreed to become a party to a criminal act. So, police work now entails gathering evidence on those who conspire to commit a criminal act in the United States, even if they live in a foreign country far from American shores.

Since the nature of crime has changed, so too has the approach to immobilizing criminals been transformed. To immobilize a criminal, law enforcement agents must accomplish five separate tasks.[49] They must identify who is breaking the law, locate and arrest those criminals, seize their assets, gather the evidence necessary to convict them, and securely imprison them.

One can readily imagine how internationalized those tasks have become with regard to the most serious crimes. While in the past police officers rarely ventured beyond their jurisdictions, authorities now might have to go to Hong Kong to identify the leader of a gang importing heroin into New York City. They might have to range far from an American city to find and arrest a fugitive, whether he or she is accused of business fraud or terrorism, drug dealing or kidnapping, or any of a myriad of other crimes. While seizing a criminal's assets once involved searching houses and cars and investigating local bank accounts, it may now involve holdings in a Sicilian bank or investments in a Mexican beachfront hotel. To gather the evidence necessary to convict a drug kingpin, authorities may be every bit as interested in an organizational flow chart discovered in a police raid in Kingston, Jamaica, as they are in questioning a drug courier in Harlem.

The tasks of investigating international crime, collecting evidence of international conspiracies and other criminal law violations, and cooperating with other police forces intent on capturing international criminals occupies an increasing proportion of police work. In 1989 U.S. Attorney General Richard Thornburgh observed: "Often more than 50 percent of my day is devoted to some matter relating to our international involvement in fighting drug trafficking, money laundering, international organized crime and business fraud, environmental depredations, terrorism, or espionage."[50]

[48] Some legal systems, most notably in Latin America, did not traditionally recognize conspiracy as a crime. Consequently, successfully prosecuting a sophisticated criminal organization proved to be very difficult. In recent years various countries have passed conspiracy statutes patterned on American laws. See Nadelmann, *Cops Across Borders,* p. 12.

[49] Ibid., p. 4.

[50] Ibid., p. viii.

THE ROLE OF THE POLICE IN THE LEGAL SYSTEM

In any society, difficult tradeoffs must be made between permitting individual liberty and upholding peace and order in the community. Americans have sought guidance in making such tradeoffs by looking back to their constitutional tradition and by trying to interpret how the ambiguous words of the U.S. Constitution ought to be applied to new circumstances. Judges deciding constitutional questions regarding police behavior must often decide how to balance order and liberty under the terms of the U.S. Constitution. To what extent ought the interests of society be subordinated to the rights of the defendant? What about the interests of the victim? Which prevails when social interests clash?

As American law enforcement has tried to cope with increasingly difficult criminal challenges and as the public has become increasingly concerned both with rising crime rates and continued police misconduct, the constitutional limits on police behavior have loomed large. What exactly is the role that the police play within the legal system? What types of police misconduct occur? What constitutional limits have been imposed on police behavior?

The Arrest

Despite public concern with high crime rates, victims often do not report crimes. Some are occupied with busy schedules. Others know or are related to the suspect.[51] Others hope to avoid publicity or lack faith in the criminal justice system. Still others fear retribution by the criminal.

When an alleged crime is reported, the first step in the criminal process is often the **arrest,** that is, the seizure of a person by the authorities to answer for a criminal offense. The American legal system permits two types of arrests: those pursuant to an arrest warrant and certain **warrantless arrests.** For a magistrate to issue an arrest warrant, a complaint must be filed that demonstrates probable cause to believe that a particular person committed the crime.[52] Police officers may also legally arrest if they see a suspect commit a crime or if they have probable cause to believe that he or she has committed or is about to commit a felony.[53] Such warrantless arrests must eventually be supported by a sworn statement declaring the probable cause for the action. As many as 95 percent of all arrests are warrantless.[54]

[51] One source estimated that "less than half of all rapes and considerably less than half of all cases of child molestation are ever reported to the police." Carp and Stidham, p. 167.

[52] One authority noted: "In 'victimless crimes,' such as gambling and prostitution, offenders have customers rather than victims. When arrests are made, the complainant usually is the arresting officer." Silberman, p. 265.

[53] A warrant is usually required for any minor crime committed outside the presence of the police officer. Thus, an officer who sees a purse-snatching may arrest the purse-snatcher. But, if the officer has probable cause to believe that someone snatched a purse, then no emergency exists to justify a warrantless search, and he or she should get a warrant for the arrest to be legal. See *Payton v. New York,* 445 U.S. 573 (1980).

[54] Carp and Stidham, p. 165.

In the course of any arrest, and prior to any **interrogation,** police officers are obligated to remind defendants of their **Miranda rights.**[55] The arresting officer states, often in hurried fashion, that the suspect has the right to remain silent, that anything the suspect says can and will be used against him or her in a court of law, that the suspect has the right to the presence of an attorney, and that, if he or she is unable to afford one, an attorney will be appointed to represent the suspect prior to any questioning, if so desired.

Police will often issue a warning to a suspect, rather than make an arrest, unless they know charges will be pressed by a prosecutor. For instance, if a group of drunken teenagers were caught knocking over trashcans and otherwise disturbing the peace in a city alley, a police officer might take the teens to the police station to frighten them, call their parents to come pick up the teens, and then release them with no charges filed. To take another example, a senior police officer stated: "[I]f respectable groups are engaged in gambling, such as church groups, only a warning is issued—and even then only after a complaint has been received. . . . If Sister Rosita is running a church bingo game, I'm sure not going to arrest her."[56]

One study found that police failed to make an arrest in more than half the instances when they had probable cause to believe that a suspect committed a misdemeanor.[57] Of course, the police cannot make an arrest if a suspect has not yet been identified. And, in many cases the police are unable to apprehend a suspect because they lack information or are too busy to investigate carefully.[58]

Booking

Shortly after the arrest the police officers take the suspect to the city police station (or the *station house*) to carry out a routine procedure known as **booking.** For many years, a policeman would actually write down in a large book basic facts about the arrested individual such as the date and reason for the arrest, the suspect's height, weight, and age, and his or her address. The police would also enter into the *book* the suspect's photograph and fingerprints. These days, of course, much of this information is commonly stored in a computer.

Once the booking procedure is complete, if the police officer decides the matter is so minor as not to be worth prosecuting, the officer in conjunction with the prosecutor's office may have the discretion to release the arrested person and the case may well be over. Especially in past years, when domestic violence was only

[55] The U.S. Supreme Court declared the Miranda rule in *Miranda v. Arizona,* 384 U.S. 436 (1966).

[56] Carp and Stidham, p. 166.

[57] Wrightsman, p. 93, citing A.J. Reiss, Jr., *The Police and the Public* (New Haven, CT: Yale University Press, 1991).

[58] One authority reports that of 15 million serious crimes reported in 1990, police arrested suspects in only 3 million of those cases. Henry R. Glick, *Courts, Politics, and Justice,* 3d ed. rev. (New York: McGraw-Hill, 1993), p. 207.

rarely considered worth prosecuting,[59] police often arrested abusive husbands, took them to the station house, and then released them. Along with unenlightened ideas about a man's home being his castle, the lack of prosecution in domestic violence cases also occurred because victims often dropped charges and refused to testify at trial. To this day, prosecutors remain unwilling to devote resources to cases that are unlikely to result in convictions.[60]

Interrogation

The *Miranda* requirement that an officer inform an individual of his or her right to remain silent is derived from the long-standing privilege against **self-incrimination** found in English common law and in the Fifth Amendment to the U.S. Constitution. (To *self-incriminate* means to serve as a witness against oneself.) Under the accusatory American legal system, with its innocent-until-proven-guilty premise, the state must prove guilt and is not permitted to compel someone to **testify** against himself or herself.[61]

The Supreme Court designed the *Miranda* warnings as a **prophylactic rule,** that is, one designed to prevent the law from being violated. The warnings are meant to ensure that subjects of police interrogation know their fundamental constitutional rights. American courts have viewed self-incrimination as inherently untrustworthy when it is the product of browbeating or exhausting a suspect. Moreover, the authorities have been required to prove their case independently in order to protect the privacy rights of the innocent. The Founding Fathers saw the potential for dangerous abuses if a government that had imprisoned a suspect was permitted to try to extract a confession.

Once a suspect is taken into custody, the police must act correctly or any statements[62] extracted in violation of the Constitution may be excluded as inadmissible evidence at the criminal trial. Thus, police are not to interrogate for extraordinarily lengthy periods. If a suspect asks for an attorney, police are not to ask additional questions until the attorney is present. No confession is to be obtained by overcoming the suspect's will through fatigue, official pressure, and false appeals to sympathy.[63]

Despite these restraints, however, the American system does not bar police from questioning a suspect. If an individual has not yet been arrested and is free to

[59] For an overview of changes in American views toward family violence see Wrightsman, pp. 88–89.

[60] For various other instances in which victims are unlikely to seek prosecution, see Carp and Stidham, p. 167.

[61] An exception is the *transactional immunity rule* by which the state may compel testimony from an unwilling witness by giving that witness immunity from use of the testimony and from any evidence derived from it in subsequent criminal proceedings. See *Kastigar v. United States,* 406 U.S. 441 (1972).

[62] Suspects can be compelled to produce physical evidence that incriminates them, such as a diary, blood-stained clothing, and other items.

[63] *Spano v. New York,* 360 U.S. 315 (1959).

leave, any incriminating statement he or she makes will be admissible at trial. In addition, whether or not an arrest has occurred, any incriminating **spontaneous statement,** not made in response to an officer's question, will be admissible. If a suspect voluntarily and intelligently waives the right to remain silent, any incriminating statements are admissible.[64] Under the public-safety exception, the police may be excused from giving *Miranda* warnings and any incriminating statement will still be admissible if the question asked the suspect was primarily prompted by a concern for public safety.

Early critics of the *Miranda* decision argued that criminals would no longer confess to crimes and that, since confessions are an important source of evidence against criminals, fewer convictions would result. It is true that anyone intimately familiar with the American system—prosecutor, defense counsel, or experienced criminal—would be likely to agree that a suspect is usually foolish to answer any questions during police interrogation. The wiser counsel is to keep quiet and let the state try to build its case unaided. It is also true, however, that many criminal defendants now simply confess at a later stage in the proceedings in return for a lighter sentence or other considerations during plea-bargaining, a subject taken up in detail in Chapter 7.[65]

Clearly, the privilege against self-incrimination and the restraints on police interrogation are tied directly to America's sharply adversarial criminal justice system. The criminal justice system has long distinguished between the general investigation of a crime and the specific accusation of a particular individual. When official attention has turned to an accused person and the authorities would like to try to elicit a confession, then the adversarial system has started to operate and the accused must be permitted to consult with an attorney. Such an approach to police questioning differs markedly from that in civil law legal systems, in which the attitude of the courts is that all citizens are responsible for their acts and should either answer questions about them or freely acknowledge their wrongdoing.

The Police Report

Upon returning to the police station shortly after the arrest, the officer who seized the suspect will take his or her field notes and write a report. This **police report**[66] briefly describes the nature of the crime, how the police responded, and whatever facts the police relied upon in deciding to make the arrest. Like so many other aspects of American criminal justice, the appearance of a police report varies from state to state. Most, however, include a standard form on which the officer is to list

[64] The waiver of the right to an attorney during questioning need not be made expressly, orally, or in writing; rather, in some cases a waiver can be inferred from the actions and words of the person being interrogated. *North Carolina v. Butler,* 441 U.S. 369 (1979).

[65] See also Calvi and Coleman, p. 169, citing Richard H. Seeburger and R. Stanton Wettick, Jr., "*Miranda* in Pittsburgh: A Statistical Study," *University of Pittsburgh Law Review* 29 (1967): 1–26.

[66] For an example of a police report see Chapter 7.

facts, and a supplemental section in which the officer is expected to write a narrative account of what occurred.

A police report serves primarily as an internal memorandum, not a legal document.[67] It has no value in and of itself as evidence. However, police reports and attached statements by witnesses are often significant because they establish the basic facts that the prosecution will work with at trial and that the defense will attempt to refute or qualify. In many minor cases, like shoplifting or purse-snatching, all the information that the prosecution will present at trial is contained in the police report and accompanying documents.[68] The police report thus amounts to an important first step in the trial process in the United States.

So far as the police are concerned, the arrest and the police report will likely end their direct involvement with a simple case like shoplifting, other minor theft, or even burglary. Normally, the officers will consider the case "cleared by arrest" and will take up other law-enforcement tasks until they are called as witnesses at the trial, if one occurs.[69] In more serious and complicated cases or in cases in which an investigation is ongoing, police detectives will help the prosecutor to gather the evidence necessary to convict the criminal should the case go to trial. The role of the police in investigating crime raises the Fourth Amendment search-and-seizure issues explored subsequently.

POLICE MISCONDUCT

Although many countries experience illegitimate police behavior that dwarfs that in the United States, the proper functioning of the American legal system has been distorted by several types of police misconduct. Certain officers have brutalized suspects. Others have accepted bribes from criminals. Still others have ignored legal rules, especially constitutional prohibitions protecting the rights of defendants. The breaking of legal rules by the police might be termed illegitimate crime control.

Brutality

In the United States, a leading legal historian observed, "[p]olice brutality has a long, dishonorable history, not only on the street, but also in the station house."[70] In patrolling the streets, police have used nightsticks, fists, feet, and guns to quell disorder. Force has long been used not just in self-defense, but in an effort to teach criminals a lesson and thus deter crime. "Rough halters for rough donkeys" might

[67] The following discussion draws on Weinreb, p. 48.

[68] Ibid.

[69] Occasionally, in a case that might not be prosecuted, police officers will "shop around" the local prosecutor's office to find a prosecutor willing to take on their case. See George F. Cole, "The Decision to Prosecute," in Sheldon Goldman and Austin Sarat, eds., *American Court Systems: Readings in Judicial Process and Behavior* (San Francisco: W. H. Freeman, 1978), p. 100.

[70] Friedman, p. 361.

have been the credo of many a police unit. When officers brought suspects to the police station, the notorious "third degree" entailed eliciting information during interrogation by "inflicting 'suffering, physical and mental' . . . a whole world of torture and abuse—beatings with nightsticks and rubber hoses, and sometimes worse."[71]

In the early years of the twentieth century, authorities gave local police considerable leeway in maintaining law and order. Unfortunately, police forces in certain parts of the country routinely abused their power. One authority wrote of this era as follows:

> [T]he police enjoyed an enormous amount of discretion as far as the lower levels of society were concerned. Southern blacks were always fair game. And what the police did to drunks, hoboes, and the poor in general was largely invisible. It happened in the back alleys, in the station houses, on the streets, out of sight of the bright lights and boulevards of due process. In the realm that was theirs, the police *were* the law; they beat, they harassed, they hounded drunks, prostitutes, bums. And they arrested thousands of men and women every year for vagrancy, loitering, and similar 'crimes'; or simply hauled them in 'on suspicion.'[72]

Along with ignorance of the law and disdain for criminals, the stress of a police officer's life helps to explain occasionally brutal behavior. In the course of a single week, or even sometimes a single night, a city cop might fill out a stack of lengthy forms, arrest a drunk, dash after a purse-snatcher or drug courier, break up a barroom fight, calm a bitter family argument, deal with various citizen complaints, and inspect a bloody crime scene.

A psychologist noted: "Every day every police officer realizes that there is a possibility of being in a life-endangering situation; furthermore, the police must deal with human law breaking, distress, and misfortune on an ongoing basis. Having to investigate sex crimes or child abuse, for example, plus the long hours of some investigations, requires police officers to combine a tough shell, for their own protection, with a sensitivity to others."[73] It is no wonder that their spouses report that police officers come home from work: "upset, angry, tense, and anxious."[74] Brutal treatment of suspects may be one unfortunate method that police use to take out their frustrations.

In any event American police misconduct persists, though doubtless at lesser levels than if reformers and the courts had chosen to ignore it. In recent

[71] Ibid.

[72] Ibid., citing the findings of the Wickersham Commission of 1929, chaired by Attorney General George W. Wickersham. See U.S. National Commission on Law Observance and Enforcement, *Lawlessness in Law Enforcement* (1931).

[73] Wrightsman, p. 92, citing K. Ellison and R. Buckhout, *Psychology and Criminal Justice* (New York: Harper & Row, 1981).

[74] Wrightsman, p. 92, citing S. E. Jackson and C. Maslach, "Burnout in Organizational Settings," *Applied Social Psychology Annual* (1984): 134.

years public attention has focused on urban police brutality, especially the years of mistreatment of minority suspects in Los Angeles, Detroit, Philadelphia, and other large cities. In the most visible case to date, a jury acquitted police officers of misconduct in beating Rodney King, a black motorist who had attempted to resist arrest. The jury acquitted the police even though a passing driver captured much of the beating on a videotape that showed Mr. King lying helplessly on the ground while the police officers repeatedly struck him.

While public attention is focused on the most egregious incidents, in truth, local police forces vary widely in their reputations for professionalism and upstanding behavior. A few police forces retain virtually unblemished records. Most cities have had problems with particular officers who use too much force to subdue suspects, but have not had the epidemic of official violence found in Los Angeles. Still police brutality is a serious ongoing problem for law enforcement.

Graft

Alongside official brutality, issues of **graft** and corruption in the police continue to surface, especially in the area of vice control. Recently, narcotics-related bribery of police officers has made headlines in Washington, DC, New York, and other large cities.[75] Such narco-corruption is only the latest chapter in a cycle "of police corruption, investigatory commission, reform, and corruption once again . . ."[76] that has characterized urban law enforcement for decades.

Police graft can, of course, take different forms.[77] An officer who is bribed to look the other way and take no action while criminal activity occurs might be considered in passive cooperation with the criminals. When an officer aids a criminal enterprise by supplying information, he or she has committed an even more serious offense. Corrupt officers have facilitated criminal activity by selling information regarding "the time and place of police raids; the identity of informants; the fact that . . . [a criminal] is under surveillance; the radio frequencies used by police to communicate with one another, and any other information that can help [the criminal] . . . to avoid seizure of [evidence] . . . and his own apprehension, arrest, and/or prosecution."[78] Finally, some officers have actually initiated or actively participated in crime in exchange for a cut of the profits of the criminal enterprise. These most corrupt officers sell seized goods, arrange criminal deals, pro-

[75] See, for instance, Robert Daley, *Prince of the City* (New York: Granada, 1978) and Alan Dershowitz, *The Best Defense* (New York: Random House, 1982).

[76] Nadelmann, *Cops Across Borders,* p. 263. For different forms of corruption in the New York City police department compare Peter Maas, *Serpico* (New York: Bantam Books, 1973) with Commission to Investigate Allegations of Police Corruption and the City's Anti-Corruption Procedures, *The Knapp Commission Report on Police Corruption* (New York: George Braziller, 1973).

[77] The following typology is drawn from Nadelmann, *Cops Across Borders,* pp. 267–269.

[78] Ibid., p. 268.

vide muscle and protection to further a criminal enterprise, or control police activity.

Illegitimate Crime Control

On practically a daily basis American police officers are charged with ignoring procedural rules designed to protect the rights of defendants. Since the courts may exclude illegitimate evidence from a trial, this third type of police misconduct frames certain highly controversial legal issues.

Charges of police misconduct in handling evidence or preparing for trial have been raised more frequently against local than federal police forces. While this may reflect differences in training, hiring standards, and professional cultures,[79] perhaps most important is the different environment and tasks that face various types of police forces. In explaining why arrests by local police are more often considered unlawful than those by the FBI, one scholar wrote:

> When [police patrol officers] . . . go to the scene of a fight, they are trying to restore order and ascertain who started the fight and who wielded the knife. An arrest, if any, is often the culmination of a long, subtle, low-visibility process of interviewing victims, observing people, and questioning suspects, all done on the street in the absence of a supervisor and all based on making inferences from incomplete and disputed assertions. The essence of this process is judgment: deciding whose conduct, demeanor, and appearance make it likely that he has committed a crime.[80]

In contrast, FBI agents usually act as detectives, called to crime scenes after order has been restored.[81] The timing of their intervention in a normal case, and the opportunity for reflection and careful preparation, puts FBI agents in a position more conducive to following legal rules. Often a city police officer at a crime scene will be primarily concerned with restoring peace in a volatile situation and with avoiding injuries or deaths. Under such circumstances gathering evidence according to the rulebook may be a secondary concern. The FBI agent tends to arrive at a crime scene that has already been secured, and he or she focuses on conducting a professional investigation aimed at producing a conviction.

Curbing Misconduct

All forms of police misconduct poison community relations and make controlling and investigating crime substantially more difficult. One law professor and former federal prosecutor declared: "As long as the citizens do not believe in the criminal

[79] While FBI agents have long prided themselves on acting coolly and intelligently, certain other police forces display an arrogant or a "macho" professional ethos.

[80] Wilson, *Bureaucracy*, p. 327.

[81] Ibid.

justice system, even ordinary crime cannot be satisfactorily investigated. Citizen co-operation is simply the ***sine qua non*** for every country that I know of in investigating ordinary crime."[82]

In deciding scores of cases alleging illegitimate crime control, the American judiciary has created an elaborate network of rules to govern police work.[83] How to interrogate a prisoner, search a house, seize evidence, and arrest suspects have all become part of laws of criminal procedure, though one should certainly question the extent to which such laws have become part of the practice of police forces.

The most interesting and controversial limits on the police are found in the U.S. Constitution and, especially, in the extensive judicial decisions regarding the meaning of its general principles. The Fourth Amendment declares that "the right of the people to be secure in their persons, houses, papers, and effects, against unreasonable searches and seizures, shall not be violated." Furthermore, "no Warrants shall issue, but upon probable cause . . . particularly describing the place to be searched, and the persons or things to be seized."[84] Just when is a search and seizure unreasonable? When is a warrant necessary? What is meant by probable cause? The role of the police as investigators of crime is bound inextricably to proper interpretations of the meaning of those ambiguous phrases.

Search and Seizure

Unlike legal traditions in many other countries, Anglo-American law has long respected the rights of citizens to be left alone by the state. A person's home, in particular, has been viewed as a special sanctuary into which authorities should not intrude unless absolutely necessary. The special concern of Americans with "illegal" searches and seizures may be traced to the colonial period. One of the underlying causes of the American Revolution, and an important early stimulus for the anti-authoritarian strain in American culture, was the anger that ordinary American citizens felt toward British troops regarding unreasonable search and seizures. Among the Founding Fathers, John Adams had even led protests against aggressive searches carried out by British soldiers.

High-handed treatment by colonial authorities led early American leaders to fear creating a police state in which officials might enter houses at will and tear through possessions in an attempt to find evidence to use against the inhabitants. Great Britain had long barred such behavior at home, though not necessarily in its colonies, and the Founders wanted to ensure that intrusive searches and seizures

[82] Philip Heymann, Director of the Center for Criminal Justice at Harvard Law School, in congressional testimony, as cited in Michael Ross Fowler and Julie M. Bunck, "Legal Imperialism or Disinterested Assistance?: American Legal Aid in the Caribbean Basin," *Albany Law Review* 55 (1992): 825.

[83] Much of this judicial attention occurred during the 1960s, which may be viewed as an unusual period in which courts shook off their customary laissez-faire attitudes toward law enforcement and tried to curb abuses.

[84] U.S. Constitution, Amendment IV.

would be strictly circumscribed in their new legal system. In 1791 the Fourth Amendment thus imposed strict constitutional limits on how authorities could search for and seize evidence of crime. In particular, the Fourth Amendment required police to secure the agreement of a neutral third party, a judicial authority, before a warrant could issue authorizing the search of a citizen's home, papers, or belongings.

The chief problem with the constitutional protection against unreasonable searches and seizures has not usually been that obtaining a search-warrant is especially difficult or time-consuming. The police officer must simply specify to the magistrate or other judicial officer what the search is after, where the search will be conducted, and why the search should be authorized. Occasionally, questions are raised as to whether adequate grounds for a search exist. In assessing probable cause, the magistrate must ask whether sufficient evidence of wrongdoing has been marshaled to support a warrant. Moreover, judicial officers understand that issuing search-warrants promptly is essential for effective police work, and they are ordinarily prepared to grant them around the clock. Most important, the Supreme Court has not erected a probable cause standard that is especially difficult to meet. In 1983 the Court declared: "The task of the issuing magistrate is simply to make a practical, common sense decision whether, given all the circumstances set forth in the affidavit before him, including the 'veracity' and 'basis of knowledge' of persons supplying **hearsay** information, there is a fair probability that contraband or evidence of a crime will be found in a particular place."[85]

Since any adequately supported request for a warrant will likely be upheld in short order, the real problem is that police often view the constitutional warrant requirement as unnecessary and inconvenient paperwork. Indeed, the very fact that search-warrants are readily obtained may have contributed to the prevalent view that they are extraneous red tape and not a necessary safeguard. Certainly, the decisions of the Supreme Court regarding the scope of the Fourth Amendment have directly affected police officers, the targets of police searches and seizures, and the many Americans concerned about maintaining law and order in their communities. In particular, the fact that American courts frequently bar illegally seized evidence from being used in court has long sparked controversy.

Establishing the Exclusionary Rule

The **exclusionary rule** states that evidence obtained in violation of the U.S. Constitution cannot be used at the trial of the defendant.[86] Thus, when police undertake a search and seizure that violates the Fourth Amendment, the evidence that was illegally procured will not be allowed in the criminal prosecution. Statements unconstitutionally obtained in violation of the Fifth and Sixth Amendments will likewise be excluded. In addition, if the police use the illegal evidence to find ad-

[85] *Illinois v. Gates,* 462 U.S. 213 (1983). Italics furnished by author.

[86] See *Mapp v. Ohio,* 367 U.S. 643 (1961).

ditional evidence, then, under the "fruit of the poisonous tree" doctrine,[87] that evidence is also normally excluded.[88]

Thus, the exclusionary rule does not prohibit prosecution of criminals after illegal searches and seizures; rather, the prosecution may go forward but any evidence obtained from the illegal search must be excluded. One authority noted: "[T]he exclusionary rule merely places the government in the same position it would have been in had the illegal search . . . not taken place. Moreover, if a conviction is overturned on appeal because the illegally obtained evidence was used to secure it, the defendant can be retried with that evidence excluded from consideration."[89]

The case that first framed the exclusionary rule was *Weeks v. United States*.[90] Federal authorities investigating a postal offense had conducted an illegal search in which certain letters and papers had been seized. Mr. Weeks moved to have these items returned to him, arguing that the Court should not permit them to be used as evidence against him at trial. The Supreme Court considered the issue and held: "[T]he Fourth Amendment . . . put the courts of the United States and Federal officials . . . under limitations and restraints [and] . . . forever secure[d] the people, their persons, houses, papers and effects against all unreasonable searches and seizures under the guise of law." The Court concluded: "If letters and private documents can thus be seized and held and used in evidence against a citizen accused of an offense, the protection of the Fourth Amendment declaring his right to be secure against such searches is of no value, and . . . might as well be stricken from the Constitution."

In 1957 another landmark exclusionary rule case arose in Cleveland, Ohio. Someone advised police officers looking for a fugitive that the man was hiding at Dollree Mapp's house. Without bothering to obtain a search-warrant, three policemen arrived at Mapp's house and ordered her to open the door. She refused and called her attorney, who counseled her to do nothing until he arrived. When the lawyer arrived, however, the police barred him from the house, while seven officers broke through the back door.

When Mapp asked for a search-warrant, one officer waved a scrap of paper at her, which turned out not to be a warrant. Dolly Mapp grabbed the paper as evidence of police misconduct and stuffed it down her dress, but the policeman immediately forced his way into her clothes to retrieve it. The police seized Mapp, handcuffed her, and ransacked her house looking for the fugitive. Although the police officers did not find any sign of the suspect, they did discover a locked trunk. Upon breaking open the trunk, they found several pictures, four small pamphlets, and a pencil drawing that they seized, claiming it was obscene material. Ohio au-

[87] See *Wong Sun v. United States,* 371 U.S. 471 (1963).

[88] If the authorities can prove that they learned of evidence independently of the information derived from the illegal search, that evidence would be admissible. *Nix v. Williams,* 467 U.S. 431 (1984). For a summary of other exceptions, see *U.S. v. Leon,* 468 U.S. 897, 910 (1984).

[89] G. Alan Tarr, *Judicial Process and Judicial Policymaking* (St. Paul, MN: West, 1994), p. 211.

[90] *Weeks v. United States,* 232 U.S. 383 (1914).

thorities eventually brought Mapp to trial and convicted her of knowingly possessing "lewd and lascivious" materials.

After the *Weeks* case any evidence found during the course of such an illegal search had to be excluded from a federal trial. However, authorities brought the case against Mapp under Ohio law in an Ohio court. Although the federal exclusionary rule did not apply, the Supreme Court considered whether, under the terms of the Fourteenth Amendment,[91] the federal ban on illegal searches might apply to the states as well. The argument was that any state which tries to sanction such police incursions into privacy has violated the due process of law that the U.S. Constitution protects for each American citizen.

The Supreme Court agreed, ruling that evidence discovered in illegal searches cannot be used in court, whether the court is federal or state. The majority reasoned: "This Court has not hesitated to enforce as strictly against the States as it does against the Federal Government the rights of free speech, and of a free press, the rights to notice and to a fair, public trial, including . . . the right not to be convicted by use of a coerced confession. . . . Why should not the same rule apply to what is tantamount to coerced testimony by way of unconstitutional seizure of goods, papers, effects, documents, etc.?"

And, the Court concluded: "[T]he imperative of judicial integrity . . . [counsels that] [t]he criminal goes free, if he must, but it is the law that sets him free. Nothing can destroy a government more quickly than its failure to observe its own laws, or worse, its disregard of the charter of its own existence. . . . Our decision . . . gives to the individual no more than that which the Constitution guarantees him, to the police officer no less than that to which honest law enforcement is entitled, and, to the courts, that judicial integrity so necessary in the true administration of justice."

In short, the rationale for the exclusionary rule is that a strong disincentive to illegal behavior will deter police from committing unconstitutional searches and seizures and encourage them to obtain search-warrants. Police are likely to be embarrassed and frustrated if a court feels compelled to throw out evidence seized illegally. Indeed, the theory is that in the face of a strict exclusionary rule police would ordinarily have no incentive to undertake unconstitutional searches and seizures.

Analyzing the Exclusionary Rule

Since no one but the defendant enjoys overturning a conviction because of the exclusionary rule, its worth has been the subject of bitter ongoing debate. The supporters of the rule argue that, for all its imperfections, it remains the best way to curb illegal searches.[92] Evidence illegally seized must be excluded, they argue, or

[91] The Fourteenth Amendment reads: "[No State shall] deprive any person of life, liberty, or property, without due process of law . . ." U.S. Constitution, Amendment XIV.

[92] See, for instance, Yale Kamisar, "The Exclusionary Rule in Historical Perspective: The Struggle to Make the Fourth Amendment 'More Than an Empty Blessing,'" *Judicature* 62 (February 1979): 337–350.

the Fourth Amendment will be drained of meaning. If the courts permit evidence seized in illegal searches to be admitted at trial, then what would stop police from consistently taking the easier route of conducting warrantless searches? And, if police routinely carry out warrantless searches, then the Fourth Amendment would be nothing but hollow words.

The critics respond that *society* is punished when the criminal goes free, *not* the police officer who acted unlawfully. Sometimes the evidence excluded will be critical to the prosecution's case, and hence a dangerous criminal may be released because of a legal technicality. The critics suggest that, as in virtually all other countries, the evidence should be admitted, but the police officers who conduct the warrantless searches should be punished. Police charged with undertaking illegal warrantless searches might be prosecuted, be penalized with sanctions handed down by their superiors, or be made subject to civil litigation by the defendant whose rights were violated.[93]

Supporters of the exclusionary rule, however, find all these suggestions to be flawed. Since prosecutors have to gain police cooperation to pursue other cases, and since some prosecutors face reelection campaigns or plan to run for other public office, relying on a prosecutor to bring unpopular cases against officers who had engaged in illegal searches seems unsatisfactory. Most prosecutors most of the time would be far more likely to exercise prosecutorial discretion and neglect to pursue such allegations against the police.

Relying upon the police department to discipline its own officers seems equally problematic. The supporters of the exclusionary rule claim that state law-enforcement authorities for many years routinely ignored the Fourth Amendment. Since neither prosecutors nor police departments could or did stop illegal searches and seizures in the states, the courts had to step in.[94] In fact, with the defendant often imprisoned and with little public outcry, high-level officials would be tempted to sweep aside such claims of police misconduct. Moreover, if higher-level officials did fine or suspend officers engaged in illegal warrantless searches, the police might become overly hesitant to undertake any warrantless searches under any circumstances. So long as they were the slightest bit unsure of their legal footing, police officers would be inclined to refrain from acting for fear of personal consequences.

As for civil litigation, the supporters reason that juries would not be likely to favor convicted criminals who had been the victims of illegal searches over po-

[93] Under the terms of 42 U.S.C. sec. 1983 a state authority (technically, anyone acting under color of state law) is forbidden from depriving anyone in the United States of any constitutional or federal rights or privileges. Two authorities noted: "When a police officer is alleged to have acted improperly, say, in conducting an illegal search, that officer can be sued in a federal court by alleging that he or she deprived the person searched of his or her constitutional right under the Fourteenth Amendment to be free from unreasonable searches and seizures and did so while acting within the scope of his employment as a local police officer." Charles R. Swanson and Leonard Territo, *Police Administration: Structures, Processes, and Behavior* (New York: Macmillan, 1983), p. 292. For the liability of federal police agents for unauthorized searches, see *Bivens v. 6 Unknown Federal Agents,* 403 U.S. 388 (1971).

[94] See Tarr, p. 212.

lice officers who had conducted the searches.[95] If favorable jury verdicts proved difficult to obtain in these cases, private attorneys would be disinclined to take them on. Moreover, legal services attorneys, already overloaded with work, might also resist wasting scarce resources on bringing such fruitless cases to court. Hence, civil litigation also appears to be a poor alternative to the exclusionary rule.

Studies of the effects of the exclusionary rule cast doubt on the claim by the critics that the rule permits considerable numbers of dangerous criminals to go free. The National Institute of Justice studied prosecutions in California and found that prosecutors decided not to press charges because of illegal searches and seizures in less than 1 percent of the cases they considered.[96] Similarly, a legal scholar reported that in a sample of federal court cases about 10 percent of criminal defendants moved to suppress evidence, but only one of ten succeeded.[97]

Various studies of cases in state court systems in the East, West, and Midwest found similar results.[98] In one study,[99] defense attorneys filed motions to suppress evidence because of illegal searches and seizures in about 7 percent of their cases. Ninety-five percent of those motions failed. Of the small number that succeeded, the prosecutor still managed to convict the defendant with other untainted evidence in a third of the cases. And, many of the cases that were affected did not involve violent crime. Thus, the data collected to date suggests that "very few defendants escape conviction because of the exclusionary rule."[100]

Changing Search and Seizure Standards

After the *Mapp* decision, the courts for a time interpreted Fourth Amendment cases according to a set of fairly clear questions. First, a court would ask: "Did the suspect have a protected interest?" The Fourth Amendment, after all, guarantees that Americans will be secure against illegal searches and seizures only in "their persons, houses, papers, and effects." So, if a suspect took a flight on a commercial airplane, the police would be free to search around the seat without getting a war-

[95] See Jonathan D. Casper, Kennette Benedict, and Jo L. Perry, "The Tort Remedy in Search and Seizure Cases: A Case Study in Juror Decisionmaking," *American Bar Foundation Research Journal* 13 (Spring 1988): 279–303, cited in Tarr, p. 228.

[96] National Institute of Justice, *Criminal Justice Research Report—The Effects of the Exclusionary Rule: A Study in California* (Washington, DC: Department of Justice, National Institute of Justice, 1982), cited in Tarr, p. 228.

[97] Glick, p. 433, citing Yale Kamisar, "The Warren Court (Was It Really So Defense-Minded?), The Burger Court (Is It Really So Prosecutor-Oriented?), and Police Investigatory Practices," in Vincent Blasi, ed., *The Burger Court: The Counter-Revolution That Wasn't* (New Haven, CT: Yale University Press, 1983), p. 81.

[98] See Silberman, pp. 262–264 ("It is only in cases of . . . 'victimless' crimes that any significant number of seemingly guilty offenders go free because tainted evidence—evidence acquired as a result of an illegal search, seizure, or arrest—is excluded from court; and even here, the number is considerably smaller than critics assume").

[99] See Peter F. Nardulli, "The Societal Cost of the Exclusionary Rule: An Empirical Assessment," *American Bar Foundation Research Journal* (Summer 1983), p. 585, cited in Tarr, p. 228.

[100] Tarr, p. 214.

rant since American citizens do not have any protected interest in such a public place as an airplane seat.[101]

Once the court had determined that a protected interest existed, it would ask: "Did the suspect consent to the search?" If so, the search would be constitutionally valid, even if the police had not obtained a warrant. A search or seizure must be reasonable, the courts concluded, if the target fails to object.[102] Next, the court would ask: "If a protected interest existed and the suspect did not consent to a search, did the police get a search warrant?" If the search-warrant were properly obtained, the search would not be ruled unconstitutional. If the search-warrant were flawed, the evidence could still be admitted under a good faith exception. Evidence will not be suppressed if it is discovered by police officers who acted in good faith and in a reasonable, though mistaken, belief that they had been authorized to conduct the search.[103]

Finally, if the police did not get a warrant, the court would ask whether an exception to the warrant requirement applied. And, in a series of cases the court listed various important exceptions. For instance, the police need not get a warrant when they search a person during an arrest or when they stop an automobile.[104] Nor is a search-warrant needed when the police **stop and frisk** a suspect, that is, when they halt someone and pat down the person's sides to ensure that he or she is not carrying a concealed weapon.[105] Police officers need not obtain a warrant when they come across evidence of a crime in plain view or when they are in hot pursuit of a criminal.

Under this line of constitutional interpretation, an illegal search, such as the one found in the *Mapp* case would occur only under a set of especially unreasonable circumstances. The person had to have a protected interest, as Mrs. Mapp did in her house. The person had to object to the search, as Mrs. Mapp had done. The police had to ignore their duty to get a search-warrant, as they did in *Mapp*. And, no exception to the warrant requirement could apply. If all those conditions were met, the search would be held unreasonable, and the evidence would be excluded from either state or federal trials.

This interpretation of the Fourth Amendment seemed practical, since police departments could train officers to follow its dictates relatively easily. It also seemed faithful to the original intent of those, such as John Adams, who had helped to draft the Fourth Amendment. Nevertheless, over time, police continued

[101] The Fourth Amendment, it is sometimes observed, protects people and not places, yet just how much protection is afforded a person often depends on where that person is located.

[102] Two legal scholars argued: "A police officer's *request,* such as, 'Do you mind if I look in your trunk?" becomes a *command* to most people. . . . Is 'permission' under such circumstances an intelligent waiver of constitutional rights?" James V. Calvi and Susan Coleman, *American Law and Legal Systems,* 2d ed. rev. (Englewood Cliffs, NJ: Prentice Hall, 1992), p. 165. For a case dealing with this issue see *Schneckloth v. Bustamonte,* 412 U.S. 218 (1973).

[103] *United States v. Leon,* 468 U.S. 897 (1984).

[104] An automobile, after all, can be moved before a search-warrant is obtained. See *Carroll v. United States,* 267 U.S. 132 (1925) and *Chambers v. Maroney,* 399 U.S. 42 (1970).

[105] *Terry v. Ohio,* 392 U.S. 1 (1968).

to engage in warrantless searches. When the excluded evidence proved important in various cases, the Supreme Court softened application of the exclusionary rule. Under the leadership of Chief Justice Warren Burger, the Supreme Court at first seemed merely to be creating more and more exceptions to the warrant requirement. But, eventually, the Court seemed to arrive at a new standard altogether. The justices began to ask: "Was the search 'reasonable' under all the circumstances?" Intent on improving the capability of the police and less sympathetic to the rights of criminal defendants, the Burger Court and then the Rehnquist Court adopted this new approach to Fourth Amendment issues.

Unfortunately, however, the idea of using a reasonableness standard to determine the legality of searches and seizures has created its own nest of difficulties. In a typical case, the prosecutor emphasizes that the search was reasonable since society does not want to protect criminals. The defense counsel emphasizes that the search was unreasonable on account of the privacy interests of all the noncriminals who might be subject to such searches if the police were permitted to engage in this sort of conduct. Under the new standard the former emphasis on whether the police officer could have obtained a warrant in a timely fashion and without endangering the safety of innocents is a matter of secondary, and sometimes negligible, importance.

This approach places in a difficult position the police officer who is trying to decide whether to stop to get a warrant or to skip that step. He or she must try to figure out how a court, months or years later, is going to assess the situation. Is it reasonable under the totality of the circumstances to proceed with a warrantless search? Since what seems reasonable to one judge may seem unreasonable to another, the more ambiguous standard has left the police and citizens largely uncertain about just when warrantless searches can take place.

Although some feel that the new vague standard has helped law enforcement by keeping evidence from being excluded in certain high-visibility cases, others argue that it has encouraged police to gamble that a warrantless search will be approved. Therefore, Fourth Amendment issues come up more frequently, and convictions are overturned more often, than they would have been under the former, clearer approach.

REFORM OF LAW ENFORCEMENT

A survey of law enforcement in the United States thus uncovers various problems. Most thoughtful observers would probably agree that the American system is not the most rational and effective method of administering criminal justice. Too often both the search for truth and the desire for the efficient and fair administration of justice get lost in the shuffle of technical arguments or in the adversarial contest in the courtroom.

Fundamentally contradictory perspectives on criminal justice lie at the heart of American culture and explain much of the tension in caselaw and policy. One scholar observed:

> The average . . . [American couple], if they heard a speech about defendants' rights, about the presumption of innocence, about the wonders and fairness of the system, would no doubt nod in solemn agreement. This was America, by God! But the same pair also wanted an efficient, effective system; they wanted to sleep soundly at night; they wanted security, law and order; they wanted the police to sweep vagrants and tramps off the street, to get rid of the scruffy, disgusting human flotsam that disfigured their cities; they wanted the police to catch dangerous criminals who robbed and stole and assaulted; they wanted the system to convict these men and put them away. The system, in real life, was equally ambivalent; it bounced from one pole to another.[106]

Americans have customarily chosen to sacrifice a degree of efficiency in order to retain liberties. Americans want to maintain order and curb crime, yet they do not want to live in a police state. They want to be left alone to enjoy their privacy and to be secure from overly intrusive authorities, yet they fear a system that seems weighted in favor of the criminal suspect. Too often the courts have responded with a scheme that asks police, along with all their other responsibilities, to become experts in law and to gauge the reaction of some future judge to their actions in situations that are frequently tense and dangerous.

Indeed, as courts have tried to assess how reasonably the police acted, the rules have become less coherent and less useful as guidelines for behavior. The courts may well have done a disservice to police by failing to declare a set of clear rules that can be readily applied to criminal process, that are guided by the Constitution and *stare decisis,* and that strike a rational balance between social needs. Instead, the system is now supposed to function through numerous rules that are increasingly complicated and technical and, hence, likely to be ignored by police.

Students of the legal system ought to realize that police need not operate as they do in the United States. Other advanced societies take quite different approaches to law enforcement.[107] For instance, U.S. police conduct far more covert operations than do their counterparts in Europe,[108] yet they are hemmed in by stricter procedural rules in many other respects. One scholar observed:

> The exclusionary rule that denies police the use in court of illegally gathered evidence, the privilege against self-incrimination . . . , restrictions on interrogation while in custody, and limitations on search and seizure and arrest have indirectly encouraged undercover work.
>
> This contrasts with many European countries where the standard of suspi-

[106] Friedman, p. 251. Although Friedman was referring to the views of nineteenth-century Americans, much the same views hold true today.

[107] See, for instance, John Roach and Jurgen Thomanek, eds., *Police and Public Order in Europe* (London: Croom Helm, 1985); Maurice Punch, *Policing the Inner City: A Study of Amsterdam's Warmoesstraat* (London: Macmillan, 1979); Philip John Stead, *The Police of France* (New York: Macmillan, 1983); and Robert C. Fried, *The Italian Prefects: A Study in Administrative Politics* (New Haven, CT: Yale University Press, 1963).

[108] One scholar observed: "[U]nlike their American counterparts, police in most European countries require a prosecutor's approval to conduct an undercover operation, pay an informant, and take a variety of other investigative steps." Nadelmann, *Cops Across Borders,* p. 219.

> cion for a search or arrest is lower, persons can be held and interrogated for a longer period of time without charges being brought, self-incriminating statements need not be corroborated, and even evidence obtained through illegal searches and seizures can generally be introduced in court. . . . [W]ithin democratic societies, the greater the restriction on police in overt investigations, the greater will be their use of covert investigations.[109]

In critically analyzing American police work, one might first explore the tradeoffs. How much efficiency in law enforcement should be sacrificed to ensure vigorous protection of liberties and individual rights? Which is more important—strict procedural safeguards or noninterference with police work? More particularly, is the American desire for liberty and privacy met more satisfactorily by a system that encourages covert operations, yet restricts arrests, interrogations, and searches and seizures?[110] Or, should Americans restrict stings, unmarked cars, and plain-clothes police, yet permit more leeway in **search-and-seizure law?** Unfortunately, such issues are rarely raised; even more infrequently are they thoughtfully assessed.

Specific Reforms

How, then, might the system be reformed? Some have argued that the answer to America's criminal justice problems is to make ever finer distinctions about constitutional issues. Others would like to go back and reverse Supreme Court precedents in order to give police more power at the expense of individual liberties and defendant's rights. Still others rue the judicial activism of the Burger and Rehnquist courts in rolling back the precedents set in the Warren court era to reflect the more conservative attitudes of the justices.

In fact, certain problems of criminal process in the United States arise or are exacerbated because the American system requires its police also to investigate crimes.[111] After an arrest in the United States, police are in charge of booking and interrogating suspects, conducting lineups for eyewitness identifications, searching for evidence, and many other functions that properly relate to crime investigation. At the same time, Americans expect their police to maintain the peace, quickly and forcefully, and to ensure law and order in each community.

An evident tension exists between these roles. To curb street crime and catch criminals, patrol officers must be vigorous, courageous, and decisive. They must be able to command authority, and they are often advised to be constantly suspicious. A Chicago police training bulletin read as follows:

> Actions, dress, or location of a person often classify him as suspicious. . . . Men loitering near schools, public toilets, playgrounds, and swimming pools

[109] Marx, p. 47.

[110] In Europe one source noted: "A search can be made without a warrant whenever police can reasonably claim that the police were looking for a weapon." Nadelmann, *Cops Across Borders,* p. 219.

[111] See Weinreb, p. 14.

> may be sex perverts. Men loitering near bars . . . or any other business at closing time, may be robbery suspects. Men or youths walking along looking into cars may be car thieves or looking for something to steal. Persons showing evidence of recent injury, or whose clothing is disheveled, may be victims or participants in an assault or strong-arm robbery.[112]

To maintain law and order, Americans want innately suspicious patrol officers prepared to act and to act swiftly and forcibly. Whether the impulse comes from a hunch, intuition, experience, or keen powers of observation, the goal is to stop the burglary, robbery, rape, or murder before it happens or at least before injuries occur. If the crime has already happened, the goal is to seize the fleeing suspect.

Among those who investigate crime, however, Americans look for a somewhat different set of characteristics. They want their detectives to be careful, thoughtful, fair-minded, and painstakingly thorough. They do not want investigators who act impulsively and rush forward without a warrant or without a very good reason to proceed in the absence of a warrant. They do not want clumsy or hurried analyses of a crime scene. They do not want the police to jump to hasty conclusions on the basis of prior suspicions. Above all, modern Americans do not want racist detectives injecting personal prejudices into assessments of crime and perhaps manipulating the evidence to suit their biases.

The O. J. Simpson trial, by highlighting the biases, carelessness, and lack of oversight of police detectives in Los Angeles, has brought unprecedented publicity to this very problem. In short, the qualities we look for in an individual charged with maintaining the peace by breaking up a fight, tackling a purse-snatcher, chasing an armed suspect, or stopping a rape, differ dramatically from those of the person we want to investigate a crime by questioning suspects, obtaining search-warrants, searching premises, seizing evidence, taking blood samples for DNA matching, conducting lineups to identify a suspect, and ensuring that physical evidence is handled in a proper and secure manner so that it cannot be successfully challenged at trial.

The dual function that they are required to perform frustrates American police officers and causes tensions that can eventually bring about a range of ills, from lies by the police to tampering with the evidence, from brutal or unfair treatment of suspects to the delay that leads prosecutors to negotiate plea bargains to speed the administration of justice. Such deep-seated problems can poison the good relations between police and citizens that are essential for the efficient administration of justice.

To some extent, of course, the American criminal justice system recognizes the gulf between these roles. Police forces do, after all, divide officers on patrol from detectives. Prosecutors do inject a lawyer's perspective into police investigations. However, in the United States, those charged with maintaining order and those charged with investigating crime both operate in the same police force with

[112] Wrightsman, p. 86, citing M. S. Greenberg and R. B. Ruback, *Social Psychology of the Criminal Justice System* (Monterey, CA: Brooks/Cole, 1982), p. 72.

common superior officers and, often, a shared professional ethos. Furthermore, for fear of being reminded of legal constraints, many detectives keep prosecutors at arms length for as much of the investigation as possible.[113]

In contrast, many civil law countries actually place the investigation of crime under the authority of the judicial branch. The ultimate boss in a judicial police force, the one who issues orders to the detectives, supervises ongoing investigations, and determines assignments, promotions, and seniority, is trained in law. In this way the job of keeping the peace is explicitly separated from the job of investigating crime. The incidence of sloppy detective work and of illegitimate investigatory techniques might well be lower and the rate of convictions might well be higher if the United States adopted such an alternative system.

Wholly consistently with the U.S. Constitution, one might reform this problematic aspect of the legal system by charging the police with keeping the peace and arresting suspects.[114] After arrest the suspect would become the responsibility of a quasi-judicial, quasi-prosecutorial official, which many other countries call the *investigating magistrate.* The magistrate would then take responsibility for directing a judicial police force, men and women who would be largely drawn from the ranks of current police detectives, but who would be assigned the sole task of investigating alleged crimes under the guidance of a judicial official.

The investigating magistrate would then gather and assess evidence, determine whether probable cause was evident, and write a report that would either dismiss the case or send it on to the prosecutor's office for trial. This revamped process might improve the professionalism and effectiveness of police investigations, reduce the incidence of tampering and brutality, and increase the confidence of the public in crime-solving by inserting a responsible judicial official into the investigatory stage of a criminal case.[115]

Given the extent to which actors in the American criminal justice system resist change, especially of a sweeping variety, such a proposal is bound to be criticized as unrealistic. Perhaps those who would like to reform law enforcement might better focus attention on useful incremental changes. Courts might discard the foray into assessing "reasonableness" and instead articulate clear rules of police behavior that do not call on officers to try to act as lawyers and figure out how justifiable their actions will appear in some future court case. To the greatest extent possible, the police might peel apart the roles of patrol officer and investigator, and police and prosecutors might better coordinate their supervision of detectives.

[113] One scholar wrote: "Police in every country . . . tend to avoid involving prosecutors in investigations until it is absolutely necessary." Nadelmann, *Cops Across Borders,* p. 219.

[114] For a more detailed rendition of a similar proposal see "An Alternative Model" in Weinreb, especially pp. 119–144.

[115] The addition of an investigating magistrate could actually streamline the system since neither a police station booking, nor a probable cause hearing, nor a grand jury indictment would have to occur. If the case were to be prosecuted, the magistrate could oversee any negotiations that might occur between the defense lawyer and the prosecution toward a plea-bargain arrangement. With the assistance of a magistrate who was familiar with the case, the judge could then be encouraged to exert more influence in rejecting inappropriate plea bargains. Various stages of a criminal trial are investigated in more detail in the next chapter.

Such steps might improve the record of law enforcement, foster better community relations, and present prosecutors with more solid and winnable cases.

SELECTED ADDITIONAL READINGS

BAYLEY, DAVID H. *Police For the Future.* New York: Oxford University Press, 1994.

FRIEDMAN, LAWRENCE M. *A History of American Law.* 2d ed. rev. New York: Simon & Schuster, 1985.

———. *Crime and Punishment.* New York: W. W. Norton, 1993.

JOHNSON, DAVID R. *American Law Enforcement: A History.* Arlington Heights, IL: Forum Press, 1981.

MARX, GARY T. *Undercover: Police Surveillance in America.* Berkeley: University of California Press, 1988.

NADELMANN, ETHAN A. *Cops Across Borders: The Internationalization of U.S. Criminal Law Enforcement.* University Park: Pennsylvania State University Press, 1993.

SARAT, AUSTIN, AND KEARNS, THOMAS R. *Law's Violence.* Ann Arbor: University of Michigan Press, 1992.

SILBERMAN, CHARLES E. *Criminal Violence, Criminal Justice.* New York: Random House, 1978.

SKOLNICK, JEROME H. *Justice Without Trial: Law Enforcement in Democratic Society.* 2d ed. rev. New York: John Wiley & Sons, 1975.

SPARROW, MALCOLM K., MOORE, MARK H., and KENNEDY, DAVID M. *Beyond 911: A New Era for Policing.* New York: Basic Books, 1992.

WEINREB, LLOYD L. *Denial of Justice: Criminal Process in the United States.* New York: The Free Press, 1977.

WILSON, JAMES Q. *Crime.* San Francisco: ICS Press, 1995.

———. *Thinking About Crime.* New York: Basic Books, 1975.

———. *Varieties of Police Behavior: The Management of Law and Order in Eight Communities.* Cambridge, MA: Harvard University Press, 1978.

7

Criminal Proceedings

With the roles of the principal participants in the American criminal justice system in mind we shall now turn to the criminal trial. How do the police and prosecutor, judge and jury, defense counsel and defendant interact? What preliminary steps lead up to the actual trial in court? What happens during the court proceedings? How might a prosecutor or defense lawyer plot trial strategy? And how is a criminal case finally resolved?[1]

AMERICAN CRIMINAL JUSTICE IN ACTION

Not long ago a very ordinary crime occurred. A man stole a small car, and at about 2:30 A.M. crashed it into the side of a university dormitory. Let us imagine that the police in an American city managed to catch a suspect to put on trial for having allegedly stolen the car. To clarify the manner in which criminal cases are resolved in the United States, we will follow that hypothetical case through the legal system.

First, the police officer making the arrest would file a detailed report of the incident and of the steps that led to the arrest of the individual suspected of stealing the car. The police report in this case might look something like the example that follows on pages 196–97.

[1] Since *misdemeanors* are often dealt with in cursory fashion, with the defendant pleading guilty rather than taking the time and spending the money necessary to contest the charges, we shall focus in this chapter on *felony* cases.

POLICE REPORT

Officer Name: Julie Brown — Time/Date: 3:30 a.m. 6/12/96

Arrest Number: 10046 — Location: 2546 Maryland Road

Other Officers Present at Arrest: Ted Howard

Name of Arrested Individual: Michael Jones

Address: 1601 Main Street, Andersonville

Offense: Stolen car

Witnesses: Sidney Thompson, Room 204, College Hall

Evidence:	Item Description:	Storage Location:
Car seized	White Honda	Lot C-2—warehouse

SUPPLEMENTAL NOTES

At 3:30 a.m. on Friday, June 12, I arrested suspect Michael Jones and charged him with stealing an automobile belonging to George Doe. On the above date I was on patrol with Ted Howard. At 11:30 p.m. on June 11 headquarters issued a radio report that a Mr. Doe had just seen a single white male steal his car out of his driveway on Tulip Avenue. The stolen car was reported to be a white Honda with a license plate reading KYG-503, but no identifying marks. Registration and serial numbers were unknown.

At 1:05 a.m. Howard and I saw a white Honda speed through the intersection of Old Mill Road and Gizzard Avenue. By the time we gave chase the car was at least five blocks ahead. It did not slow down even after we pursued with siren and emergency lights on. We radioed to headquarters and chased the suspect to the university campus. The car had crashed into the side of College Hall. There was heavy damage to the fender and right front end. The suspect had apparently fled on foot. I looked inside the car with my flashlight and saw blood on the steering wheel and on the floor below. It looked to me as though the driver had hit his head after running the stolen car into the wall.

Just after we arrived, college student Sidney Thompson came out of the dorm and reported that he had seen a man, dressed in a blue, striped shirt and blue jeans, running down the hill away from the building just after he heard the car crash into the wall of the building. The window of his room is on the first floor just to the right of the place of impact.

Howard called headquarters to report our location and to request back-up assistance. Almost immediately, Officers Clark and Smith arrived. Howard,

Clark, and I then searched the immediate area and found no sign of the driver. Smith photographed the scene, supervised the towing of the car to headquarters, and further interviewed the witness, taking his statement (attached).

Hoping to find the suspect nearby, Howard and I resumed our patrol of the neighborhood in our cruiser. At 3:28 a.m. I spotted a man walking alone about one-half mile from the place where the car had been abandoned on the university campus. As we approached, we could see that the man was wearing a blue shirt and dark pants and he had a bandanna around his forehead, perhaps covering a cut.

Upon seeing the police car, the man quickly turned into the all-night convenience store at 2546 Maryland Road. I entered the store to investigate. I saw the suspect was Michael Jones. I arrested Jones last June in another stolen car case. I saw his clothes matched the description of the suspect. When he saw me, he said: "I knew I was headed for trouble again."

Howard and I then read Jones his rights and arrested him, charging him with stealing George Doe's car. The driver's license and a credit card in his wallet confirmed my identification of him as Michael Jones of 1601 Main Street.

Signature: Officer Julie M. Smith
Attachment: Statement by witness who saw the man running from the scene of the accident.

Should a criminal trial occur, officers Smith and Howard will probably be called as witnesses. If not, their role in the case ends upon filing their report.

The Criminal Complaint

In any case that is likely to be of interest to a prosecutor, the police will ensure that a formality known as a **criminal complaint** is issued.[2] In the given hypothetical case, the arresting officers or their colleagues would make out a complaint, or the police would ask Mr. Doe to come before a magistrate to serve as the **complaining witness.** The police or the victim would then sign an official written declaration, under oath, stating that George Doe had been the victim of a crime when someone stole his car on Thursday night, June 11. The magistrate might require the police or Mr. Doe to answer questions about the affair, and the magistrate might call the eyewitness in the dormitory for another sworn statement. If the suspect were not already in custody, the magistrate would then normally issue an **arrest warrant,** an order directing the police to arrest a suspect and bring that individual to court to answer to some specific charge.

Under the U.S. Constitution, a defendant is entitled to the assistance of le-

[2] In some states the criminal complaint is called an **affidavit;** in others it is part of the information proceedings.

gal counsel, however unpopular the defendant may be or however heinous the alleged crime, once the police start to **interrogate** or when criminal charges are filed. Thus, at a very early stage in the criminal process all willing defendants are represented by legal counsel, either their own private attorney or a court-appointed public defender paid by the government. Since the right to an attorney is designed to benefit the accused, a defendant may waive it, just as he or she may waive the right to a trial by jury.

In the American adversarial and accusatorial system no defendant shall be convicted if the legal decision maker has a reasonable doubt[3] as to whether he or she in fact committed the alleged crime. The job of the defense attorney, whether private or public, is to represent the accused zealously and ensure that he or she enjoys every protection from an unjust conviction that is available under law.

In some places the prosecutor's office decides whether to pursue the case before it presses for a complaint to be filed. Elsewhere, the complaint is issued, and then the prosecutors decide whether or not to pursue it. Whichever is the case, authorities in most states do not hold a suspect for more than a day or so while a crime is being initially investigated.[4] After that time formal criminal charges are filed or the individual is released. Hence, prosecutors often find the timing of a criminal complaint to be a significant detail.

Once the suspect has been arrested, the prosecutor's office must determine whether it intends to prosecute or dismiss the case. This discretionary decision, only rarely subject to internal or external review, depends upon various factors. The seriousness of the crime and the extent of evidence against the suspect are, of course, most important. Other significant secondary factors might include the results of prior similar cases, including the severity or leniency of the judge at sentencing, any errors made by the police that raise serious legal difficulties for successful prosecution, and the flow of cases being handled by the prosecutor's office at the time. In addition, the decision may be influenced by the relationship of the prosecutors with the police, the views of the arresting officers, and in certain cases the relationship of the prosecutors with the defense counsel.[5]

Since it is not easy to gather proof beyond a reasonable doubt, prosecutors dismiss at once as many as one-half of all felony cases brought before them.[6] Addi-

[3] The precise meaning of *reasonable doubt* is elusive. A prominent court of appeals opinion explained the concept as follows: "[Reasonable doubt which will justify acquittal] is a doubt based on reason which arises from evidence or lack of evidence. It is doubt which a reasonable man or woman might entertain. It is not fanciful doubt; it is not an imagined doubt; it is not a doubt that a juror might conjure up in order to avoid performing an unpleasant task or duty." *United States v. Johnson,* 343 F.2d 5, 6 (2d Cir. 1965).

[4] While interpretations of state constitutions vary, holding a suspect in jail for more than forty-eight hours without charging him or her with a crime violates the U.S. Constitution.

[5] See George F. Cole, "The Decision to Prosecute," in Sheldon Goldman and Austin Sarat, eds., *American Court Systems: Readings in Judicial Process and Behavior* (San Francisco: W. H. Freeman, 1978), pp. 97–100.

[6] See G. Alan Tarr, *Judicial Process and Judicial Policymaking* (St. Paul, MN: West, 1994), p. 194, and Glick, p. 206. Some of those cases may be downgraded to misdemeanors and sent to a *court of limited jurisdiction,* where they might or might not be dismissed.

tional cases are dismissed at a later date as the prosecution encounters problems in preparing for trial. This does not, however, mean that those whose cases are dismissed entirely avoid punishment.[7] Before the prosecutor finally decides to dismiss the incident, the suspect will have been arrested and booked, matters that remain part of his or her criminal record. Moreover, the suspect may have had to hire a lawyer, spend time in jail, and explain the circumstances to his or her employer and spouse. One scholar wrote: "Stress on family, fear of losing a job, and the trauma of being ordered about, photographed, finger-printed, and handled by police and jailers is a short experience that lasts a lifetime. Being arrested and going through the mill has led some observers to conclude that a defendant 'might beat the rap, but he won't beat the ride' . . ."[8]

Bringing Charges

The purpose of officially bringing charges in the American criminal process is to ensure that before a case is brought against a felony suspect it is reviewed by a body of impartial citizens or a judicial official and not just by police and a prosecutor. As Chapter 5 noted in detail, in prosecuting a serious crime the government ordinarily attempts to gain an indictment through a grand jury proceeding. While all federal crimes require a grand jury indictment, the reader will recall that some states use a slightly different system. In an *information,* the prosecutor brings the case before a judge or magistrate to determine whether enough evidence has been compiled to suggest that the alleged crime really occurred and that the particular suspect before the court may have committed it. In essence, a judicial officer is substituted for the grand jurors, and the name of the formal accusation changes. In either case, the formal accusation by the government against the suspect typically includes multiple **counts,** or particular offenses, that the prosecution believes the suspect may have committed.

Whether the prosecutor moves for an indictment by a grand jury or an information is normally determined by the process adhered to by the courts of that state. However, in some jurisdictions the prosecutor is allowed to choose whether to pursue an indictment or an information. Whichever process is used, the charges must describe the alleged crime, including when and where it occurred. If the suspect is not already in custody when the indictment or information is handed down, a clerk of the court issues an arrest warrant directing the police to seize that individual.

In the information system, once the charges have been brought to court, the suspect moves onto center stage. While prosecutors dominate grand juries, information proceedings are more evenly balanced. At a preliminary (or **probable cause**) hearing the government must show the magistrate reasonable grounds for believing that the defendant committed the crime. The accused attends the

[7] See Henry R. Glick, *Courts, Politics, and Justice,* 3d ed rev. (New York: McGraw-Hill, 1993), pp. 222–223.

[8] Ibid., p. 223.

preliminary hearing and is permitted to **cross-examine** the government's witnesses and to present evidence on his or her own behalf. For instance, in our hypothetical case the defense counsel might point out that the police failed to find the defendant's fingerprints on the steering wheel or some other exculpatory argument. Since a preliminary hearing has been incorporated into the trial process for the defendant's benefit, the accused retains the right to waive this procedural step. Often, a suspect will do so if the authorities have already collected considerable evidence.

Just as probable cause is necessary to justify an arrest, so must the government show probable cause to continue holding the suspect in jail and to proceed with a criminal trial. If the court finds reason to believe that the defendant did commit the crime, the magistrate will order the accused individual held to answer the charges, and he or she will be **bound over** for trial.

The chief purpose of the complaint and probable cause hearing is to form a legal basis for holding a suspect in custody. Since no one is accused secretly of a crime under the U.S. Constitution, such a preliminary hearing will be public, unless the defendant requests that it be closed. If little evidence exists that links the suspect to the alleged crime, or if the criminal offense is very minor, the suspect is released and the case is over unless the police discover additional evidence and rearrest and recharge the suspect. Although the numbers vary from one locality to the next, the release of the suspect occurs in a large number of cases, approximately one-half the cases in some jurisdictions.

At a preliminary hearing in our hypothetical case the prosecutor would point out that at the time of the arrest the police found the suspect, Michael Jones, within walking distance of the abandoned car. He was wearing a blue shirt and dark blue jeans that matched an eyewitness's description of the suspect, and he was bleeding from the forehead, an injury that matched the blood stains on the steering wheel. If the magistrate agreed that the government had probable cause to pursue the case, as seems quite likely in such circumstances, the case would move to the next stage of the trial process.

The Arraignment

The subsequent stage is called the **arraignment.** If the suspect is in jail, he or she is brought into court. Otherwise, the court issues a **summons** to the suspect, now correctly termed a *defendant,* requiring him or her to appear to answer the charges in the criminal complaint.

If an indigent suspect remains unrepresented by counsel, the court may ask at the arraignment if the services of a public defender or other court-appointed attorney are desired.[9] The clerk of the court then reads the charges against the sus-

[9] Exactly what constitutes an "impoverished" defendant has never been finally settled. One authority noted: "A defendant who is unemployed and has no cash may still be required to hire a lawyer even though it means selling personal possessions. Other judges, however, may permit defendants to obtain free legal help simply by stating that they cannot afford to hire their own attorney." Ibid., p. 220.

pect from the indictment,[10] and in most states the defendant immediately pleads guilty or not guilty.[11] In some states and in federal courts with judicial permission, a defendant has the option of a ***nolo contendere*** plea. This Latin phrase is translated "I will not contest it." The defendant does not admit or deny the criminal charges, but allows the court to proceed with sentencing as if guilt had been admitted or proven.[12] If the defendant pleads guilty, no criminal trial takes place. Rather, the court sets a date on the **court calendar** for a hearing to determine the proper sentence. If the defendant pleads not guilty, the court will then schedule a criminal trial.

Although relatively few persons charged with serious crimes plead guilty at the arraignment, such is not the case with those accused of committing minor offenses. Rather than contesting the charges, one accused of a minor crime will likely admit guilt in order to avoid time-consuming and expensive court appearances. In such cases the magistrate may impose a sentence at once.

What might happen in our hypothetical case at the arraignment of the defendant accused of stealing a car? Despite the evidence against him, Michael Jones is likely to plead not guilty. In fact, at this stage many defendants plead not guilty, whether they in fact committed a crime or not.[13] Knowing how unpredictable a jury trial can be, many defendants hope to be acquitted, especially if the law prescribes a lengthy sentence for the crime they allegedly committed.

A technical reason that defendants accused of serious crimes customarily plead not guilty at the arraignment is that no defendant can be convicted of a crime other than those listed in the indictment, or "lesser, included offenses." This rule provides an incentive for American prosecutors to "throw the book" at the defendant, that is, to "load up" every criminal charge that the defendant could possibly be proven guilty of. For instance, imagine that after a 17-year-old uses a knife to break into a car one night, he steals a checkbook from the glove compartment, outruns pursuing police, and eventually writes ten bad checks to local stores. Depending on the content of state law, a prosecutor might charge the teenager with **grand larceny, petty larceny, vandalism,** possession of stolen property, possession of a weapon, possession of a concealed weapon, ten counts of writing bad checks, fleeing to avoid arrest, and even violating a juvenile cur–

[10] To simplify, I have used the term *indictment* throughout the discussion. The same process occurs in an *information*.

[11] In a few states the charges are read at the arraignment, and the formal plea of guilty or not guilty occurs at a later hearing.

[12] A *nolo* plea is useful to a defendant chiefly in one of two contexts. First, it might save face for a defendant, like a politician or celebrity, who recognizes the strength of the government's case yet wishes to avoid admitting guilt. Second, many cases involve both criminal and civil charges, and although a guilty plea or conviction in a criminal case may be used against a defendant in a later civil lawsuit involving the same acts, a *nolo* plea may not be used in that manner. Consequently, under circumstances such as a price-fixing antitrust case involving potentially serious civil liability, a defendant may prefer to enter a *nolo* plea on the criminal charges rather than risk facing the civil charges with a prior criminal conviction on the record.

[13] For a more detailed discussion see Lloyd L. Weinreb, *Denial of Justice: Criminal Process in the United States* (New York, The Free Press, 1977), pp. 57–58.

few.[14] In many cases of overloaded charges, the defendant will likely believe that he or she is innocent of some of the charges filed. In any event, the defendant may well believe that the prosecution cannot prove guilt beyond a reasonable doubt on every one of the charges listed.

Plea-Bargaining Negotiations

Defendants accused of serious crimes frequently plead not guilty at their arraignment for a more practical reason as well. Many times, even after authorities press charges, American criminal trials do not occur. Instead, a negotiation known as *plea bargaining* occurs between prosecutor and defense counsel. In eight or nine out of every ten cases,[15] at some point before the trial is scheduled to start, the defendant will agree to plead guilty to certain charges. In exchange, the government will agree to drop other charges, to reduce a serious charge to a less serious ("included") offense, or to recommend to the judge that a lighter sentence be imposed. Often, the prosecutor will offer some combination of these incentives in order to gain the defendant's guilty plea. The need for bargaining chips to use in these plea-bargaining sessions also helps to explain why prosecutors so often "load up" charges against a suspect.

When the evidence against a defendant is very strong and the likelihood that the case will be dismissed at a preliminary hearing is negligible, plea bargaining may occur even before the arraignment. If so, the defendant pleads guilty, the prosecutor carries through with the agreed deal, the judge issues a sentence, and the case is over. Often, however, the defendant will want to wait for the preliminary hearing to see if the court agrees that the prosecutor can demonstrate probable cause. Hence, most defendants accused of serious crimes plead not guilty at the arraignment and anticipate future plea-bargaining negotiations.

During the negotiations the prosecutor and defense lawyer usually focus upon three issues.[16] First, they will spar over the strength of the case against the defendant, with the prosecutor emphasizing how persuasive the physical evidence and witnesses would likely be in court, and with the defense lawyer probing the weaknesses of the case, especially any indications of unlawful police activity in searching for and seizing evidence and in arresting and interrogating the suspect. The two sides will also analyze the criminal charges in an effort to determine how serious they are. Did injuries or death occur? Was a weapon used? How was the victim harmed? Finally, the prosecutor and defense counsel may discuss the suspect's criminal record, if any. After exploring their different perspectives on the case, the two sides will try to arrive at a proposal that the defense lawyer can take to the defendant and recommend that he or she accept in lieu of going to trial.

[14] For a similar example see Glick, p. 227.

[15] See Weinreb, p. 71, Glick, p. 13; and Robert A. Carp and Ronald Stidham, *Judicial Process in America,* 3d ed. rev. (Washington, DC: Congressional Quarterly Press, 1996), p. 154. The exact percentages vary from state to state.

[16] See Glick, p. 226.

This bargaining process between the lawyers aims to avoid the time, expense, and uncertainty of a criminal trial. The defendant is rewarded for cooperation with a lighter penalty. The prosecutor gains another conviction without having to devote resources to actually trying the case. Often, at the next election the prosecutor's office will publicize its high conviction rate in order to cultivate a public image of being tough on crime without drawing attention to the fact that many of those guilty pleas came at the cost of dropped charges and light sentences.

In our hypothetical case, after having been accused in the indictment of the crime of grand larceny, Michael Jones will not be likely to plead guilty to that crime. Rather, even if he committed the crime, Jones will plead innocent. Then, the defense lawyer will try to plea bargain and persuade the prosecutor to eliminate the grand larceny charge in exchange for a guilty plea. In all likelihood the prosecutor will eventually come to Jones's defense lawyer and say something like this: "The grand jury indictment accuses your client of the crime of grand larceny[17] of an automobile—which carries a sentence of one to five years in prison. We feel we have a fairly good case against him. But, if your client is willing to plead guilty to the crime of **joyriding,**[18] which carries a sentence of not more than one year, we will drop the grand larceny charge." And, the defense counsel may advise Jones to accept such a plea bargain.

Bail

At this early point in the criminal proceedings a magistrate must also decide whether to release the suspect until further proceedings, hold the person in jail until trial, or set **bail.** The idea of bail is that if the judge requires the suspect to deposit some significant sum with the court—perhaps $5,000, $20,000, or $50,000—then the individual will be likely to return for trial in order to recover the deposit. If the individual flees and does not return for trial—an offense known as **jumping bail**—then the state keeps the bail money and the police issue an arrest warrant for the suspect, who is now termed a **fugitive.**[19]

A magistrate who determines that a defendant is very likely to appear in court may allow that individual to leave on his or her own *recognizance,* that is, on the person's promise to appear in court at a later date. However, if the magistrate has some reason to fear that the suspect poses a very dangerous threat to the community or is likely to deposit a large amount of money and nevertheless flee in or-

[17] In certain states *grand larceny* means that an individual has taken and carried away the personal property of another worth more than a particular amount of money, perhaps $100. The theft of personal property worth less than that amount would be termed *petit larceny,* and would be considered a less serious offense.

[18] Whether a defendant is guilty of larceny of an auto or joyriding depends upon intent: Did the defendant intend to permanently deprive the owner of the use of the motor vehicle? Joyriding is sometimes known as *use without authority,* that is, using someone else's property without permission.

[19] The term *fugitive* includes any person who flees from arrest, prosecution, or imprisonment. Hence, *jumping bail* is simply one of the various sets of circumstances that will lead the authorities to term a person a fugitive.

der to avoid trial, the magistrate can deny bail altogether. Since the U.S. Supreme Court has held that the denial of bail does not violate the Eighth Amendment's prohibition against excessive bail, in most states a suspect charged with murder is no longer even eligible for release on bail.

One case involving the issue of whether or not to deny bail arose some years ago when American authorities arrested a Honduran diplomat named Rigoberto Regalado Lara, after catching him trying to pass through Miami International Airport with twelve kilos of cocaine hidden in his luggage.[20] After his arrest, Regalado Lara's attorney asked the magistrate to set a reasonable figure for bail. The prosecution, however, argued that Regalado Lara was part of a dangerous and wealthy narcotics network and might well decide to flee the United States. The prosecutor also pointed out that under the constitution of Honduras no Honduran citizen may be **extradited,** that is, may be sent to another country for a criminal trial. Because of these special factors, the prosecutor persuaded the magistrate to deny bail and to hold Regalado Lara in prison until his case was heard.[21]

Should the suspect be unable to raise the amount of bail set by the magistrate or judge, many states allow individuals (or companies) called **bondsmen** to put up bail for a suspect in return for a fee. The bondsman signs a **promissory note** to the court covering the amount of the bail, then charges the suspect a fee, perhaps 10 percent of the bail figure.[22] If the suspect then jumps bail, the bondsman will lose the entire amount of the bail set by the court. Consequently, the bondsman may require the suspect or his family or associates to put up **bond** or **collateral**—that is, some valuable item as security—to ensure that he or she will not jump bail. Even in states that allow bondsmen to help suspects raise bail, some accused individuals simply lack the resources to raise the requisite sum, whether it is to be paid to the court or to the bondsman. Such individuals must remain in jail until the trial occurs.

In a case in 1991, U.S. authorities arrested a prominent Cuban-American drug trafficker named Carlos Rafael Duque,[23] and the magistrate set bail at $200,000.[24] Duque paid a percentage of that money to a bondsman, who offered

[20] "Destituido Coronel Regalado y puesto a su disposición de EE. UU." [Colonel Regalado Fired and Put in the Hands of the United States], *La Prensa* [Honduras], May 17, 1988, p. 3. "En plástico y rodeado de café iba la 'coca'" [The "Coke" Arrived Wrapped in Plastic and Surrounded by Coffee], *La Prensa* [Honduras], May 17, 1988, p. 3.

[21] "Niega libertad provisional a Rigoberto Regalado Lara" [Rigoberto Regalado Lara Is Denied Bail], *La Prensa* [Honduras], May 25, 1988, p. 4. See also "10 años de cárcel para Regalado Lara" [10 Years In Jail for Regalado Lara], *La Prensa* [Honduras], Sept. 2, 1989, p. 2.

[22] See Tarr, p. 196.

[23] For Duque's links to Manuel Noriega see "Narcotraficante es plagiado y llevado a Miami" [Narcotics Trafficker is Kidnapped and Taken to Miami], *La Prensa* [Panama], Aug. 17, 1991, p. 3A. See also "Noriega ofreció FAP a traficantes" [Noriega Offered Panamanian Air Force to Traffickers], *La Prensa* [Panama], Nov. 5, 1991, p. 1A; "Kalish compró protección oficial para actividades de narcotráfico" [Kalish Bought Official Protection for Narcotics Trafficking Activities], *La Prensa* [Panama], Nov. 6, 1991, p. 1A; "Involucran a Alfredo Orange en contrabando de marihuana" [Alfredo Orange Involved in Marijuana Smuggling], *La Prensa* [Panama], Nov. 7, 1991, p. 1A.

[24] "Condenado a 30 años Carlos Rafael Duque" [Carlos Rafael Duque Sentenced to Thirty Years], *La Nacion* [Costa Rica], Nov. 2, 1991, p. 10A.

the court the remainder. Duque later jumped bail. The bondsman, who had now lost a very considerable sum, hired private investigators to track down Duque.[25] The men eventually found Duque on a ranch in Costa Rica. His girlfriend later reported that two armed men suddenly appeared at the door, forced their way in, handcuffed Duque, and compelled him to return to the United States, where a court sentenced him to thirty years in prison. Since Duque had been returned for trial, the government repaid the bondsman the deposit.

Rather than denying bail altogether, some magistrates will request such a large amount for bail that the suspect will be very unlikely to be able to pay it and, hence, must remain in custody awaiting trial. Since bail is set at the court's discretion and since jumping bail is not uncommon, this type of decision is difficult to challenge successfully. Occasionally, however, a judge clearly abuses the bail system in this manner, as when courts in the South set extraordinarily high bail for civil rights protestors arrested after engaging in nonviolent demonstrations.[26]

Although many defendants cannot meet bail and the court denies others the opportunity for bail, virtually all defendants hope that the magistrate sets a reasonable figure that can be raised at once to release them from custody. Not only are jails often crowded and uncomfortable, but one released on bail can live a normal life until the case goes to trial or is plea-bargained. A bailed defendant need not be separated from family and friends. He or she can continue to work. In addition, a defendant out on bail may be better situated to help defense counsel prepare for trial.[27]

Since bail decisions depend upon the assessments of individual magistrates or judges, it is very difficult to predict at what level a court might set bail in our hypothetical case. The magistrate might consider the prosecutor's recommendation, the defense counsel's argument on behalf of the defendant, the degree to which the jail is overcrowded, and various other factors. Although the figure would be likely to vary from one jurisdiction to another, a suspect with a prior criminal record accused of stealing a car might expect bail to be set at between $5,000 and $10,000.

Trial Preparation

In the weeks following the suspect's arrest, if the prosecutor and defense counsel cannot agree on a plea bargain, both sides begin to prepare for trial. Trial preparation starts off with a period called **discovery** in which both sides try to determine what actually happened. The prosecution will interview potential witnesses and collect its physical evidence. It will also marshall the experts who will testify on the government's behalf. In a case involving the firing of a weapon, expert testimony regarding ballistics usually occurs. Even more common is expert testimony regarding

[25] Ibid.

[26] Glick, p. 221.

[27] See ibid., pp. 220–221.

forensic medicine—that is, the branch of medical science that applies to legal ends knowledge in fields as diverse as anatomy, botany, chemistry, medicine, physics, physiology, and surgery. The forensic medicine scientists at the FBI crime laboratory examine more than one million pieces of evidence each year and testify at trial in hundreds of state and federal courts.[28]

Meanwhile, the defendant's lawyer will prepare the defense in a somewhat similar manner. Unlike the occasional trial in which the defense is well-stocked with resources, as in the O. J. Simpson murder case, the defense lawyer ordinarily has very limited time to devote to an independent investigation of the facts. Rather, the prosecution is required to turn over to the defense lawyer much of the evidence the government has collected, so the suspect will know at least the outlines of the government's case before the trial begins. Hence, the defense typically relies heavily on the defendant's version of the events and the prosecutor's developing case.[29]

In this regard, it bears emphasizing that the privilege against self-incrimination, introduced in the prior chapter, protects a defendant from being compelled to answer questions regarding the criminal accusation as well as from testifying at the trial. In this regard, of course, America's innocent-until-proven-guilty system contrasts markedly with the demonstrate-your-innocence system favored by civil law countries. A criminal defendant in a civil law state would ordinarily be ill-advised to refuse to divulge any information, since a burden rests on the defendant's shoulders to clear his or her name of the accusation. The civil law systems provide the authorities with a substantial advantage in their quest to determine the truth of what happened, especially since a guilty defendant will be likely to make up an **alibi** that can itself be investigated by the authorities.

During this pre-trial period, the court will frequently hold an **omnibus hearing** in which the judge considers many different, and often unrelated, legal issues raised by the two sides. Such a hearing provides an opportunity for both sides to bring preliminary legal matters to the judge for decision before the trial begins. Such preliminary matters often include attempts by the defense to have the case dismissed, to exclude certain pieces of evidence, to object to various aspects of the complaint, or to challenge the jurisdiction of the court over the alleged offenses or over the defendant. At this stage either side may request the judge to grant a **continuance,** that is, a postponement of the trial to allow for additional preparation.

Toward the end of the trial preparation period the prosecutor and defense attorney meet with the judge in a pre-trial conference. At this stage the two sides with the judge's assistance will identify any facts that are not in dispute and a trial date will be set. After this conference the only remaining stage before trial is the jury selection, or *voir dire,* described in detail in Chapter 5.

[28] Pierre Thomas and Mike Mills, "F.B.I. Crime Laboratory Being Probed," *Washington Post,* Sept. 14, 1995, p. A12.

[29] See Weinreb, pp. 64–65. In order to avoid the possible intimidation of witnesses, their statements to the police—an extremely important part of most criminal cases—are not usually turned over to the defense.

THE STEPS IN A CRIMINAL TRIAL

The Opening Statement

The prosecutor customarily begins a criminal trial with an **opening statement.** In some states the defense counsel follows the prosecutor with an opening statement on behalf of the defendant. In other jurisdictions the defense is allowed to postpone, or "reserve," its opening until the end of the prosecution's case. Opening statements preview the case that is to be presented, introduce the lawyers and the dispute at issue to the jury and court, and often set the tone for the remainder of the trial.

In the opening statement each lawyer lays out, often in narrative form, the essential facts that he or she intends to prove. Since one's initial view of an event can have a powerful psychological effect in influencing the interpretation of later facts, trial attorneys usually try to set forth some theme for the jury to consider as the two sides present their evidence. While at first glance this task may appear to be straightforward, the opening address often turns out to be one of the most difficult and delicate stages of a trial. One experienced trial lawyer observed: "Strange as it may appear, there is nothing more difficult in the art of advocacy than to effectively open a case to a jury."[30]

An opening statement is not permitted to be an exhaustive rendition of the case. Judges also do not allow openly argumentative addresses. Rather, the court expects each lawyer to sift through the matters that he or she expects to prove at trial and briefly identify certain vitally important points. An ideal opening will begin to win over the decision maker by marshaling key facts in a clear narrative that places one's side of the case in the most favorable possible light. The objective of the opening statement is to leave an advantageous initial impression in the mind of the jury and judge.

While a lawyer is unlikely to win a case with the opening address, he or she will certainly want to avoid losing it at this early stage! An experienced lawyer will take special care not to alienate the judge and jury by words or appearance. He or she will avoid foolish **admissions,** that is, confessions, concessions, or voluntary acknowledgments that the other side might put to use. (For instance, a prosecutor would be making an admission by saying: "This witness is so important that if you don't believe her, we might just as well set the accused free and all go home.") Trial lawyers especially do not want to overstate matters in the opening statement to their client's initial advantage but ultimate disadvantage. In the closing argument the opposing counsel may be able to harp on such misstatements and compare the facts actually proved at trial with the overstated prediction of what would be proved.

Experienced trial lawyers will thus try to ensure that nothing is said in the opening that will end up gravely damaging their client's cause. Nevertheless, a

[30] Lloyd Paul Stryker, *The Art of Advocacy: A Plea for the Renaissance of the Trial Lawyer* (New York: Simon & Schuster, 1954), pp. 59–60.

lawyer may well want to face up to certain weaknesses in the case on the theory that the damage will be compounded if the opposing counsel is allowed to introduce them. A noted litigator and defense counsel advised: "There is never a case in which there is not some unanswerable fact or circumstance that is strong against you. Face it boldly, . . . at the start . . . 'Why this can't be so bad,' the jury is saying to itself, 'or why should the man's own lawyer be telling us about it?' So, . . . tell it all, even as you would pluck a splinter from an infected finger. It is over and done with then, and it will become a stale and twice-told story when your adversary mentions it."[31]

In their efforts to craft a statement that neither says too much nor too little, lawyers spend much time and effort strategizing about the most effective way to open the case. For example, in 1992 a woman in Florida accused William Kennedy Smith, a member of the famous Kennedy family, of raping her. The most widely publicized rape trial in American history followed, concluded by Smith's acquittal on all charges. Just before the trial the *Miami Herald* asked various well-known attorneys, both prosecutors and defense lawyers, to describe how they might phrase an effective opening statement.[32]

Susan Dechovitz, one of the most experienced prosecutors of rape cases in Florida at the time, said: "[I would emphasize that] every woman has the right to say no [to a man who wants sex]—to say no to any man, under any circumstances, even to a Kennedy." Rebekah Poston, a criminal defense lawyer who formerly served as a federal prosecutor, advised the defense as follows: "Keep the case simple. You don't have to make the woman out to be a bad person to convince the jury to acquit William Kennedy Smith. It is important to make the jury understand what aspects of the woman's conduct that evening led Smith to reasonably believe she had consented [to have sex with him.]" Poston continued: "Often, intimate relationships are not carved out of direct communications. One person's impression is another person's misimpression. Here Smith's reasonable impression from her conduct was that she desired to have an intimate relationship with him." She concluded:

> I would not attack the alleged victim or be discourteous. I would set out objectively what transpired that evening. How she displayed her interest in him. Whether they drank. Whether they danced. How closely they danced. The fact that she returned home with him. And that she remained there despite numerous opportunities to leave.

Professor Alan Dershowitz of Harvard Law School similarly advised the defense: "If this is a trial at which it is handsome, charming Dr. Smith's word against

[31] Ibid., p. 61.

[32] "Rape Trial Strategy," *Miami Herald* (Int'l Ed.), Dec. 2, 1991, p. 11A. Two notable recent works on rape are Susan Estrich, *Real Rape* (Cambridge, MA.: Harvard University Press, 1987) and Leslie Francis, ed., *Date Rape: Feminism, Philosophy and the Law* (University Park: Pennsylvania State University Press, 1996).

the word of a woman he took home at 3:00 A.M. for a walk on the beach, he will win." Dershowitz continued: "I think the lawyer has to be a gentleman. If the lawyer is aggressive toward the woman, then the jury will think that Smith was aggressive to the woman. [The jury will identify] the way the lawyer behaves toward her . . . as the way William Kennedy Smith behaved toward her."

Each of these examples demonstrates how lawyers think strategically in an effort to phrase an effective opening statement that leaves a positive impression without raising expectations beyond what can reasonably be met by the evidence to be presented at trial. In our hypothetical example involving the stolen car the prosecutor would be likely to use the opening statement to lay out the facts in a chronological narrative that pointed toward the defendant's guilt. Through the remainder of the case the prosecutor would try to use **circumstantial evidence** to extinguish any doubt in the minds of the jurors that the authorities had the real culprit on trial. In contrast, the defense lawyer would use the opening statement to emphasize the gaps in the prosecution's case. For instance, the defense would want to point out that a rather long period elapsed between the time the car crashed into the building and the sighting and arrest of the suspect by police.

The Case-in-Chief

After the opening statements, the prosecution begins its **case-in-chief.** The case-in-chief encompasses the main portion of a criminal trial in which the prosecutor lays out the evidence of guilt, after which the prosecution **rests** while the defense presents its case. After the defense rests, the judge will often allow the prosecution to **reopen** its case or offer **rebuttal** testimony to speak to issues not adequately addressed in its case-in-chief. The same opportunity is then given to the defense to reopen its case or to rebut.

Direct Examination of Witnesses

The prosecutor starts the case-in-chief by questioning the government's witnesses on **direct examination.** Witnesses often include the victim or individuals who observed the crime being committed or who came upon the scene of the crime shortly after it occurred.[33] Alternatively, the witnesses may be experts such as a doctor, **medical examiner** or **coroner,** or a laboratory professional skilled in analyzing blood, hair, flesh samples, fingerprints, bullets, or other physical evidence.

In our hypothetical case one obvious choice for a witness would be a laboratory technician expert in analyzing blood samples. Deoxyribonucleic acid (or **DNA**) is the chemical that codes the genes in the cells in a human body in a pattern unique to each human being. In a process sometimes called **DNA fingerprinting** American authorities increasingly use DNA samples to link suspects to

[33] For an interesting analysis of the problems posed by children serving as witnesses, see Lucy S. McGough, *Child Witnesses: Fragile Voices in the American Legal System* (New Haven, CT: Yale University Press, 1994).

physical evidence, such as blood, semen, or hair, bone or skin fragments, found at the crime scene or on the victim. DNA testing is a controversial but ever more important part of American criminal trials. Thus, in the case of the stolen car an expert would examine the blood sample taken from the steering wheel and compare it to a sample of blood taken from the defendant to determine if the DNA matched.[34]

Each witness, brought to the stand by the bailiff, must swear to speak truthfully.[35] A witness who lies commits **perjury,** which may be defined as a false material statement made under oath in an official proceeding by a person who knows the statement to be untrue. On the day they are scheduled to testify, the witnesses will sometimes be present in the courtroom, waiting to **take the witness stand** and listening to the other witnesses testify. However, the prosecutor or the defense counsel may call for the "rule on witnesses." The judge will then order the **separation of witnesses.** This means that all the remaining witnesses will be excluded from the courtroom and separated from one another until they are called to take the witness stand.

Ordinary witnesses simply testify to facts that they know: what they saw or heard at the crime scene or know about the crime. Attorneys also use witnesses to identify the exhibits that their side wishes to introduce into evidence. Witnesses are not to discuss irrelevant matters, nor are they to report hearsay.[36] Technically, hearsay means an out-of-court statement offered to prove the truth of what it asserts. Generally, the prohibition against hearsay bars evidence that comes not from personal knowledge, but from repeating what a witness has heard another say. Ordinary witnesses are not generally permitted to state their opinion; however, a qualified **expert witness** may give an opinion and support that opinion with reasons.

Once an attorney moves from asking a witness routine questions such as name, address, and occupation, he or she may not ask **leading questions** on direct examination. That is, the attorney may not ask his or her own witness questions phrased so as to suggest to that witness the answer that is desired. For example, in our hypothetical case a prosecutor would not be permitted to ask Officer Julie Brown: "I understand that upon arriving at the scene of the crime you found blood on the steering wheel?" That would constitute a leading question regarding a substantive matter at issue in the trial.

Often, in the course of examining witnesses, the lawyers will introduce

[34] In various other countries the use of DNA is even more extensive than in the United States. In the United Kingdom, for instance, authorities sometimes engage in mass DNA screening; that is, taking "voluntary" samples of blood, hair, or saliva from thousands of men in an attempt to match their DNA with evidence from a crime scene. Although the sampling is said to be "voluntary," anyone who refuses to give a sample automatically becomes a suspect in the case. Since such methods might constitute an unreasonable *search and seizure* under the U.S. Constitution, American authorities collect other evidence against a particular suspect before requesting samples. See Fred Barbash, "Crime-Solving by DNA Dragnet," *Washington Post,* Feb. 2, 1996, p. A21.

[35] Witnesses traditionally declare: "I swear to tell the truth, the whole truth, and nothing but the truth, so help me God."

[36] For a readable introduction to this complicated subject see Irving Younger, *Hearsay: A Practical Guide Through the Thicket* (Clifton, NJ: Prentice Hall, 1988).

physical evidence and ask that it be held by the court and marked for identification.

Cross-Examination of Witnesses

When the prosecutor completes his examination of each witness, the defense lawyer asks questions of that same witness either about some subject the witness has already discussed during direct examination or about a different aspect of the case. This practice is called **cross-examination.**

Since the perspectives of those on opposing sides of a case naturally conflict, since testimony is often ambiguous, biased, or fragmentary, and since witnesses often contradict or qualify one another, allowing an attorney to question an adverse witness is supposed to help to reveal what truly occurred. The lawyer doing the questioning, the cross-examiner, will have an opportunity to raise doubts about whether the testimony of each witness accurately reflected what really occurred. During this highly adversarial portion of the trial, a lawyer who is cross-examining a witness is permitted to ask leading questions.

To counter the fallibility of witnesses, legal systems that function justly must somehow test and critically examine testimony before the court accepts it as valid. Cross-examination has been called "beyond any doubt the greatest legal engine for the discovery of the truth."[37] One trial attorney noted:

> Witnesses are historians . . . reconstructing past events. Many of them to the best of their ability attempt to do it honestly, but it is not strange to find the grossest of imperfections even in the memory of an honest man. Not only may his hearing and eyesight be defective, but all his recollections . . . are the product of an association of ideas, conmingled and confused with rationalization, and all his memory may be tinctured by a bias, sometimes subconscious, or colored by suggestion.[38]

Of course, a stressful cross-examination may induce witnesses to stumble, forget, or misspeak. Certain studies have suggested that "rather than forcing truth to the surface, [cross-examination] impairs memory and reduces the accuracy of testimony."[39]

However that may be, it seems fair to conclude that "[A]s yet no substitute has ever been found for cross-examination as a means of separating truth from falsehood, and of reducing exaggerated statements to their true dimensions."[40] While cross-examination is not without faults and pratfalls, the American legal system uses it to illuminate the biases of witnesses, to question their character, verac-

[37] Sir John Henry Wigmore, cited in Stryker, p. 75.

[38] Stryker, p. 94.

[39] Stephen J. Adler, *The Jury: Trial and Error in the American Courtroom* (New York: Times Books, 1994), p. 210.

[40] Francis L. Wellman, *The Art of Cross-Examination,* 4th ed. rev. (New York: Macmillan, 1936), p. 7.

ity, and credibility, to flush factual errors out of their testimony, and, most dramatically, to expose the gross inconsistencies and, occasionally, the outright lies in their testimony. In *The Art of Cross-Examination,* Francis Wellman concluded that to cross-examine skillfully "requires the greatest ingenuity, a habit of logical thought, clearness of perception . . . ; an infinite patience and self-control; power to read minds instantly, to judge . . . character by . . . faces, to appreciate . . . motives; ability to act with force and precision; a masterful knowledge of the subject-matter itself; . . . and above all the *instinct to discover the weak point* in the witness under examination."[41] Some of the most compelling cross-examinations "become a speech in the form of questions."[42]

For an example of a lawyer cross-examining a witness, one might consider the following short but effective cross-examination by Chicago attorney Weymouth Kirkland. Kirkland was defending insurance companies that were convinced that a ship's engineer named Peck had faked his death by pretending to fall overboard in order to collect life insurance payments. The plaintiff found a witness, a cook on another ship, who claimed to have seen Peck's drowned body. Kirkland's job was to convince the jury this witness was lying.

KIRKLAND: How long had you known Peck?
WITNESS: Fifteen years.
KIRKLAND: You knew him well?
WITNESS: Yes, sir.
KIRKLAND: How did you happen to see his body?
WITNESS: I looked out of the porthole.
KIRKLAND: You recognized it beyond doubt as the body of Peck?
WITNESS: Yes, sir.
KIRKLAND: Did you make any outcry when you saw the body?
WITNESS: No sir.
KIRKLAND: Did you ask the captain to stop the ship?
WITNESS: No, sir.
KIRKLAND: What were you doing when you happened to look out of the window and saw the body?
WITNESS: I was peeling potatoes.
KIRKLAND: And when the body of your old friend, Peck, floated by, you just kept on peeling potatoes?
WITNESS: Yes, sir.

After such a cross-examination it would be difficult for any juror to find such testimony very credible!

[41] Ibid., p. 8 (*italics* in original).

[42] One English authority, Sir James Fitzjames Stephens, traced this style of cross-examination through English legal history to a period in the seventeenth and eighteenth centuries when courts did not permit defense counsel in felony cases to address the jury directly. Without the benefit of an opening statement or closing argument, the attorneys used the questions during cross-examination to tell the story of the case from their client's point of view. Ibid., p. 72.

For an example of a cross-examination gone awry, consider the following **driving while intoxicated** (or **DWI**) case.[43] The prosecutor on direct examination questioned a policeman who had stopped a defendant allegedly driving a car while under the influence of alcohol. In order to raise doubts among the jury members as to how reliable a witness the policeman was, the defense lawyer tried the following cross-examination.

DEFENSE LAWYER: And, officer, you say you are absolutely sure the defendant was intoxicated?

POLICE OFFICER: Yes sir.

DEFENSE LAWYER: And how long have you been with the state police?

POLICE OFFICER: Six months.

DEFENSE LAWYER: And, after only six months on the force, you are able to say, to *know* that the defendant was intoxicated?

POLICE OFFICER: Well, before I joined the police force, I was a bartender for sixteen years.

Plainly, this cross-examination did not proceed as the defense counsel wished since he ended up not attacking the witness's credibility, but making the testimony seem even stronger. The cross-examination revealed that what the jury had been viewing as simply the opinion of an inexperienced policeman, on whether the defendant had been drunk, was actually the opinion of an expert, who had been judging when a person was drunk by working in a bar for sixteen years!

This highlights the important issues that trial lawyers face of whether to cross-examine at all and when to stop questioning a witness. If an adverse witness has actually strengthened the client's side of the case, or even if the adverse witness has simply done nothing to damage it, there may be little to gain and something to lose by engaging in cross-examination. By waiving cross-examination, a lawyer may induce jurors to think: "There couldn't be much in that testimony if the opposing lawyer does not wish to question it."[44] Moreover, a lawyer who has elicited favorable points on cross-examination wants to avoid asking that one question too many that opens up new difficulties. Before becoming the second U.S. president, John Adams was a skillful defense counsel. On one occasion he is said to have admonished an associate: "You, Josiah, are a man of zeal. In the heat and inspiration of cross-examination, do not, my young friend, press your examination beyond the necessity of the case. . . . Cases at law . . . are often won by what is left unsaid."[45]

Throughout examination and cross-examination, the attorney who is not questioning the witness may object to any inappropriate questions put to that wit-

[43] This exchange also appeared in the Boule article noted above. For a more extended example of a frustrated, and amusing, cross-examination see the fictional account of questions put by attorney Duffield to witness Colonel Brain in the novel by British judge Henry Cecil, *According To The Evidence* (Chicago: Academy, 1958), pp. 88–91.

[44] Stryker, p. 92.

[45] Ibid., p. 97.

ness. Although the rules of evidence contain many possible grounds for an **objection,** lawyers commonly object to leading questions, questions that ask an ordinary witness for an opinion, and questions that ask the witness for an answer based on hearsay. During redirect examination an attorney might object to questions that deal with matters that go beyond the scope of the cross-examination. The judge, then, either sustains the objection or denies it. If the judge sustains the objection, the attorney must move on to another question or reformulate the question so that it is asked in an unobjectionable manner.[46] If the judge denies the objection, the question is allowed to stand. However, the objecting attorney is usually free to raise the issue on appeal.[47]

In considering the role of objections at trial, one should remember that an American trial is a contest in which each side is striving for victory. It is not an attempt to come up with a model of how to conduct a trial in strict accordance with the laws of evidence. A lawyer will often choose whether or not to object on the basis of the extent to which the matter damages the client, rather than on the extent to which the rules of evidence have been violated. In a case I argued in municipal court, the opposing lawyer introduced photographs that he felt buttressed his argument. A quick glance at the pictures, however, led me to believe that they would further my client's case far more than that of her opponent. Hence, rather than objecting to the authenticity of the photos, I was happy to have the court examine them.

Jurors often think of objections as technical ways that attorneys try to obstruct their view of what really happened. Occasionally, one will see an attorney attempt to use this to advantage by asking a question that he or she must know will raise a valid objection that will be sustained by the judge. Even though the question is overruled, the attorney may feel that the jury has been influenced by hearing it. In most instances such behavior would be considered a minor ethical transgression by the attorney and would be soon forgotten.

It may also be true that the irritation jurors often feel toward all objecting attorneys is compounded if the judge then overrules a particular objection. Consequently, experienced trial lawyers will sometimes allow certain breaches of the rules of evidence to slip by without objection in order to retain the jury's confidence. One authority on trial advocacy advised: "Let trivial and unimportant breaches of the rules of evidence pass unnoticed and never . . . make an objection without good grounds for believing that it will be sustained unless it relates . . . to some fundamental legal proposition . . . in which you must have a ruling to pre-

[46] When the judge sustains an objection, the attorney whose question has been ruled inappropriate may make an *offer of proof.* That means that the attorney gives the court reporter the answer that the witness was prepared to give to the question, if he or she had been permitted to do so by the judge. Thus, the offer of proof becomes part of the record of the case and can be considered by an appellate court.

[47] In some states any such denied objection may be raised on appeal. In other states, the attorney whose objection has been denied must *take an exception.* That means that he or she must formally object to the court's ruling at the time the ruling is made in order to preserve the right to appeal that issue at a later date.

serve some basic right upon appeal. For every time that you are overruled, the jury thinks that you do not know your business or that you are merely there to obstruct, and every answer given after an unsuccessful objection is doubly emphasized."[48]

After cross-examination the first lawyer has the opportunity to question the witness again on any statements made during the cross-examination. This is called **redirect examination.** Then, the other attorney is given the opportunity to conduct **recross-examination.** Eventually, the questioning of that witness ends, and the process starts off again for the next individual to be called to the stand.

Throughout the examination of witnesses and the introduction of physical evidence the opposing lawyer must object if he or she believes the question posed by the examining attorney, the answer of the witness, or the physical evidence submitted to the court violates a rule of evidence. Once an objection is made, the judge issues an immediate ruling sustaining or denying it. If the judge rules that an objection to a question posed by an examining attorney is valid, the question is withdrawn, and the witness is not allowed to answer it. If the judge denies the objection, the court **stenographer** notes the exchange which becomes part of the record of the case. After the trial, if the losing party believes that the judge erred in sustaining or denying an important objection, that decision may form grounds for an appeal. However, attorneys must be alert. They are not normally permitted to object after the moment in which the question is asked or answered or the evidence is submitted, and they may not be permitted to appeal a matter to which they neglected to object at trial.

Since a cross-examination can be such an important part of the trial, experienced lawyers plan very carefully how they will cross-examine a witness. Before the William Kennedy Smith rape trial, for instance, prosecutor Susan Dechovitz was asked how she might go about cross-examining Smith, if he took the witness stand. She advised as follows:

> [Smith is] going to be an extremely well-trained witness. The Kennedys obviously have endless financial resources for this defense. I might therefore ask just how well trained [Smith] has been, how many times he has rehearsed his testimony, how many times he has been videotaped, how many times he has practiced in front of mock juries, how many changes he has made in his testimony as a result, and just whose idea it was to buy him a dog and photograph him walking on the beach.[49]

Experienced trial attorneys often maintain that good lawyers never ask a question at trial to which they do not already know the answer. Christopher Darden, one of the prosecutors in the O. J. Simpson trial, later ruefully conceded that he violated this fundamental precept in asking Simpson to try on a bloody glove

[48] Stryker, p. 90.

[49] "Rape Trial Strategy," p. 11A. Some observers claimed that a widely publicized photograph of William Kennedy Smith walking with a dog on the beach had been planted in the media to remind the public, and perhaps jury members as well, of a famous picture of President John Kennedy walking with a dog on a beach.

found by police behind the football star's mansion on the night of the murders. As it turned out, Simpson seemed to have trouble getting the glove on his hand, leading defense attorney Johnnie Cochran in his closing to the jury to use the slogan: "If it doesn't fit, you must acquit."[50]

Skillful lawyers thus attempt to use the discovery period and the preliminary hearings, including the omnibus hearing, to determine what an adverse witness will say at trial. Through interviews, a lawyer may even find out the weak spots of witnesses: their demeanors and tempers and the extent to which they yield under pressure. Such a strategy, of course, helps to explain why American lawyers sometimes wish to spend so many hours probing different aspects of a case. Yet, apart from delay, excessive fishing about in the pre-trial period can be dangerous. For instance, a lawyer may inadvertently prepare a witness for future questions. The witness may be able to answer those questions in a more compelling manner at trial since he or she has heard them once before.

The Defendant's Case

Once the final witness for the prosecution has finished testifying, the prosecutor will announce that the prosecution rests. That declaration ends the prosecution's case-in-chief. In the American accusatorial system, the government has the burden of proof in a criminal trial. The defendant need not prove his innocence; rather, the state must prove the defendant's guilt. Thus, once the prosecution rests, the defense counsel can raise a **motion for a directed verdict** on the ground that the prosecution has failed to meet its burden of proof—that it has not introduced sufficient evidence to prove that this defendant committed this crime.

If the motion is sustained, the judge directs a verdict in favor of the defendant and the case is over. If the motion is denied, the defense counsel may, but is not obliged to, present its own evidence. It may, but is not obliged to, have the defendant take the witness stand to testify. Of course, if a defendant does voluntarily take the stand in an effort to help his or her own cause, the prosecutor is free on cross-examination to try to elicit evidence that will damage the defendant's case.

The extent of the defendant's case will depend upon the defense counsel's judgment as to how strong the prosecution's case has been and what **exculpatory evidence** exists that the judge or jury has not yet heard. The shape of the defendant's case is also determined by what prejudicial or other negative material might be revealed to the decisionmaker, judge or jury, if a particular piece of evidence were presented or line of argument were pursued in court. A defense lawyer will not want the jury to be wrongly influenced by facts that are irrelevant to the case, but that place the defendant in a bad light. Some lawyers refer to such facts as "skunks": "'Once you let a skunk into the courtroom,' according to an old country lawyer's saying, 'you can't ever completely remove its stink.'"[51]

[50] See "Christopher Darden Speaks," *Washington Post,* March 20, 1996, p. B8.

[51] Alan M. Dershowitz, *The Best Defense* (New York: Random House, 1982), p. 393.

After examination of all the defense witnesses, the prosecutor has the opportunity to ask additional witnesses to testify or to introduce additional evidence so long as the new witness or evidence is designed to rebut testimony or evidence set forth by the defense. After the prosecutor has had the opportunity to rebut, the defense may also counter the new evidence introduced by the prosecutor.

The essential point, then, is that the lawyers exchange roles as testimony is taken during the trial. Each attorney conducts direct examination of his or her own witnesses, and each is allowed to cross-examine the other side's witnesses. If later testimony or evidence seems to demand a response, the court will allow for rebuttal evidence. In this way the system attempts to serve justice by fully exploring the relevant legal issues. Indeed, the American criminal trial provides such ample opportunities for the introduction of evidence that in all but the most unusual circumstances neither side can justifiably claim that the case would have been won if only a particular witness had been allowed to speak.

Closing Arguments

Once all the evidence has been presented, the defense may, once again, move for a directed verdict. So long as the judge denies that motion, one final, exceptionally important stage of the trial process remains—the **closing arguments** (sometimes called **summations** or **closing statements**). The prosecutor first addresses the court and closes the government's case. Concluding remarks by the defense follow. Finally, since the burden of proof rests on the government, the prosecutor is permitted to have the last word and answer (or *rebut*) the defendant's closing argument.

Although in past generations the closing of the case afforded lawyers their opportunity for dramatic speeches,[52] flowery oratory is now usually scorned, though emotional appeals are still sometimes used. Today, each lawyer attempts to set forth the key evidence in the strongest manner possible for his or her side of the case. Neither is permitted to raise irrelevant matters or new evidence. If the defendant chose not to take the stand, the prosecutor is prohibited from making any reference to that decision and what it might imply. However, both lawyers are permitted to make arguments about the case by interpreting the facts reviewed at the trial. In addition, so long as their arguments are supported by evidence introduced at trial, the attorneys may attack and try to discredit the case presented by the other side, including the testimony of opposing witnesses. Thus, a closing argument normally summarizes the evidence a lawyer feels he or she has established and the other side has failed to establish.

Closing remarks usually aim to accomplish several objectives. First, the attorney defines the issue in dispute, thereby clearing the table of all unnecessary factual controversies.[53] A closing argument should also summarize briefly the outstanding points of the case so that the jury can easily recall them. As one trial

[52] See, for instance, Frederick C. Hicks, ed., *Famous American Jury Speeches* (Littleton, CO: Fred B. Rothman, 1990).

[53] See Stryker, p. 120.

lawyer instructed: "[A summation should be] such a systematic arrangement and presentation of the facts that each bit of evidence fits into the pattern of your theory and every circumstance advances your contention."[54] While discussing the evidence frankly and thoughtfully and reasoning with the jury rather than talking at them, a defense lawyer will emphasize why the jury ought to set the suspect free and a prosecutor will stress why the jury ought to decide the suspect is guilty. Finally, and more ambiguously, lawyers attempt in their closing statements to leave a strong, final impression to influence the jury in favor of their side. Lloyd Paul Stryker describes the task of crafting a closing argument as follows:

> The trial, for the lawyer, is what research is for the author. Histories and biographies, letters, memoirs, diaries, and the archives of . . . libraries are the material from which a book is made. The evidence, documents, and the demeanor of the witnesses are the stuff from which the advocate's summation must be constructed.
>
> But the author works . . . alone, with time for reflection and for reconsideration. The advocate . . . must . . . write his book in the floodlight of the public gaze and send it forth to the . . . jury . . . without correction or amendment, and yet . . . he must be as accurate, as clear, as logical, and as interesting as the author, and his book must be so written as to withstand the hostile reviewer in the person of opposing counsel. . . .
>
> [A writer] . . . chooses his material from those facts and incidents that illuminate and explain his central point. . . . So, too, the lawyer, from perhaps six or maybe thirty weeks of testimony must be able to discern which are the points worth dwelling on when he sums up and just how those facts should be marshaled.
>
> But there is one respect in which the advocate has an advantage over the author: he has seen and watched the jury. . . . The author . . . cannot watch [his readers] . . . and change his text to suit their moods.
>
> The advocate, on the other hand, observes . . . those who listen to him and knows . . . whether what he is saying is having its effect or is creating the desired impression. The advocate has direct contact with those whom he is seeking to convince and for whom he molds and shades his words and sentences . . . [55]

One example of a powerful summation occurred in a murder case years ago.[56] Authorities in New Hampshire arrested three suspects, and the state asked Daniel Webster, the famous nineteenth-century American politician and lawyer, to act as **state's attorney** and prosecute the case. During his final remarks to the jury, Daniel

[54] Ibid., p. 128.

[55] Ibid., pp. 113–115.

[56] This example is drawn from Victor Alvin Ketcham, "The Seven Doors to the Mind and How to Open Them," unpublished speech. Webster's argument in the White murder trial may be found in James Milton O'Neill, *Models of Speech Composition: Ninety-five Complete Speeches* (New York: Century, 1921), pp. 3–47. For the full transcript of another famous legal argument by Webster see William L. Snyder, *Great Speeches by Great Lawyers: A Collection of Arguments and Speeches Before Courts and Juries* (New York: Baker, Voorhis, 1923), pp. 67–83.

Webster wanted, in one sentence, to express the idea that the three suspects were hired killers. He said: "Gentlemen of the jury, this was the weighing of money against life—the counting out of so many pieces of silver against so many drops of blood."

It is instructive to analyze how Daniel Webster crafted that sentence. Instead of simply saying, "These men were paid to commit a murder," Webster asked the jurors, in essence, to see in their minds the act of counting out money to these hired killers and the drops of blood falling from the attacked victim. To make the image more vivid, he also appealed to their sense of sound by speaking of "pieces of silver," that is, silver coins that make a special noise—clink, clink, clink—as they are counted out on top of a table. Webster might also have left an especially strong sensory impression since members of a jury at that time could easily recognize the feeling of hard, cold coins.

As might be expected, Daniel Webster proved to be quite a convincing prosecutor. In short order the jury convicted the men of murdering Mr. White.

The Verdict

After the closing arguments the judge gives an instruction (or *charge*) to the jury that outlines the issues they must decide. The judge then sends the jury off to deliberate, that is, to determine whether the suspect is guilty or not guilty. The bailiff accompanies the jury to the jury room and, while remaining outside the room, ensures that no one enters to influence (or "tamper with") the jurors while they deliberate.

When the jury has reached its verdict, the judge reassembles the parties in the courtroom. The **foreman** or **forewoman** then announces the decision: whether the defendant is guilty or not guilty on each count. As noted in Chapter 4, a hung jury will be disbanded, and a new trial may be held. When a jury does return a verdict, the judge listens to the verdict and then polls the jurors to check the accuracy of the verdict. The jury is then formally dismissed.

Once the case is over, the court often permits the lawyers to discuss the proceedings informally with the jurors. They can try to determine what the jurors thought of the case, which witnesses proved to be most and least compelling, and how the jury determined which facts were vitally important as it reached its verdict. In this way lawyers hope to improve their trial advocacy skills for future cases.

After criminal convictions the next step in the trial process is a **sentencing** hearing at which the judge imposes punishment on the guilty.[57] Some convictions and sentences are then followed by a request for a new trial or for a **pardon,** or more customarily by an **appeal.** Appeals in American criminal trials differ from those in many other countries in that they focus on some technical legal matter that arose during the proceedings. As one legal scholar noted:

> In some legal systems (but not ours), an appeals court goes over everything—facts, testimony—in effect, retrying the case. In American law an appeals court

[57] In some states the jury determines the sentence; in others a special board or commission determines the length of the sentence for felonies.

> only corrects "errors"; it does not rehash everything that went on at the trial. The convicted defendant (or his lawyer), on appeal, must be able to point out some technical flaw in the indictment, in the procedures followed or in the way the trial was run. Did the judge allow forbidden bits of evidence? Did he keep proper evidence out? Did he give the jury erroneous instructions?[58]

Whether the defendant wins the appeal or not is considered a matter of law, not of fact. Hence, it is determined by judges interpreting the law, rather than by a jury considering the facts.

PRISONS

Of every five persons convicted of a crime in the United States, courts incarcerate only about two.[59] Judges sentence the remainder to some other form of punishment, perhaps fines, work release, house arrest, community service, or electronic monitoring.[60]

Two very common punishments that are often confused with one another are **probation** and **parole.** A criminal sentenced to probation is released into the community under the supervision of a probation officer, but only so long as he or she abides by certain conditions. For instance, an individual on probation pledges not to break any additional laws for a specified period. He or she is often not allowed to leave the state without permission from the probation officer. And, he or she must check in with the probation officer at regular intervals.

Parole means release from confinement after the criminal has actually served a portion of the sentence. Authorities grant parole when a prisoner seems reasonably likely to live at liberty without violating additional laws. Like one on probation, a *parolee* must comply with the terms provided in the parole order or parole may be revoked. The U.S. Parole Commission determines when federal prisoners should be granted or denied parole, when parole should be revoked, and how the parole order should be supervised. Bodies often known as parole boards or commissions fulfill the same responsibilities in the states.

Types of Prisons and Prisoners

U.S. prisons currently hold about 300,000 **inmates.** In addition, 50,000 prisoners are being held temporarily in U.S. jails. Stealing or damaging property is not considered as serious a crime as one that injures another human being. Since property offenders are not viewed as particularly dangerous for society, they are usually not

[58] Lawrence Friedman, *Crime and Punishment* (New York: W. W. Norton, 1993), pp. 255–256.

[59] Of these, some spend less than a year, though most spend substantially more than a year.

[60] See Anthony Duff, et al., eds. *Penal Theory and Practice: Tradition and Innovation in Criminal Justice.* (Manchester, Lancashire: Manchester University Press, 1996), and Franklin Zimring and Gordon Hawkins, *Incapacitation: Penal Confinement and the Restraint of Crime* (New York: Oxford University Press, 1995).

punished with as lengthy prison terms as violent offenders. Nevertheless, because so many property crimes occur, of the group that is sent to prison more than half have committed crimes against property, not against people.

Although the terms *jail* and *prison* are often used synonymously, they actually have distinct meanings. A **prison** is a place of incarceration to which an individual is sent after being convicted of a crime at a criminal trial. A **jail** is a place to which an individual is sent before the trial begins, often on a temporary basis before he or she pays bail to gain freedom until the trial occurs.[61] Jails are run by local governments and do not usually hold prisoners for long periods. Although the quality of American jails varies from place to place, many are old, small, and extremely overcrowded.[62] Nevertheless, a jail will not usually hold large numbers of hardened criminals. For those who recognize the distinction between the terms, going to jail will carry less of a social stigma than going to prison, since one who is jailed has not yet been convicted of any crime.

Just as the United States has state and federal courts, so it has state prisons for those convicted of crimes in state courts, and federal prisons for people convicted of federal crimes. Throughout the United States men are incarcerated separately from women, though this was not always the case. Children who commit crimes and whose cases are heard in juvenile court may be sent to juvenile detention centers or correctional institutions.

Both state and federal prison systems are also customarily divided into levels. An individual convicted of a crime and sentenced to serve time is thus assigned to one of three different types of state or federal prison: maximum-, medium-, or minimum-security. The decision of where to send a prisoner is determined on the basis of how likely he or she is to try to escape, to cause disciplinary problems, or to injure other prisoners. In the federal prisons, the U.S. Marshals Service is ultimately responsible for deciding which prison is appropriate for which offender.

The most important prisons are designated "maximum-security" **penitentiaries,** or "pens." The buildings in a maximum-security prison are generally very old,[63] but have been built quite securely. The principal emphases in a maximum-security prison are on preventing escapes and controlling prisoners.[64] Hence, such prisons are characterized by massive external walls with multiple guard towers, scores of spotlights, and various electronic devices to trigger alarms in the event of

[61] In the United States and many other countries bound by human rights treaties, people who are merely awaiting trial are detained in a separate location from those who have already been convicted of a criminal offense.

[62] One authority noted: "Paradoxically, efforts to relieve overcrowding in state prisons have increased congestion in local jails, where living conditions are generally worse than in most prisons." Charles E. Silberman, *Criminal Violence, Criminal Justice* (New York: Random House, 1978), p. 375.

[63] About half of America's maximum-security pens were built prior to 1900, and approximately a fifth are more than 100 years old.

[64] Different prisons take different approaches to trying to handle inmates. For the distinction between the rule-oriented approach that characterized a Michigan maximum-security prison and the control-oriented approach adopted by the Texas Department of Corrections, see James Q. Wilson, *Bureaucracy: What Government Agencies Do and Why They Do It* (New York: Basic Books, 1989), pp. 19–20.

escape attempts. Inside the buildings the prison cells are often arranged in long rows, the most famous of which is *death row,* which houses criminals who have been sentenced to death and are awaiting the results of appeals of their death sentences. The cells have barred doors and windows, and television surveillance cameras are placed throughout the interior, including the showers and bathrooms. Most such prison complexes also include a medical clinic, a gymnasium and recreation yard, meeting rooms, and a dining hall.

In some maximum-security prisons inmates must have passes to move from one area to the next and are often accompanied by guards when they move about. Inmates also find themselves subject to frequent head counts, strip searches, and cell "shakedowns" to ensure that no one is unaccounted for, and that concealed weapons are located and confiscated. In a maximum-security prison inmates may be barred from receiving visitors, or they may be required to communicate with them only through plexiglass windows. In some states, mostly in the South, maximum-security prisoners have been put to "hard labor," working on public works projects under the eye of armed guards.

Although maximum-security pens hold approximately half of American inmates, critics have long argued that perhaps only a quarter of the prison population really requires such extreme security measures. Certainly, mass or multiple murderers and organized crime leaders, such as a major narcotics trafficker or the head of a mafia chapter, belong under maximum security. Yet, half of all American inmates do not really pose such a grave danger to other prisoners or to society if they escape. And it may go without saying that maximum-security prisons do not boast impressive records in rehabilitating inmates. A former jail warden and director of a university research center in criminal justice once declared: "If . . . [the authorities] had deliberately set themselves the task of designing an institution that would systematically maladjust men, they would have invented the large, walled maximum-security prison."[65]

Nevertheless, prison officials understandably prefer to err on the side of having prisoners locked up too securely, rather than not securely enough. Certainly, the administration and guards at a prison are likely to be blamed if a prisoner escapes and the criticism will mount if he or she commits another crime while "on the lam." Another reason that so many are assigned to the maximum-security "pens" is that they are the largest in the system: the prison at Jackson, Michigan, for instance, holds 5,000 prisoners. However, the tendency of assigning too many prisoners to maximum-security penitentiaries has the unfortunate consequence of placing criminals who might be rehabilitated into the midst of the most hardened and dangerous prisoners in the system.

The somewhat less dangerous inmates sent to medium-security prisons also find themselves confined within secure, though often smaller, facilities with strict regulations on prisoner conduct. Medium-security prisons, however, tend to emphasize more rehabilitation programs for inmates. Moreover, strip searches,

[65] Hans Mattick, former director of the University of Illinois Center for Research in Criminal Justice, quoted in Silberman, p. 382.

head counts, and shakedowns are not so frequent, privacy is respected a bit more, and visiting hours tend to be more liberal.

While the maximum- and medium-security prisons resemble one another in many respects, the minimum-security prisons differ markedly. Minimum-security inmates tend to have committed property and white-collar crimes. Since they have been judged unlikely to attempt escape and not especially dangerous if they do, minimum-security prisoners are permitted to live a more normal lifestyle. In particular, relatively little emphasis is placed on preventing minimum-security prisoners from fleeing.

A minimum-security prison may consist of a series of detached buildings, surrounded by a fence, often located in a rural area. Inside minimum-security prisons, one may find private rooms with locking doors to ensure that prisoners enjoy some privacy. Meals tend to be taken at small tables with a handful of other inmates, rather than at long tables with constant supervision by guards, as in the medium- and maximum-security pens. Most important, minimum-security prisons emphasize giving the inmates basic training and experience at various jobs. Since rehabilitation is seen as a more realistic goal for these inmates, prison administrators regularly call on psychologists, social workers, religious leaders, and others who might help the inmates to reform themselves, to stay "clean" of crime, and to become more productive and responsible members of society. In keeping with this approach, minimum-security prisons tend to have relatively generous policies regarding visitors. Some even have special buildings where the inmate's family can come for visiting periods of as long as several days.

Eventually, minimum-security prisoners are often placed in work-release programs in which they work at jobs outside the prison during the day and return at night, or sometimes they may merely come back to prison each evening to sign a registration book. Other such prisoners graduate to *halfway houses,* where they can attempt to get a fresh start in life, while still living under penal supervision.

Early Problems in American Prisons

In early American history imprisonment was unusual; instead, courts punished criminals with fines, forced labor on public works (such as cleaning the streets), banishment from the community, infliction of pain, or execution. Prisons began to be built only in the early nineteenth century. In 1829, for instance, authorities constructed a mammoth prison near Philadelphia. A legal historian described it in the following terms:

> Cherry Hill was built in the form of a grim fortress, surrounded by walls of medieval strength. Great stone arms radiated out of a central core. Each arm contained a number of individual cells connected to tiny walled courtyards, one to a cell. The prisoners lived in cell and courtyard, utterly alone, night and day. Sometimes they wore masks. Through peepholes, the prisoners could listen to religious services. . . . [A]bsolute silence was imposed—a punishment

> perhaps more inhumane than the flogging and branding that were supposedly supplanted.[66]

Onlookers differed on the social worth of such new prisons. In the 1830s, French observers Alexis de Tocqueville and Gustave de Beaumont visited Cherry Hill and were impressed by its "moral and just" discipline, though they did note its severity, stating: "While society in the United States gives the example of the most extended liberty, the prisons . . . offer the spectacle of the most complete despotism."[67] They continued: "We have often trod during night those monotonous and dim galleries, where a lamp is always burning: we felt as if we traversed catacombs; there were a thousand living beings, and yet it was a desert solitude."[68]

The Cherry Hill experiment utterly shocked and appalled another famous observer, Charles Dickens. He visited and wrote: "Those who devised this system of [silent] Prison Discipline . . . do not know what it is that they are doing. [This] dreadful punishment [inflicts] immense . . . torture and agony. . . . [It is a] slow and daily tampering with the mysteries of the brain . . . immeasurably worse than any torture of the body." "The silence," Dickens went on, was "awful . . . Over the head and face of every prisoner who comes into this melancholy house, a black hood is drawn; and in this dark shroud . . . he is led to the cell. He is a man buried alive."[69]

In this early period of American penal history prisoners had no rights at all. Upon being convicted of a crime they became what one judge called "slaves of the state." One legal scholar described the prisons of this era as follows: "Ordinary prisons, state and local, were starved for funds, filthy, sometimes debauched. . . . Prisoners were whipped, starved and tortured in prisons all over the country, . . . though not in all prisons at all times. . . . Young and old, men and women, were heaped together, under conditions of 'dirt, vermin, offensive air and darkness.'"[70] He continued:

> [I]n the 1870s, at Sing Sing, investigators found incredible corruption: guards sold forbidden items to prisoners; convicts were allowed to lounge about idly, or play games. . . . Yet at the same time, there was incredible brutality in some prisons: prisoners were whipped and beaten; or they were tortured with pulleys, iron caps, or "cages," or afflicted with the lash, the paddle, or . . . a fiendish form of water torture. . . .

[66] Lawrence M. Friedman, *A History of American Law,* 2d ed. rev. (New York: Simon & Schuster, 1985), p. 296.

[67] Ibid., p. 297, citing Gustave de Beaumont and Alexis de Tocqueville, *On the Penitentiary System in the United States and its Application to France* (1833; reprinted, Carbondale: Southern Illinois University Press, 1964).

[68] Friedman, *Crime and Punishment,* p. 79, citing Beaumont and Tocqueville, p. 65.

[69] Friedman, *A History of American Law,* p. 296, citing Charles Dickens, *American Notes* (Philadelphia: T. B. Peterson and Brothers, 1859), pp. 118, 121. See also Friedman, *Crime and Punishment,* pp. 80–81.

[70] Friedman, *A History of American Law,* p. 600, citing James Leiby, *Charity and Correction in New Jersey: A History of State Welfare Institutions* (New Brunswick, NJ: Rutgers University Press, 1967), pp. 126–128.

> The story was always the same. Somehow reforms never took hold, or were perverted in practice. The fact is that convicts . . . were at the very bottom of American society; powerless, their wants and needs had no American priority. On the other hand, middle-class society had a definite program. People detested crime, and were afraid of it. They wanted criminals punished, and severely; even more, they wanted bad people kept out of sight and circulation.

Reform of the Prison System

Over the years American prison reform movements have regularly sprung up, accomplished a bit, and faded.[71] One historian wrote: "[Each generation] discovers anew the scandals of incarceration, each sets out to correct them and each passes on a legacy of failure. The rallying cries of one period echo dismally into the next."[72]

Few with first-hand familiarity of American prisons would argue that prisoners are coddled. For many years overcrowding has been the norm, with many prison systems doubling or even tripling the prisoner population beyond the original design capacity intended. Living conditions are characterized by poor sewage, rodent and insect infestation, and soiled bedding. The routines of prison life and the prison surroundings are designed to inspire terror and degradation: heads are shaved, bodily orifices are probed for concealed weapons, numbers are substituted for names, and prisoners are incarcerated in cold and often dirty structures of metal, concrete, and barbed wire. One observer wrote: "Until one has experienced it, it is hard to imagine how oppressive is the overwhelming grayness of the prison environment; the unrelieved harshness of the metallic surfaces, which seem to amplify every sound; the absence of flowers, plants, and trees, indeed, of any direct contact with nature or the outside world."[73]

Even more disturbing, modern American prisons have long been plagued by a lack of security. The numbers of prison guards are chronically insufficient. Although brutality sometimes occurs, especially after a guard has been injured or killed, outnumbered guards tend to be afraid to use force since they fear being beaten or taken hostage: ". . . in the tinderbox atmosphere of a prison yard or cellblock, striking an inmate may invite retaliation, and the slightest scuffle may be the spark that sets off a riot or a massed assault on a single guard or group of guards."[74]

Lack of sufficient internal security can result in frequent prisoner fistfights, stabbings, and homosexual gang-rapes, and it encourages the occasional violent riot. For their own safety, the outnumbered authorities must rely on the inmates to control one another to some degree. This is unfortunate since "prison life

[71] See Friedman, *Crime and Punishment,* pp. 159–163, and Silberman, p. 372.

[72] David J. Rothman, "Decarcerating Prisoners and Patients," *Civil Liberties Review,* 1 (Fall 1973): 8–9, cited in Silberman, p. 372.

[73] Silberman, p. 384.

[74] Ibid., p. 393.

is a crucible of intimidation and conflict."[75] The most powerful inmates may be the most brutal, and protection by the powerful may come at a high price in money, drugs, or other goods, in homosexual relations, or in other things valued behind bars. One observer wrote:

> [S]tatus is in such short supply in prison that it can be gained only at someone else's expense—by putting him down verbally, physically, financially, or sexually. Since manhood cannot be demonstrated by heterosexual prowess, there is an exaggerated emphasis on toughness: the ability to either victimize others or withstand victimization, especially by people who appear to be bigger and stronger. By the same token, every slight—every presumed slight—must be countered, lest the person being slighted be branded as a weakling or "punk," a characterization that will make him the target of anyone eager to improve his status by downing someone else. The most casual interactions (brushing against someone in line, using the "wrong" tone of voice) may erupt into lethal violence.[76]

He concluded: "[I]nmates must constantly reaffirm the credentials on which their fragile identity is based. Every challenge must be met; and the challenges are endless, because of the shifting composition of the inmate population. Each inmate who arrives represents an opportunity to victimize inmates, who may be able to improve their status by downing the newcomer; [or the new arrival may be] a threat to the victimizers, who may themselves be victimized if the newcomer is tough enough."[77]

The most recent movement advocating wholesale reform of American prisons is of relatively recent vintage, dating to the post–World War II era and especially the 1960s. It has attracted more broad-based support than its predecessors: most notably, the support of the American Bar Association, church groups, public interest law firms, and civil rights and liberties lobbying groups. However, building better prisons or improving the living standards of inmates has never proved to be a very popular program with the public or their elected representatives. Occasionally, as part of a crime-fighting package, legislatures authorized the construction of new prisons, yet for the most part state and federal politicians have not given prison administrators adequate funding. Since prison reform has no lasting appeal as a political issue, it has been especially well suited to the current era in which effecting social change through litigation is often preferred to political persuasion. Many effective reforms have come about through court orders by judges less

[75] Ibid., p. 387.

[76] Ibid., pp. 386–387. Among the other interactions that Silberman mentions that are frequently used to "down" another inmate are disputes over who enjoys candy, cigarettes, desserts, and radios; who controls the ping pong table, television set, or seating at a movie; who gets the sunniest or shadiest spot in the recreation area; and who enters the showers first. He concluded: "Almost any aspect of prison life can provide an opportunity for some inmates to 'mess over' others, i.e., to demonstrate their domination and other inmates' submission." Ibid., p. 388.

[77] Ibid., p. 387. Silberman continued: "The more frequently inmates come and go, therefore, the more volatile the atmosphere is likely to be—which is why jails are often more brutal than prisons."

concerned with charges of judicial activism and policymaking than their predecessors.

Over time, the long-standing view of prisoners as slaves of the state changed and courts became more willing to step in when prison officials grossly mistreated prisoners. In the years immediately following World War II, courts agreed to intervene in disputes between prisoners and prison officals, but only when necessary to protect prisoners from death or serious bodily harm at the hands of prison authorities. Many judges and state and federal legislators frowned upon interfering with prison officials engaged in a difficult, thankless, and dangerous job without adequate funding.

In the 1960s, amidst other social turmoil and debate, a vigorous movement arose to reform American prisons. American prisoners eventually came to be viewed by some reformers in the same light as minorities and women and others who had long been discriminated against. Equally important, during these years certain civil rights workers deliberately violated unjust laws in order to be imprisoned and to draw national attention to the unfair treatment of minorities. While detained, these civil rights workers saw first-hand the terrible state of many American jails and prisons. When they were eventually freed, the civil rights workers often became vigorous advocates of prison reform. And, when the Nixon administration and the U.S. Congress devoted more money to fighting crime, funds were also set aside to build and improve prison systems.

Prisoners' Rights

The U.S. Constitution prohibits the inflicting of "cruel and unusual punishments."[78] To succeed in proving that punishment is excessively cruel and unusual, a prisoner must demonstrate to the court that the punishment either "inflicts unnecessary pain" or is "grossly disproportionate" to the severity of the crime that was committed. Thus, courts have ruled that whipping prisoners or denying them necessary medical care violates the "cruel and unusual" clause. Likewise, placing a prisoner in *solitary confinement* for periods exceeding 15 days is also cruel and unusual. (Solitary confinement means placing a prisoner in a small room alone with no contact with other human beings.)

Perhaps the most important development in prisoners' rights came when the courts ruled that an inmate deserved due process of law under particular circumstances. In 1970 prison officials discovered that an imprisoned Black Muslim political activist had radical literature in his cell. Upon being questioned, he adamantly refused to tell prison officials where he had received the writings. As punishment, the officials placed him in solitary confinement for more than one year.

When this man challenged his treatment in court, a federal judge ruled that prisoners retain their constitutional rights, except those that must be re-

[78] U.S. Constitution, Amendment VIII.

stricted as part of their imprisonment. Thus, the judge held that the Black Muslim prisoner had the same rights to read literature as any other American, limited only by whatever reasonable rules and regulations were necessary to maintain prison discipline. Most important, the judge ruled that placing prisoners into solitary confinement was unconstitutional without first providing them due process of law. Thus, when officials wish to make prisoners suffer additional punishment, the prisoners are entitled first to receive written notice and to have a formal hearing with lawyers. They have the right to cross-examine witnesses, and eventually to have a written record of the proceedings that may be appealed to higher authorities.

The prisoners' rights movement has resulted in more humane treatment of many inmates—not only is the food more frequently decent and the medical care more often adequate, but devices such as the "Tucker Telephone," a device which guards in Arkansas used to shock the genitals of inmates, have been banned. The changes have also been widespread: The majority of state prison systems have been ordered to improve their conditions.[79] Nonetheless, serious problems persist.[80] The prisoners' rights movement has focused more on correcting abuses and neglect by guards and other prison officials than on curbing brutality by inmates against other inmates. Yet, as one prisoner explained, "It's not the screws you have to worry about, it's the other cons."[81]

Indeed, certain reforms may have made matters worse for the prisoner who simply wants to serve the time without being humiliated, attacked, or sexually exploited by other inmates. While introducing due process to the prison system has given inmates the opportunity to challenge abusive mistreatment by authorities, it has also encouraged unruly prisoner behavior and demoralized prison guards, who on a daily basis must try to decide how to handle some of the most volatile and dangerous people in society under the most adverse circumstances. One scholar wrote: "The need to get the approval of a superior officer and then of a disciplinary board before an inmate can be punished makes guards even more reluctant to enforce the rules. When their judgments are questioned by their superiors, guards feel that they, rather than the inmate, are on trial; and when their disciplinary recommendations are overturned, guards feel that they have been made fools of in front of the inmates they are expected to control."[82]

Thus, reforms aimed at curbing brutality by the authorities may have encouraged guards to be passive and to cut deals with inmates. So long as prisoners do not injure one another so seriously as to draw the attention of higher officials, guards may look the other way or pretend not to know about serious infractions.

[79] For a comparison of the largely positive penal conditions that once existed in a maximum-security prison in Texas and the serious problems found in Michigan and Massachusetts, see John J. DiIulio, Jr., *Governing Prisons: A Comparative Study of Correctional Management* (New York: The Free Press, 1987).

[80] See William I Selke, *Prisons in Crisis* (Bloomington: University of Indiana Press, 1993); Friedman, *Crime and Punishment,* pp. 309–316; and Silberman, pp. 371–423.

[81] Silberman, p. 410. Silberman argued that prison reform may have left "inmates more vulnerable to intimidation and brutality on the part of other inmates." Ibid., p. 379.

[82] Ibid., p. 407.

Even the most conscientious guard may fear to enforce a rule that others freely allow to be broken. Such insights into prison culture help to explain how narcotics have circulated so freely and why rapes have occurred so commonly, even within maximum-security penitentiaries.

As one might expect, the reactions among prison officials to the reform movement have varied. Many felt that federal courts should stop interfering with the operations of prisons, for the courts were making the handling of dangerous criminals even more difficult. Others, however, had been genuinely concerned by the poor standards of care found in the prison system. Unable to gain funding through appeals to legislators, they have welcomed prison reformers and have felt that even prisoner lawsuits might focus attention on egregious problems and help to bring about positive change. For example, after a case in which a federal judge ruled that living conditions in Alabama's prison system were so inhumane as to violate the Constitution, the attorney defending the state observed: "Many of the things the judge ordered are things the Department of Corrections has wanted to [do] for fifty years and couldn't because it was hamstrung by a lack of funds."[83]

WITH JUSTICE FOR ALL?

Criminal process in the United States moves through various distinct phases: the booking, the initial appearance and bail hearing, the complaint, the grand jury indictment or information, the preliminary (or probable cause) hearing, the arraignment, the plea-bargaining negotiations, the discovery period, and the *voir dire* jury selection. Then, the trial itself includes the opening statements, the examination of witnesses (direct, cross, redirect, and recross), the closing statements, the instructions to the jury, the jury deliberations and verdict, the sentencing, and perhaps an appeal. This process often results in prison time for the defendant within a penal system that, for all its reforms, remains rife with problems and largely unable to rehabilitate prisoners effectively.

While the steps in the criminal process may seem comfortable and normal to American lawyers and students of law, they are by no means the only method of determining criminal guilt. Nor are they necessarily the best way. The extent to which the American legal system does justice in criminal cases certainly remains open to debate. Even the most vocal supporters of the criminal justice system would be likely to concede that the United States has a complicated and lengthy criminal trial process that strongly emphasizes the traditional over the efficient.

Once again, if sweeping reforms of American criminal proceedings are unlikely, perhaps incremental changes might be considered. For instance, certain steps in the trial process were designed principally to protect defendants from arbitrary prosecution. One may well question whether arbitrary prosecution remains as ominous a problem as it seemed to the Founders and other eighteenth-century Americans. We live in an age with excessively high crime rates, when the authori-

[83] Ibid., p. 375.

ties cannot close many cases and when antiquated state and federal criminal processes are ordinarily clogged and backlogged. To keep such an unwieldy system from thoroughly malfunctioning, prosecutors must dismiss large numbers of cases, even regarding felonies, and the authorities must lean heavily on plea bargaining with its lesser sentences and dropped charges. It is worth pondering whether under such circumstances American society is better off having indictments and informations and preliminary hearings exhaust so many legal and judicial resources. If streamlining the system is unlikely to bring about justice for all, it might well bring about more justice for more defendants and for more victims.

SELECTED ADDITIONAL READINGS

BIANCHI, HERMAN. *Justice as Sanctuary: Toward a New System of Crime Control.* Bloomington, IN: University Press, 1994.

EISENSTEIN, JAMES, et al. *The Contours of Justice: Communities and their Courts.* New York: HarperCollins College, 1988.

EISENSTEIN, JAMES, and JACOB, HAROLD. *Felony Justice.* Boston: Little, Brown, 1977.

MATHER, LYNN M. *Plea Bargaining or Trial?* Boston: Lexington Books, 1980.

STRYKER, LLOYD PAUL. *The Art of Advocacy: A Plea for the Renaissance of the Trial Lawyer.* New York: Simon & Schuster, 1954.

WEINREB, LLOYD L. *Denial of Justice: Criminal Process in the United States.* New York: The Free Press, 1977.

WELLMAN, FRANCIS L. *The Art of Cross-Examination.* 4th ed. rev. New York: Macmillan, 1936.

8

Civil Proceedings

In a criminal case, the government proceeds against an individual suspected of having committed an offense regarded as criminal under American law. In a civil case an individual, business, or government agency believes that another party has committed a wrong against it and asks the court to settle the dispute, usually by awarding some amount of money as damages. Rather than asking whether and how someone should be punished,[1] the courts in civil litigation ask whether a party has wronged another and how the wrongdoer should compensate the victim. Many new students of American law are surprised to learn that the vast bulk of American court cases involve civil litigation, not criminal trials. In 1995 litigants filed 14 million civil cases in the state courts alone.[2]

This chapter explores the several stages of an American civil trial and examines the following questions: What bodies of law form the basis for civil litigation? What is a class-action lawsuit? What is the nature of a civil trial? How does the course of a civil lawsuit parallel and differ from that of a criminal trial? What role do administrative proceedings play in resolving civil disputes? What principal problems are associated with civil litigation?

[1] A civil lawsuit typically involves no criminal offense. However, on occasion a case does arise in which a criminal offense occurs that also gives rise to civil liability. For instance, one man might punch another in a fight in a bar. The police might arrest the aggressor, and the government might or might not choose to prosecute. However, the victim might also pursue a civil lawsuit to gain money damages for the wrong inflicted. One well-known example arose in 1992 when Indiana authorities successfully prosecuted championship heavyweight boxer Mike Tyson for raping a beauty pageant contestant. The woman also pursued a civil lawsuit against the boxer.

[2] Benjamin Weiser, "Tort Reform's Promise, Peril," *Washington Post,* Sept. 14, 1995, p. A10.

CIVIL CAUSES OF ACTION

Various bodies of law can form the basis for a civil lawsuit, including most notably **contract,**[3] **tort,** and **property** law. Perhaps the easiest way to envision these bodies of law is through illustrations of several ordinary civil **causes of action,** starting with a typical contract case.

Imagine that a university fires a tenured professor.[4] The university claims that the professor violated the terms of his employment contract, in which he agreed to carry out certain teaching responsibilities in exchange for which the university would pay a certain salary supplemented by certain benefits. In particular, the university argues that the professor repeatedly harassed female staff and students and persisted in this conduct despite warnings and disciplinary action by university administrators. The professor, however, charges that he is really being fired because the administration and influential faculty members found his political views to be unpopular. After receiving notice of the termination of his employment, the professor files a civil lawsuit to contest the university's decision.

In such a case the university's legal counsel might advise the dean: "My review of the professor's record suggests that he has not yet committed any criminal offense. However, I do believe that his conduct violates the terms of his employment contract and thus provides a legal basis for his dismissal." After a civil lawsuit, a court would decide how the terms of this particular employment contract should be applied to this dispute. It would determine whether the professor or the university violated the terms of the contract.

An employment contract, of course, is merely one of various types of contracts. Many contracts delineate how one party will provide services to another, such as the contract a university might sign with a landscaping company to cut grass and trim bushes around campus. Other contracts might involve the transfer of goods, such as the contract that a university might sign with a company supplying pork for the campus dining hall. In the United States, when a serious dispute arises that deals with how each party is supposed to act under the terms of a contract, a civil lawsuit is often initiated. Under the broad rubric of contract law, one might also include such related fields or subfields as insurance law, dealing with the rights of parties to insurance contracts, and bankruptcy law, dealing with the rights of

[3] Several well-regarded works on the development of contract law are Patrick S. Atiyah, *The Rise and Fall of Freedom of Contract* (Oxford: Oxford University Press, 1981), Grant Gilmore, *The Death of Contract* (Columbus: Ohio State University Press, 1974), and Lawrence M. Friedman, *Contract Law in America: A Social and Economic Case Study* (Madison: University of Wisconsin Press, 1965).

[4] After an assistant professor works for an American university for seven to ten years, the faculty of his or her department votes, in conjunction with the university administration, on whether to award that faculty member tenure. A tenured professor is a permanent employee of the university who cannot be fired barring exceptional circumstances, such as violations of the law or grossly unprofessional conduct. The tenure system, while criticized by some for eliminating the incentives for continued hard work among senior professors, is designed to insulate the permanent faculty from political or other popular pressures. Universities hope that job security for tenured professors will ensure that they are not afraid to adopt unpopular positions in their fields and with their students.

debtors and creditors. Indeed, commercial law has many contractual elements, dealing as it does with the buying, selling, and exchanging of items.

Contracts, however, form just one of the diverse bodies of law that can form the basis for a civil lawsuit. For instance, tort law concerns conduct that violates a legal duty and results in a private injury or wrong committed against the person or property of another. The most common example of a tort is an automobile accident. One driver fails to operate a vehicle according to legal standards; an accident occurs and injuries result. The driver has committed a tort against those who have been injured by the unlawful activity.

To illustrate a slightly different sort of tort lawsuit, one might consider the case of an American teenager who buys a tape recorder. When she takes the recorder home, her younger brother plugs it into an electrical outlet and is badly shocked. Her brother is rushed to the hospital for emergency medical care, and her family must pay hospital bills. The family might well file a civil lawsuit in the boy's name against the company that manufactured the tape recorder that caused such an injury. Such a case would rely on **product liability law**—a body of law that concerns the duty companies have to sell products that do not injure consumers because of manufacturing defects.

Product liability law might be envisioned as just one subsection of tort law. Another common variety of tort lawsuit is a **slip-and-fall case.** In one such case, an elderly woman suffered severe injuries after falling off a railroad station platform. The lawyer hired by the elderly woman sued the railroad company and alleged that the company had failed to repair the platform lights, creating an unnecessarily hazardous condition for passengers. He argued that the **negligence** of the railroad company resulted in the plaintif's being unable to see where she was going. That, in turn, caused the elderly woman to fall off the platform and severely injure herself. The plaintiff's attorney concluded that the "tortious" conduct of the railroad company must be viewed as the legal cause of the injury.

The lawyer in such a slip-and-fall case might also cite state property law under which the owner of a public property has a duty to keep public buildings and grounds in good repair so that visitors are not injured. American property law primarily encompasses legal matters concerning real estate.[5] Civil disputes often arise with regard to ownership, boundaries, and the use of land. Moreover, civil causes of action may be derived from related bodies of law, such as those regarding inheritance, which determine how property is to be passed after the death of an individual to his or her heirs.

Examples of modern property law disputes abound. For instance, much real estate falls under the terms of zoning ordinances, which specify the permissible uses for particular tracts of land. One area may be zoned residential; another may be designated for light or heavy industry. Farming, renting a residence, or leasing business space may qualify as a suitable land use in one area, but not in another. Since zoning ordinances often regulate such detailed matters as permissible archi-

[5] Disputes regarding possessions and other personal property often fall under contract, bankruptcy, and commercial laws.

tectural designs for buildings, the extent to which structures must be set back from roads, and even the percentage of open spaces that must be retained between structures in a neighborhood, disputes often arise as to whether an individual is complying with a zoning ordinance and whether a local government has exceeded its legal authority in mandating particular zoning requirements.[6]

Every day the legal system sees a rainbow spectrum of different shades of civil lawsuits, from broken contracts to torts, such as legal or medical malpractice suits, to property violations, such as **trespass** to marriage, divorce, child custody, and other family disputes. All involve some alleged civil wrong in the sense that someone claims to have suffered some loss, detriment, or injury through the unlawful acts of another. The illegal nature of the act, however, could also be defined in common law or statutory law terms. Unlawful acts could range from a deceitful practice intended to injure another, as in **fraud,** to a mistaken interpretation of laws regarding wills and estates, to a physical blow, as in assault and battery. Such acts might also be subject to criminal prosecution as well as civil litigation.

Moreover, the injury that is the subject of civil litigation might have been suffered by an individual or by a group. The American legal system permits **class-action lawsuits;** that is, large numbers of persons are allowed to sue together as a group so long as their individual claims—ordinarily, relatively small ones—deal with the same matter. For example, many civil rights, consumer protection, and antitrust cases have been brought by some named person or persons on behalf of a class of hundreds or thousands of similarly situated individuals.[7] Mass tort actions have also been brought with increasing frequency concerning matters such as asbestos contamination and agent orange herbicide injuries. Women who used malfunctioning Dalkon shield contraceptive devices have pursued class-action suits against the company that manufactured those products.[8]

A class action, of course, distributes the financial burden of bringing a lawsuit among many plaintiffs and brings to court cases that a single individual might not find worth pursuing. Successful class action suits "provide a way for the claims of many individuals to be settled at one time, eliminating repetitious litigation and establishing an economical route to obtaining redress, since the legal fees can be taken from the total damages awarded."[9] Businesses, however, often view class action suits as nuisances that drain profits, contribute to soaring legal costs, and pro-

[6] For an introduction to zoning issues see William A. Fischel, *An Economics of Zoning Laws: A Property Rights Approach to American Land Use Controls* (Baltimore, MD: Johns Hopkins University Press, 1985).

[7] To maintain a class-action suit, so many persons must make up the class that it would be impractical to bring each of them before the court. The class must have a well-defined common interest in the questions of law and fact at issue in the suit, and the named individuals must be able to represent adequately the other members of the class. See, for instance, *Daar v. Yellow Cab Co.,* 67 Cal.2d 695, 433 P.2d 732 (1967).

[8] See, for instance, Peter H. Schuck, *Agent Orange on Trial: Mass Toxic Disasters in the Courts* (Cambridge, MA: Belknap Press of Harvard University Press, 1986).

[9] Henry J. Abraham, *The Judicial Process: An Introductory Analysis of the Courts of the United States, England, and France,* 6th ed. rev. (New York: Oxford University Press, 1993), p. 350, n. 13.

vide a competitive advantage to international competitors in countries such as Japan that ban class action proceedings.

While the extent to which such lawsuits are encouraged or discouraged varies among state courts and between state and federal courts, the class action lawsuit has long been an important feature of civil trials in the United States. This is especially true since the lawyers who represent the class often benefit the most from the proceedings through collecting substantial legal fees. Hence, American lawyers are tempted to bring such lawsuits and regularly do so.

INITIAL STEPS IN A CIVIL TRIAL

The first step in civil litigation occurs when the person who believes he or she has been wronged contacts a lawyer to start the process of marshaling the facts and identifying the legal issues pertinent to the dispute. Both tasks often require additional research and numerous meetings and phone conversations. During the initial planning period, the lawyer's attention will focus upon identifying the proper cause of action, the legal **claims,** all potentially relevant legal arguments, and the remedy sought from the court.

Before any formal step is taken, the plaintiff's attorney often contacts the other side, preferably through its lawyer, to determine whether an out-of-court settlement is possible, which would spare each side the time and costs, and perhaps the stress, uncertainty, and embarrassment, that accompany much civil litigation.

The Civil Complaint

A civil case in the United States actually commences when the lawyer for the person who is complaining **files suit,** that is, sends documents to court that initiate litigation. The term *plaintiff* designates the person who brought the lawsuit to the attention of the court, complaining of some other's actions.

Just as a criminal case in the United States is started by a criminal complaint, so a civil case is started by a **civil complaint.** That document, written by the plaintiff's lawyer, must include certain cardinal features. First, the complaint identifies the alleged wrongdoer, called the defendant, and summarizes the principal facts relevant to the case. Second, it identifies all the laws that the plaintiff believes have been violated by the defendant. Third, the complaint describes just how the plaintiff has been harmed by those violations of law. Finally, it declares what the plaintiff wants the court to do about the situation. That is, it suggests the remedy, or **relief,** the plaintiff would like the court to order.

This process might be illustrated by the example mentioned above of the elderly woman who fell off a platform and decided to sue the railroad company. Her lawyer would file with the clerk of the court a civil complaint that would briefly describe the most important facts. Next, the complaint would argue that the railroad company had violated its duties under state law to keep the platform safe and well lit. As noted previously, in such circumstances the lawyer would be likely to cite either a specific state law that imposes a duty of care on those who operate a public place or a general negligence cause of action, or both. By *negligence* lawyers mean an individual's failure to use such care as a reasonably prudent person, guided by ordinary considerations, would use under those circumstances. (Patrick Atiyah, a distinguished British legal scholar, once remarked: "The figure of The Reasonable Man forever stalks the law of torts.")[10]

The plaintiff's lawyer in such a slip-and-fall case would also assert in the complaint that the violation of law caused the plaintiff serious injury and bodily harm since the elderly woman fell off the platform, badly injured herself, and paid substantial hospital bills. Finally, the complaint would lay out a possible remedy that the plaintiff would like the court to adopt. In most cases the plaintiff hopes to receive some substantial sum of damages.

State laws and legal practices differ on whether a plaintiff is expected to request a specific amount of damages in the complaint or is actually prohibited from doing so. Many states allow a plaintiff to request both *general damages* to compensate the plaintiff for the harm caused by the defendant's violation of the law, and **punitive** or **exemplary damages,** to penalize the defendant for wanton, reckless, or reprehensible behavior. If particular sums are to be designated, lawyers, of course, tend to err on the side of asking for more damages than the court is likely to award, rather than less. In this case, the lawyer might ask for a sum like $500,000, or $1 million or more.

At the same time that the plaintiff's lawyer files the complaint in court, or immediately thereafter, he or she also sends a copy of the complaint and a *court summons* to the opposing party or parties so that the defendant is immediately informed of the lawsuit. This is called **service of process,** that is, the formal notification to the defendant that a lawsuit has been filed and an official request to respond to the allegations within a fixed period of time.

Jurisdiction, Venue, and Standing

In initiating a civil lawsuit an attorney is invariably concerned with sifting through that imposing array of tribunals reviewed in Chapter 2 to determine the court or courts in which the case could properly be filed. In particular, the lawyer needs to ensure that the court would have jurisdiction to hear the case.

While most people have some sense for what *jurisdiction* means, the term has unfortunately been stretched to encompass various usages. For instance, if a university decided to seize and hold cars whose owners had parked illegally on campus and had failed to pay past parking fines, a student might wonder: "Does the university have jurisdiction to take such an action?" Here, the issue is one of **legislative jurisdiction,** that is, the ability of a particular group to make binding laws. Issues of legislative jurisdiction arise in such diverse instances as challenges to an executive order on grounds that the president has exceeded the authority of the

[10] Lecture, Harvard Law School, Cambridge, MA, September 16, 1982.

office, to a state law on grounds that it conflicts with the U.S. Constitution or preexisting federal law, and to a local ordinance on grounds that a municipal body has exceeded the powers delegated to it by the state.

For an alternative use of the term *jurisdiction* consider the following example. After the United States Drug Enforcement Administration (DEA) masterminded the kidnapping from Mexico of a suspect in the murder of a DEA agent,[11] a commentator declared: "I don't know why our government thinks it has jurisdiction to engage in illegal acts abroad." Here, the issue is one of **executive jurisdiction**—that is, the principle in international law that a state is the final authority regarding government matters within its own territory, and in peacetime government officials are only to act abroad with the express consent of the foreign state in whose territory they wish to act. Issues of executive jurisdiction arise when one state wishes to have its officials act in another state. One common example would be police who wish to tail a suspect or conduct an undercover operation abroad.[12]

Although the term *jurisdiction* thus has special meanings in the legislative and executive domains, it most commonly refers to courts. Issues of **judicial jurisdiction** concern the question of when a particular court may lawfully recognize, hear, and decide a particular legal question. In the American judicial system, a key preliminary issue in a civil trial is whether a court has jurisdiction over the individual or subject matter in dispute. Plainly, a specialized federal court like the U.S. Tax Court would have jurisdiction over a case in which the government alleged that a corporation had paid insufficient taxes, but it would not have jurisdiction over a dispute between two neighbors regarding conflicting interpretations of their boundary line.

The breadth of a court's jurisdiction is ultimately derived from the political process. Although certain state constitutions speak to jurisdictional issues, much as the U.S. Constitution lays out the jurisdiction of the U.S. Supreme Court, the extent of a court's jurisdiction is usually found in the legislative statute that created the court, which the court then interprets.

A state *court of limited jurisdiction,* such as a small claims court, municipal court, or police court, may be limited to hearing civil cases that do not exceed some fixed threshold amount and that arose within some fixed geographical boundary, such as a county or metropolitan area. In addition, some courts of limited jurisdiction, such as a juvenile court or probate court, may hear cases that deal with one field of law, such as family matters or **wills,** trusts, and estates. A state *court of general* or *unlimited jurisdiction* will be able to hear any legal issue that arises under the laws or constitution of that state.

In Article III the U.S. Constitution specifies the type of cases that the fed-

[11] See *United States v. Alvarez-Machain,* 504 U.S. 655 (1991). See also Michael Ross Fowler and Julie Marie Bunck, *Law, Power, and the Sovereign State: The Evolution and Application of the Concept of Sovereignty* (University Park: Pennsylvania State University Press, 1995), p. 15.

[12] See Ethan A. Nadelmann, *Cops Across Borders: The Internationalization of U.S. Criminal Law Enforcement* (University Park: Pennsylvania State University Press, 1993).

eral courts may hear.[13] Since in most matters Congress has granted federal courts *concurrent jurisdiction,* rather than *exclusive jurisdiction,* an attorney may at times choose to file a case in either federal or state court. In considering where a case might best be brought, a lawyer might consider such strategic questions as which judges appear most sympathetic to the plaintiff's cause of action, which court might be expected to award the most damages if the case is won, and how state and federal jurisprudence might have developed differently on the key substantive and procedural legal issues in the case.

Along with ensuring that a particular court has jurisdiction over the case at hand, a lawyer must also determine the proper **venue** for the trial, that is, the county or district where the case may be heard and tried. Thus, the term *jurisdiction* deals with the authority that a court has to hear a case; the term *venue* deals with the proper location for the case to be brought. In a civil case involving property the lawyer's first instinct will be to discover in which county or federal district the property is located. Normally, the case will then be brought in that county court or, perhaps, in that federal district court, depending upon whether or not a federal question is involved.[14] In a personal injury case to be heard in state court, the plaintiff's lawyer will first discover in which county the defendant is located. Usually, the lawyer will then have the complaint and summons served on the defendant in that county and will file suit in the corresponding state court. Under federal law the proper venue for a case is either the district in which the injury occurred or the district in which the plaintiff or defendant lives. All this correctly implies that lawyers will sometimes find that multiple courts would constitute a proper venue for a case.

As legal proceedings get under way, the venue for a case may be changed for reasons ranging from the mundane to the highly controversial. A court in a different location might simply prove to be substantially more convenient for witnesses. An attorney might file papers in the wrong court, then wish to refile in a different venue. Or the parties might agree to move the trial for practical or strategic purposes. Alternatively, if the facts and allegations in a criminal or civil case have been widely publicized to the possible prejudice of one party, the venue may be changed in order to convene a neutral jury. If the judge who would have presided has some possible stake in the outcome of a trial, such as a personal relationship with the parties or attorneys, a trial is occasionally moved to a different location, though ordinarily substituting a different judge from the same court will suffice to ensure judicial impartiality.

Nevertheless, in most cases the choice of venue creates few problems. The attorney chooses properly and logically, and the action proceeds in that court until a final decision is rendered, unless, of course, the parties settle out of court or the case is withdrawn for some other reason.

Finally, another preliminary jurisdictional issue, often straightforward but

[13] Chapter 2 reviewed what constitutes a question of federal law and what constitutes a sufficiently significant amount of money between citizens of different states as to warrant the attention of a federal court.

[14] See Chapter 2 for a discussion of when a federal court will hear a case.

occasionally troublesome, relates to the phrases **standing to sue** and *case or controversy.* In an adversarial system courts do not settle a point of law on the basis of an argument from a party that is only tangentially interested in the subject matter of the dispute. Rather, courts want plaintiffs to be sufficiently involved in the litigation that they can be counted on to argue their side of the case as strongly as possible. Thus, in order to bring a civil lawsuit, a plaintiff must have *standing to sue,* that is, a legally protectible and tangible interest at stake in the litigation.

Similarly, American courts do not resolve hypothetical legal issues. For a court to hear a case, the litigants must have a genuine and immediate dispute, not an imaginary one or some possible future conflict. In the states one can sometimes receive a considered judgment on a hypothetical legal issue by asking the state attorney general, or in certain states under certain circumstances, asking a state court, to issue an advisory opinion. An advisory opinion is an interpretation of the law indicating how a legal issue would be resolved if a case occurred in which that issue arose. However, these sorts of answers to hypothetical scenarios are never binding; they are never issued by U.S. federal courts[15] and only rarely by certain state courts.

If a standing to sue issue is raised, the court will ask is this plaintiff the proper party to bring the lawsuit? The court may also inquire as to whether a genuine conflict of interests exists. If not, the case will be dismissed.

The Answer

After receiving service of process, the defendant is responsible for filing in court an **answer** to the plaintiff's complaint. This written document sets forth in technical legal terms the defendant's reply to the charges brought by the plaintiff. Usually, the answer admits certain facts and contests others that are alleged in the complaint. Answers typically deny liability for the harm allegedly caused the plaintiff. This is accomplished by having the defendant plead one of a handful of popular defenses. For instance, the defendant could simply deny the allegations as factually inaccurate. He or she could reply by claiming that the complaint is too vague to respond to. In the initial exchange of pleadings a defendant occasionally strikes back by alleging a *counterclaim* or filing a **cross-complaint** that states a cause of action and a legal claim against the plaintiff.[16] The plaintiff is then responsible for answering those charges.

One popular defense is a relic from the English common law called **contributory negligence.** This ancient legal doctrine originally stated that if the plain-

[15] The federal court practice of refusing to issue advisory opinions extends to the decision of the first chief justice, John Jay, to reject requests by Treasury Secretary Alexander Hamilton and President George Washington for advisory opinions. See Robert A. Carp and Ronald Stidham, *Judicial Process in America,* 3d ed. rev. (Washington, DC: Congressional Quarterly Press, 1996), pp. 27–28.

[16] A defendant's cross-complaint, which may be filed as part of an answer or as a separate pleading, may be asserted against one who is not a plaintiff so long as the defendant's cause of action arises out of the same transaction or occurrence as the cause raised by the plaintiff, or asserts a claim, right, or interest in the property or controversy that forms the subject of the plaintiff's suit.

tiff, by his or her behavior, helped to bring about the same problem that the plaintiff has now taken to court, then the plaintiff would be denied recovery.

Over time, American legislatures and courts have softened the sometimes harsh doctrine of contributory negligence. Instead of automatically eliminating suits because a plaintiff was partially at fault, courts have come to examine which party was more at fault, and to assess responsibility accordingly. Some states now allow a plaintiff to recover so long as his or her fault was slight. In certain states only plaintiffs who are more than 50 percent at fault are denied recovery altogether. Many states have enacted **comparative fault statutes** that allow a plaintiff to recover damages proportionate to the defendant's fault. In other words, if the court found a particular defendant to be 20 percent at fault, a plaintiff could recover from that defendant 20 percent of the damages sustained. In all jurisdictions, demonstrating the plaintiff's contributory negligence will dramatically diminish the defendant's liability. Hence, in appropriate circumstances it is a most popular defense.

The example of the tape recorder that shocked the little boy could illustrate the idea of contributory negligence. Depending upon the facts of the case, the defendant's lawyers might be able to argue that the little brother contributed to his own accident, perhaps by spilling a glass of water on the electrical plug just before inserting it into the wall. The defendant's lawyer might argue in the answer that the company should not have to pay damages to someone who disregarded clear instructions on the tape recorder by placing a wet electrical plug in a wall socket.

The purpose of this exchange of **pleadings**—as the complaint, answer, and follow-up documents are called—is to narrow the issues in dispute between the parties. The initial exchange forces the defendant to read carefully through the plaintiff's complaint and decide which facts and charges to accept as true and which to deny and challenge in court. That process of narrowing the issues in dispute forms the essence of the initial written stage of a civil lawsuit.

Participation in the Court Process

One might wonder why a defendant in civil litigation would bother to participate in the court process at all? Why not just ignore the complaint and go on about daily life? Many Americans, of course, are law-abiding citizens and are thus motivated to act in a manner that respects the court process. A more technical answer, however, relates to the summons that the clerk of the court issues to the defendant.[17] The summons is a court order addressed to the defendant requiring the defendant to reply to the charges by filing an answer within a certain number of days, usually twenty or thirty depending on the court. If the defendant fails to respond, the

[17] The procedure for issuing a summons varies from state to state and has changed over time. In some states, the plaintiff's attorney files with the clerk a document requesting the clerk to issue the summons and directing the county sheriff to serve the defendant with a copy. Elsewhere, the summons is simply a court form that the plaintiff's lawyer attaches to the complaint and then serves on the defendant and files with the court.

court may award the plaintiff a **default judgment,** perhaps providing the remedy the plaintiff originally requested. (A *default judgment* is a judgment in favor of one party that a judge may award should the other party fail to appear in court or to plead within a specified time period.)

Some lawsuits are primarily disputes regarding property, rather than money. When each of two parties claims to own property, the court may **attach** the property and hold it until the dispute is resolved. Perhaps the most readily understandable illustration of the process of attachment arises in car sales. When a teenager buys a first car, he or she often wonders: "Why is this car dealer letting me buy a car worth $13,000, when I'm paying only a **down payment** of $5,000 and am simply promising to pay the remainder in the future? What if I never pay the dealer the other $8,000 that I owe?" The answer is that if the buyer does not pay the owed money, the dealer will hire a repossession company to repossess the car. In fact, the process of repossessing cars is such an ordinary part of American life that some years ago a popular movie traced the adventures of a **repo-man,** that is, a person in the business of repossessing cars after the buyer has **defaulted** on payment.

Imagine that a clever teenager fails to make car payments but hides the vehicle away in a place that makes repossession extremely difficult even for the most ingenious and skillful repo-man. Perhaps the teenager parks the car inside an enclosed yard, surrounded by a high fence and containing a watch dog. In that case the car dealer would be likely to send the company's lawyer to court to ask a judge to issue an order that gives the sheriff, as head of the local police force, the authority to attach the property. Once that court order is issued, the sheriff can forcibly take possession of the car awaiting the outcome of the lawsuit between the car's seller and its buyer.

This process of attaching some kind of property, pending the outcome of a lawsuit, is very common. Every day sheriffs across the United States take possession of various types of property because someone has gone into a court with a claim against that property. The lawyer has persuaded a judge to grant an attachment order instructing the local sheriff to seize that property pending the outcome of a civil trial to determine who really owns it.

TRIAL PREPARATION

Conducting Discovery

Just as a criminal trial begins with a period in which the prosecution and defense investigate and exchange facts about the case, so does a civil trial start in much the same manner. In order to allow the two sides to try to learn what actually happened in the case, the federal rules of civil procedure require mandatory disclosure of certain categories of information. Civil lawsuits in state and federal courts thus include a **discovery** period during which lawyers make a record to help them in pretrial preparation, trial advocacy, and later appeals.

Early in the discovery stage of a civil lawsuit a lawyer acquires books, letters, contracts, memoranda, maps, diagrams, records, and other documents relevant to the case through a *document request* addressed to the opposing party. The production of documents and their inspection by the opposing counsel normally takes place before the other steps in the discovery process since attorneys will always want to have had the chance to review relevant documents before they question an individual. If a witness in a civil case resists producing tangible evidence that is pertinent to the issues in controversy, the opposing attorney may have the court issue a ***subpoena duces tecum.*** The judge then orders the party withholding the evidence to produce it in court. Continued resistance may cause the judge to declare the party to be in contempt of court and, perhaps, to order sanctions against that party.

Another initial step often taken in the discovery stage of a civil trial is collecting **affidavits,** that is, voluntary, written statements of fact made under oath and before a proper authority. A noteworthy complementary tool is a *request for admission.* In such a request the attorney asks the other party to admit to certain mundane, noncontroversial matters. For example, in a lawsuit dealing with an auto accident an attorney might send requests that the other side admit that an accident occurred, that medical records are authentic, and that the party was in his or her auto at the scene where the accident took place. Such requests for admission serve to narrow the legal issues in dispute and reduce the time and costs of litigation by limiting the number of witnesses needed at trial.

Another useful discovery tool, an **interrogatory** is simply a series of questions that one lawyer sends to the other party that must be answered in writing **under oath** within a given time period. To illustrate the use of interrogatories, one might consider once more the case of the elderly woman who fell off an unlit train platform after disembarking from a train late at night and who claimed the railroad company to have been negligent for failing to maintain adequate lighting. The lawyers for the railroad company might require the woman to answer a set of interrogatories that ask questions dealing with the facts of that dispute. For instance, if the railroad's lawyers were exploring a contributory negligence defense, they might ask questions such as the following:

QUESTION 1: Do you wear glasses?

QUESTION 2: If the answer to Question 1 was yes, were you wearing your glasses the night that you claim to have fallen off the platform?

QUESTION 3: If the answer to Question 1 was no, when was the last time a certified eye doctor checked your eyesight?

Each of those questions would be aimed at discovering whether the woman fell off the platform not because of any problem with the railroad platform lights but because she had a preexisting problem with her eyesight.

A **deposition,** another popular form of discovery, is like a set of interrogatories in the sense that a lawyer asks one of the parties to the lawsuit or a knowledgeable third party a series of questions that are to be answered under oath. However, a deposition differs from an interrogatory and from courtroom examination in that the questions are asked orally, but in some private forum. Under the rules of discovery the witness must answer honestly any question relevant to the trial that is not the subject of several narrow and restricted matters of **privilege**—that is, matters about which the court does not require witnesses to speak.

The ultimate objective of a deposition parallels that of other forms of discovery: to learn crucial facts about the case that may be useful at the upcoming trial. Unlike testimony in open court, depositions are not public records, open to the media and other interested parties. Rather, they are private trial preparation documents, which become public only through a court order or through their use at trial.

A lawyer who takes a deposition thus preserves the sworn, out-of-court statements of a witness in order to use them in court or in trial preparation. This can be especially important when a witness is likely to be unable to appear in court, perhaps because of a terminal illness or residence in another state or foreign country. In such cases any relevant portion of the witness's deposition may be read into evidence at trial. Most frequently, however, a lawyer deposes a witness to determine how he or she would testify, if called at trial. Moreover, if a witness who has been deposed testifies in some inconsistent manner at trial, the deposition may be read in court to challenge the witness's credibility.

At a deposition the lawyers, and sometimes one or both parties to the lawsuit, meet with the person to be deposed. A stenographer attends to record all that is said. The stenographer first places the witness under oath by having him or her swear to tell the truth. Then, the lawyer who is taking the deposition begins to ask questions of the witness. Most frequently, the individual being questioned will be an *adverse witness;* occasionally, however, a *friendly witness* might also be deposed.

As in a criminal trial, attorneys are expected to object to questions and answers that violate the rules of evidence. Thus, although a judge never attends a deposition, a stenographer takes down all the proceedings and the defending lawyer or lawyers of the deposed witness will be present to note **objections** to any inadmissible questions. However, often the attorneys who take and who defend the deposition agree that objections need not be made at once or that the grounds for each objection need not be specified immediately.

Although many lawyers expert at taking depositions advise that the best way to get most witnesses to talk freely about an event is to act friendly, the nature of a deposition is such that examining a witness typically becomes a rather stressful, even hostile, undertaking for all involved. Since the judge is not immediately available to act as referee, depositions often become quite antagonistic with heated exchanges between the lawyer defending the witness and the lawyer taking the deposition. One distinguished attorney recently observed: "Some lawyers bully witnesses at discovery proceedings in ways a judge would never permit; others wheedle in a way jurors would find distasteful."[18]

Under the surface of a deposition, of course, lie tactical considerations. At times the lawyer taking the deposition may believe that a witness will blurt out a

[18] Sol M. Linowitz with Martin Mayer, *The Betrayed Profession: Lawyering at the End of the Twentieth Century* (New York: Charles Scribner's Sons, 1994), p. 170.

statement in anger that he or she would not make unless provoked. Sometimes a lengthy, difficult deposition will serve to "soften up" a party to the lawsuit. In other words, it will make the party more amenable to settling the case in order to avoid further exchanges. Alternatively, the defending lawyer may believe that the witness is talking too freely and is forgetting the adversarial nature of the proceeding. Or, the defending lawyer may grow impatient with what might be characterized as an extended *fishing trip,* that is, an effort by the deposing lawyer to poke around in the witness's background in an effort to find some useful bit of information.

At still other times, a lawyer may purposefully provoke hostility during the deposition, not to intimidate the witness so much as to influence the opposing lawyer. The defending lawyer may believe that the lawyer deposing the witness is young or inexperienced and might be easily intimidated. When I prepared for my first deposition, a senior litigator advised me to pay no attention to the other lawyers in attendance should they try to throw me off the line of questioning I intended to pursue. He recounted one deposition in a case with multiple parties at which the senior lawyers laughed and hooted derisively at every opportunity simply in order to rattle the young lawyer doing the questioning.

Lawyers also sometimes "grandstand" or "showboat" to impress clients in attendance at a deposition. For instance, a lawyer might provoke hostility to show that he or she is working zealously on the client's behalf and thus earning the large legal fees that will eventually be charged. Given these various motives leading to antagonistic or even unprofessional conduct, it is no wonder that, as Judge Richard Posner once observed, "The transcripts of depositions are often very ugly documents."[19]

One final observation about discovery may not be self-evident to beginning students of American law. Document requests, affidavits, requests for admission, interrogatories, and depositions are all tools designed to root out the facts in a case. This explains the origin of the term *discovery.* Yet, while lawyers constantly, and glibly, refer to "*the* facts" of a case, a case of any sophistication will be so full of facts that all of them will never be known by the court, the lawyers, or even the parties.

In reality, a court can usually do no more than aim to discover and consider all the relevant, critically important facts and also the less vital, contributing facts that happen to be brought to the court's attention. As one experienced district judge once observed: "[O]ne comes to realize that the search for 'the facts' is never-ending. . . . Perhaps there is no such thing as 'the facts' of any particular case, when one considers that an ordinary civil suit of even reasonable complexity involves dozens of conversations which must be reconstructed against the background of letters, diary entries, telegrams, and what not. What a fascinating task it is to study and restudy the documents and fit them in to affidavits, depositions, and perhaps testimony in other cases while preparing for the cross-examination of an adverse witness!"[20]

[19] *DF Activities Corp. v. Brown,* 851 F.2d 920 (7th Cir. 1988), cited in Linowitz, p. 170.

[20] Judge Harold R. Medina in his introduction to Lloyd Paul Stryker, *The Art of Advocacy: A Plea for the Renaissance of the Trial Lawyer* (New York: Simon & Schuster, 1954), p. ix.

Policing Discovery

Theoretically, discovery is expected to work almost entirely through the parties without judicial intervention.[21] In practice, while lawyers often threaten to take discovery disputes to a judge to be resolved, they hesitate to do so since judges tend to become angry when asked to deal with such preliminary matters. Judges usually assume that both sides are being childish or unreasonable in their inability to work out disagreements regarding the discovery of relevant facts. And, judges are empowered to deal sternly with a party who refuses to submit to discovery. In egregious cases judges may even dismiss a case or enter a default judgment against the party who is flagrantly violating the standard rules of discovery.

Some years ago, I was able to use to my client's advantage the anger that most judges feel when confronting discovery disputes. In this case, I represented a young couple who had submitted a large down payment to buy a house under construction. Unfortunately, the financing to buy the new house collapsed, and the real estate developer tried to keep a portion of the deposit as an "architectural design fee," contrary to the explicit terms of the **purchase and sale agreement.** On four occasions I attempted to depose the real estate developer who had wrongfully retained my clients' deposit. Each time, the man came up with some excuse at the last minute to keep him from attending the deposition.

On the eve of the first scheduled deposition he fired his lawyer. Next, just before the deposition, he orally agreed to settle the case, but then failed to make the requisite payment. Then, he claimed sickness. Finally, at the fourth scheduled deposition he simply failed to show up without offering any excuse, later phoning his attorney to report that he had driven someone to the hospital rather than attend the deposition. At that point I filed with the court a preliminary motion, which I termed a Motion for Sanctions for Willful Failure to Appear for Deposition, recounting in detail my efforts to proceed with discovery.

I argued that the court should handle this discovery dispute by ordering the developer to appear at a deposition at my convenience, not at his, and by requiring the developer to pay the expenses and attorney's fees I had compiled in having to force him to carry out his duty of participating in the discovery process. Should the developer fail to abide by the court's order within thirty days, I asked the court to award my client a default judgment. A default judgment is a final decision in favor of one party that a judge may award should the other party fail to appear in court or to plead within a specified time period.

I filed my motion with the clerk of the court at about 3:00 P.M. and scheduled it for hearing the following morning, expecting at a minimum that the judge would strongly criticize the real estate developer and his attorney and order them to attend the next scheduled deposition or lose the case by default. As is customary, I also sent a messenger to the opposing lawyer with a copy of the document. Before I could even prepare my oral argument for the motion before the judge,

[21] One exception is when a party requests that the court order a physician to undertake a mental or physical examination of some individual involved in a suit.

the opposing lawyer called. By midnight we had nullified the discovery dispute by settling the entire case, and I had a check in hand to present to my clients in the morning.

The decline of legal professionalism noted in Chapter 4 raises the issue of how frequently such safeguards fail to prevent abuses of discovery. The discovery process, along with other aspects of the civil lawsuit, can and sometimes is exploited by unscrupulous attorneys. Just as some clients will want to have a lawsuit filed simply in order to harass an enemy, so other clients may wish to use discovery to probe the secrets of a rival business, a former spouse, or some other person or entity of interest to them.

To guard against such misuse of discovery, a lawyer is permitted to subpoena and depose witnesses, compel the production of documents, and otherwise pursue civil litigation only under the court's authority. One distinguished attorney recently observed:

> It was understood that [an attorney] was not to use these gifts of the court for his own advantage or to help further the designs of clients whose cause could not make at least a *prima facie*—"first look"—claim that the law was on their side. The purpose of the elaborate "pleadings" by which lawyers introduced their clients' cases to the courts was to establish a reason why these "impositional powers" of the judge should be placed at the disposal of a litigant. Judges expected that, as officers of the court, lawyers would *always* make some investigation of their clients' claims before asking for such powers—that, in the fine phrase of Chief Justice Warren Burger, "a lawyer's signature on a pleading or motion was something like a signature on a check: there was supposed to be something to back it up."[22]

In practice, however, judges grant discovery powers as a matter of course, and lawyers do not always fulfill judicial expectations of honorable professional conduct.

The Rationale for Discovery

The guiding principle behind the idea of discovery is that both sides should know roughly the same facts when entering the courtroom for trial. Thus, both lawyers attend the depositions, have the opportunity to examine and cross-examine witnesses, and receive transcripts from the stenographer. Both may review interrogatories, results of physical examinations, and other material that has surfaced during discovery. The lawyers exchange lists of witnesses to be called at trial and reveal the evidence they expect to produce. With this in mind, one might wonder why the American legal system, one that prides itself on an adversarial trial process, forces the parties to reveal so much information to one another before the trial begins?

In fact, the rules of civil procedure did not always compel American lawyers to reveal much of their cases to one another before trial. That initial ap-

[22] Linowitz, pp. 9–10.

proach, however, came to be viewed as flawed in three respects. First, it seemed to encourage litigation since the strength of a case could best be assessed during the trial when many of the facts about the dispute emerged. Second, attention at trial became focused on what tricks or surprises each lawyer was going to suddenly reveal, rather than on the merits of the case. Third, lawyers often entered trials with highly fragmentary information. Not only might their investigations of the facts and dispute have been flawed, but their client might not have revealed the whole truth to them. Discovery might bring the lawyer's attention to "certain facts left out of the client's version of the events . . ."[23] One rationale for extensive discovery is that if both sides have the opportunity to know the core facts ahead of time, they may be more likely to drop cases of negligible merit or to settle problematic cases and not waste the court's time in trying to determine the legality of the actions of either or both parties.

Equally important, reforming the rules of civil procedure aimed to enable lawyers to use the discovery process to narrow the particular legal and factual issues in dispute between the parties. If the fundamental facts of a case are ambiguous before the trial, the court will have to be convened throughout the time-consuming process of learning exactly what happened. But, if the basic facts are known, then the court can immediately focus on the most significant unresolved factual and legal issues. From this perspective, extensive discovery constitutes a shortcut in an otherwise drawn-out civil trial process. It helps to identify the facts that both sides agree are true and reduces the scope of legal decision making.

If the objectives of reforming the rules of civil procedure to permit discovery are clear, the issue of whether the arrows launched by the reformers have struck the bull's eye is far more controversial. In fact, lawyers often use discovery proceedings as an exploratory or delaying tactic or as a punitive weapon. A dishonorable party can use discovery to explore the business or personal secrets of another. Even more commonly, a party with more resources can use discovery to wear down an opponent. For instance, a large corporation might unleash lawyers on a smaller competitor, forcing that business to endure exorbitant and sometimes exhaustive costs in responding to discovery requests.

The reformed system also lends itself to waste and abuse. Lawyers run up billable hours by conducting extensive discovery. Large portions of cases are essentially tried twice—once in deposition and once on the witness stand in court. Throughout the process judges are not immediately available to prevent fishing expeditions by attorneys willing to consume hours trying to find some relevant piece of evidence. One authority wrote:

> The worst aspect of discovery . . . is the fact that lawyers conduct it away from the courtroom and away from the direct supervision of the judge. Every wrong instinct of adversarial advocacy is thereby brought into play. . . . There is gold to be mined in lines of questioning that elicit an apparent "admission" of something that will look embarrassing in the context of the evidence to be introduced at the trial—or a statement that could be construed, even twisted, to

[23] James V. Calvi and Susan Coleman, *American Law and Legal Systems,* 2d ed. rev. (Englewood Cliffs, NJ: Prentice Hall, 1992), p. 70.

appear to contradict the testimony this witness can be expected to give at trial.[24]

Abuses of discovery thus raise questions about the efficacy of the reforms of civil procedure. Years ago, Charles Elias Clark, once a federal judge and a dean of Yale Law School, and an influential force behind reforming the rules, argued that the new system would "secure the just, speedy and inexpensive outcome of an action."[25] The experience of the ensuing decades suggests to the critics that, in fact, discovery may make the resolution of civil disputes slower, costlier, and in certain respects less just. Whether the situation might be improved by further reforms of the rules of civil procedure or by judges policing the discovery process more actively[26] remains subject to debate. Few, however, wish to return to the former rules of civil procedure, plagued by their own serious problems.

Motions

While a criminal case often includes an omnibus hearing or some other pre-trial proceeding to settle subsidiary legal issues, civil cases frequently involve a lengthy series of **motions** in which the parties argue about various technical legal matters after the complaint is filed. Many such motions, though far from all of them, are argued before the trial begins. In many courts a judge sits in **motion session** every morning to listen and rule on the many preliminary motions that routinely arise during civil litigation.

Normally, motion session proceeds without a court reporter present to record the questions posed and arguments made. Typically, the judge listens to the arguments by each attorney, glances over the relevant pleadings (which he or she may have reviewed in advance), and then issues a ruling on the spot or later that same day. Despite the brevity and relative informality of the proceedings, civil litigators spend many hours preparing and arguing preliminary motions in order to have a case dismissed, in whole or in part, or even to gain a slight advantage at trial or in negotiations leading to an out-of-court settlement.

Like most new litigators, I made my first appearance in court arguing a motion in a civil case. In fact, the vast majority of attorneys who engage in civil litigation, and some who later move to criminal trial practice, make their initial court appearances in motion session. This form of oral advocacy can be quite challenging, especially for an inexperienced attorney. Judge Paul Garrity of the Massachusetts Superior Court once observed: "When arguing a motion, counsel is engaged in a dissimilar kind of advocacy than when either at trial or on appeal. With appellate advocacy, which is stylized and focuses solely on the law, facts are incidental. With trial advocacy, where flexibility is essential and the focus is exclusively on

[24] Linowitz, p. 170.

[25] Ibid., p. 171.

[26] Linowitz argued: "Judges could be receptive to complaints by witnesses or opposing lawyers that the discovery process was being abused, and could refuse to permit the use at the trial of statements from an abusive discovery." Ibid.

evidence, facts are all. With motion session advocacy, counsel must know all of the facts, the relevant law, and any applicable rules of civil procedure . . . and also have prepared a set . . . argument which he or she should be ready to modify and even to abandon when pressed by the motion session judge."[27]

The spectrum of motions in civil litigation is quite broad. The **motion for an order compelling production of documents** arises in discovery disputes when one party is withholding important documents requested by the other side. In a **motion to strike** one party asks the court to order the other party to delete material from a pleading that is irrelevant, redundant, prejudicial, or scandalous. A **motion for a more definite statement** calls upon the court to rule that a pleading (usually the complaint) is so unnecessarily vague that the other party cannot reasonably be required to respond to it. Such a motion compels a party to set forth the facts, injury, or remedy more clearly or precisely.

Perhaps the most important preliminary motions are the **motion to dismiss** and the **motion for summary judgment.** A motion to dismiss, still known as a **demurrer** in certain state courts, asks the judge to dismiss the case for failure to state a claim upon which relief can be granted. Thus, the lawyer will argue that the judge should dismiss the case because, even if the defendant were to admit that all the facts alleged by the plaintiff were true, the complaint would still fail to state a legally sound claim against the defendant.

A summary judgment motion, often argued at the close of discovery, requests the judge to dispose of a case or parts of a case since both sides agree on all the essential facts and a question of law is all that remains. For instance, a defendant would ask for summary judgment if no material fact remained in dispute and the law did not entitle the plaintiff to receive any damages under such circumstances. Since such a motion requires technical legal expertise rather than fact-finding, a judge—not a jury—decides. Either the plaintiff or the defendant can move for summary judgment.

Summary judgment decisions have become critical to the health of the overloaded American legal system since a successful motion can end a lawsuit that has no merit. Even a partially successful summary judgment motion can narrow the issues in dispute and save time and expense for both parties at trial. By granting summary judgment on certain issues, a judge might reduce a five- or six-day trial to two or three days.

Pre-trial Conference

After the exchange of pleadings and the close of discovery, many courts opt to conduct a pre-trial conference.[28] Ordinarily, such a hearing is presided over by the judge and is attended by the attorneys on each side, usually with all their documents,

[27] Paul G. Garrity, *Guide to Civil Motion Practice: Law and Advocacy* (Boston: Boston Bar Association, 1985), pp. 111-145–111-146.

[28] An interesting article on pre-trial conferences by a well-known federal judge is J. Skelly Wright, "The Pre-trial Conference," in Sheldon Goldman and Austin Sarat, eds., *American Court Systems: Readings in Judicial Process and Behavior* (San Francisco: W. H. Freeman, 1978), pp. 119–121.

including their lists of witnesses. The aim is twofold. First, a successful pre-trial conference will streamline the trial process by narrowing the legal issues and having the parties agree to stipulate to undisputed facts and, occasionally, to points of law. Second, a judge presiding at a pre-trial conference can encourage settlement of the case. The attorneys will meet face-to-face, but without the distracting presence of their clients, on their best behavior in a relatively informal environment in which the legal issues may be outlined in a detached and professional manner under the judge's watchful eye.

The judge at a pre-trial conference may also participate actively by formulating the issues as he or she sees them at this early stage of the case. While the parties will normally have negotiated with one another before the pre-trial conference, the judge will certainly inquire about settlement efforts and, perhaps, prod the lawyers toward a negotiated resolution. He or she may even signal where a compromise appears reasonable. Regardless of the likelihood of a future settlement, the judge will attempt to narrow the scope of the trial by having the attorneys stipulate to all uncontested factual issues and share lists of witnesses and documents that will be entered into evidence. Ultimately, the judge sets a trial date and issues an order to govern the conduct of the attorneys at trial that embodies the terms agreed to during the pre-trial conference. He or she may also order the parties to try to **mediate** the case before they bring it to court. (Mediation is discussed in more detail below.)

THE CIVIL TRIAL

The Course of the Civil Trial

Once the preliminary motions and the pre-trial conference (or conferences) are over and the actual trial begins, the course of a civil trial parallels the course of a criminal trial in many respects. Although fewer civil trials than criminal trials are heard by a jury, the *voir dire* process of selecting jurors for a civil jury trial resembles that in a criminal jury trial. The trial is held in the same setting, and in both cases the lawyers engage in such familiar matters as opening and closing statements and direct and cross-examination of witnesses. In a civil trial the plaintiff's attorney delivers his or her opening statement before the defendant's lawyer speaks. At the end of the trial the defendant's lawyer closes his or her case first, allowing the opposing attorney the final word in the plaintiff's summation.

Just as defense counsel in a criminal case may move for a directed verdict at the close of the government's case-in-chief,[29] so counsel for either party may do likewise in a civil case. If the judge finds that the evidence is insufficient to justify a verdict for one party, he or she should direct a verdict for the other side. However,

[29] That the prosecutor cannot ask for a directed verdict but the defense counsel can illustrates once more the manner in which American procedural rules favor the defense over the prosecution. Calvi and Coleman, p. 86.

usually the trial will have included conflicting oral testimony or other factual disputes that need to be resolved by a fact-finder, and the motion for a directed verdict will be denied.

The Judgment

As in a criminal case, the initial trial court decision is usually of utmost importance in a civil lawsuit. In a jury trial the jurors will withdraw and deliberate and then issue their verdict, just as they do in the criminal context. However, although jury verdicts in federal criminal cases must be unanimous, the parties to a civil lawsuit in federal court may stipulate before the trial that a verdict of some stated majority of jurors shall suffice. In the states practices vary as to how many jurors make up a sufficient majority to decide the case.

In a criminal case a convicted offender is usually sent to prison to serve a sentence. In a civil case, by contrast, a court often redresses the violation of a right by granting damages to the injured party. For example, a famous actress might sue a tabloid for **libel** after publication of a malicious and false article that injures the celebrity's reputation. If the actress won the case by proving that the tabloid had published the material either knowing it to be false or recklessly without regard to its truth,[30] the court might award a remedy of $1 million or some other amount to be paid by the tabloid to the celebrity. Legal systems around the world commonly award money in this manner to compensate an injured person for the violation of his or her rights.

The example in Chapter 2 of the niece who locked an elderly woman out of her own house illustrates another possible remedy under American law. Plaintiffs also sometimes sue in an effort to persuade a court to enforce their rights. The housing court that issued an injunction ordering the niece to allow the woman back into her home opted for injunctive relief to enforce a right, rather than monetary damages to redress a wrong. Legal efforts aimed at enforcing a right may be traced back to the English *courts of equity,* which spent much of their time considering such cases.

Along with injunctions of various sorts, courts frequently recognize other forms of equitable relief. For instance, one avid collector might contract to purchase a Honus Wagner baseball card from another collector. Since a Honus Wagner is perhaps the most unusual baseball card a collector can own, the buyer may not be satisfied with money damages if the seller attempts to break the contract. Instead, the purchaser's lawyer might ask the court to order **specific performance** of the agreement. The doctrine of specific performance states that if damages would be inadequate compensation for the breach of a contract, a court may order a party to carry through with its obligations as the agreement stipulated.

Incidentally, specific performance is not an available remedy after the breach of an employment agreement. Thus, if a theater company has contracted

[30] See *New York Times v. Sullivan,* 376 U.S. 254 (1964).

with a famous diva to sing during an opera season, and if the diva decides instead to break her contract and retire to her villa in the South Pacific, the theater company will not be able to persuade a court to compel the diva to fulfill her obligations, though it might gain damages and even an injunction barring the singer from performing for a rival company during the term of her employment contract.

POST-TRIAL PROCEEDINGS

After the verdict is reached, the court issues a judgment determining the money damages or other relief to be accorded the victorious party. The losing side may opt to move for a **judgment notwithstanding the verdict.** Such a motion asks the judge to declare that no reasonable jury could have reached the verdict announced in the case. Alternatively, within ten days the losing party may move for a new trial, arguing that new evidence has come to light, that the evidence does not support the verdict, or that the damages assessed are plainly inadequate or exceptionally excessive.

Sometimes parties also choose to appeal a decision to a higher court. Within a specified number of days after the lower court's decision, the lawyer first files a notice of appeal. Thereafter, he or she serves the **appellee** with notice of the appeal and prepares a written argument known as a *brief* for the appellate court to consider. A brief always includes the legal questions to be presented to the court, a statement of the facts of the case, and a legal argument favoring the lawyer's client, complete with citations to supporting legal authorities. Ordinarily, after reviewing the appellant's brief, the appellee then files a brief and, after another shorter period of review, the appellant has the opportunity to file a reply brief.

Then, after a prehearing conference to narrow the issues in dispute, the two sides square off in oral argument before the court. Ultimately, the appellate judges render a decision either to affirm or overrule the trial court. Although the decision by the federal or state court of appeals ordinarily ends the case, some parties may wish to pursue appeals to the U.S. Supreme Court, or in states that have intermediate appellate courts to the state court of last resort. Once all appeals have been exhausted, the only step of the civil trial that remains concerns enforcement of the judgment.

To succeed on appeal, the lawyer will ordinarily[31] have to find a legal issue that the trial court mishandled and that substantially affected the course of the trial. For instance, the lawyer might review those objections that he or she made at trial that the trial judge overruled. If the trial judge were mistaken, and the matter were sufficiently serious, an appellate court might conclude that **reversible error** had occurred. Reversible error means a mistaken view of the law or a mistaken application of the law to the facts so serious as to warrant reversal of the lower court's judgment.

[31] Sometimes, of course, lawyers appeal not the decision of the court but the size of the damages awarded.

All appeals tend to be expensive; thus, the **appellant** must be willing to absorb more attorney's fees in an effort that may or may not result in a more satisfactory conclusion. Hence, the vast bulk of the civil cases that go to trial are not appealed to a higher court. However, a higher court does occasionally reverse a lower-court decision and allow an appellant to emerge victorious at the end of the lengthy appeals process.

Enforcement of the Judgment

Since money damages are awarded in many cases, one might wonder how a court enforces such a judgment in a civil case? In the example given previously, suppose that the court agrees with the elderly woman who fell off the train platform that the railroad company acted negligently in failing to light the platform adequately, and decides that she is entitled to $100,000 in damages. How can that woman compel the railroad company to pay the money it now owes her?

The answer relates to the notion of attachment. If a plaintiff attaches some disputed property before trial, then after the case is won the court may award the plaintiff that property. One might think back to the example of the teenager who stopped paying for the new car. Since the car had been hidden and could not easily be repossessed, the dealer persuaded the court to attach the car. When the dealer wins that case, the court will simply award him or her ownership of the car.

Consider, however, the somewhat different case of the elderly woman who fell off the train platform. She was not in a dispute over a piece of property that could be readily attached, like a car, and held by the court. If the railroad company ignores the court order, how might she force it to pay her the money the court has awarded in damages? The answer involves another important phase in civil litigation: **execution of judgment.**

If a plaintiff has already gone into court, and the court has decided in his or her favor and awarded damages, but the defendant has not paid, then the plaintiff can ask the court to attach some piece of property owned by the defendant in order to **execute,** or **satisfy,** the judgment. The court will then attach the property, eventually sell it at a court auction, and pay the plaintiff the money owed out of the proceeds of the sale. For example, if the railroad company did not pay the elderly woman, her lawyer could request that the court attach two locomotives sitting in the railroad's train yard. Then, if the company still refused to make payment, the court could auction off those locomotives and pay the woman her money out of the proceeds from that sale.

Executing a judgment in this manner can be problematic, however. Before a sheriff will act, the plaintiff must be able to prove that the defendant who owes the money really owns the property. Moreover, even though victorious in court, the plaintiff must ordinarily pay a deposit to the sheriff to cover the costs of finding, seizing, and storing the property. The plaintiff, sometimes in conjunction with plaintiffs in other cases who are facing similar circumstances, must also cover the costs of holding the auction, including the costs of advertising and reimbursing the auctioneer. Thus, if the value of the property to be seized is negligible or the amount owed is small, the considerable expense and bother of executing the judgment may cause the plaintiff to drop the matter.

Another method of enforcing a judgment involves placing on the public record a **lien** against the defendants' property. A lien is a claim, encumbrance, or charge on property that gives a creditor the right to retain property to secure payment of a debt. Thus, a victorious plaintiff who has not otherwise been able to enforce a judgment could file public notice of the debt with the clerk of the court. If the defendant tried to sell the property, its title would be defective. The defendant would be compelled to pay off the debt in order to gain the full ownership necessary in order to sell the property. Yet another way to enforce a judgment is to obtain a court order that **garnishes** the defendant's salary. That is, a judge can order an employer to send a percentage of the employee's paycheck to the court in order to pay off an adverse judgment.

Any party who flouts the authority of a judge may also be held in **contempt of court.** Any party who willfully disobeys the lawful orders handed down in a court, or acts to hinder or obstruct the administration of justice, or attempts to embarrass the court or detract from the dignity of the judge risks being held liable for contempt.

Of course, despite these considerable incentives, some defendants never do satisfy a judgment against them. Frequently, the losing party is insolvent and simply cannot pay the plaintiff the sum that is due. In such a state of affairs the defendant is said to be **judgment-proof.** On account of the defendant's insolvency, a judgment for money damages is of no practical effect. However, since many Americans are law-abiding[32] and since the court process can clearly be used to try to execute a judgment against those who might be inclined to ignore it, a solvent party will normally pay the damages awarded.

DIFFERENCES BETWEEN CIVIL AND CRIMINAL TRIALS

Preceding chapters have outlined both the courtroom setting and many of the fundamentals of an American trial, such as the opening and closing statements and the examination and cross-examination of witnesses. Much of this information applies equally to civil and criminal trials. However, civil litigation also differs from criminal proceedings in important respects. In particular, the standard of proof, the settlement process, and the frequency of bench trials differentiate civil from criminal proceedings.

Standards of Proof

In a criminal case the government bears the burden of proving that the defendant is guilty. In a civil case, by contrast, the plaintiff must prove the case against the defendant. Moreover, the decision in a civil case must meet a different standard of

[32] For a work exploring this subject in various contexts see Tom R. Tyler, *Why People Obey the Law* (New Haven, CT: Yale University Press, 1990).

proof than in a criminal case. A criminal prosecutor must prove that the defendant is guilty beyond a reasonable doubt. In a civil case the standard is substantially easier to meet: the plaintiff must prove his or her case by a **preponderance of the evidence.** This means that the plaintiff must prove that it is more than 50 percent likely that the law supports the plaintiff's version of how the dispute should be resolved.

The difference between the standards of proof in civil and criminal proceedings is well illustrated by the cases against O. J. Simpson. In the criminal case, the prosecutors had to prove Simpson's guilt on the murder charges beyond a reasonable doubt. The jury ruled that the prosecution failed to meet that high standard, and hence it acquitted Simpson. In the civil case brought by the survivors of the murder victims, however, the plaintiffs had to prove merely that Simpson was more than 50 percent likely to have caused them injury. This different standard made the civil litigation substantially more difficult for Simpson to win.

Settlement

Only a relative handful of the multitudes of civil cases that are filed eventually go to trial. The parties settle all the rest. Parties often find settlement to be attractive in order to cut the high costs of ongoing litigation and provide a certain compromise outcome, rather than have the parties rely on the court to determine which side wins and which loses and what consequences result.

The high costs of extended civil litigation have also contributed to the increasing popularity of alternative dispute resolution, or ADR. Forms of ADR include **conciliation, mediation,** and **arbitration.** Each of these methods takes a dispute out of the hands of the trial court;[33] each may be viewed as occupying a position on a dispute settlement spectrum. One pole on that spectrum might be marked "privately discussing a settlement," or *negotiation;* the other pole might be marked "going to court to have a judge determine the outcome," or *adjudication.*

The idea of *arbitration* is relatively close to the adjudication pole in that the decision maker hears arguments about a dispute, considers the evidence on both sides, and issues a binding decision. However, arbitration differs from adjudication in various ways. The proceeding is not public. Nor is it necessarily governed by the same strict rules of evidence and procedure that the parties would abide by in court. Since it is informal, arbitration is usually a much quicker method of resolving a dispute than adjudication.

While judges are assigned to cases, the parties to an arbitration usually choose the arbitrator or panel of arbitrators or, at least, they influence the method by which the arbitrator is selected. The parties may also influence the scope of the arbitrator's authority. Unlike a judge, the arbitrator is customarily paid by the par-

[33] Practical and theoretical issues regarding alternative dispute resolution (ADR) are analyzed in the *Negotiation Journal,* affiliated with the Program on Negotiation at Harvard Law School. For overviews of ADR methods see Carp and Stidham, pp. 220–226 and G. Alan Tarr, *Judicial Process and Judicial Policymaking* (St. Paul, MN: West, 1994), pp. 254–260.

ties. Although much arbitration is voluntary, courts in certain jurisdictions occasionally order the parties to arbitrate a dispute, usually one of minor dimensions. While exceptions do exist, both parties to an arbitration normally agree beforehand to abide by whatever award is issued by the arbitrator.

Mediation may be thought of as a large step closer to the *negotiation* pole. In mediation a dispute is referred to a neutral third party who assists the parties in resolving the dispute through negotiation and compromise. The best intermediary, of course, is someone who can communicate with both sides better than they can communicate with one another. Rather than making a binding decision, as a judge or arbitrator normally does, a skillful mediator aims to keep discussions centered on solving the immediate problem, rather than allowing the parties to go off on tangents that raise irrelevant and distracting issues. Mediators differ in the extent to which they adopt active or passive and procedural or substantive roles.

The least common of the three chief ADR methods, *conciliation* means the investigation of a dispute by a third party who has the responsibility of submitting suggestions to the parties for settlement. While a *mediator* will often either sit down with the parties or hear out one and the other with the aim of helping them to find a mutually agreeable resolution, a *conciliator* normally makes an independent analysis of the situation, then outlines a proposal for the parties to consider in their later negotiations. One of the advantages of conciliation is the opportunity the conciliator has to think creatively about how the problem might best be resolved. For instance, rather than determining who owned legal title to disputed property, a conciliator might consider how both sides might profit by sharing the benefits of that property.

Some statutes also promote settlement by threatening the defendant with punitive damages. Although often the extent of such damages is unlimited, certain statutes cap recovery for punitive damages. A cap set at three times the actual injury is called **treble damages.** An example of a treble damages claim leading to an out-of-court settlement arose in my law practice some years ago when I represented an elderly woman in a dispute with a claims agent for her insurance company. Just after her husband died, a flood from a broken water pipe had ruined much of the first floor of her house. An unscrupulous agent had come upon the woman in her grief and persuaded her to sign, without reading it, a document that settled a claim worth at least $30,000 for $3,000. In fact, the agent told the woman to trust him, rather than to waste time finding her glasses in order to read the settlement carefully. Once the agent realized that I had prepared a civil lawsuit under Massachusetts consumer protection laws that alleged the agent had **defrauded** my client and requested treble damages, the case settled immediately.

Since individuals rarely have the experience necessary to judge the worth of a claim and the likelihood that the case would be won in court, they tend to rely on their lawyer's advice as to whether and when to settle. Thus, another reason that so many cases do not go to trial is that the lawyers involved may want to move on to other matters and may persuade their clients that a settlement would satisfy their interests and would be preferable to further litigation.

This is perhaps especially true of lawyers who take cases on a contingency fee basis. Rather than spending days preparing and then arguing a case, and rather than risking a possible adverse judgment that reflects poorly on the lawyer and eliminates legal fees, a lawyer in a contingency fee arrangement may well prefer to settle and take on another client. Settling a case is obviously attractive if it keeps the lawyer from having to turn away other clients and eliminates the possibility of losing the case and having to shoulder all the trial expenses without any compensation. Thus, while artful negotiation may explain why some civil cases settle, the incentives to compromise that are incorporated in a legal system that permits contingency fee arrangements also help to explain why so many cases are settled.

Frequency of Bench Trials

An even higher percentage of civil than criminal cases are heard with a judge, not a jury, as the chief courtroom decisionmaker. In order to waive the right to a jury trial, both parties must agree that a bench trial is preferable. Yet, often such agreement is readily secured. Some cases are so simple and minor that a jury is not convened. In other cases, the dispute is so complex that the parties opt not to exercise their right to a jury.

As one might expect, lawyers tend to approach a civil trial before a judge somewhat differently than one before a jury. In an effort to influence a judge trained in legal reasoning, rather than a jury, lawyers tend to couch their arguments in more technical terms and to orient them more to the law than to the facts. Thus, those watching the course of different cases may find more complicated legal arguments in the many civil cases argued before judges than in the many criminal cases decided by a jury.

ADMINISTRATIVE PROCEEDINGS

Administrative proceedings are yet another legal process by which disputes are resolved in the United States. Congress and state legislatures have delegated the power to make rules and regulations[34] to various federal and state government agencies. These rules and regulations have the force of law. Alongside the courts, administrative tribunals associated with these agencies also decide legal questions involving the extent to which parties are abiding by government regulations. Although occasionally administrative laws specify certain types of behavior as criminal, most administrative proceedings are civil in nature.

The rise of American administrative law may be traced to 1887, when Congress created the Interstate Commerce Commission (ICC) to supervise railroads

[34] By rules and regulations I mean an agency statement "designed to implement, interpret, or prescribe law or policy." Cornelius M. Kerwin, *Rulemaking: How Government Agencies Write Law and Make Policy* (Washington, DC: Congressional Quarterly Press, 1994), p. 3. (Kerwin writes: "Rules are byproducts of the deliberations and votes of our elected representatives, but they are not themselves legislation.")

and protect farmers and others from unreasonable rates. As society grew more complex, Congress created additional agencies charged with regulating different aspects of life to try to ensure safety and fair dealings. The bureaucratic arms of the federal government came to include a host of administrations, agencies, boards, commissions, and departments. Think, for instance, of the Federal Aviation Administration (FAA), the Food and Drug Administration (FDA),[35] and the Occupational Safety and Health Administration (OSHA); the Environmental Protection Agency (EPA) and the National Labor Relations Board (NLRB); the Federal Trade Commission (FTC), the Federal Communications Commission (FCC), the Securities and Exchange Commission (SEC), the Equal Employment Opportunity Commission (EEOC), and the Consumer Product Safety Commission (CPSC); even the cabinet-level departments of Agriculture, Labor, and Transportation, and the Internal Revenue Service (IRS).

The states soon followed suit, creating their own administrative agencies, ranging from departments of environmental protection to workers' compensation boards and even driver's license revocation boards. Each administrative agency's bureaucratic staff was supposed to use its special expertise to deal justly and efficiently with all the applications, claims, inspections, reviews, and other matters that arose under that agency's regulations.

Throughout the twentieth century, but especially in the 1970s, state and federal bodies of administrative law grew rapidly in size and scope. Legislatures continued to delegate broad rule-making powers and to call on the agencies to pass regulations to fill in multiple gaps in very general laws. Moreover, the courts ruled on such fundamental issues as how much due process was to be accorded people appearing before administrative agencies.[36] This, in turn, caused more and different rules to be crafted. Yet in the 1980s, before many of the gaps had yet been filled, a political backlash against government rules at least slowed the momentum of the regulatory machine.

As an administrative agency carries out its rule-making and rule-enforcing functions, disputes often arise. An applicant may be denied a license to operate a radio station or to provide cable services to a neighborhood; a welfare recipient may have his or her benefits terminated; a factory may be fined for violating health, safety, or environmental regulations. When a party believes that an administrative agency has wrongly taken action against it or, perhaps, has failed to take action that it believes is legally required, an administrative dispute-resolution process comes into play.

Administrative agencies have often been delegated quasi-judicial duties so that aggrieved parties may challenge an agency decision. Such proceedings, often

[35] For a recent critique of the FDA see Herbert Burkholz, *The FDA Follies* (New York: Basic Books, 1994).

[36] For a useful introductory overview of these issues, see Calvi and Coleman, pp. 192–213, and Kerwin, *Rulemaking*. See also Peter H. Schuck, *Foundations of Administrative Law* (New York: Oxford University Press, 1994); James Q. Wilson, *Bureaucracy: What Government Agencies Do and Why They Do It* (New York: Basic Books, 1991); and Christopher F. Edley, Jr., *Administrative Law: Rethinking Judicial Control of Bureaucracy* (New Haven, CT: Yale University Press, 1990).

held before administrative law judges, are designed to curb unfair, illegal, and arbitrary bureaucratic decisions. The judgment of the administrative tribunal is then subject to judicial review; that is, a court can overturn the agency's decision if it conflicts with the U.S. Constitution.

As administrative law has developed and administrative proceedings have become more frequent, various controversies have arisen. Some have questioned whether administrative agencies have become unduly zealous in rule-making and have produced inflexible, overly detailed, and sometimes contradictory codes of regulations that have become increasingly onerous, counterproductive, and irrational.[37] For instance, OSHA regulations dictate that the height of railings within a workplace measure 42 inches, not 40 or 44 inches.[38] As one critic noted: "Once the idea is to cover every situation explicitly, the words of law expand like floodwaters that have broken through a dike. Rules elaborate on prior rules; detail breeds greater detail. There is no logical stopping point in the quest for certainty."[39]

Others have questioned the extent to which administrative agencies can act fairly in carrying out their quasi-judicial function. In 1970, a landmark Supreme Court case, *Goldberg v. Kelly*,[40] delineated the minimum due process requirements expected of administrative proceedings, including the right to adequate and timely notice and the right to a hearing with an attorney present, in which evidence may be presented, adverse witnesses may be confronted and cross-examined, leading to a formal record with an explanation of the decision reached. While clarifying certain troublesome ambiguities, the *Goldberg* decision raised other issues that concern the extent to which justice is served via administrative proceedings. In fulfilling their quasi-judicial functions, to what extent have administrative agencies faithfully complied with the Supreme Court's announced requirements? To what extent do extensive due process requirements invite challenges to bureaucratic decisions both within the agency's processes and through judicial review? To what extent do these challenges slow agency operations and detract from the agency's ability to fulfill the objectives it was created to meet?

WITH JUSTICE FOR ALL?

This introduction to the various stages of civil lawsuits has explored the preliminary steps leading up to the actual trial, the nature of a civil trial and its principal distinguishing features, and the final resolution of civil disputes. A critical examination of these topics raises difficult issues as to whether the American legal system truly does justice in civil litigation. Certainly, the system differs sharply from that in

[37] See Philip K. Howard, *The Death of Common Sense: How Law Is Suffocating America* (New York: Warner Books, 1994).

[38] Ibid., pp. 12–13.

[39] Ibid., p. 27.

[40] *Goldberg v. Kelly*, 397 U.S. 254 (1970).

other countries,[41] and it is far from self-evident that the American system is the most just or equitable.

In analyzing this issue, Judge Posner wrote: "[T]he last quarter century has witnessed an astonishing rise in the amount of litigation in the country . . . to which the legal profession has responded with all the imagination of a traffic engineer whose only answer to highway congestion is to build more highways, or of a political establishment whose only answer to increased demand for government services is to print more money."[42] While judicial resources have been stretched far too thin in many parts of the country, Posner correctly questions whether building more courthouses and hiring more judges is the whole answer to increased caseloads.

When one considers how the quality of judicial work and the legitimacy of the court has been questioned in recent years, one might conclude that the American system of resolving civil disputes could usefully be transformed. The rules of civil procedure might be reformed again, not to eliminate discovery, but to protect parties against its abuses and to ensure that it in fact helps to bring about the just, speedy, and inexpensive resolution of disputes. Just before his retirement Chief Justice Earl Warren remarked: "[The] most important job of the courts today is not to decide what the substantive law is, but to work out ways to move cases along and relieve court congestion."[43] What was perceptive in 1968 is of even more pressing concern three decades later. The American civil trial system is far from a model of efficiency.

SELECTED ADDITIONAL READINGS

CARP, ROBERT A., and STIDHAM, RONALD. *Judicial Process in America.* 3d ed. rev. Washington, DC: Congressional Quarterly Press, 1996.

FRIEDMAN, LAWRENCE. *American Law.* New York: W. W. Norton, 1984.

GLICK, HENRY R. *Courts, Politics, and Justice.* 3d ed. rev. New York: McGraw-Hill, 1993.

HAZARD, GEOFFREY C., JR., and TARUFFO, MICHELLE. *American Civil Procedure: An Introduction.* New Haven, CT: Yale University Press, 1993.

HUBER, PETER W. *Liability: The Legal Revolution and Its Consequences.* New York: Basic Books, 1990.

KRITZER, HERBERT M. *The Justice Broker: Lawyers and Ordinary Litigation.* New York: Oxford University Press, 1990.

SARAT, AUSTIN, and KEARNS, THOMAS R., eds. *Law in Everyday Life.* Ann Arbor: University of Michigan Press, 1993.

SCHUBERT, FRANK H. *Grilliot's Introduction to Law and the Legal System.* 6th ed. rev. Boston: Houghton Mifflin, 1995.

ULMER, S. SIDNEY. *Courts, Law, and the Judicial Process.* New York: The Free Press, 1981.

[41] In explaining that a civil law judge "conducts every aspect of the proceeding and questions all witnesses himself," one authority noted: "In many civil-law nations witnesses are not placed under oath before they testify, and cross-examination is virtually unknown. Evidence taken by the judge automatically becomes part of the record in the case, even though no verbatim transcript of the proceedings is made. Instead, the judge summarizes the testimony, which may be subscribed by the witness later. Furthermore, many countries regard it as improper for the lawyers to talk with the witnesses before they testify." R. Doak Bishop, "International Litigation in Texas: Obtaining Evidence in Foreign Countries," *Houston Law Review* 19 (1982), pp. 363–364, cited in Ethan A. Nadelmann, *Cops Across Borders: The Internationalization of U.S. Criminal Law Enforcement* (University Park: Pennsylvania State University Press, 1993), pp. 331–332.

[42] Richard A. Posner, "The Decline of Law as an Autonomous Discipline: 1962–1967," *Harvard Law Review 100* (1987): 771, cited in Glendon, p. 130.

[43] Fred P. Graham, "Warren, Justice 15 Years, to Seek Speed in Courts," *New York Times,* Sept. 30, 1968, p. 1, cited in Carp and Stidham, p. 72.

9

Training and Regulation

Exploring how the American legal system functions in civil and criminal cases leads to questions about the education and supervision of its participants. How are lawyers trained? What is the law school experience like and how might a legal education be assessed? What is meant by legal thinking? How are lawyers regulated? What role is played by bar associations and bar examinations? Why does the United States have so many lawyers? Has the legal system become oversupplied with attorneys? Will there be still more attorneys in the years ahead or fewer?

TRAINING WITHIN THE LEGAL SYSTEM

In civil law systems the training of a judge usually differs from that of a lawyer. Those who aim to serve in the judiciary ordinarily attend a school for judges, the first step in a judicial career. In common law systems, by contrast, judges are either appointed by the government or elected by the people from among the ranks of practicing lawyers. Hence, to understand training within the U.S. legal system, one should focus principally on the education of America's lawyers.

The vast majority of American lawyers endure at least three years of graduate education in law after completing the customary four years of college education and gaining their undergraduate degrees. All potential law school applicants take a *Law School Aptitude Test,* or *LSAT.* This standardized national exam, administered to more than 80,000 prospective law students each year,[1] attempts to measure how well each student thinks. LSAT results offer predictions, often surprisingly accurate ones, as to how well students will fare in law school. Although admissions committees also carefully evaluate a student's college grades, the LSAT is probably

[1] "The Numbers Game," *U.S. News & World Report* 116 (March 21, 1994), p. 70.

the single most important factor in determining which law school will accept a particular student.

The many American law schools differ substantially in expense[2] and prestige and vary somewhat in curricula. Students who wish to attend one of the very best law schools compete for excellent grades in college and often take a review course to prepare for the LSAT. Students from a low-ranking law school will have to graduate at the top of their class in order to land a high-paying job at a major law firm, but graduates from one of the very best law schools can have mediocre grades and still be recruited quite intensely by firms across the country. Such firms court recruits with lavish wining and dining and lucrative summer clerkships, full of perquisites such as complimentary tickets to the best entertainment in town. When I interviewed for a summer position at Skadden, Arps, at the height of the mid-1980s merger-and-acquisitions fever that the firm found so lucrative, I recall hearing of the substantial sum that was supposedly appended to each new associate's first paycheck, along with the admonition: "Dress yourself like a Skadden, Arps attorney!"

American law schools offer different programs of study leading to the several graduate degrees. Standard for those who wish to practice law in the United States is the **juris doctorate** (J.D.), which full-time students usually complete in three years. Many foreign students as well as practitioners interested in gaining special expertise in a particular area opt for a **Master's of Law** (LL.M.) degree, which can normally be completed in two years. Most master's programs focus upon a particular legal subfield, such as tax, comparative, or international law.

J.D. candidates complete a standard program of first-year courses that includes the study of contract, tort, property, criminal, and constitutional law, as well as civil procedure, legal writing, and professional responsibility. During the remaining two years, students select from various specialized subjects, such as tax, antitrust, and labor law; international and environmental law; and bankruptcy and commercial transactions. The larger, more expensive and prestigious law schools tend to offer a broader variety of courses, covering such fields as admiralty, negotiation, and comparative law; human rights, intellectual property, and sports law; and many advanced courses in the standard first-year subjects listed previously.

The curricula of law schools also vary dramatically in regard to *clinical education,* that is, a course of study outside the law school in which students learn certain technical skills useful to practicing law, usually complemented by classroom discussion of the legal and ethical issues raised by the experience. After an initial period of resistance, virtually all law schools now have some clinical programs that permit students to earn credits working at a legal aid clinic or for a judge or practicing lawyer of some sort. Certain law schools, such as Northeastern University Law

[2] The cost of tuition alone at Harvard Law School more than doubles that at various reputable state universities.

TABLE 9.1 **Top Twenty Law Schools—1996**[3]

1. Yale University
2. Harvard University
3. Stanford University
4. University of Chicago
5. Columbia University
6. New York University
7. University of Michigan at Ann Arbor
8. University of Pennsylvania
9. University of Virginia
10. Duke University
11. Cornell University
12. Georgetown University
13. University of California at Berkeley
14. Northwestern University
15. University of Southern California
16. Vanderbilt University
17. University of California at Los Angeles
18. University of Texas at Austin
19. University of Illinois at Urbana-Champaign
20. Washington and Lee University

Source: *U.S. News & World Report* (March 18, 1996), p. 82.

School in Boston, especially emphasize having their students work for prosecutors and public defenders, and in courts, law firms, and government agencies.

Because so many individuals want to become lawyers, admission to law school is more difficult than is admission to many other university programs. Only about one-half of those who take the LSAT exam are admitted to a law school, and so many students apply to the top law schools that even the very best students are not assured of admission. Law students at Harvard or Yale usually graduated in the top 10 percent of their college class and received an LSAT score that placed them in or near the top 1 percent of the 80,000 students who took the test. Each year certain excellent students who meet those two criteria still find themselves rejected by a high-ranking law school. A list of the top twenty law schools, according to one national publication, appears in Table 9.1.

Those unable to gain admission to a top law school or unwilling to pay its considerable tuition may still earn a law degree at one of the many other law schools accredited by the American Bar Association. A recent ABA report listed 171

[3] The rankings are drawn from *U.S. News & World Report* (March 18, 1996), p. 82. The law schools are ranked on five scales: student selectivity, placement success, faculty resources, reputation according to deans and faculty members, and reputation according to lawyers and judges. The five rankings are then merged into overall scores.

accredited law schools, staffed by 5,600 full-time law professors and enjoying a total enrollment of almost 130,000 law students.[4]

The Law School Experience

Of the college graduates and the older professionals who have eagerly sought admission to law school, a surprisingly large number soon comes to dislike intensely their law school experience. One might wonder why this is so.

Perhaps the most distinctive characteristic of the American law school education is the **Socratic method,** a phrase that describes the manner in which most classes are conducted. American law professors, like the Greek philosopher Socrates many centuries before, rarely lecture. Instead, they teach by asking questions about the law cases the students have been assigned to read.[5] The professor's questions are intended to lead the class toward discovering important principles of law and toward gaining the ability to analyze problems as a good lawyer might.

New students at law schools thus arrive in a very large classroom and sit down in an assigned seat, surrounded by perhaps 100 others. The professor then comes in with a large chart showing the assigned seats of all class members. The professor looks over the chart, selects a student, and questions that student about one of the assigned cases for anywhere from several minutes to an hour or more.

"The task of the law professor," one authority has written, "is often to change a student's mind, and then change it back again, until the student and the class understand that in many situations that will come before them professionally they can with a whole heart devote their skills to either side. Then they have to block out much of that part of their mind that saw the other side, finding ways to diminish and combat what they once considered the strong points of the opponent's argument. In the public forum, they are expected to be aggressive for their client . . ."[6] Ultimately, the focus is on examining past legal disputes, usually at the appellate level, in order to learn the legal principles in a judge's reasoning. Hypothetical situations are used to illustrate how a rule might be applied or altered to suit different circumstances. The weaknesses and limitations of arguments by lawyers and courts are carefully scrutinized.

Unfortunately, since law schools contain so many students these days, this questioning by professors often occurs in an atmosphere that is at least occasionally uncomfortable and for some students can be terrifying. Since few professors excel at asking a series of truly illuminating questions, the teaching method can be both confusing and intimidating. Professors inadept or inexperienced in using the

[4] American Bar Association, "Legal Education and Professional Development: The Report of the Task Force on Law Schools and the Profession" (Chicago: American Bar Association, 1992), pp. 112–113, cited in Sol M. Linowitz, with Martin Mayer, *The Betrayed Profession: Lawyering at the End of the Twentieth Century* (New York: Charles Scribner's Sons, 1994), p. 114.

[5] For an interesting critique of the case method see Jerome Frank, *Courts on Trial: Myth and Reality in American Justice* (Princeton, NJ: Princeton University Press, 1973), pp. 225–246.

[6] Linowitz, p. 116.

Socratic method to analyze cases can easily obscure already complicated legal subjects.

Some law students are also shy about speaking out in public, particularly when they are being questioned in front of 100 other students. Professors often assign so many lengthy cases to read each night that students find it very difficult to come to class thoroughly prepared. As a result, a student is sometimes being questioned on a case that he or she has not read in full or has only skimmed over quickly. To force students to do as much work as possible, professors occasionally try to punish unprepared students by inducing other students to laugh at their efforts. After several years of this type of teaching, the most jaded law students come to view law school as a most unpleasant experience, revolving around an almost endless succession of dull cases and tedious classes full of far-fetched hypotheticals.

Testing in law schools is also quite unusual. Although some seminars require a research paper, most courses conclude with a final exam that is the sole grade a student receives. Exams almost invariably consist of **issue-spotters**—that is, tests that call on the student to read through a lengthy hypothetical scenario that contains multiple legal issues that are to be identified and then related to the relevant law in an in-class essay.

Along with reading vast quantities of cases for classroom work, many law students spend considerable time working on a law journal of some sort. Often, their chief aim is to improve their resume with an impressive credential. Students edit the great majority of the more than 800 American law journals published, usually quarterly, by the different law schools. In most law schools, intense competition determines who *makes law review*—that is, which students are chosen to manage the chief law journal of the school, selecting its articles, editing the prose, and especially proofreading and correcting the citations to ensure that they correspond with proper legal form. Typically, a handful of the students with the top first-year grades are invited to join the law review (they are said to "grade on" to the journal), and others attempt to win a writing competition (and "write on" to the journal).

Apart from the principal law review, students at large law schools often publish more specialized journals as well, on topics ranging from international law to law and economics; from human rights to law and public policy; from transnational law to feminist approaches to legal philosophy. Although practices differ from one law school to another, interest in the subject matter of the journal is normally more important than grades or writing ability in determining who participates in editing the more specialized journals.

Frankly, most law students probably find law review work to be mostly drudgery, relieved a bit by the camaraderie of the journal staff. Articles in law reviews tend to be highly specialized and narrowly focused; many are excessively lengthy, theoretical, impractical, and obscure. Most are never widely read. Recently, the dean of Yale Law School went so far as to declare that most law journals contain "unreadable junk that goes on endlessly."[7] Although that assessment may

[7] See Rosa Ehrenreich, "Look Who's Editing," *Lingua Franca* (Jan.–Feb. 1996), p. 60.

be unduly harsh, students editing law reviews often find themselves bogged down, trying to escape from a mire of minutiae under a tight time deadline exacerbated by a plethora of outside pressures. A cynic might call that excellent preparation for the practice of law!

On the basis of such in-class and outside activities many popular accounts of the American law school experience, like *One L* by popular author Scott Turow[8] or the movie *The Paper Chase,* portray law students as anxious, overworked, and very tired. One Yale University study found graduate students in law far more stressed than students in other fields, like medicine or nursing.[9] Rare is the law student who is not more than ready to leave law school behind and move on to the actual practice of law.

Assessing Legal Education

This negative image of the American law school raises the issue of whether this type of education should be reformed. Do American law schools produce good lawyers? What are the positive and negative consequences of a legal education?

The law school experience, as disagreeable and uncomfortable as it may be, does provide students with tools that good lawyers find useful. The American law school tries to teach its students to work hard, think quickly, and master extraordinary quantities of material. The intense questioning in class, although often carried to an unfortunate extreme, does help to prepare students for court appearances where they have to argue matters for their clients in highly partisan and sometimes hostile settings. One attorney observed: "Whether in negotiation or on trial . . . or in conference with clients . . . , lawyers must be quick on their feet, able to handle even the questions they cannot answer in a confidence-inspiring way. Most important of all, they must have the ability to suspend judgment, to see both sides of a case that is presented to them, for they may be called on to argue either side."[10]

Since law is so essential to daily life in the United States, another substantial benefit of a legal education is that it provides much information about society that is important to educated Americans. In law school one learns not just about broad areas of American law and about how the American court system functions, but also a wealth of information about related subjects from taxes to crime, from welfare to accounting, from real estate to prison systems, from business to the environment, from international affairs to marriage and divorce.

Unfortunately, law schools also neglect various aspects of legal training and emphasize certain traits that may not be beneficial for the profession or the individual practitioner. Despite the continued proliferation of "legalese" within the legal profession, law schools are not leading the way in improving the clarity of legal writing or providing law students with the skills necessary to weed out useless

[8] Scott Turow, *One L* (New York: G. P. Putnam's Sons, 1988).

[9] Lawrence S. Wrightsman, *Psychology and the Legal System* (Pacific Grove, CA: Brooks/ Cole, 1987), p. 72.

[10] Linowitz, p. 116.

archaic expressions and produce sound and intelligible documents. Faculties typically treat legal writing as a third-class course, inferior to clinical education and far beneath the core curriculum. Customarily, legal writing is worth fewer credits than "real" courses and is taught by less-experienced instructors who have yet to gain the credentials necessary for a tenure-track post. A law professor who would just as soon teach legal writing as one of the more prestigious, substantive courses would likely be viewed by colleagues and students alike as most eccentric.

Moreover, with one very important exception many law schools have been curiously reluctant to embrace interdisciplinary approaches to legal subjects. The sole exception is the marriage of the study of law with that of economics. The dean of Yale Law School recently observed:

> Law and economics is today a permanent, institutionalized feature of American legal education. Specialized journals are devoted to it, and its presence is pervasive in the older law reviews as well; faculty positions at many law schools are explicitly reserved for its adherents; and it is now represented by a professional organization of its own, the American Association of Law and Economics. Even these external markers of success do not fully measure the movement's influence, which is nearly unrivaled in some fields (corporations and commercial law) and dominant in others (torts, contracts, and property). The law-and-economics movement has transformed the way that teachers in these fields think about their subject and present it to their students.[11]

Apart from the law-and-economics movement, however, the study of law has been kept more rigorously separated than might be expected from other related fields, like history, sociology, anthropology, or political science. Those few law schools that have attempted to recruit faculty members who are expert in two disciplines have tended to do so in only one direction. For instance, both the University of Chicago Law School and George Mason University Law School have led the effort to merge the study of law with that of economics. However, neither of those law schools has embraced other relevant disciplines as readily.

The ability to think logically and analytically is heavily stressed throughout American legal education. The ability to provide legal services to businesses is also emphasized, especially in such common second-year "elective courses" as antitrust, commercial transactions, labor, and tax law. Accounting is more likely to be a required course than is consumer protection or family law. In contrast, most law schools give relatively short shrift to honing the ability to think about how government should function or even how legislation should be drafted.

This state of affairs is not entirely the fault of legal educators. American society has more slots for business lawyers than for legal historians or philosophers. Their eyes set on passing the bar exam and landing a lucrative job, law students who might choose electives like jurisprudence, human rights, legal history, local

[11] Anthony Kronman, *The Lost Lawyer: Failing Ideals of the Legal Profession* (Cambridge, MA: Harvard University Press, 1993), p. 166.

government law, and judicial decisionmaking, instead flock to courses like securities, corporations, federal courts, appellate advocacy, corporations, debtor-creditor law, and corporate taxation. While subtle cues from the faculty may help to guide students toward abandoning idealistic public interest or policymaking careers in favor of more pragmatic, business-oriented ones, the social realities of a materialistic culture, a costly education, high student debt, and a tight job market help to explain why the audience for business-oriented courses is so large and receptive. Thus, with the blessing of many law students, law schools continue to focus primarily on teaching how legal principles might logically be applied to different factual circumstances in a case brought to court.

While in past eras liberal law professors, in particular, might focus attention on the consequences of different possible legal rules and interpretations for American society, discussion of social issues is now often viewed as the province of the *critical legal scholars,* a school of legal philosophy that maintains that law may be manipulated endlessly to suit political objectives.[12] Yet, the attitude of many law students seems to be that, while "the crits" may make for stimulating theoretical dialogue, obtaining the skills necessary to garner a lucrative job offer must be their first priority. For all these reasons, American law schools tend to produce graduates who approach subjects from a rather narrow perspective, without having as broad a vision of the roles of the lawyer and of law and society as might be hoped.

Finally, the modes of behavior taught aspiring lawyers in law school may be questioned. A fine line divides being assertive and persuasive from being arrogant and intimidating. Rather than emphasizing how interpersonal skills might be cultivated and used advantageously, law professors tend to glorify the "take-no-prisoners" trial attorney. By their classroom behavior many professors illustrate the power of the cynical or glib rejoinder and the clever or abrupt put-down. In accord with the adversarial nature of the action in American courts, when law professors discuss cases they tend to emphasize gaining the ability to argue either side of a case far more than determining which side of the case one ought to be arguing.[13]

Such dimensions of legal education may harm the profession and the individual practitioner. As Dean John Sexton of New York University Law School observed: "Real people don't find themselves in cases; they find themselves in situations. Lawyers don't encounter their clients in cases; they encounter them in situations. . . . [E]ven the closest reading of an appellate opinion misses the human element of the lawyer's job. How, for example, does a lawyer interact with a client? How does a lawyer provide guidance, both legal and moral? When and how should a lawyer say no to a client? How does a lawyer confront the possibility of taking action that does not violate any law but does offend the underlying spirit of the law—for example, using discovery to exhaust an adversary?"[14]

Another critic wrote, "Because litigation produces the cases the students

[12] Perhaps the leading book-length explication of the principles of the movement is Roberto Mangabeira Unger, *The Critical Legal Studies Movement* (Cambridge, MA: Harvard University Press, 1986).

[13] See Linowitz, pp. 116–118.

[14] Ibid., pp. 128–129.

study, the model is one of conflict . . ."[15] Although understanding how legal disputes have been argued and resolved in court is obviously important to a budding lawyer, the proportion of time spent counselling clients and negotiating mutually satisfactory, and often amicable, resolutions to disputes suggests that the cooperative elements of law practice are given less attention than is deserved. A challenge for the American law school is to broaden legal education so that it better prepares law students to handle the circumstances they will encounter in their professional lives.

In this regard it is worth noting that a tension has long existed in American law schools between two streams of thought.[16] The first views law as a science. It may be traced to Christopher Columbus Langdell, dean of Harvard Law School from 1870 to 1895, best known for revolutionizing legal education by introducing and institutionalizing the case study method.[17] Langdell might be termed a legal taxonomist: "[H]e appears to have conceived the aim of legal science to be the construction of a comprehensive scheme of classification in which every individual case might be fit under its controlling rule in much the same way that a biologist fits individual birds, fish, and so on under the appropriate species-type."[18]

Moreover, Langdell seems to have had something of the mathematician, and especially the geometrician, in him. The astute legal scholar, according to Langdell, closely examines the caselaw in a particular legal subfield in order to identify fundamental principles from which a series of secondary principles may logically be drawn. In this way the legal scholar extrapolates "a well-ordered system of rules that offers the best possible description of that particular branch of law—the best answer to the question of what the law in that area is. . . . [I]ndividual cases that cannot be fit within this system must be rejected as mistakes."[19]

This new legal science rejected the view of law as a craft that might be mastered by a long apprenticeship at the knee of a wise master. Rather than emphasizing experience, it stressed logic. One legal scholar explained:

> At the end of this process of analysis, what one possesses is a system of ordered propositions like those that appear in a textbook of geometry. Together these exhaustively describe the law. There is nothing more to the law than what they state, nothing in the law that cannot be stated in their terms, and if a case should arise that appears to present a novel issue, that is only because the relevant propositions have not yet been worked out in sufficient detail. . . . [T]he proper way of deciding such a case is simply to carry the process of

[15] Ibid., p. 119.

[16] The following discussion draws on Kronman, pp. 168–180. The political scientist may find it interesting to compare Kronman's analysis with that of Jim Ceaser. See James W. Ceaser, *Liberal Democracy and Political Science* (Baltimore, MD: Johns Hopkins University Press, 1990).

[17] As Kronman points out, this approach to law can be traced even further to the works of Thomas Hobbes, who attempted to repudiate the Aristotelian view of politics and law. See Kronman, pp. 174–180.

[18] Ibid., pp. 170–171.

[19] Ibid., p. 171 (*italics* in original).

> analysis further, until one reaches an implied subrule specific enough to resolve it. Thus even in cases of first impression, Langdell's method offers a procedure for determining what the law is and hence how the case should be decided . . .[20]

One may still detect considerable sympathy with this approach in modern American legal training. The casebook method, the manner in which cases are analyzed by many professors, the style of examination requiring mastery of *black-letter law,* and the resistance, or at least bias against, clinical legal education and skills-oriented courses like legal writing and negotiation reflect something of a Langdellian perspective.

Langdell's continuing influence is also apparent in recruiting law school faculty. More law professors than might be expected have little practical experience. Rather, they have graduated at the top of their law school classes with prestigious positions on law reviews, then clerked for an appellate judge and perhaps a Supreme Court justice, before settling into a teaching career. If the study of law is primarily a matter of principled reasoning, hiring committees will search for theoretical or philosophical brilliance at the expense of the practitioner's experience. To reverse Justice Holmes' famous dictum, the law for these professors has been logic, not experience.[21]

Competing with this approach is the view that legal training requires the gathering of experience, prudence, and practical wisdom. Law is conceived primarily as an intellectual craft, rather than a logical science that requires, above all, the mastery of fundamental principles. This contrary perspective stresses the lack of legal orderliness in a common law legal system, the need for high professional standards, and the natural differences of opinion among reasonable minds on how law is and should be applied.

In this tradition one scholar wrote: "The judgment an experienced lawyer possesses . . . can never attain the level of precision to which one properly aspires in geometry for the simple reason that the complexity and contradictoriness of the relevant precedents often leave room for disagreement as to how specific cases should be decided. Even the most skilled lawyers acknowledge that there may be reasonable differences of opinion regarding the resolution of particular disputes. While each believes his own position is the one that best meets the law's requirements, he nevertheless concedes that other positions may reasonably be defended on the basis of the same ambiguous precedents."[22]

Thus, the elements of the assault on the Langdellian view included: "the recognition of judicial creativity; the insistence that law is not a self-contained and self-serving realm of norms but a tool to be used for the advancement of social ends; and a confidence in the power of the nascent social sciences, and in particu-

[20] Ibid., p. 174.

[21] This phrasing is drawn from Linowitz, who used it in a considerably narrower context involving the teaching of legal ethics. See Linowitz, p. 122.

[22] Kronman, p. 178.

lar of economics, to settle the issues of policy that a judge must address."[23] One can, of course, trace variations of these ideas through the history of American legal philosophy from Oliver Wendell Holmes to the legal realists like Jerome Frank and Karl Llewellyn to the law and economics scholars and critical legal scholars of today.

Naturally, this vein of thought is also evident throughout modern American legal training, countering, contradicting, and perhaps balancing the Langdellian perspective. Law faculties do welcome experienced practitioners, especially as adjunct colleagues. The growth of clinical programs and the popularity of skills-oriented classes attest to the demand by law students for practical, and not just theoretical, learning.

I would guess that most lawyers feel that real legal training occurs in the practice of law and that law school, at best, lays a foundation of fundamental knowledge that may prove useful in later years. Few doubt that the assistance of senior attorneys is critical to developing into a competent lawyer, perhaps especially a competent trial attorney. One judge observed: "I know of no child prodigies among trial lawyers. A certain seasoning of actual experience is a necessary ingredient in the trial advocate. He can learn a good deal from books, and should of course have the rules of evidence at his finger tips, and be well grounded in the law affecting his case. But to develop beyond the point of adequacy, he must learn from his own mistakes and successes and from watching other lawyers in action."[24]

Legal Thinking

One often hears nonlawyers say, usually with a hint of admiration in their voices, that lawyers approach problems from a unique perspective. American law students sometimes go to law school with the idea of becoming schooled in "legal thinking." Indeed, committees often invite one or more lawyers to join their deliberations to take advantage of their analytical skills.

Much legal reasoning, of course, is merely reasoning by example passed down from the common law tradition of deciding cases.[25] That is, a person engaged in legal reasoning compares a set of facts with the facts and application of law found in prior judicial decisions. The legal reasoner then tries to determine whether the rule of law announced in prior cases ought, logically and justly, to be extended to cover the current facts. Two legal scholars explained this process as follows:

> The facts in a current case never exactly duplicate the facts of an earlier case. Thus there is constant opportunity to contend that a rule of law previously applied to an apparently similar case is not really applicable to a current dispute.

[23] Ibid., p. 185.

[24] Bernard Botein, *Trial Judge: The Candid, Behind-the-Bench Story of Justice Bernard Botein* (New York: Simon & Schuster, 1952), quoted in Lloyd Paul Stryker, *The Art of Advocacy: A Plea for the Renaissance of the Trial Lawyer* (New York: Simon & Schuster, 1954), p. 193.

[25] Edward H. Levi, *An Introduction to Legal Reasoning* (Chicago: University of Chicago Press, 1948), p. 1. For a criticism of Levi, see Frank, pp. 320–323.

> Counsel may argue, for example, that the facts in an earlier case were A, B, C, and D, whereas here they are A, B, C, and E. Judges must then decide whether the similarities are so close that they should apply the same rule. If so, they must reformulate the rule to cover situations where the facts are A-B-C-E as well as A-B-C-D. Alternatively, judges may decide that replacement of D by E so changes the situation that they must apply a different rule; in that event, they may merely modify the older rule or create a new one.[26]

Yet while becoming adept at such legal reasoning helps to explain what is commonly meant by "thinking like a lawyer," it provides only a partial explanation. When a neighborhood group or a board of directors or an industry council decides to add a lawyer to their deliberations, they probably do not expect to gain someone who is experienced at reasoning by example alone. Rather, they also expect a particular brand of analytical problem-solving. A respected judge once characterized good legal thinking as "clarity of expression, precision of definition, organization of thought, and more generally the capacity to deal argumentatively."[27]

The subject of precisely how lawyers apply their "legal thinking" to the varied problems presented to them is extraordinarily elusive. The notion that lawyers literally "think differently" than do others skilled in analytical reasoning ought to be treated skeptically. I recall how, after listening to convoluted legal arguments, British legal scholar Patrick Atiyah used to admonish his law students: "Try to forget for a moment that you are lawyers, and remember that you are reasonable and intelligent human beings!"

In fact, what may be most interesting about watching lawyers at work is not how similarly they all think, but instead is how differently they seem to think. A group of first-rate lawyers is likely to approach the same problem in quite distinct manners. The ability to call upon the different approaches of other partners and associates is one advantage to practicing law in a firm.[28] To contend that lawyers think differently than nonlawyers should not imply that all lawyers think alike.

Still, one should not completely discard the notion that legal training has some effect on how most lawyers approach most problems. In part, individuals who have attended law school and have started to practice law have acquired considerable stores of information about different fields of law, about the reasoning of prominent judges, about the historical development of legal philosophies, and about legal principles that link one rule with another. Moreover, in regularly draw-

[26] Walter F. Murphy and C. Herman Pritchett, *Courts, Judges, and Politics,* 3d ed. rev. (New York: Random House, 1979), p. 487.

[27] Linowitz, p. 116.

[28] Solo practitioners can, of course, call upon professional colleagues, often through networks like the American Bar Association (ABA) or the American Trial Lawyers Association (ATLA), to gain advice and expertise on difficult or unusual legal issues. However, it is debatable whether calling upon such a network of professional acquaintances is as straightforward, efficient, and comprehensive as calling upon one's own colleagues in a law firm, who have immediate pecuniary interests served by offering their assistance.

ing on this mass of information, lawyers often seem to develop a subconscious, almost intuitive, sense for how some new legal issue will be resolved. One often hears an experienced lawyer tell a junior associate who has a question about some field of law or about the possible solution to some problem: "Yes, that sounds right" or "No, that seems mistaken to me."

Legal training does emphasize rigorous analytical skills to a greater extent than do many other fields. When I started to practice law, I recall sitting in a senior partner's office and marvelling at how he was able to slice to the core of the client's problem. He had developed the ability to brush aside irrelevant matters and focus attention on precisely what was vitally important. Once the critical issue or issues had been defined, he would lead the client to think through the problem carefully: probing for important facts, clarifying ambiguities or contradictions, creating alternative courses of action, weighing the advantages and disadvantages of different possible actions and their consequences, laying out the various steps that had to be taken to reach a given goal, and finally arriving at a logical conclusion as to what should be done.

Similarly, legal training places a premium on seeing the subtle complexities in a problem. For instance, assume that your neighbor arrived at your back door very upset because a delivery man had just slipped on the front steps and broken his collarbone. Most Americans would realize that the neighbor might well be liable for the injuries caused in such a *slip-and-fall case.* The attention of someone with legal training, however, would likely be drawn toward the possible complexities of the incident. The lawyer's mind is trained to review a plethora of possible hypothetical situations in order to find and focus upon the facts that are legally significant: What was the condition of the steps? Had they been kept in good repair and free of ice and snow? Had any other visitor been injured on the neighbor's property? If the stairs were dangerous, perhaps because of a hole or a loose plank, had the neighbor posted a sign? Had he warned the delivery man of the dangerous condition on some previous occasion? How had the delivery man behaved before he fell? Had he sprinted up the stairs to save time or had he proceeded cautiously? Had the neighbor taken out a homeowner's **personal** ("umbrella") **liability policy** with his insurance company? If so, what were its terms relating to such accidents? All these and many other conceivable subtleties in the situation, subtleties that a lawyer is trained to watch for, would help to determine whether the homeowner would be liable or not.

Perhaps the German and American legal scholar Edgar Bodenheimer offered the clearest and most sensible philosophical explanation of how American lawyers think through a type of "dialectical reasoning." In the following passage a law professor illuminated Bodenheimer's philosophy of legal thought in a common law system:

> The dialectic method . . . attends to available data and experience, forms hypotheses, tests them against concrete particulars, weighs competing hypotheses, and stands ready to repeat the process in the light of new data, experience, or insight. But unlike the method of the natural sciences, dialectical reasoning

> begins with promises that are doubtful or in dispute. It ends, not with certainty, but with determining which of opposing positions is supported by stronger evidence and more convincing reasons.[29]

Thus, the approach taken by a lawyer to a particular problem may be likely to reflect not just the lawyer's superior knowledge of the law, but an analytical approach that is more rigorous, comprehensive, and dialectical than that taken by the typical layperson. But whether such an approach amounts to a new and different way of thinking remains a debatable proposition.

THE REGULATION OF LAWYERS

The manner in which legal expertise is used has rippling consequences that extend far beyond the lawyer and his or her client. The influence of the American legal profession has neighborhood, metropolitan, state, national, and international dimensions. An intensely competitive and highly lucrative legal system, rife with stress and temptation and highly influential in society, cries out for supervision of some sort. How do lawyers abuse professional standards? Who supervises the work of American lawyers? How does one acquire a license to practice law? What happens if an attorney acts in an abusive or unprofessional manner? To what extent do lawyers ignore professional obligations, such as serving as a fiduciary to their clients? In short, how is the legal profession regulated?

The Bad Eggs of the Profession

One reason that lawyers are so often held in low esteem is that they do not always act reputably. Since it is not especially difficult to launch a lucrative career in law, the legal profession attracts its shady characters intent on getting rich as quickly as possible. The intense competition and high pressure that characterize the practice of law lead still more attorneys to desert responsible behavior, abandon traditional ethical principles and professional ideals, and act in a disreputable, underhanded, or downright disgraceful manner.

It may also be true that such a markedly *adversarial system* naturally breeds some measure of dishonesty. Certainly, in attempting to represent a client zealously, attorneys are often sorely tempted to skirt ethical rules or shade the truth in order to satisfy their client or bring their side closer to victory. An unscrupulous attorney might litter a trial with sly innuendos, inflame a jury with irrelevant but prejudicial matter, or influence future jurors by a campaign of pre-trial publicity designed to favor the client. They might coach a witness to lie for a particular cause,

[29] Mary Ann Glendon, *A Nation Under Lawyers: How the Crisis in the Legal Profession Is Transforming American Society* (New York: Farrar, Straus & Giroux, 1994), pp. 237–238. Glendon explains a central premise of Bodenheimer's philosophy drawn from his "A Neglected Theory of Legal Reasoning," *Journal of Legal Education* 21 (1969): 373–402, and *Jurisprudence: The Philosophy and Method of Law* (Cambridge, MA: Harvard University Press, 1974).

purposefully misstate or misrepresent facts or legal provisions, or bring a lawsuit merely to harass or annoy an opponent.

One common tactic, filing intellectually spurious motions simply to bankrupt another party or to delay a judicial decision, is now considered no more than a peccadillo by various aggressive corporate attorneys. A noted law professor recently commented: "In many ways, contemporary federal litigation is analogous to the dance marathon contests of yesteryear. The object of the exercise is to . . . hang on to one's client, and then drift aimlessly and endlessly to the litigation music for as long as possible, hoping that everyone else will collapse from exhaustion."[30] A high-powered New York lawyer boasted: "I was born . . . to be a protractor. . . . I could take the simplest antitrust case and protract for the defense almost to infinity. . . . [One case] lasted fourteen years. . . . Despite 50,000 pages of testimony, there really wasn't any dispute about the facts. . . . We won that case, and, as you know, my firm's meter was running all the time—every month for fourteen years."[31]

As lawyers become expert in manipulating legal rules for the benefit of their clients, as they become arrogant and cynical about their position in society, they may also come to manipulate the rules of professional conduct to suit their own self-interest. While the legal profession is now, and probably always has been, first and foremost a business, the single-minded pursuit of profits has led increasing numbers of irresponsible lawyers into trouble. They overstaff cases, inflate billable hours, and overcharge clients.

A law professor recently wrote: "Just as sexual self-expression has few limits in a culture where chaste behavior is mocked, lawyers' self-interest is apt to run amok when anyone who places court and client above profit is branded a hypocrite or a chump."[32] After noting that past leaders of the bar valued their reputation above all else, another distinguished attorney observed ruefully: "Law, of course, is not alone in the deterioration of its morals and manners. Much of American life has lost our old reverence for reputation."[33]

Attorneys obsessed with improving the bottom line also take on legal business that they are ill-equipped to handle, as when an attorney expert in one field of law ventures into a new area without adequate preparation or an attorney accustomed to counselling clients enters the relatively unfamiliar surroundings of the courtroom. The extent to which this is a pressing problem is subject to debate; however, ill-prepared lawyers are by no means unheard of in the legal profession. In 1978 Chief Justice Warren Burger reportedly made the astonishing claim that up to one-half of all trial attorneys were "inadequate."[34]

[30] Glendon, p. 56, citing Nick Armstrong, "Discovery, Abuse and Judicial Management," *New Law Journal* (July 3, 1992): 927 (quoting Professor Arthur Miller of Harvard Law School).

[31] Glendon, p. 56, citing "Those #*X!!! Lawyers," *Time* (April 10, 1978), pp. 56, 59.

[32] Glendon, p. 83.

[33] Linowitz, p. 18.

[34] Henry J. Abraham, *The Judicial Process: An Introductory Analysis of the Courts of the United States, England, and France*, 6th ed. rev. (New York: Oxford University Press, 1993), p. 167.

The Bar Examination

The first professional effort to screen inadequacy from the ranks of lawyers comes at the bar examination. After graduating from law school,[35] a student must pass a bar exam in order to be licensed to practice law in a particular state in the United States or in Washington, DC. Each state also requires prospective attorneys to take and pass a test concerning that state's *code of professional responsibility,* the ethical guidelines that govern the practice of law within that state.

In theory, at least, the two days of testing ensure that all attorneys in a state possess the minimum qualifications deemed necessary to represent clients competently. A national standardized test known as the **multistate exam** occupies one half of the testing period. Its multiple-choice questions cover in considerable detail the legal rules that would be found in most states in diverse fields of law. The state-specific half of the bar exam takes the form of written essays on the content of that state's laws.

The subjects tested during the state-specific half of the bar exam differ significantly from state to state. For example, Delaware, home to the headquarters of many business corporations, tests its applicants extensively on business law. New York, where many lawyers deal with issues involving the stock exchanges, tests its applicants on securities laws. Texas, with all its oil production, tests its applicants on laws relating to natural resources. Perhaps the most difficult exams are those held in New York, California, Florida, and Hawaii, in which numerous students are tested and high percentages fail. Each year in each state many people, anywhere from 20 to 50 percent, fail the bar exam. Because the two days of testing can be so rigorous, and because many consider failure to be a black mark on a law student's record, almost all recent law school graduates take a two-month cram course in preparation.

Once an individual passes the bar exam and fills out a questionnaire leading to a routine character check, he or she then attends a formal "swearing-in" ceremony and officially becomes a lawyer. However, since state laws differ substantially, if that lawyer moves to another state, he or she will ordinarily have to pass that state's bar exam as well.[36]

The Bar Associations

Different species of bar associations exist. One, the voluntary bar association, ranges in size from the enormous American Bar Association (ABA) or the more specialized Association of Trial Lawyers of America (ATLA) to municipal bodies

[35] Several states still allow individuals to take the bar examination and to attempt to become officially sanctioned as lawyers without first having graduated from an accredited law school. In Virginia, for instance, several dozen "law readers" study under tutors each year in hopes of passing the bar exam and avoiding the expense of law school. Since Thomas Jefferson successfully took this route in the late eighteenth century, a small number of law readers pass each Virginia bar exam and are duly admitted to the practice of law.

[36] In most states and in Washington, DC, a sufficiently experienced lawyer may be able to waive at least the standardized part of the bar exam, thus dramatically reducing the burden of studying for another exam.

like the Boston Bar Association or the Bar Association of the District of Columbia. The ABA has long striven to improve the administration of justice in the United States. Among its most important accomplishments, the ABA sponsored the drafting and updating of legal canons of ethics, which are codes of professional responsibility for attorneys. It also provides its members with various services, ranging from favorable credit card and insurance terms to continuing legal education training programs in a wide array of fields of law. And, as noted in Chapter 3, the ABA also evaluates candidates for positions in the federal judiciary.

Voluntary bar associations are, for better or worse, highly social groups. Members meet at conferences and receptions to socialize, often in lavish surroundings, and to try to make a name for themselves and their law firms. However, as one bar organization official noted, "As firms grew into 'law factories' with hundreds of lawyers in their employ, they began to provide the training, the social environment, the camaraderie and the entertainment rooms for clients that lawyers once sought at bar groups."[37] This, combined with rising dues in a tight economy, helps to explain why so many voluntary bar associations are losing members.[38] Those that continue to increase in size tend to be clustered in rising fields of law (the American Intellectual Property Association, for instance) or tend to have target memberships that feel a special need to come together (the Women's Bar Association of the District of Columbia or the National Bar Association, which is predominantly African-American).[39]

Apart from the voluntary bar associations, in most states the organization that administers the bar exam also supervises the work of lawyers, at least to a limited degree. Under this system, sometimes called a "unified" or an "integrated" bar, all attorneys admitted to practice law must pay annual dues to a state bar association. The bar then draws on those resources to fund educational programs for lawyers, to publicize issues regarding professional duties, to print compilations of ethics opinions, and to investigate lawyers who commit crimes, poorly represent their clients, or violate other professional responsibilities.

In licensing a lawyer, the state certifies that this professional in law is competent to handle the problems of clients. In return, the state imposes professional obligations on the lawyers it certifies.[40] Since nonlawyers might not be able to judge professional competence in law, the licensing and supervision of lawyers is undertaken by groups of reputable lawyers within the bar associations. Some measure of regulation is thus thought to benefit American society and the legal profession.

In most states, the integrated bar associations investigate misbehavior, but the courts actually discipline attorneys for unprofessional conduct. Among the

[37] Saundra Terry, "Shrinking Bar Associations Work to Make Their Case," *Washington Post,* Washington Business section, July 8, 1996, p. 7, citing Randall Scott, former director of the Bar Association of the District of Columbia.

[38] The ABA, with dues of $50 to $275 a year, reached its membership peak in 1991 with more than 362,000 members. Since then the numbers have declined to 339,000 in 1995. Ibid.

[39] See ibid.

[40] Linowitz, p. 11.

common penalties assessed against lawyers who violate a state's code of professional responsibility are formal public reprimands, orders to restore fees to a client, and, for very serious offenses, suspension of the license to practice law for some designated period. In states that do not have an integrated bar, a special body, such as a state commission, is delegated the task of supervising wayward attorneys and non-lawyers engaged in the unauthorized practice of law.[41] Under either system, however, few if any states have been lauded for aggressively and consistently pursuing illegal or unethical legal practices.

Critics of such bar organizations have long argued that they exist primarily to keep other individuals who are not lawyers from doing legal work that sometimes is quite simple. For instance, helping a couple in a **no-fault divorce** without substantial property issues to settle will involve a sequence of events and a number of standard forms that no great amount of legal expertise is necessary to master. Changing names, drafting wills, adopting children, distributing estates, and transferring property titles, might be placed in the same category. While each of these activities might involve complications that require a lawyer's expertise, one may question whether a lawyer's services are always vitally needed.

For years some bar associations resisted having real estate agents handle the purchase and sale of houses without legal assistance, and even having accountants prepare tax returns without a lawyer at hand.[42] Today, tax lawyers no longer prepare returns, and states permit a range of real estate transactions to occur without legal counsel on both sides.[43] The dimensions of what qualifies as the illegal practice of law seem to be narrowing and may continue to narrow in the future.

Nonetheless, state bar organizations do periodically pursue persons accused of engaging in the unauthorized practice of law in that state. The critics claim that bar associations have been unduly authoritarian in demonstrating their power over all who would practice law within the state. By putting the influence of the bar behind having attorneys undertake even the simplest kind of legal work, the bar association simply ensures that fees continue to flow into the pockets of lawyers and that lawyers maintain a firm grip on many mundane tasks, some might say the "make-work" of the profession.

In my experience, the bar associations that guard the gates of the legal profession and oversee the activities of lawyers can be unreasonable and obsessed with protocol and tradition. Increasingly, their rulemaking is divorced from the effort to craft high professional ideals. Rather than exhorting lawyers toward lofty conduct, the rules now regulate the legal profession as a business. They focus upon finding a lowest common denominator of minimally appropriate conduct that all lawyers should maintain in order to avoid facing disciplinary proceedings.[44]

[41] In Washington, DC, for instance, the District of Columbia Committee on Unauthorized Practice of Law reports to the District of Columbia Court of Appeals.

[42] See Linowitz, pp. 157–158.

[43] See Glick, p. 84, citing Herbert Jacob, *Justice in America,* 4th ed. rev. (Boston: Little, Brown, 1984), p. 63.

[44] See Glendon, pp. 5, 79–80.

Nevertheless, bar organizations also do some unequivocally positive work for society by disciplining underhanded or incompetent attorneys. Of course, lawyers who cheat their clients, take fees without providing services in return, or represent them very poorly are already subject to civil claims on malpractice and other grounds. Lawyers who misappropriate their client's funds may be subject to criminal penalties as well. Yet, the scrutiny of state bar authorities remains useful. Not all cheated clients have the time, energy, resources, or inclination to sue their former attorney. Since lawyers have specialized knowledge that the general public lacks, a bar organization may be able to search out incompetence and fraud in the legal profession better than the victims ever could, acting alone. By instituting disciplinary proceedings and keeping public records concerning the unprofessional conduct of all attorneys brought before them, the state bar association can serve as an information clearinghouse[45] for clients who become suspicious of their attorney or are concerned about hiring a particular lawyer or firm.

The adverse publicity associated with disciplinary action as well as the actual penalties, such as **disbarment,** or suspension of the license to practice law within the state, likely serve to deter some unprofessional conduct. Unfortunately, however, most bar associations are very reluctant to pursue complaints against lawyers aggressively. One study found that the disciplinary committees of state bar associations took action in fewer than 2 or 3 percent of all client complaints.[46] Moreover, the standards set by bar associations are not especially high. While a disciplinary committee might well pursue an attorney accused of bilking a client of a large sum, it would be much less likely to take on the more ambiguous and challenging task of reprimanding a lawyer devoted to assisting clients in evading the law.

Bar organizations in various states have also led movements to pressure, or even to require, attorneys to perform more *pro bono* service and to attend more continuing legal education conferences. They have brought attention to the low numbers of women and minority partners in law firms. Thus, along with sponsoring social events, issuing memoranda and directives, and focusing attention on nonlawyers practicing law on the sly, bar organizations also set minimum professional standards and exert pressure on lawyers and law firms to reach positive goals for society.

AN OVERSUPPLY OF LAWYERS?

In describing the lawyers of the late Roman Empire, Edward Gibbon noted: "[that] splendid and popular class are described . . . as . . . rapacious guides, who conducted their clients through a maze of expense, of delay, and of disappointment,

[45] In an era in which lawyers commonly practice in different states in the course of a single career, it has been suggested that a national computerized service, perhaps through the American Bar Association, be made available to the public that would list action taken against lawyers and, if desired, the lawyers' explanation for what occurred. The ABA's current informal list of lawyers punished in just one of the states exceeds 40,000 names. See Linowitz, p. 143.

[46] Henry R. Glick, *Courts, Politics, and Justice,* 3rd ed. rev. (New York: McGraw, 1993), p. 93.

from whence, after a tedious series of years, they were at length dismissed, when their [clients'] patience and fortune were almost exhausted."[47] King Ferdinand of Spain once declared to his subjects departing to colonize the West Indies: "no lawyers should be carried along, lest lawsuits should become ordinary occurrences in the New World."[48] After moving to the United States in 1754, French writer J. Hector St. John Crèvecoeur observed: "Lawyers are plants that will grow in any soil that is cultivated by the hands of others; and when once they have taken root they will extinguish every other vegetable that grows around them."[49]

Today, although the United States contains only 6 percent of the world's population, two out of every three lawyers in the world are American. An even higher percentage of the world's attorneys has received legal training at an American law school. Within a total population of approximately 255 million, America has about 950,000 people who have had legal training.[50] That amounts to about one lawyer for every 310 people in the United States, more than four times as many lawyers as in 1960, and more than twenty-five times more lawyers per capita than in Japan. Great Britain, a country with an even longer legal tradition than the United States, would have to triple the number of its lawyers to achieve an equivalent number of lawyers per capita. In fact, more people practice law in Los Angeles county than in all of France, a country with seven times the population of that single American county.[51] Why does the U.S. have such extraordinary numbers of lawyers?

A simple answer, though one that begs the question, is that practicing law has become ever more profitable. American lawyers have earned a comfortable living since colonial times. However, during the last quarter of the twentieth century attorneys in the United States increased their earnings more than six times and began to take home a total of more than $100 billion a year.[52] In the 1980s the

[47] Glendon, p. 57, citing Edward Gibbon, in D. M. Low ed., *The Decline and Fall of the Roman Empire* (New York: Harcourt, Brace, 1960), p. 259.

[48] James V. Calvi and Susan Coleman, *American Law and Legal Systems,* 2d ed. rev. (Englewood Cliffs, NJ: Prentice Hall, 1992), p. 31, citing Walter M. Chandler, *The Trial of Jesus From a Lawyer's Standpoint* (Norcross, GA: Harrison, 1976), p. 62.

[49] Lawrence M. Friedman, *A History of American Law,* 2d ed. rev. (New York: Simon & Schuster, 1985), p. 304, citing J. Hector St. John de Crèvecoeur, *Letters from an American Farmer* (1782; reprinted Franklin Center, PA: Franklin Library, 1982).

[50] In 1985, the American Bar Foundation reported that 655,191 Americans practiced law. See Barbara Curran, ed., *Supplement to The Lawyer Statistical Report: The U.S. Legal Profession in 1985* (Chicago: American Bar Foundation, 1986), p. 3. By 1991 that figure had risen to 805,872 lawyers, of whom 36,971 listed themselves as inactive or retired. *Statistical Abstract of the United States* (Washington DC: U.S. Government Printing Office, 1994), p. 210. By 1996 more than 946,000 American practiced law. Terry, "Shrinking Bar Associations," p. 7.

[51] For the comparative statistics, see Wrightsman, p. 66. Naturally, all these lawyers are not evenly distributed across the United States. In 1985 the densely populated urban area of Washington, DC, had the highest per capita ratio of lawyers, reporting one practicing lawyer for every twenty-two residents. The second highest percentage of lawyers in the United States came in New York with a lawyer for every 244 people, while the largely rural states of South Carolina, North Carolina, and West Virginia reported one lawyer for every 657, 665, and 669 residents. Among the states with surprisingly high percentages of lawyers were Colorado, which ranked fifth with one lawyer for every 284 residents, and Alaska, sixth with one for every 286 persons. See Curran, p. 166.

[52] Linowitz, p. 101.

amount Americans spent for legal services more than doubled: from less than $40 billion to more than $80 billion.[53] In 1989, perhaps the most profitable year the American lawyer ever enjoyed, the average compensation for partners at seven New York firms exceeded $1 million dollars.[54] If the idea of law as a modern-day gold rush helps to explain why so many people want to become lawyers, it also raises the question of why legal services are in such demand? Why is practicing law in the United States such a profitable endeavor?

Modernization

Modernization and urbanization have brought in their train crowding, transformed values, impersonal relationships, a highly mobile population, different surrounding cultures, constant interactions with unfamiliar people, and many other stresses. An increasingly developed, urban society helps to explain why the current generation of Americans is more inclined to go to court to resolve differences and why so many lawyers are earning such handsome salaries.

"It stands to reason," one lawyer wrote, "that 100 people living in one building will have more disputes and problems than 100 people scattered over 100,000 acres."[55] Moreover, the U.S. population has continued to diversify ethnically and culturally, and the cities and suburbs have continued to expand. A transient, heterogeneous, urban population has resulted in many people losing their sense of community and feeling as though they are individuals living among strangers.[56] For many Americans even the idea of *community* has gained certain negative connotations. Where once *community* implied friendly neighborhoods and common social, religious, cultural, ethnic, and athletic bonds, community now also conjures up images of meddling and officious homeowner, condominium, and neighborhood associations attempting to influence or even dictate the condition of yards, the planting of trees, and the color and architectural design of residences.

On account of changed values, American divorce rates have risen dramatically, eclipsing those in all other advanced countries.[57] This has created a boom for divorce lawyers. As the American economy has expanded and shifted to a post-industrial phase, complicated business disputes, especially those dealing with patents and contracts, have soared. This has greatly increased the profits of the corporate law firm. The need for more thorough and sophisticated environmental protection suitable for a highly developed industrial state has led to a strong de-

[53] Ibid.

[54] Ibid.

[55] Charles W. Joiner, *Civil Justice and the Jury* (Westport, CT: Greenwood Press, 1962), p. 10.

[56] For an interesting analysis of the term *community*, see Inis L. Claude, Jr., "Community and World Order," *Virginia Quarterly Review* 50 (1974): 481–496.

[57] See David Popenoe, *Disturbing the Nest: Family Change and Decline in Modern Society* (New York: Aldine de Gruyter, 1988), p. 287, and William J. Goode, *The World Changes in Divorce Patterns* (New Haven, CT: Yale University Press, 1993), p. 153, cited in Seymour Martin Lipset, *American Exceptionalism: A Double-Edged Sword* (New York: W. W. Norton, 1996), pp. 49–50.

mand for environmental lawyers. Thus, as American society has changed, the demand for lawyers has skyrocketed.

Increased Lawmaking

While Americans are not an especially law-abiding group, they are remarkably legalistic in passing extraordinary numbers of laws and regulations, in emphasizing due process guarantees, and in resolving disputes in court. Plainly, the explosion in American laws has contributed mightily to the population explosion in lawyers.[58] While scholars debate whether the United States ranks as the most litigious society, it seems certainly to be the most legislative. At every level of the federal system, government bodies regularly make law. A host of state and national agencies also occupy themselves with passing rules and regulations. Despite periodic efforts to deregulate, reduce red tape, and streamline the statute books, Americans have had to contend with steadily growing and ever more complex bodies of law.

If the federal tax code remained the fifteen-page document it was in 1913, rather than growing to the present stature of more than 9,400 pages, one might expect that American society would employ fewer tax attorneys. However, as the government has sought to increase tax revenues and to carve out tax breaks that are popular with important constituents or that encourage positive social behavior, the Internal Revenue Code has become an ever more ponderous set of laws. Moreover, as one corporate attorney put it, "the profitability of an enterprise [has become] . . . in no small measure the result of the cleverness of its tax lawyers."[59]

The trend evident in tax law appears throughout many diverse fields of American governance. One authority declared: "Lawyer-dominated legislatures and bureaucracies now extend their reach into every corner of contemporary American life—taxing, subsidizing, licensing, attaching conditions, granting dispensations, mandating or encouraging this and forbidding or discouraging that."[60] Certainly, from Franklin Roosevelt's New Deal forward, American government has expanded and evolved into a vast administrative and regulatory state. The laws and regulations under which that state operates, whether the subject matter is agriculture or the environment, welfare or finance, civil rights or military procurement, or any of a host of other subjects, have created a voracious demand for lawyers in government and private practice.[61]

Moreover, government agencies justify their budgets by showing Congress that they are actively engaged in controlling those subject to their various jurisdictions.[62] One authority noted: "The discovery that the government may have a reason for action under the law is a moment of satisfaction for the agency, a moment

[58] For an extended discussion of various of the points below, see John G. Kester, "Cluttered Statute Books," *Washington Post*, Feb. 9, 1996, p. A21.

[59] Linowitz, p. 80.

[60] Glendon, p. 12.

[61] See Glick, p. 97.

[62] This point is drawn from Linowitz, p. 77.

of dismay for the client."[63] One might add that it can be a moment of unbridled glee for the attorneys on all sides.

The work done by state and federal legislatures and administrative agencies is especially problematic since law-making often takes place quite sloppily. In contrast to the efforts in civil law states to create logical encompassing codes, American laws and regulations are often formulated with little regard for how best to splice together new and old legislation. One scholar wrote: "Legislatures and administrative agencies rarely take the trouble to fit new statutes and regulations into the framework of existing law. Rather, they leave it up to judges to make some sense of a welter of federal, state, and local enactments that are often conflicting or overlapping—some overly detailed, others airily vague."[64]

In a highly partisan political era, characterized by high campaigning costs, politicians often seem to be more than happy to have the courts decide difficult issues, rather than enter a political debate that may prove unpopular and cost them support or even their jobs.[65] Yet, resolving disputes by legal means that could be dealt with by political means plainly brings business to the legal profession. From this perspective, the quantity of American lawyers is simply a symptom of an underlying reality—the constant law-making engaged in by American legislatures, themselves full of lawyers, and the law-enforcing undertaken by government agencies, also well stocked with attorneys.

The Structure of Legal Education

The structure of American legal education also contributes to the high numbers of lawyers. Unlike many countries that permit only a small elite to receive legal training,[66] for many years American law schools have admitted quite large classes of students. They have done so to expand legal services and to ensure that legal training is available for all qualified applicants, whether they hail from the country-club set atop the social order or from immigrant or working-class backgrounds. In part, also, law school admissions policies may have been crafted to pay the salaries of the many lawyers who would like careers as law professors!

Law schools employ approximately 10,000 American lawyers, and universities typically pay law professors substantially better salaries than other university faculty. Hence, competition to become a law professor has steadily increased, as has the size of law school faculties and curricula, and student bodies. Such trends, coupled with the serious financial difficulties that characterize so many American universities in the late twentieth century, help to explain why law schools admit so many students.

In addition, the government has long provided financial assistance to the

[63] Ibid.

[64] Glendon, p. 167.

[65] See ibid., p. 168.

[66] See Alan G. Tarr, *Judicial Process and Judicial Policymaking* (St. Paul, MN: West, 1994), p. 252.

many qualified applicants who wish to attend law school. In this, legislators have responded to the American value that endorses providing opportunities for graduate education to intelligent individuals from all strata of society. A country such as Japan strictly limits those admitted to practice law by passing and providing licenses to those with only the very top scores on national law exams. In contrast, American state bar associations pass thousands of applicants each year, a licensing decision that plays a role in attracting law school students and ultimately results in an annual crop of incoming attorneys that is larger than the group leaving the profession.

The Drumming Up of Legal Business

One sometimes hears the argument that lawyers breed lawyers. An old joke tells of a town that was too small for one lawyer, but once two had hung out their shingles they became rich men![67] The idea is that every time a new attorney appears and is hired by a client to do legal work, some other person, company, or government agency will also be likely to need its own lawyer in order to be adequately represented in the legal battle of wits. This argument assumes, not wholly without cause, that American lawyers are able to "drum up" business from clients who might otherwise ignore the legal issues that arise in their lives or resolve them through negotiation, mediation, or other methods that do not necessarily require a lawyer's assistance.

For many years state bar associations banned advertising by lawyers, viewing it as professionally unbecoming. The state bars were, of course, often firmly in the grip of attorneys from large law firms who neither needed nor wanted to advertise. This group maintained that legal professionalism would suffer if attorneys were to advertise their services. In contrast, solo practitioners and lawyers in small firms generally felt that advertising would help them to reach the new clients they needed to attract. Whatever the merits of the policy arguments on both sides, the U.S. Supreme Court ruled in 1977 that the Arizona ban on lawyer advertising amounted to an unconstitutional infringement of free speech.[68]

Since that landmark decision, attorneys have taken to advertising on television, in the newspapers, and now on the Internet in increasingly aggressive fashion. One of the most common methods of luring in customers is by publicizing the contingency-fee basis. The television announcer might declare something like this: "If you're injured, call Smith, Jones, and Johnson today. Remember no legal fee is charged unless we recover money for you."

Thus, one reason that litigation may be increasing is that lawyers can use advertising to convince potential clients that taking a grievance to the legal system may result in a sizeable payoff. A firm in Washington, DC, took to the airways with the message: "If you have a phone, you have a lawyer."[69] Lawyers in Chicago adver-

[67] Linowitz, p. 92.

[68] *Bates v. State Bar*, 433 U.S. 350 (1977).

[69] Linowitz, p. 111.

tised: "We are pleased to announce that we obtained for our client THE LARGEST VERDICT EVER FOR AN ARM AMPUTATION—$7.8 MILLION."[70] A New York firm ran the following radio advertisement: "Have you or someone you know been injured in any type of accident? Just call toll-free, 1-800-EX-JUDGE. . . . Let the ex-judge help you get everything you're entitled to. . . ."[71]

Systemic Encouragement of Lawsuits

Perhaps an even weightier factor is that other legal systems commonly include disincentives to sue that are wholly absent from the American trial process. For instance, although in the United States any attorney can file and argue a lawsuit, in Britain all major cases are taken to court by an elite class of trial attorneys known as **barristers.** A client first goes to an office attorney known as a *solicitor.* If after interviewing the client the solicitor believes that the client's claim has merit, he or she takes the case to a barrister who decides whether to accept it or not. The structure of such a system may well bring about fewer negligible, harassing, or false claims since the barrister has a reputation with court and colleagues that needs to be nurtured and protected.[72] Such feelings, while not wholly absent in the United States, seem to be much less compelling in a system in which any licensed attorney is free to take a case to court.

Even more important, in Britain and various other countries a plaintiff who brings a civil lawsuit and then loses the case can expect to pay the defendant's legal fees and court costs. Under such a system the plaintiff risks losing a considerable sum, just as the defendant does. A potential plaintiff must carefully consider whether the likelihood of winning the case is strong enough to justify the financial risk of losing the case and paying off the other side's costs. However, this disincentive to sue is often partly balanced by state medical insurance and social benefits packages, absent in the United States, that help to restore the injured person to the position he or she occupied before the accident or other damage occurred.

The American system, by contrast, seems designed to encourage lawsuits. Rather than relying upon national medical insurance or a social security system that replaces lost income after all accidents, Americans prefer to have issues regarding compensation after accidents resolved in court. With certain exceptions, such as **no-fault automobile insurance,** Americans opt to try to assign blame judicially, rather than simply make the victim whole. Contingency-fee arrangements, banned in many countries, provide American clients with a strong incentive to go to court to settle disputes.

Even workers' compensation systems, which for certain categories of workers restore lost income after work-related accidents, without regard to negligence

[70]"Quotes," *ABA Journal* (Nov. 1989): 39, cited in Glendon, p. 5.

[71] Linowitz, p. 22.

[72] A useful comparison of the American and English trial systems that argues in favor of adopting a barrister and solicitor division in the legal profession in the United States may be found in Stryker, pp. 251–270.

and other causal factors, have become more litigious over time. In various states, courts have heard and qualified dubious injuries, and legislatures have increased the size of possible awards as well as the fraction that lawyers can take as legal fees.[73] Arguably, comprehensive social insurance would cost society less and benefit victims of accidents more than the current system. However that may be, to date Americans have opted to use litigation to resolve most issues concerning accidents.[74]

The American system also seems especially prone to litigation in comparison with legal systems in other developed countries since American courts rarely order plaintiffs to pay the defendant's legal fees. Ordinarily, each party must pay its own lawyers, though poor plaintiffs and defendants may sometimes take advantage of free public legal services. In fact, American courts more frequently order a losing defendant to pay the plaintiff's legal fees to punish an unlawful act, than order a losing plaintiff to pay the defendant's legal fees to discourage frivolous lawsuits. This may be explained, in part, by the value Americans have long placed on innovative legal arguments. What to one judge might appear frivolous could seem brilliantly progressive to another. Hence, for fear of chilling innovation, judges have been reluctant to punish lawyers bringing odd arguments to court.[75]

Among the other positive inducements to sue that characterize the American trial system are the class-action lawsuit, banned in various countries, and the many laws that allow for punitive damages over and above those necessary to restore plaintiffs to the position they occupied before the unlawful acts occurred. Certain statutes specifically authorize recovery of attorneys' fees in order to encourage particular types of litigation, such as civil rights cases. American courts also recognize the "infliction of emotional distress" to be a valid legal claim. Since juries and judges often have an especially difficult time determining genuine emotional distress, and since the magnitude of potential damages to compensate for psychological injuries can be staggering, litigants are tempted to pursue such claims, whether genuine or spurious.

Moreover, when a lawyer takes a case on a contingency-fee basis, the client need not worry about spiraling legal costs or receiving only negligible damages that will not cover attorneys' fees. Instead, the attorney shoulders the costs of the suit, and the client merely waits breathlessly to hear the amount of the settlement or award. With lawyers counselling clients that virtually any injury could be attributed to some wealthy defendant—one with "deep pockets," as lawyers like to put it—little risk and a potentially large payoff seems a recipe designed to bring parties to litigate their problems.

[73] See Linowitz, pp. 155–156.

[74] This helps to explain why tort costs as a percentage of Gross National Product (GNP) are substantially higher in the United States than in other developed Western countries. While in 1987 such tort costs averaged 0.5 to 0.6 percent in England and Wales, France, Italy, and West Germany, and accounted for only 0.3 percent of GNP in Japan, they reached 2.4 percent in the United States. See Seymour Martin Lipset, *American Exceptionalism: A Double-Edged Sword* (New York: W. W. Norton, 1996), pp. 50, 228.

[75] For an especially interesting discussion of this point see Linowitz, pp. 176–177.

Structuring the system in this way leads to many American lawsuits handled by many American lawyers. Contingency fees are banned in many countries for fear that they "promote harassing litigation designed to exact settlements, as well as . . . tempt lawyers to put their own interests ahead of their clients."[76] Nevertheless, permitting contingency fees also ensures that the courtroom door is open to people who might otherwise be shut out, especially those without substantial financial resources.

In a country that bans contingency fees and compels unsuccessful plaintiffs to pay the defendant's costs, an injured retiree living on a fixed income or many others in serious financial straits might not care to risk meager savings on a lawsuit. The influence and resources of a large corporate opponent or insurance company and the possibility that the court could award hefty attorneys' fees if the case were lost would act as strong disincentives to sue.[77] An American in the same position would be likely to find an attorney willing to take on the case on a contingency fee basis. From this perspective the American system may make more sense for a society that is more intent on redressing individual grievances than on protecting businesses from unwarranted claims.

Whether the aggressive assertion of rights through litigation is a blessing, a curse, or a mixed blessing may be debated. Some feel that the system might be improved by a cap on the size of the contingency fees that a lawyer can collect. For instance, the Supreme Court of New Jersey has instituted a scheme that establishes maximum fees so that lawyers do not take more than 10 percent of any award over $100,000.[78] However, public support for the principles that all should be equal before the law and that rich and poor alike should be able to take advantage of the judicial system do help to explain why American society supports so many lawyers.

Familiarity with the Legal System

Despite its complexity, Americans may also be more accustomed to their judicial system these days. Though the state court system can accurately be characterized as a patchwork quilt, it is nonetheless a reasonably comfortable one for many Americans. While media coverage and popular books, movies, and television shows do not always accurately depict the legal system, what goes on in court is not as unfamiliar and intimidating as it once may have been. Common citizens, often fascinated by American legal process, may have become more inclined to take disputes before a court than were their parents or grandparents. And, as the money damages awarded by juries in many types of cases have risen sharply, the potential payoff for a successful lawsuit has come to overwhelm feelings of insecurity or unfamiliarity. One is likely to be prepared to endure far more embarrassment, con-

[76] Glendon, p. 54.

[77] It is true that in some cases a British plaintiff would be aided in bringing suit by devices unfamiliar to Americans: insurance policies that cover legal bills, litigation funds sponsored by unions and other groups, and extensive public legal assistance programs. See Linowitz, p. 175.

[78] Tarr, p. 134.

fusion, and frustration for a potential payoff of tens of thousands, hundreds of thousands, or even millions of dollars than for much lesser damages.

An Innovative Court System

Furthermore, as American courts have exercised their powers of judicial review more actively and have used innovative legal reasoning from established principles to resolve novel disputes, interest groups and reformers of various stripes, intent on resolving social issues, have come to favor going to court over trying to advance their cause through politics.[79] This trend has also helped to stimulate the litigation explosion that partly accounts for the growing numbers of American lawyers.

Benefits and Drawbacks

If all these factors help to explain why the United States has so many attorneys, one might wonder what benefits and drawbacks might be associated with America's plentiful supply of lawyers? With a storehouse of close to a million lawyers on hand and additional increments of 35,000 freshly minted newcomers joining the profession each year, the system is certainly well stocked with legal talent. While the sheer numbers of American lawyers may lead to excessive litigiousness on the part of their clients, they also ensure that information about the law and representation in the legal system may be readily obtained.

Nevertheless, Americans often fear that too much of their intellectual talent is being devoted to legal wrangling. Would not the country be better off if those hundreds of thousands of intelligent Americans put their minds toward more productive work than settling legal disputes? Is there not at least a glut of litigators, all ready to rush into court, or threaten to do so, if the stakes are high enough? Is it not self-evident that the United States is overly litigious?

One might respond by pointing out first that so long as the state and federal governments persist in making illegal so many different aspects of human behavior, and so long as substantial numbers of crimes are committed, society will need considerable numbers of prosecutors, defense counsels, and judges. Moreover, the majority of America's lawyers are not courtroom advocates. Many still try to steer their clients away from lawsuits. Hence, asking whether American society has not become overly litigious is a somewhat different question from asking whether the United States has too many attorneys. As one legal scholar put it: "[T]here are currently at large in the land legions of law-trained individuals whose powers exceed their self-control and whose ambitions for law outrun its capacity. But like long-legged water striders playing on the surface of a woodland pond, they are only the most visible and acrobatic inhabitants of a complicated world. To a passerby who stops to watch their feats on a summer day, the slow, deep movements of life below remain invisible."[80]

An exceedingly legalistic country needs a robust legal profession not just

[79] See Glendon, p. 141.

[80] Ibid., p. 291.

to go to court and help to frame legal arguments, but to provide counsel on what laws mean, how courts are likely to interpret them, and how to stay out of the trouble that may arise if the rules are broken. Moreover, the frequency with which attorneys are hired suggests that Americans need legal experts ready to advise on when to sue and also when not to sue, when settlement is preferable to protracted litigation, and how to go about reaching a useful and binding agreement. No other group can fill the role of negotiator, consensus builder, troubleshooter, and dealmaker as skillfully and readily as America's lawyers.[81]

Many Americans are certainly prepared to go to court to settle their problems. Yet, so, too, are the people of many developed western states. Thus, American **litigiousness,** while undeniable, is not terribly out of line with the propensity to sue found in many other advanced countries. The number of civil cases in U.S. courts per 1,000 citizens is roughly comparable to the numbers in Australia, Canada, Denmark, England, Israel, and New Zealand.[82] Moreover, while litigation rates in the United States have been rising, the number of cases has been very high in particular parts of the country in past eras as well. For instance, for every 1,000 citizens living in St. Louis in the 1840s, 36 filed civil cases each year,[83] a litigation rate higher than that found in many American cities today. Thus, while litigiousness may indeed be an ongoing problem, litigation rates in the United States are about where an informed observer might expect them to be.

Certainly, American society would function more efficiently if more value were placed on negotiation and compromise and less on adversarial encounters in court. Yet, rather than wishing for a quota on the number of American lawyers, perhaps Americans should wish to restrain their instinctive impulse to make ever broader realms of human activity the subject of law. One scholar observed: ". . . that law has limits; that there are aspects of life which the state wisely refrains from regulating; that not every injustice can or should be adjudicated; and that few people would enjoy living in a society where every insult or injury gave rise to legal remedies."[84] In the final analysis, if the books full of state and federal laws and regulations were to shrink, the numbers of American lawyers would be likely to follow suit. So long as the law books grow ever fatter, the American legal profession is likely to be correspondingly stout.

SELECTED ADDITIONAL READINGS

BONSIGNORE, JOHN J., et al., eds. "Part III: The Legal Profession and the Legal System," in *Before the Law: An Introduction to the Legal Process.* Boston: Houghton Mifflin, 1994, pp. 281–369.

BURTON, STEVEN J. *An Introduction to Law and Legal Reasoning.* Boston: Little, Brown, 1985.

GLENDON, MARY ANN. *A Nation Under Lawyers: How the Crisis in the Legal Profession Is Transforming American Society.* New York: Farrar, Straus, & Giroux, 1994.

KRONMAN, ANTHONY. *The Lost Lawyer: Failing Ideals of the Legal Profession.* Cambridge, MA: Harvard University Press, 1993.

[81] For a parallel observation see ibid., pp. 100–101.

[82] See Tarr, p. 251 and Glick, p. 187.

[83] Glick, p. 187.

[84] Glendon, p. 264.

LEVI, EDWARD. *An Introduction to Legal Reasoning.* Chicago: University of Chicago Press, 1949.

LIEBERMAN, JETHRO K. *The Litigious Society.* New York: Basic Books, 1983.

LINOWITZ, SOL M., and MAYER, MARTIN. *The Betrayed Profession: Lawyering at the End of the Twentieth Century.* New York: Charles Scribner's Sons, 1994.

NELSON, ROBERT L., TRUBEK, DAVID M., and SOLOMON, RAYMOND L., EDS. *Lawyers' Ideals/Lawyers' Practices: Transformations in the American Legal Profession.* Ithaca, NY: Cornell University Press, 1992.

10

Assessing Justice in America

Three cardinal questions relating to the nature of modern American justice have occupied our attention thus far. What is the role of law in society? How does the legal system function? And, what are the chief issues, the most striking successes, and the most glaring failures of the system today? In conclusion, I would like to focus on the third question and challenge the reader to put the U.S. legal system on the examining table to diagnose the state of its health. To what extent does the system provide justice for all? To what extent does it fall short? Students of American law ought to try to understand and critically assess both the signs of good health and the symptoms of encroaching illness. Possible antidotes should also be assessed—to gauge the likelihood of their ever being adopted and to determine the probability of their successfully curing the problems.

Students of American law engaged in a critical assessment of the legal system should also consider just what is meant by justice.[1] As one of America's most distinguished judges noted: "Justice is a concept by far more subtle and indefinite than is yielded by mere obedience to a rule."[2] One might also ask: Is justice a matter of having legal disputes appear to an informed, unbiased observer to be resolved fairly and equitably? That is, is justice a matter of the relative fairness of outcomes? Or, is justice served when a court follows legal rules, treats those before it respectfully, and scrupulously and conscientiously weighs the evidence and the law in coming to a decision, whatever the particular outcome? That is, is justice principally related to procedural fairness? To what extent are the ideas of procedural justice and substantive justice linked? If the procedures are just, how often will the outcome still seem unjust? These are broad philosophical issues upon which rea-

[1] For a more detailed discussion of these matters, see Henry R. Glick, *Courts, Politics, and Justice,* 3d ed. rev. (New York: McGraw-Hill, 1993), pp. 12–16.

[2] Justice Benjamin Cardozo cited in Philip K. Howard, *The Death of Common Sense: How Law Is Suffocating America* (New York: Warner Books, 1994), p. 52.

sonable minds can differ. Although properly the subject of books and courses on legal philosophy and jurisprudence,[3] these issues form the backdrop against which people view the particular positive and negative aspects of a legal system. Thus, they merit some thought by all students of law attempting to examine critically the American system.

POSITIVE ASPECTS OF THE AMERICAN LEGAL SYSTEM

Its Adversarial Nature

One broad criticism of the American system is that it is too markedly adversarial—that the truth too often gets lost in the rush to win the contest in court. While Americans expect a court proceeding to be adversarial, they are often put off by the partisan zeal shown by the participants.[4] Some are shocked by aggressive prosecution or by lawyers attempting to gain for an injured client every dollar possible in compensation. Others are disturbed by a criminal defense attorney trying to gain the freedom of a client accused of a violent crime, even though the public and even the attorney may believe the individual is guilty. Still others find objectionable the work of attorneys for unpopular corporate clients: perhaps a bank, a cigarette or insurance company, a manufacturing concern that emits pollutants, or a business that has produced defective products that have caused serious injuries.

One view is that a country should have a fully adversarial system or should opt for a different method of resolving legal disputes, such as the method found in inquisitorial civil law systems. Americans, however, seem reluctant to discard their traditional legal system, yet they are repelled by lawyers fulfilling their responsibilities of zealously representing their clients within that system. While Americans readily acknowledge that doctors have a right and a duty to tend to a patient regardless of the patient's moral character, they are not so comfortable in asserting that lawyers have a parallel right and duty to represent a client regardless of the client's moral character.[5] This may be explained in part by the many formal legal proceedings that do not seem to have been resolved fairly. The idea seems to be that lawbreakers are entitled to an effective defense, but not a defense so effective that it fails to serve justice.

An effective right to counsel, however, implies a duty on the part of lawyers to provide counsel to all. If Americans really believe in the virtues of an adversarial

[3] See, for instance, Conrad Johnson, *Philosophy of Law* (New York: Macmillan, 1993); Judith N. Shklar, *The Faces of Injustice* (New Haven, CT: Yale University Press, 1990); and George W. Spiro and James L. Houghteling, Jr., *The Dynamics of Law,* 2d ed. rev. (New York: Harcourt Brace Jovanovich, 1981).

[4] For a parallel observation see G. Alan Tarr, *Judicial Process and Judicial Policymaking* (St. Paul, MN: West, 1994), p. 109.

[5] Lloyd Paul Stryker, *The Art of Advocacy: A Plea for the Renaissance of the Trial Lawyer* (New York: Simon & Schuster, 1954), p. 214.

system, how can they fairly criticize lawyers for accepting unpopular clients or doing their best to represent them? Perhaps something might also be said in favor of the adage, "A horse worth a ride is a horse worth a gallop." If the adversarial system does not always administer justice at full speed, is it likely to do better at half speed? While Americans would expect a basketball game played at half speed to be sloppy and error-filled, they seem to believe that the adversarial process could be usefully toned down if only the lawyers would act more moderately. Yet, a defense lawyer zealously defending a client provides a strong incentive for the authorities to act reasonably and carry out their jobs legally and effectively, since a hasty investigation that cuts legal corners may well lead to an acquittal.

A related critique of the American legal system is that its adversarial, competitive nature encourages lawyers to confuse the decisionmaker and to shade, distort, or manipulate the truth. Federal judge Henry Friendly once remarked: "Under our adversary system the role of counsel is not to make sure the truth is ascertained but to advance his client's cause by any ethical means. . . . Causing delay and sowing confusion not only are his right but may be his duty."[6] Another longtime member of the federal judiciary, Jerome Frank, argued: "[F]requently the partisanship of the opposing lawyers blocks the uncovering of vital evidence or leads to a presentation of vital testimony in a way that distorts it."[7] As an example he pointed to the treatment of witnesses, arguing that if the legal system were really designed to uncover the truth, the judge and lawyers would do everything in their power to ensure that witnesses did not distort their testimony.

Instead, Frank claimed, in order to discredit adverse witnesses, American lawyers tend to agitate, embarrass, hurry, and intimidate them. Such tactics are considered normal, and to some extent are sanctioned by judges, law professors, and trial practice manuals. A lawyer will play on the timid aspect of one witness, the unfamiliarity of another with court procedures, the emotional or irritable manner of a third. In their effort to win the contest, lawyers try to preclude adverse witnesses from explaining inconsistencies in their testimony. Rather, they try to keep such information from the judge and jury, unless or until the other counsel raises it on redirect examination. Judge Frank concluded:

> The purpose of these tactics—often effective—is to prevent the trial judge or jury from correctly evaluating the trustworthiness of witnesses and to shut out evidence the trial court ought to receive in order to approximate the truth.
>
> In short, the lawyer aims at victory, at winning the fight, not at aiding the court to discover the facts. He does not want the trial court to reach a sound educated guess, if it is likely to be contrary to his client's interests. Our present trial method is thus the equivalent of throwing pepper in the eyes of a surgeon when he is performing an operation.[8]

[6] Howard, p. 86.

[7] Jerome Frank, *Courts on Trial: Myth and Reality in American Justice* (Princeton, NJ: Princeton University Press, 1973), p. 82.

[8] Ibid., p. 85.

The problem may be especially troublesome in cases that hinge on scientific or technical matters. Although jurors and judges may be expected to see through obfuscation in a simple criminal case, they may be less able to do so in more complicated cases. As a report of the National Academy of Sciences stated: "Confrontation and the adversary process do not create an atmosphere conducive to the careful weighing of scientific and technical knowledge, and distort the state of scientific and technical agreement and disagreement."[9]

One can, however, admit to the American system's excesses without also denying its benefits. Years ago, an English historian and philosopher argued in favor of the adversarial system by stating that the fairest possible decision is attained "when two men argue, as unfairly as possible, on opposite sides . . . [since then] it is certain that no important consideration will altogether escape notice."[10] The competition between two adversarial sides is intended to provide the decisionmaker, whether judge or jury, with all the information needed to make a fair and just decision about the dispute. The theory is that the objective of doing justice will be well served if a neutral decisionmaker watches a skillful competition between two sides, each side representing one view of what really happened in the dispute and one view of how the law ought to be applied to that dispute.

So, the fact that a system is highly adversarial does not necessarily mean the participants are ignoring justice; rather, they are pursuing justice in an indirect manner. The strengths of the adversarial system may stand out in sharp relief if one imagines oneself in the position of an innocent suspect languishing in jail awaiting trial. Would it be preferable to have a partisan lawyer zealously interviewing witnesses, planning trial strategy, and arguing the case? Or, would it be preferable to rely upon a neutral figure, like an investigating judge, who might well lack the financial and professional motivation to explore and assert every conceivable line of argument on behalf of just one more in a long line of prisoners coming before the bench?

Surely, a strongly adversarial system is not well suited for every culture. Yet, for all its drawbacks, many of the features of the adversarial system in the United States seem to be tailored quite nicely to American culture. Americans tend to be more personally combative, aggressive, and outspoken than are people in various other countries. Since competition is ingrained in American culture, from athletics to business to politics, a legal system that also capitalizes on the benefits of competition may fit the country's psyche.

Moreover, through long experience the American public, as well as the participants in the court system, have come to understand the general features of how such an adversarial system works. Perhaps the public also allows for its excesses, at least to some degree. Jurors tend to understand that lawyers are called upon to represent their side of the case as zealously as possible. In hearing a case argued, they tend to allow for the fact that a lawyer is wearing the hat of advocate and not the robes of a disinterested judge.

[9] Howard, p. 86.

[10] Thomas Babington Macaulay, cited in Frank, p. 81.

For all these reasons I would be disinclined to sacrifice the benefits of the adversarial system by substituting a wholly inquisitorial approach, even if that were practically plausible. Rather, Americans should be focusing on eliminating the extraneous or counterproductive features of the adversarial system and on tempering those aspects of the adversarial system that seem to be working less well.

Citizen Involvement

Another strength of the American legal system, and one that foreigners tend to see more clearly than Americans, is the extent of citizen involvement. A Mexican commentator recently observed: "Keeping track of the course of justice is a far more complicated task in Mexico than it is in the United States, where the jury system guarantees both access to criminal cases and a drama-laden context in which to understand them."[11] Certainly, the common citizen plays an integral role in the application of American law.

In the United States voters in many states elect judges. Trials are held in open court with ample seating for spectators and, increasingly, with television cameras broadcasting the proceedings to viewers. Citizens are also deeply involved in reporting crime and serving as witnesses in court. In fact, law enforcement can function effectively only with substantial citizen support for police and prosecutors. To investigate a crime and successfully prosecute the criminal, the authorities must enjoy a substantial measure of popular cooperation. In a more homogeneous society, like Japan, that critical element of citizen assistance is perhaps more readily secured than in a country like the United States where so many people hail from such divergent cultural backgrounds. Citizen involvement thus strengthens the American legal system in various ways.

Perhaps most important, relying on a jury, while problematic in various cases, directly involves Americans in applying their laws. Average Americans serve both as critical spectators and key decision makers. The jury represents democracy within the judicial system, and the drama of a jury trial in open court holds the attention of the public and media alike. As compared with the secretive nature of various civil law legal systems, such as those in Central America,[12] this outside scrutiny helps to maintain the public's faith that an American criminal trial—whatever else it might be—is not a rigged farce, regularly distorted by bribery and other forms of blatant corruption. Instead, one can actually see a court assess and often struggle with the evidence in trying to determine which party should prevail.

Indeed, since voting is not mandatory in the United States, and since voter turnout is less than 50 percent in most elections, serving on a jury is one of the few civic duties that many Americans find themselves obliged to carry out on behalf of their democratic system. My impression is that most jurors most of the time believe that their actions are supporting the powerful cultural norm that

[11] Alma Guillermoprieto, "Whodunnit?," *The New Yorker,* Sept. 25, 1995, p. 50.

[12] See Michael Ross Fowler and Julie Marie Bunck, "Legal Imperialism or Disinterested Assistance?: American Legal Aid in the Caribbean Basin," *Albany Law Review* 55 (1992): 815–848.

requires a jury to act independently, impartially, and seriously in attempting to do justice.

By compelling citizens to become involved in administering the law, the jury system helps to encourage citizens to cooperate in enforcing the law. To be sure, in certain parts of America—especially the violence-ridden inner cities—some citizens have become so alienated from the police or so fear criminal gangs that their cooperation in law-enforcement tasks leaves much to be desired. This, however, is not the fault of the jury. Rather, an open judicial system, with participation by the common citizen on juries, contributes to the well-being of the legal system.

Strong Judicial Tradition

Another positive feature of the administration of justice in the United States is the judiciary. Since many trials have no jury, and since many legal issues that a judge must decide routinely arise during jury trials, the judiciary plays a critical role in courtrooms as referees and decisionmakers. In deciding cases and in ensuring that the adversarial contest proceeds in a fair manner in accordance with the rules of court and of civil and criminal procedure, American judges typically follow quite high standards of conduct. Judges are the guardians of the widely accepted idea that justice in America should be guided by a rule of law in which no one—criminal, politician, or celebrity—is too important to have to abide by the law's dictates.

Americans too often take this positive feature of their legal system for granted. In a society such as that in Guatemala[13] the rule of law is considered a radical notion, not a long-accepted social norm. Such legal systems face truly formidable problems in attempting to administer justice. In sharp distinction to their counterparts in various other countries, however, American judges are not normally corrupt. Although occasional corruption surfaces, the vast majority of American judges try to act, in and out of court, in a manner that furthers public confidence in judicial integrity and impartiality.

Although American judges make their share of biased, mistaken, or shortsighted decisions, most Americans have some faith in the ability of the judiciary to manage most affairs in the courtroom reasonably and fairly. Thus, more than police, politicians, and various other authority figures, judges tend to be held in high esteem. Though it is often overlooked by Americans, to have a respected judiciary is an enormous advantage for any legal system intent on providing justice to all.

For all of its evident strengths, however, the American judiciary might improve its performance in certain respects. For instance, one might ask just how active a referee should an American judge be? Currently, trial judges are kept on a rather taut leash with appellate courts ready to overrule them whenever a judge's statements or actions may have influenced the jury's finding of facts.[14] Students of

[13] See Fowler and Bunck.

[14] Sol M. Linowitz, with Martin Mayer, *The Betrayed Profession: Lawyering at the End of the Twentieth Century* (New York: Charles Scribner's Sons, 1994), p. 173.

American law might at least consider whether a less passive posture by judges acting as referees might bring about more just outcomes.

Appellate judges, for instance, might be better advised to encourage lower courts to exert more influence over trials, not less. In this vein the ABA Committee on Professionalism argued: "Trial judges should take a more active role in the conduct of litigation. They should see that cases advance promptly, fairly and without abuse. . . . There is a public interest in not clogging the courts with stale cases. Unfortunately, the responsibility for the efficient movement of cases must fall upon the shoulders of the judges largely by default."[15] While no one wants the judiciary to act in a highhanded or biased manner, permitting trial judges to control cases in their courts with a firm hand might improve the behavior of lawyers, speed the course of trials, eliminate many nuisance lawsuits, and aid juries to come to reasonable decisions, especially in assessing damages.

Emboldened American judges might also be encouraged to throw out of court not the odd but innovative claim, but the truly frivolous lawsuit. Indeed, by granting motions for summary judgment and motions to dismiss[16] in civil cases more readily, judges could more strictly control access to the legal system. One authority argued: "If a judge thinks it highly unlikely that a plaintiff can prevail, he has an obligation to the defendants, to the schedule of his court, and to other applicants for justice—and, indeed, to the plaintiff—not to permit the waste of their time and money. A courtroom should not be a casino where lawyers throw the dice in hopes that a jury will read them wrong."[17] Such modest changes in judicial behavior might further strengthen an already positive attribute of the American legal system.

Protection of Defendants' Rights

The American legal system also does an especially good job at protecting the rights of defendants to a fair trial. The burden of proof in a criminal trial lies squarely on the shoulders of the government. Thus, if a reasonable doubt of guilt exists, the defendant is to go free. Furthermore, even unpopular or poverty–stricken defendants are provided legal counsel, sometimes through the *pro bono publico* work of private attorneys and, even more frequently, at the expense of the government through the state and federal public defender programs. And, while public defenders have a solid record of ably representing their clients, any defendant who is very poorly represented may ask for, and occasionally receives, a new trial.

The American legal system is quite unusual in the extent to which it is tilted in favor of the defendant, at least in the sense that convicting the innocent is viewed as a more serious flaw than acquitting the guilty. In crafting the U.S. Constitution, the Founding Fathers decided to err on the side of the accused rather

[15] American Bar Association, "Report of the Committee on Professionalism," 112 *Federal Rules Decisions,* pp. 289–290, cited in ibid., p. 174.

[16] For a description of these preliminary motions see Chapter 8.

[17] Linowitz, p. 178.

than the government, a decision that stemmed from the colonial period when many Americans thought the British authorities had persecuted politically troublesome Americans by jailing them with little regard for procedure or evidence.

Thus, while all judicial systems are prone to human error and prejudice, the American system infrequently violates the human rights of defendants. It does not normally abuse prisoners to coerce them into confessions. Indeed, the constitutional prohibition against self-incrimination means that the prosecutor must usually build a case against a defendant independent of any admission of guilt. The criminal justice system—its rules of procedure and traditions—is thus firmly oriented toward ensuring that only those clearly guilty be punished. Of course, in any legal system tragic mistakes will occur, either through strange coincidence or bias or human error. The safeguards that protect defendants' rights in the United States, however, ensure that the authorities only very rarely convict an innocent person, after a full trial, of a serious crime that he or she did not really commit.

Thus, the most encouraging aspects of the American legal system may be its open, participatory trial system, the rectitude and impartiality of the judiciary, the commitment to the rule of law, and the protection of defendants' rights.

A CRITIQUE OF THE AMERICAN LEGAL SYSTEM

The preceding chapters have identified various imperfections and flaws in the American legal system of greater and lesser note. Justice is plainly not served when prisoners rape other prisoners and when police brutalize suspects or participate in criminal enterprises. The system does not provide justice for all when attorneys act unprofessionally, bringing frivolous claims and nuisance lawsuits, twisting the truth, lying, and defrauding clients. Justice for all seems an ephemeral ideal in the face of foolish jury decisions and extraordinary damage awards far out of proportion to the injuries sustained. Any fair but critical assessment of the modern legal system must account for a large number of worrisome signs of ill health. The following difficulties rank high among them.

Justice to the Wealthy

One leading problem concerns the issue of whether the American legal system really provides justice to all or merely to those with the wealth to use the system to their advantage. Since the American system is stocked primarily with lawyers intent on making money, those, such as O. J. Simpson, who have considerable sums to spend will have their legal claims and defenses advanced more carefully and expertly than those with fewer resources. That the system seems to fall short of providing *equal* justice for all is disturbing.

Although having considerable money to spend certainly does not ensure victory in court, a poverty-stricken individual, one from the middle class, and a wealthy individual or corporation do not operate within the legal system on an entirely equal footing. A poor defendant is likely to be represented by an overworked public defender or an attorney who, perhaps through lack of work, has volunteered to be assigned cases by the court for modest sums. A national or multinational corporation will have elite legal expertise on its in-house staff, and the pick of the finest law firms in the country eager to represent it with all their high-powered means.

Even among clients with less stark differences in wealth, perfunctory representation by a mediocre lawyer contrasts markedly with zealous representation by a leading member of the bar. One can wonder how frequently justice is really done if the chances of attaining a satisfactory resolution of a legal problem differ sharply from one attorney to the next. Moreover, even when legal talent is fairly distributed on both sides of a case, those with wealth can unleash their attorneys: allow them to run up more expenses in researching difficult issues, bringing preliminary motions, and exhausting appeals. For all these reasons a wealthier client enjoys advantages that may well affect the outcome of a case.

To its credit, however, the American legal system has not been wholly blind to such flaws. Certain features ameliorate the disadvantages faced by clients with less resources. The system would be even more heavily weighted toward providing justice for the rich if it were not for the public defenders and legal services lawyers supported by state and federal taxpayers. Contingency fees and class-action suits, while imperfect devices, do create incentives for lawyers to bring promising cases against wealthy corporations. The fact that lawyers may set their own fees, rather than adhere to a national, standardized fee structure,[18] may bring about more zealous advocacy as the lawyer attempts to please the client and justify the ensuing bill.

Still, many who might take a claim to the legal system for resolution continue to have a hard time finding an able attorney prepared to represent an individual who is not wealthy, without charging crippling legal bills. This problem affects not only the poverty-stricken underclass, but students, single parents, struggling businesses, and others trying to make ends meet. Legal clinics run by private attorneys charging modest sums for their services or by law school students gaining experience without charge have addressed this problem to some extent, as have prepaid legal services plans (similar to medical insurance programs) sponsored by unions and employers. Public defenders, legal services attorneys, and *pro bono* work by private attorneys also help to fill this gap.

Nevertheless, despite the sheer number of American attorneys, a pressing need remains for more and better inexpensive legal services. This is especially true when the political climate has turned against nationalized health insurance and against welfare benefits. If the government is not going to fulfill medical and social needs to the extent that it has in the past, people who have suffered accidents and other misfortunes will want to turn to the courts to gain recompense. However, in the spirit of downsizing government the budget of the Legal Services Corporation

[18] G. Alan Tarr wrote: "In Germany . . . legal fees for various types of cases are established by law. Whether one wins or loses, devotes countless hours to case preparation or not, one receives the same fee. Thus inquisitorial systems not only discourage excessive zeal in advocacy but also remove the material incentives to engage in it." Tarr, pp. 110–111.

has also been slashed. An ultracompetitive legal marketplace has resulted in less liberal *pro bono* policies among certain law firms.

Rather than welcoming the services of nonlawyers who might help poor clients with routine problems that merely have some legal dimension to them, bar associations continue to guard their prerogatives jealously. Indeed, they sometimes seem to pursue those accused of the unauthorized practice of law more zealously than they pursue misbehaving attorneys. Moreover, with law school tuitions rising and new attorneys facing increasing student loan debts, ever fewer numbers of law school graduates are in a financial position that would enable them to accept low-paying careers in government and public interest law.

One measure that might help to ensure that legal services are available to all would be for the government to follow its own example in luring graduates to careers in the military, teaching, and social work by forgiving some amount of student loan debts in return for government service by new lawyers in understaffed offices of prosecutors, public defenders, and legal services.[19] However, when the public perceives that far too many American lawyers exist, and not just too many lawyers practicing in overcrowded categories of the legal profession, it may be difficult to gain political support for a program that forgives a portion of the debts incurred in law school.

For all these reasons, the problem of a legal system that fails to provide equal justice for all appears to be a hardy perennial and not a weed easily uprooted by legal reformers.

Excessive Delay

Another issue that must arise in any thorough, critical assessment of the American legal system is the time taken to dispose of legal disputes. Certainly, some courts have responded to a glut of cases by operating haphazardly: injecting an assembly-line quality into their work, stripping the parties of a full opportunity to present their case, and robbing judges of the chance to spend as much time as they would like deliberating on cases and crafting thoughtful judgments and opinions. An even more serious defect, however, concerns the excessive delay that adversely affects so many criminal and civil cases. To exert maximum influence on a wrongdoer and to deter other potential criminals, punishment should follow swiftly on the heels of arrest. Similarly, in civil litigation, respect for law is enhanced when its violation is remedied in short order. When matters are tied up interminably in the courts, factual circumstances become blurred in the memory of the parties and the public. The possibility of a long period of thumb-twiddling or even adverse public-

[19] Sol Linowitz noted: "If ten thousand graduates a year went to work for public agencies and legal services programs and claimed forgiveness of $20,000 of their debt to the student loan programs, the price would be $200 million of the $7 billion the service corps program is expected to cost when up and running at the end of the decade. And there would be great benefits in the provision of legal services to ordinary people, to the profession, and within the law schools." Linowitz, pp. 134–135.

ity while a lawsuit drags on can lead law-abiding businesses to settle a dispute that they might well win in court. Indeed, if cases linger too long, their eventual resolution may be obscured or quickly forgotten. All this promotes popular cynicism and frustration. The more rapidly civil disputes are resolved, the more quickly can the parties move forward with the rest of their lives.

When measured against the urgent need for speedy trials, civil litigation and criminal justice in the United States operate far too slowly. Learned Hand, a most widely respected federal judge, candidly observed: "I must say that, as a litigant, I should dread a lawsuit beyond almost anything else short of sickness and . . . death."[20] One problem is that the large number of complicated procedural rules and customs—statutory, constitutional, and judge-made—cause the system to work in a painfully deliberate manner.

In this regard one might reflect upon all the different steps that occur even before a typical criminal trial gets under way: booking and bail, the complaint and the indictment or information, the arraignment, discovery, and the voir dire. This very cumbersome process was really designed for a more traditional society in which crimes occurred much less frequently. Though according to court guidelines a criminal trial ought to begin within four to six months of the date of arrest, it is not uncommon for substantially more time to elapse before the fate of an arrested suspect is finally determined. And, for victims and suspects alike, even a trial that does occur within four to six months of the date of the crime may not appear to be such swift justice.

While portions of the American trial process could usefully be streamlined, unnecessary delay could also be eased by the participants themselves. Bar associations might publicize the frustrations and injustices caused by delay. The bar and the media might shine the spotlight of publicity on egregious offenders. Judges could assert their power to move cases along more speedily. For instance, they could grant continuances much less readily and force attorneys to adhere to prearranged schedules. Courts and bar associations could do considerably more to discourage with stricter discipline those bringing frivolous claims and nuisance lawsuits.

Lawyers, judges, and law schools could emphasize the dangers of overtrying cases and could try to resurrect ideals that once viewed purposeful delay as an illegitimate and unprofessional tactic. The movement toward having only litigators and other trial specialists make court appearances could be encouraged on the theory that expertise in courtroom procedures and tactics, and the desire to uphold a positive reputation with the court, would likely result in speedier trials.[21] All such

[20] Frank, p. 40.

[21] One authority observed: "[An experienced trial lawyer] will not require . . . more than a quarter of the time taken by the . . . inexperienced lawyer in developing his facts. His case will be thoroughly prepared and understood before the trial begins. His points of law and issues of fact will be clearly defined and presented to the court and jury in the fewest possible words. He will in this way avoid many of the erroneous rulings on questions of law and evidence which are now upsetting so many verdicts on appeal." Francis L. Wellman, *The Art of Cross-Examination,* 4th ed. rev. (New York: Macmillan, 1936), pp. 3–4.

self-policing measures might ameliorate the problem of excessive delay. Yet this problem, too, is of such scope that it is unlikely to be expunged easily.

Plea Bargaining

To avoid lengthy and costly proceedings in court and to reduce a tremendous overload of cases, the American legal system has long relied upon plea bargaining. Today, to send every criminal case to trial would require considerably more judges and courtrooms, public defenders and prosecutors, and public and private resources. Yet the fact that this plea-bargaining process is so common[22] must raise questions as to whether the American system provides justice to all.

The prospect of a future plea bargain provides a strong incentive for guilty defendants to refrain from pleading guilty at the arraignment in order to reserve a bargaining chip for later use in plea-bargaining negotiations. At its worst, this amounts to institutionally approved lying. Authorities in most countries believe that a criminal justice system will have a better record of determining criminal responsibility and rehabilitating convicted criminals if the guilty are encouraged to admit their guilt and then are shamed and punished for committing the crime. Much of the criminal justice system in Japan, for instance, seeks to have the defendant admit guilt, so that punishment may be imposed and rehabilitation started. Even in most American families substantial value is placed on having a wayward child admit guilt, before being corrected.

Yet, in part to accommodate the plea-bargaining process, the American criminal justice system deviates from this norm. Rather than have the guilty admit their guilt, the legal system encourages criminals to deny guilt and to pretend innocence in order to gain a better position in the plea-bargaining process or the contest in court. Certainly, many legal, social, and cultural factors help to explain why rehabilitation of criminals succeeds so infrequently in the United States, yet remains a central focus in other advanced countries. Among these other factors, plea bargaining also frustrates rehabilitation.

If the plea-bargain system can provide a strong incentive for a guilty individual to plead innocent, it can also cause an individual who is really innocent to plead guilty. Consider once more the case explored in Chapter 7 of the man accused of stealing a car and crashing it on a university campus. Assume for a moment that the arrested suspect did not, in fact, steal the car, though the evidence against him is quite strong. If the jury fails to believe his plea of not guilty, the man might receive a sentence of about two years in prison. However, if the suspect had no criminal record, the prosecutor might offer him a sentence of six months on probation if he were to agree to plead guilty.

[22] Although it is true that in some states, like Alaska, plea bargaining is used very rarely (at least in certain parts of the state), most criminal courts rely heavily on plea bargaining to speed the system. In many jurisdictions as many as 80 or 90 percent of the cases are plea bargained to avoid trial.

Under such circumstances a strong incentive exists for the defendant to opt not to contest the charges but to plead guilty, even if he or she is actually innocent of the crime that is charged.[23] Of course, once a guilty plea is entered, the defendant cannot appeal the outcome or challenge the legality of the arrest. In fact, attorneys often pressure defendants to accept plea bargains. A defense counsel may hope to reduce his or her own backlog of cases by avoiding trial preparation and a time-consuming trial. A defendant may not be inclined to resist taking the advice of a legal expert who is supposedly looking out for his or her best interests and who may have painted a rather daunting picture of what a trial would entail.

The fact that the plea-bargain short-cut is so widely divorced from any effort to find out what actually happened in the incident is made perfectly clear at the court proceedings that occur when the defendant makes the plea and the result is sanctioned by the court. One legal scholar noted:

> The defendant is required to respond . . . to ensure that his decision to forgo a trial is voluntary and that he understands its consequences. He is asked if he is pleading guilty "because he is guilty and for no other reason," and if any threats or promises were made to him to induce the plea. While some judges require the prosecutor or the defendant himself to describe the crime, little if any effort is made to prove the defendant's guilt beyond his plea. . . . The judge may leave the questioning to his clerk, who asks the defendant questions in a swift monotone. The defendant answers mechanically, perhaps saying "Yes" when he should say "No" ("Have any promises been made to you?") or the reverse ("Are you pleading guilty because you are guilty and for no other reason?") until his lawyer nudges him in the ribs and he corrects himself.[24]

Thus, while an American criminal trial—with its traditional emphasis on the rights of defendants—typically convicts only those persons who are guilty of the crime charged, the American plea-bargain process is a more haphazard method of determining innocence or guilt. This is especially so since plea-bargain negotiations are often hurried affairs in which defense counsel and prosecutor sit down briefly, leaf through the papers on the case, and strike a deal, which the lawyer then strongly recommends that the accused endorse. These various flaws in the plea-

[23] One might note that the incentive to plead guilty is particularly strong if the defendant has a criminal record. The reason is that the record might influence the jury to assume that the defendant is not telling the truth. A criminal record cannot be used as evidence that a person committed a different crime; however, a criminal record may be used as evidence regarding the defendant's truthfulness. So, customarily, if a defendant testifies at trial, the prosecutor will immediately raise his criminal record for the jury to consider.

[24] Lloyd L. Weinreb, *Denial of Justice: Criminal Process in the United States* (New York: The Free Press, 1977), pp. 77–78. Weinreb pointed out: "The Supreme Court, indeed, has declared that it is not constitutionally improper to accept a guilty plea from (and to convict and punish) a person who at the same time protests his innocence of the crime." *North Carolina v. Alford,* 400 U.S. 25, 37 (1970). The New York Court of Appeals upheld a defendant's conviction after a guilty plea to a crime that the Court admitted was "logically and legally impossible." *People v. Foster,* 19 N.Y.2d 150, 152, 225 N.E. 2d 200 (1967). See also Weinreb, pp. 78, 169–170 n. 2.

bargain system, then, undercut one of the strengths of the system—protection of defendants' rights.

When incentives exist for the guilty to plead not guilty and the innocent to plead guilty, one might properly ask whether the American system really provides justice for all. In civil law systems courts explicitly focus upon finding the truth. In the American system trying to discover what really happened is a secondary matter as plea bargaining shortcuts and subverts the fact-finding process and focuses the attention of the defendant and defense counsel on finding the best deal. Such circumstances lead the public to lose faith in the system and to view American criminal justice as a charade.

Plea bargaining doubtless results in sloppy investigations by police, prosecutors, and defense counsels alike. Everyone knows that most cases are likely to be negotiated to a resolution, rather than tried in court; consequently, minimal effort is put into investigating crimes, especially routine ones. Plea bargaining also allows the participants in the system to blur the directions of legislatures. State or federal law may mandate stiff penalties for serious crimes, but so long as prosecutors and judges allow defendants to plead guilty to lesser offenses those crimes are not punished as the legislature intended.

Given the flaws of plea bargaining, it may be instructive to compare the reality of criminal process in the United States with the theories on which the system has developed. The overwhelming reliance on plea bargaining suggests that the first priority in the American system is to preserve its traditional, highly adversarial customs in the relatively few cases that do go to trial. The desire for the efficient and fair administration of justice in most cases is regularly obscured by the need to have cases cleared off the desks of judges, prosecutors, and defense attorneys.

In addition to subverting the process of discovering what really happened, plea bargaining also eliminates other positive consequences associated with trying crimes in court. The act of bringing a defendant into court demonstrates to victims, criminals, and the general public that crimes are seriously investigated and criminals are punished for illegal acts. A widespread, informal bargaining process to determine guilt and punishment thus detracts from the deterrent effect of punishment and leaves victims less satisfied than if a full criminal trial had taken place.

Americans have created such a long and costly courtroom process for determining innocence and guilt in criminal matters that the plea-bargaining shortcut for determining innocence or guilt in criminal matters has kept the legal system from being overwhelmed with cases. Neither the public nor its elected representatives have wanted to dedicate the resources necessary to provide a full criminal trial to every suspect accused of committing a crime. Often, evidence of guilt is strong and a trial does not seem worth the effort. Plea bargaining eliminates trial preparation for lawyers and eases the overcrowded dockets of judges. It allows prosecutors running for reelection to boast of high conviction rates. It keeps victims from having to appear, testify, and be cross-examined. Yet, it surely does not support the goal of providing either procedural or substantive justice for all.

THE DIFFICULTIES OF REFORM

If the legal system in the United States is defective and unpopular, why do Americans cling to it so tenaciously? Why have so few voices forcefully advocated sweeping proposals for reform? The answer lies in a combination of tradition, entrenched interests, constitutional difficulties, and a lack of detailed knowledge about the successes of alternative systems.

Although the current legal system has developed over time, in many respects it still represents the time-honored, customary manner of deciding legal cases. When the court process still includes such archaic absurdities as an official declaring "Hear ye, hear ye," at the start of a trial, one senses that self-reform in matters small and large has not been the system's greatest strength! Moreover, to date, politicians have regularly shied away from antagonizing powerful, wealthy groups like bar organizations and associations of trial lawyers.

The U.S. Constitution is a venerable document highly resistant to change. To amend the Constitution requires a favorable two-thirds majority of both houses of Congress and ratification by at least three-fourths of the state legislatures. Unfortunately, the Constitution contains some of the ideas that currently slow the legal system. For instance, when so many federal grand juries act as "rubber stamps"—routinely issuing indictments at the prosecutor's request—one must wonder whether the time of two dozen people could not be put to better use.

Whether the fault is with the Founders who drafted the Constitution or later generations who failed to amend it as needs and times changed, the Constitution now sometimes acts to obstruct thoughtful legal reform. One negative effect of American **constitutionalism,** and the large body of constitutional interpretations that have grown up around the language in the document, is that it has constricted American thinking about how the criminal justice system might be made more rational and effective.

Even more troublesome, many Americans mistakenly assume either that so many constitutional obstacles exist that proposals to reform the system are impractical, or that one should not amend the wisdom of the Founding Fathers. In this regard, toward the end of his life Thomas Jefferson warned:

> Some men look at constitutions with sanctimonious reverence, and deem them like the ark of the covenant, too sacred to be touched. They ascribe to the men of the preceding age a wisdom more than human, and suppose what they did to be beyond amendment. I knew that age well; I belonged to it, and labored with it. It deserved well of its country. It was very like the present, but without the experience of the present; and forty years of experience in government is worth a century of book-reading; and this they would say themselves, were they to rise from the dead.[25]

[25] William O. Douglas, "Stare Decisis," in Walter F. Murphy and C. Herman Pritchett, eds., *Courts, Judges, and Politics,* 3d ed. rev. (New York: Random House, 1979), p. 526.

In fact, modern American society differs vastly from that in which the Founding Fathers lived more than 200 years ago. It is no wonder, perhaps, that the criminal justice system they created does not always work so well under such different circumstances.

Lawyers, the media, and politicians in the United States seem much more content debating the original intent of the Founders than trying to form a consensus behind reasoned proposals that might help our system to operate more efficiently. Should prosecutors be given the right to appeal adverse decisions? Does diversity jurisdiction still make sense?[26] Would state courts today really discriminate against out-of-state parties? Does it remain worthwhile to offer the right to a jury trial to parties engaged in a civil dispute?[27] Could a national court of appeals take pressure off the Supreme Court and regularize and speed the federal appellate process?[28] To date, such questions have not been part of a national debate over how to improve the functioning of the American legal system.

Borrowing from Other Legal Systems

The analysis in this book is premised on the belief that criticisms of an existing institution and prescriptions for how it "should" work can be sharpened by comparison with institutions in other countries and their successes and limitations. Analyzing what other countries do, and how they do it, helps to clarify what the American system does well and poorly. Comparative analysis illuminates what a legal system might realistically accomplish and what seems, at least for the moment, beyond human capabilities. Thus, in this book I have tried to use a comparative overlay to explain something of how the American legal system works in theory and in practice. While giving credit where it is due, I have tried to analyze critically the features of the American system that are malfunctioning and suggest certain possible reforms in light of the experiences of other legal systems.

Some critics object to such an endeavor by pointing to the distinction between civil law and common law systems and claiming that reform proposals for one system that draw on practices in the other are akin to trying to grow a hybrid of two thoroughly incompatible fruits—a grape and a watermelon, for instance. In this view, the common law and civil law systems are not fit subjects for comparison, nor are they appropriate for merging. They simply differ too fundamentally.

In my view, however, the inquisitorial civil law system and the accusatorial common law system should be conceived not so much as clashing opposites, but as poles on a spectrum. In fact, many legal systems exhibit some characteristics of both ideal models. One might consider, for instance, the legal systems of Central America. The civil law system in Panama actually relies upon juries, an institution that is almost always associated with adversarial common law systems. The people of Belize, formerly the colony of British Honduras, consider themselves to have strong common law roots. Yet, for all the Belizean system's common law trap-

[26] For discussion of this issue see Tarr, p. 39, and Glick, p. 65.

[27] See Linowitz, p. 172.

[28] For one discussion of this issue see Tarr, p. 34.

pings—including even judges wearing powdered wigs, as in Britain—the magistrates, who are the workhorses of the judicial system, operate with only occasional prosecutorial assistance. Hence, in practice, Belizean magistrates take on many of the functions of an investigating judge in a civil law system.

Guatemala claims a civil law system passed down from its days as a Spanish colony.[29] However, recent changes in Guatemalan law have dramatically bolstered the prosecutor's role at the expense of the judge, creating among other things adversarial exchanges in open court, a characteristic normally associated with common law systems. The Central American experiences nicely illustrate the thesis that legal systems rarely conform to prototypes, but rather tend to mix ideal common law and civil law features.

With the passage of time the American legal system also has come to appear less strictly a common law legal system and more a mixed system. It seems to have moved down the spectrum from the common law pole toward a more centrist position. For instance, since the Civil War, statutory law has grown immensely in importance *vis-à-vis* the common law. While it is true that American legislatures tend to pass laws in incremental fashion, rather than crafting and adopting a single code covering an entire field of law, over time, the collections of American statutes in different fields of law have become sufficiently comprehensive as to resemble codes in civil law systems. Consequently, a modern American lawyer, accustomed to working with the **Internal Revenue Code,** the **Uniform Commercial Code,** so-called **restatements of law,** and various collections of state and federal statutes, would be unlikely to find the codes of France and Japan to be as unusual as would have one of America's Founding Fathers.

Indeed, increasingly, litigation regarding federal and state statutes, not the common law, has dominated the attention of America's highest court. In 1875 about 40 percent of the legal disputes at the Supreme Court involved common law litigation. By 1925 that figure had fallen to 5 percent.[30] By 1979, two distinguished observers stated: "Today the justices would rarely, if ever, accept a case unless it raised an important question of federal constitutional or statutory law . . ."[31]

Apart from the increasing codification of American law, criminal process in the United States has also taken on some characteristics commonly associated with civil law systems. To take one example, now that so many states have chosen to diminish the role of the grand jury, the initial stage of an American criminal trial increasingly resembles the same stage in many civil law countries. With the rising popularity of the information, an American judge makes decisions about initiating a criminal prosecution that do not differ so fundamentally from the initial decisions of an investigating judge elsewhere.[32]

Thus, in my view, efforts to reform the American legal system should consider cross-pollinating American legal institutions and procedures with institutions

[29] These systems are analyzed in substantially more detail in Fowler and Bunck, pp. 815–848.

[30] Felix Frankfurter and James M. Landis, *The Business of the Supreme Court* (New York: Macmillan, 1928), cited in Murphy and Pritchett, p. 527.

[31] Murphy and Pritchett, p. 527.

[32] See Weinreb, p. x.

and procedures that work successfully in other countries. A range of legal reform issues might be thoughtfully assessed with an eye cocked to the experiences of both civil law and common law countries. Should trial judges take a more active role in court? Should grand juries, or trial juries in civil cases, be eliminated? Under what circumstances should illegally obtained evidence be excluded from trial? Might an office of investigating magistrate improve the investigation and prosecution of crimes? Analysis of all such questions might be sharpened by a comparative focus.

CONCLUSION

The American legal system does many things well, yet, despite the optimistic words of the Pledge of Allegiance, Americans are now saddled with a system of administering justice that also contains serious flaws and defects. Furthermore, the current rhetoric about greedy lawyers, liberal judges, and irresponsible juries simply deflects attention from the more critical problems associated with the outmoded nature of certain American legal customs, processes, and institutions.

Americans should aim to create a more efficient process of administering justice that speeds trials, frees tangled human resources, and eases the burdens of crowded trial dockets. A less costly judicial system that distributed penalties and damages more rapidly would be likely to deter potential violations of law—both criminal offences and civil wrongs—more effectively than does the present system. Moreover, the savings that would flow from a streamlined system might permit American authorities to diminish their current reliance on such unsatisfactory shortcuts as plea-bargained criminal convictions.

The outrage of victims who see criminals go free and the frustration of plaintiffs at the delay before their injuries are redressed suggest that at present the American legal system, for all its considerable strengths, does not always administer the laws "with justice for all." Many years ago Supreme Court Justice Louis Brandeis declared: "If we would guide by the light of reason, we must let our minds be bold."[33] Americans should not allow the Constitution, or their legal traditions, to keep their minds from the bold thoughts of reform that might substantially improve the functioning of the legal system.

SELECTED ADDITIONAL READINGS

AUERBACH, JEROLD S. *Unequal Justice: Lawyers and Social Change in Modern America.* New York: Oxford University Press, 1976.

BIANCHI, HERMAN. *Justice as Sanctuary: Toward a New System of Crime Control.* Bloomington: University of Indiana Press, 1994.

FREUND, PAUL A. *On Law and Justice.* Cambridge, MA.: Harvard University Press, 1968.

FRIEDMAN, LAWRENCE M. *Law and Society.* New York: Prentice Hall, 1977.

———. *Total Justice.* New York: Russell Sage Foundation, 1985.

JACOB, HERBERT. *Law and Politics in the United States.* 2d ed. rev. New York: HarperCollins College, 1995.

WEINREB, LLOYD L. *Denial of Justice: Criminal Process in the United States.* New York: The Free Press, 1977.

[33] *New State Ice Co. v. Liebmann,* 285 U.S. 262, 311 (1932).

Glossary of Legal Terms*

ABA See *Bar association.*

accusatorial system In a *common law legal system* the government accuses a person of committing a crime, and the decision maker, either judge or jury, assumes that the defendant is not guilty. To achieve a conviction, the government must prove his or her guilt *beyond a reasonable doubt.*

acquit To absolve one who has been charged with a crime, to find one innocent.

administrative agencies *Federal* administrative agencies are arms of the national government, such as the National Labor Relations Board or the Federal Aviation Administration, charged with regulatory duties. Each state has its own network of administrative agencies, which are broadly similar to their federal counterparts.

admission A confession, concession, or voluntary acknowledgment that the opposing side in a case might use to its advantage.

adversarial system A legal system in which opposing parties contend against one another in attempting to persuade a decisionmaker, such as a judge or jury, to rule in their favor.

advisory opinion A nonbinding interpretation of the law indicating how a legal issue would be resolved if a case occurred in which that issue were raised.

*For more detailed definitions of most of the following terms see *Black's Law Dictionary* (St. Paul, MN: West, 1979).

affidavit A voluntary, written statement of facts made under oath and before proper authority. See also *complaint.*

alibi A defense against a criminal accusation in which the defendant claims to have been elsewhere when the crime occurred.

ambulance-chasers Derogatory slang used to describe lawyers who aggressively file lawsuits to recover money for claims of dubious merit.

American Bar Association See *bar association.*

amicus curiae A person or organization, having a strong interest in the subject matter of a dispute, that is granted permission by the court to file a *brief* in support of a party in a legal dispute.

answer The document filed by the defendant, after a plaintiff has initiated litigation, that sets forth the defendant's reply to the charges in a *civil complaint.*

antitrust A body of law derived from state and federal *statutes* aimed at protecting commerce from monopolies, price fixing, and other such restraints to trade.

appeal The request to have the decision of a *trial court* reviewed by a higher court.

appellant The party requesting an appeal; the *appellee* (or *respondent*) is the party not requesting the appeal and against whom the appeal is taken.

appellate courts See *court of appeals.*

appellate judge A judge sitting on a *court of appeals.* Generally, *appellate courts* conduct business through *panels* of three judges, though exceptions do exist. For instance, the U.S. Supreme Court—the ultimate national court of appeal—has nine *justices.* Moreover, appellate courts sometimes sit *en banc,* that is, with all judges attending, rather than just a panel of three. See *court of appeals.*

appellate jurisdiction See *original jurisdiction.*

appellee See *appellant.*

arbitration A process of dispute resolution in which a decisionmaker known as an arbitrator issues an award, which both parties have normally agreed in advance to accept, after a hearing at which both parties have an opportunity to present their views of the dispute.

armed robbery The taking of property from another by the use of force or the threat of force while armed with a dangerous weapon.

arraignment The stage in a criminal case in which a *defendant* comes to court to hear the *counts* in the *indictment* and to plead guilty or not guilty.

array The body of persons summoned as prospective jurors in a case.

arrest The seizure of a person suspected of committing a criminal offense by the authorities.

arrest warrant An order, issued by a judicial authority, directing the police to arrest a *suspect* and bring that individual to the court to answer to some specific charge. See also *bench warrant; search warrant; warrantless arrest.*

Articles of Confederation A legal document signed by the thirteen original states in the Union that formed a loose association for mutual support. It was in effect from March 1, 1781 until March 4, 1789, when the U.S. Constitution came into effect.

assault Under state *tort* and criminal law, a willful act by an individual that causes the victim to fear an offensive or unwanted contact. Under the criminal laws of certain states the victim need not actually fear the contact. In these states, criminal assault is committed so long as a menacing gesture occurs and the defendant intends to harm the victim. See also *battery.*

associate A salaried attorney who has usually practiced law for less than ten years and is working for a law firm that has not yet decided whether to invite that attorney to become a *partner* and share in the law firm's profits. A *permanent associate* will always be paid a salary: He or she is said to be "not on a *partnership track.*"

associate justice See *justices.*

attachment The act of seizing property under a court order, with the court then holding that property while awaiting the outcome of a lawsuit. Usually this is done to ensure that sufficient funds are available to compensate a plaintiff who has been awarded *damages* by a court. See also *execution of judgment.*

attorney general The U.S. attorney general is the head of the U.S. Department of Justice. He or she represents the United States and counsels the Cabinet and (along with the *White House Counsel*) the President on legal issues. Each of the states also has an *attorney general* who fulfills parallel responsibilities for the state and its governor. The staff lawyers in the Attorney General's office are known as *assistant attorneys general.*

bail The sum of money that an arrested or imprisoned suspect must deposit with the court in order to be set free until the court requires his or her appearance. If the suspect flees and does not return for the court appearance, he or she has committed an offense known as *jumping bail* and forfeits the money on deposit with the court.

bailiff A security officer who maintains order in the *courtroom.*

ballistics The science of gun examination, focusing on matters such as the firing characteristics of different weapons and the issue of whether a particular gun fired a particular bullet.

bankruptcy The financial state in which a person or company is unable to pay off debts as they become due.

bar The wooden fence in a *courtroom* that separates the courtroom audience and press from the judge, the lawyers, and court officials. When an individual is *admitted to the bar,* it means that he or she is duly qualified to practice law as an attorney or lawyer. See also *bar organization* and *bar examination.*

bar association A voluntary group of lawyers organized by city (for example, the Boston Bar Association), by state (for example, the Massachusetts Bar Association), or by a national grouping (for example, the American Bar Association).

bar examination An examination that must be passed by a law school graduate in order to meet the minimum requirements necessary to gain a license to practice law in one of the states in the United States or in Washington,

DC. The *multistate exam* is a national standardized test. States also require applicants to write essays on the law specific to that particular state.

bar organization The professional licensing and regulatory body found in each state. It supervises the professional conduct of attorneys and oversees the practice of law within that state.

barrister A trial attorney admitted to practice at *the bar* in England. See also *Inns of Court.*

battery Any harmful or offensive contact (often resulting in bodily injury) with another individual that is without justification or excuse. See also *assault.*

bench The large, wooden desk behind which the judge sits. When an individual is *called to the bench,* he or she has been offered employment as a judge.

bench trial A nonjury trial in which the judge decides factual as well as legal issues.

bench warrant A *warrant* issued by a judge in court (that is, *from the bench*) to arrest an individual after the issuance of an *indictment* or a *contempt of court* ruling, or to bring to court a *witness* who is ignoring a *subpoena.*

beneficiary See *trusts.*

beyond a reasonable doubt See *reasonable doubt.*

bill of indictment See *indictment.*

billable hours The number of hours that a lawyer has worked for a *client.* Billable hours would not normally include time that a lawyer spends working for a client on a *contingency fee basis.* It would also not include *pro bono publico* projects or time spent working on administrative tasks.

blanket authorization A form of general official assent that does not depend upon circumstances.

blind call A phone call, or other communication, from an attorney in private practice to a government lawyer in which the private practitioner poses a hypothetical question, while being careful not to reveal his or her *client's* identity.

bond Money or, less frequently, property deposited with the court by a criminal defendant to ensure that he or she appears in court as scheduled.

bondsman Someone who puts up *bail* for a suspect in return for a fee.

booking A routine procedure in which the police record certain basic facts about an arrested person, such as his or her height, weight, age, and address, and also the date and reason for the arrest.

bound over If the judge at a *preliminary hearing* finds that *probable cause* exists, the criminal defendant is *bound over* for trial at a later time.

Brandeis brief A written argument to an appellate court that includes economic and social data along with legal principles and citations.

brief A written legal argument submitted by an attorney to an appellate court. See also *Brandeis brief.*

burden of proof The obligation of a party to establish something that is in dispute by showing evidence that is sufficient to meet a certain standard of proof. For instance, the government has a difficult burden of proof in an American criminal case: It must prove all elements of a crime *beyond a reasonable doubt* in order to secure a conviction. In a *civil case,* a plaintiff must prove by a *preponderance of the evidence* that the law supports his or her position.

burglary The crime of unlawfully entering property with the intent of stealing money or objects from that property.

called to the bench See *bench.*

Canons of Judicial Ethics Principles of judicial behavior listed in the *Code of Judicial Conduct,* which judges are sworn to uphold.

capital felonies See *capital punishment; felonies.*

capital offenses See *capital punishment.*

capital punishment The punishment of execution for a certain category of very serious (or "capital") criminal offenses, such as murder or treason.

case-in-chief The main portion of a trial in which the prosecutor in a criminal trial or the plaintiff in a civil trial presents evidence to support their side of the case. The prosecution or plaintiff then *rests* while the defendant's lawyers present their evidence and their side of the case in their *case-in-chief.*

case report A published and bound record of a judicial decision from either the state or federal courts.

cause of action The set of facts that would entitle one to seek a judicial *remedy.* A *claim* is the legal theory upon which one seeks a remedy.

caveat emptor Latin phrase meaning "let the buyer beware." A common law doctrine placing on the shoulders of the purchaser the obligation of examining, judging, and testing the goods to be purchased.

certiorari See *writ of certiorari.*
chancery court See *county court; court of equity.*
challenge for cause See *for cause challenge.*
charge to the jury An address by a judge to a *trial* or *grand jury.* In a charge to a trial jury, the judge summarizes the issues in the case and instructs the jury as to the rules of law they must apply in reaching a *verdict* concerning those issues. In a charge to a grand jury, a judge instructs the grand jurors as to their duties.
chief justice See *justices.*
chief of police The elected or appointed leader of a police force, especially in a city.
circuit court See *county court.*
circumstantial evidence See *evidence.*
city court See *municipal court; police court.*
civil action See *civil case.*
civil case A dispute in which an individual, group, or company believes that a legal wrong has been committed against it by another. The court is then asked to resolve the dispute, usually by awarding some amount of money for *damages.* Also known as a *civil lawsuit* or *civil action.* See also *criminal case.*
civil complaint See *complaint.*
civil law legal system Legal systems found in continental Europe, Latin America, and Japan, which come to decisions by relying on codes of law rather than judicial *precedent,* and which are characterized by a very active role for the judge as both the principal investigator and the ultimate decision maker.
civil lawsuit See *civil case.*
claim See *cause of action.*
class-action lawsuit A lawsuit in which a large number of individuals sue together as a group, each individual's claim being relatively small, but dealing with the same matter.
clerk of the court Usually elected but sometimes appointed, this member of the judicial staff takes responsibility for record-keeping, organizes the *trial docket,* supervises the selection of jurors, and collects filing, docket, and other court fees. See also *court administrator.*
client A person or business that hires a lawyer to help with a legal problem.
closing argument The final remarks by a trial attorney to the judge or jury at the end of a case before the judge's *charge* or *instructions* to the jury. Closing arguments summarize the evidence that has been established by one side and the points that have not been established by the other side. They aim to focus attention on the critically important features of a case. Sometimes also called the *summation* or *closing statement.*
Code of Judicial Conduct See *Canons of Judicial Ethics.*
codes of law A systematic collection of laws usually classified by subject matter (for example, a criminal code or a commercial code). See also *Internal Revenue Code; Uniform Commercial Code.*
collateral Some valuable item or money used as security by one party to ensure that some action is taken by another party.
common law Law derived from the legal customs of a people and from the decisions and *opinions* of judges, rather than from *codes of law.*
common law legal system A legal system with a *common law* heritage that is both *accusatorial* and *adversarial* and in which the judge does not both investigate and act as a decision-maker, as in a *civil law legal system.*
community property laws Laws in force in various American states that, at the time of a divorce, divide in half the assets of a divorcing couple gained during the course of their marriage, but which were not assets derived from gifts or inheritance.
community service A penalty imposed for minor offenses which requires the convicted party to perform a number of hours of duty in public work or service.
comparative fault statutes State laws that allow a plaintiff to recover *damages* proportionate to the defendant's fault, even if the plaintiff contributed to his or her own injury; sometimes referred to as *comparative negligence statutes.* See also *contributory negligence.*
complaining witness The victim who formally complains that a crime has occurred.
complaint The U.S. legal system recognizes two types of *complaints.* A *civil complaint* is the initial document filed in a *civil case* and sets forth the plaintiff's claim. A *criminal complaint* is a formal charge that a person has committed a specified offense. In certain states a criminal complaint is called an *affidavit.*
conciliation The settlement of a dispute by friendly, nonantagonistic, and nonadversarial means.
concurring opinion See *opinion.*
confederation A league of states, such as those in America under the *Articles of Confederation,* that have come together for mutual support. See also *Articles of Confederation.*

confidential source Person who gives information to the police in confidence, but who is not charged with a criminal offense. See also *informant.*

confidentiality agreement An agreement between an employer and employee that precludes the employee from revealing the employer's secret information to competitors or others.

conspiracy Under American law a person is guilty of conspiracy to commit a crime if, to further a criminal enterprise, that individual agrees with others that they will engage in criminal conduct, or if he or she agrees to aid others in planning or committing a crime.

constitutional courts *Federal courts,* inferior to the *Supreme Court,* established by Congress under Article III of the U.S. Constitution, with purely judicial responsibilities. See also *legislative courts.*

constitutionalism The conduct of a government in accordance with that country's constitution.

contempt of court A judicial order against one who willfully disobeys the lawful orders handed down in a court, or who acts to hinder or obstruct the administration of justice, or who attempts to embarrass the court or detract from the dignity of the judge.

contingency fee A fee that is based upon an agreement between lawyer and *client* that the lawyer will take as compensation some percentage of the *damages,* if any, that are collected in court on behalf of the client.

continuance A postponement of a hearing or trial granted by a judicial officer, usually in order to enable a lawyer to undertake additional preparation.

contract An agreement between two or more legally competent parties which creates mutual obligations to act, or occasionally to refrain from acting.

contributory negligence A defense that states that since the plaintiff's behavior helped to bring about the same problem that the plaintiff has now brought to court to be redressed, the court should deny the plaintiff recovery. See also *comparative fault statutes.*

controlled delivery An investigative procedure that delays the gathering of evidence in order to build a more solid case. For example, rather than seizing evidence of criminal activity, such as a narcotics shipment, authorities allow the shipment to move forward under surveillance in order to discover more information about a *conspiracy* to commit crime.

copyright A statutory right granted to the author of certain literary or artistic productions such that the holder of the copyright has the exclusive right to reproduce copies of the work and sell them. Each published copy of a copyrighted work should include a copyright notice.

coroner A public official who inquires into the causes and circumstances of any unnatural or suspicious deaths, often by performing autopsies. In many states, coroners have been replaced by *medical examiners* who perform many of the same functions but have somewhat broader responsibilities.

counsel One who gives legal advice; also used as a synonym for *lawyer* or *attorney;* also used to refer to the advice (the "counsel") given by a lawyer to a client.

counts The portion of an *indictment* that lists the particular offenses that the prosecutor believes the suspect may have committed.

county American states are divided into smaller territorial subdivisions known as *counties* (except in Louisiana where they are called *parishes*).

county attorney See *prosecutor.*

county court The court that presides over legal matters arising within that county. In certain states, a county court may be called a *circuit court, chancery court, district court, superior court,* or *court of common pleas.*

court administrator An official on the judicial staff who looks after administrative responsibilities of a court, such as recordkeeping, managing the budget, and supervising other court personnel. See also *clerk of the court.*

court of appeals A higher court, either state or federal, that reviews *trial court* decisions. The federal *appellate courts* are known as the U.S. Supreme Court and the U.S. circuit courts of appeals. State appellate courts go by different names in different states. The highest state court of appeal is the state *supreme court,* sometimes called the *supreme judicial court,* the *supreme court of appeals,* or the *court of appeals.*

court calendar See *trial docket.*

court of chancery See *court of equity.*

court of common pleas See *county court.*

court of equity These courts formed a parallel system of justice in England, administering justice in the name of the King or Queen in accordance with general notions of fairness, rather than in accordance with the *common law.* Also called the *Court of Chancery.*

court of error Formerly the name of Connecticut's *court of last resort.*

court of error and appeals Formerly the name of the *court of last resort* in New Jersey and New York.

court of general jurisdiction See *court of unlimited jurisdiction.*

court of last resort Used in a descriptive or generic sense, this term refers to the highest court in the state or in the country. See also *courts of appeal.*

court of limited jurisdiction Any court whose *jurisdiction* is limited by amount, confined to one subject-matter, or restricted to a particular geographic region. Commonly, the term refers to a lower state court that hears cases that involve small amounts of money or property or less serious offenses (*misdemeanors*).

court of record A court with proceedings that are permanently recorded.

court of unlimited jurisdiction A *trial court* that hears *civil cases* without any maximum limit on the amount of money or the value of the property in dispute. Also referred to as a *court of general jurisdiction.*

court reporter The officer of the court who has responsibility for producing an official record of all statements and verbal exchanges during the proceedings. See also *stenographer.*

criminal case A case in which the state or federal government has formally accused an individual of committing an offense regarded as criminal under state or federal law. See also *civil case.*

criminal coercion Restricting another's freedom of action by threatening to expose a secret, to make accusations of criminal behavior, to commit a criminal offense, or to take or withhold official action. See also *criminal racketeering.*

criminal complaint See *complaint.*

criminal racketeering An organized *conspiracy* to commit the crimes of *extortion* or *criminal coercion.*

criminal record The official account of all criminal court proceedings against a particular individual.

cross-complaint A *pleading* setting forth a *cause of action* the defendant has against the plaintiff or, under certain circumstances, against other parties.

cross-examination See *examination.*

customs duties taxes on imports.

damages Money awarded by the court and paid by a wrongdoer to a party who has suffered some loss or injury to person, property, or rights through the wrongdoer's unlawful act. See also *jury award.*

declaratory judgment A binding adjudication of an actual case or controversy in which the court defines the rights and status of the parties.

default The omission or failure to perform a legal or contractual duty.

default judgment A judgment in favor of one party should another party fail to appear in court or to plead within the specified time period. A judge has the discretion to make this ruling.

defendant In a *civil case,* the party against whom the relief or recovery is sought; in a *criminal case* the person who is accused of the alleged offense and who is *standing trial.*

defense counsel The attorney representing the defendant in a *criminal case.*

defraud To cheat or trick; technically, to misrepresent a fact, knowing the representation is false and intending another to rely upon it, when the other does rely on it to their damage.

deliberations The period in a trial when the jury is isolated in order that they may determine the *verdict* in the case. See also *sequester.*

demurrer See *motion to dismiss.*

deposit Money or other assets given to a person with the idea of ensuring that a *contract* is performed. If the contract is performed, the deposit is often considered to be a part of the payment. If the contract is not performed, the deposit is forfeited.

depositions A form of civil *discovery* in which a lawyer, outside of court, asks one of the parties to a *civil case* or a potential witness in that case a series of questions. The person who will be *deposed* is placed *under oath,* and a *stenographer* is present to record the questions and responses.

deputy A police officer who serves as the top assistant to a sheriff or police chief.

dicta An incidental oral or written remark by a judge not logically necessary to resolve any legal issue involved in the case and not binding as *precedent.* Also referred to as *obiter dictum.*

direct examination See *examination.*

directed verdict A judicial order to the jury in a *civil* or *criminal case* directing it to decide in favor of one party since the other has failed to prove its case. Thus, in a criminal case a judge who has sustained a *motion for a directed verdict* would *acquit* the defendant.

disbarment Suspension of an attorney's license to practice law in a particular state or Washington, DC.

discovery In *criminal* and *civil cases,* a preparation period before the trial in which both sides attempt to determine what actually happened by requesting and obtaining evidence.

dissenting opinion See *opinion.*

district attorney See *prosecutor.*

district court In reference to states, see *county court;* in reference to the federal government, see *constitutional courts.*

district judge See *federal judge.*

diversity of citizenship If the parties to a *civil lawsuit* in which the amount in controversy exceeds $75,000 live in different states, there is a *diversity of citizenship* and one requirement for bringing a case in federal court has been met.

division of powers The principle that political power in the United States ought to be divided between the state and federal governments. See also *separation of powers.*

DNA Deoxyribonucleic acid. The chemical that encodes the genes in the cells of a human body in a pattern unique to each human being.

DNA fingerprinting *DNA* samples are increasingly used to link suspects to physical evidence such as blood, semen, bone or skin fragments, or hair strands found at the crime scene, on the victim, or on the suspect. DNA testing is a controversial but increasingly important part of many modern American criminal trials.

dissenting opinion See *opinion.*

docket See *trial docket.*

domestic dispute A quarrel or confrontation within a household.

domestic relations courts See *juvenile courts.*

double jeopardy By virtue of a clause in the Fifth Amendment to the U.S. Constitution, no one may be subjected to *double jeopardy,* that is, prosecuted a second time for the same offense.

down payment The portion of a purchase price that must be paid to the seller at the time the sale agreement is signed.

driving while intoxicated The offense committed when an individual operates a vehicle while under the influence of alcohol or drugs. State law determines the level of alcohol in the blood at which a person is deemed intoxicated and the conditions under which a person may be tested for drug use.

drug courts Courts found in certain states that deal with the legal problems related to narcotics and alcohol use.

dual court system A legal system, like that in the United States, that includes both state and national courts. See also *unitary court system.*

due process of law The regular administration of law by the courts that is constitutionally required before the government may deprive someone of life, liberty, or property. The U.S. constitutional guarantee of *due process of law* is found in the Fifth and Fourteenth Amendments. *Procedural due process* means that a person is guaranteed that fair procedures are used in judging him. *Substantive due process* prohibits a government from unfairly taking or interfering with a person's property.

duties See *customs duties.*

DWI See *driving while intoxicated.*

electronic monitoring A form of punishment in which a person is outfitted with an electronic device that may not be removed from his or her body, except by the relevant authorities. The device allows the authorities to monitor the whereabouts of the person at any time.

embezzlement The misappropriation of money or other property, whose possession had been acquired lawfully, through some position of trust.

en banc See *appellate judge.*

equal protection of the laws The legal principle that persons confronting the same circumstances must be equally protected both in enjoying their rights and in having the government prevent and provide redress for any wrongs they may suffer.

equity See *court of equity.*

estate The whole of the property owned by a person, including both personal property and real estate, before that property is distributed in accordance with the terms of that person's will. See also *trusts; wills.*

evidence *Testimony,* writings, tangible objects, or any other type of proof legally presented to demonstrate that a fact exists or does not exist. The decisionmaker in court may rely on *direct evidence,* such as *eyewitness testimony,* or on *circumstantial* or *indirect evidence,* that is, a chain of circumstances that points to the existence or nonexistence of certain facts.

examination The questions put by the lawyers to the *witnesses* at a trial. *Direct examination* refers to questions put to a witness by the lawyer who called that witness to the *stand.* After every direct examination, the opposing lawyer has the opportunity to *cross-examine* that witness by asking additional questions. Through cross-examination lawyers attempt to raise questions and doubts about what the witness just stated on direct examination. After the *cross-examination,* the first lawyer may respond with *redirect examination,* to which the second lawyer can respond with *recross-examination.*

exclusionary rule A judicial rule that evidence obtained in violation of the U.S. Constitution cannot be used at the trial of a defendant.

exculpatory evidence Evidence that tends to clear a defendant from alleged guilt.

execute See *execution of judgment.*

execution of judgment The enforcement of a court judgment, usually by having the authorities seize a debtor's property and sell it at a court auction with the proceeds going to the person awarded *damages* by the court. Also referred to as *satisfaction of judgment.*

executive jurisdiction The principle in international law that a nation-state is the final authority regarding government matters within its own territory. This principle further indicates that in peacetime government officials are only to act abroad with the express consent of the foreign state in whose territory they wish to act. See also *jurisdiction.*

exemplary damages See *punitive damages.*

exhibit Some tangible object which is displayed as evidence at a legal proceeding, marked for identification, and then formally and publicly shown to the court.

ex parte A Latin term meaning "on one side only"; a judicial proceeding, such as a hearing, that is carried out on the application of or for the benefit of only one party to the case.

expert witness See *witness.*

extortion The *felony* of obtaining property through threats to do injury to another or by actually injuring another.

extradition The surrender by one state to another state of an individual who is accused of committing an offense within the territorial jurisdiction of the other state. Extradition occurs between countries and between states within the United States.

eyewitness See *witness.*

family courts See *juvenile courts.*

federal A system of divided political power in which different governments exercise realms of authority over the same territory.

federal courts The national court system in the United States. The federal courts administer national law. The three principal categories of federal courts are the *federal district court,* the *federal court of appeals,* and the *U.S. Supreme Court.* See also *state courts.*

federal district courts See *constitutional courts.*

federal judge A judge in the national court system in the United States. The three most common categories of federal judges are the *district judges* (in the federal district court), the *appellate judges* (in the federal court of appeals), and the *justices* on the U.S. Supreme Court.

federal magistrate See *magistrate.*

federal pre-emption doctrine Under the U.S. Constitution and *federal* legislation, the federal government, rather than the state governments, has exclusive authority over certain specified matters, such as interstate commerce.

federal question A legal dispute that is under the *jurisdiction* of the *federal courts* because it arises under the terms of the U.S. Constitution, a U.S. treaty, or an act of Congress.

federalism A political system in which a government is organized by dividing its powers between national and state governing bodies.

felony A more serious crime than a *misdemeanor* and one that is punishable by imprisonment or even by death. Examples of felonies would be *armed robbery* or *murder.* In some states felonies punishable by death are known as *capital felonies.*

fence A dealer in stolen goods.

fiduciary Generally, one with a supreme duty of loyalty to another. The term has two technical meanings: one who acts as a *trustee* by managing money or property for another, and one who transacts business for the benefit of another within a formal relationship that requires the benefactor's confidence and trust and the fiduciary's good faith and expert judgment.

files suit The act by the *plaintiff's* lawyer of sending documents to court to initiate litigation.

finders See *rainmakers.*

findings of fact See *trier of fact.*

fire marshal See *marshal.*

for cause challenge At a *voir dire* a lawyer is permitted to eliminate a particular juror if the judge can be convinced that there is a compelling reason to do so, such as bias or prior knowledge of the case on the part of the juror.

Foreign Intelligence Surveillance Court This court and the Foreign Intelligence Surveillance Court of Review, both staffed by federal judges on loan from other courts, deal with legal issues that arise concerning intelligence work. In particular, the court issues warrants to government officials who wish to use wiretaps and other electronic surveillance within the United States to gain information relevant to safeguarding American national security.

foreman or forewoman The individual who speaks for the jury as a whole. Sometimes also called *foreperson* or, in the case of women, *forematron.*

forensic medicine A science that applies to legal ends knowledge in fields as diverse as anatomy, botany, chemistry, medicine, physics, physiology, and surgery.

forum shopping The effort by a party to select the court likely to issue the most favorable *judgment* or *verdict.*

fraud A deceitful practice intended to injure another.

fugitive Any person who flees from arrest, prosecution, or imprisonment.

full partner See *two-track partnership.*

garnishment A method of obtaining payment of a judgment by seizing the salary of a debtor while it is in the possession of a third party, such as an employer.

gavel A wooden hammer or mallet used by a judicial officer to initiate proceedings, signal for attention, or maintain order in a courtroom.

general counsel The head of the legal division of a corporation.

general liability policy A type of insurance policy that protects a company against debts and obligations arising from property damage. See also *personal liability policy.*

government lawyer A lawyer who works directly for a local, state, or federal government office.

graft Personal gain by a public official, such as a police officer or politician, through a dishonest or corrupt transaction.

grand jury See *jury.*

grand larceny See *larceny.*

grinders See *rainmakers.*

gun control laws Laws regulating the sale and use of guns by requiring licenses, prohibiting concealed weapons, and imposing other restrictions.

habeas corpus An order issued by a judge to bring a prisoner before the *bench* to determine whether he or she has been illegally imprisoned, not whether he or she is guilty of the crime charged.

hang out a shingle Slang phrase meaning to start a law practice by oneself without working for a law firm.

headhunters See *legal headhunters.*

hearsay An out-of-court statement, not originally made by the testifying *witness,* offered in evidence to prove the truth of the matter asserted. Hearsay evidence comes not from the witness's personal knowledge, but from repeating what the witness has heard others say out of court. This type of evidence is suspect since it may be false rumors and since the opposing lawyer is not able to *cross-examine* someone not actually present at the trial. Hearsay evidence is normally held *inadmissible,* though exceptions do exist.

hired gun Derogatory slang for a lawyer who stands ready to be hired by the highest bidder to try to win a case in court.

homicide The killing of a human being by the commission or the omission of an act.

hornbook A treatise reviewing a field of law in summary form.

house arrest A punishment in which an individual must remain in his or her own dwelling at all times.

housing court See *municipal courts.*

hung jury A jury whose members continue to disagree over an extended period, who are unable to compromise to settle the disagreement, and who therefore cannot bring a *verdict.* In cases of a *hung jury* the judge will call for a new trial to be held in front of a different jury.

impaneling a jury Determining who are to be the jurors in a trial and swearing them in so that they may properly fulfill their responsibilities.

impeachment A criminal proceeding held in the U.S. Congress against a public officer. The House of Representatives is responsible for issuing the written accusation, and the

U.S. Senate constitutes the court in which the impeachment proceedings take place.
inadmissible Something that a court will not allow to be received as evidence at a trial.
indictment A written accusation, also called a *bill of indictment,* drawn up by a *prosecutor,* that identifies the offense or offenses a *suspect* is alleged to have committed. It is formally issued by a *grand jury* after a hearing to determine if there is sufficient evidence to proceed.
individual practitioners See *solo practitioners.*
informant A criminal who supplies information to authorities on another criminal. Also known by the slang terms "snitch" or "stool pigeon." See also *confidential source.*
information A procedure used in place of a *grand jury* proceeding in certain states, in which a judge holds a preliminary hearing to determine whether the government has compiled enough evidence to justify holding a criminal trial.
in-house counsel an attorney employed by a single company to give it legal advice.
injunction An order from a court requiring that someone do something or refrain from doing something. An *interlocutory injunction* asks a court to issue a temporary order for some specified length of time in order to prevent irreparable injury, during which time the court can reach a considered decision on whether a permanent injunction should be granted or denied. Interlocutory injunctions are divided into two categories: *temporary restraining orders* and *preliminary injunctions.*
inmate A person confined to a prison.
inns of court Private associations of lawyers in London, organized in the fashion of colleges, with lectures and examinations, which confer the rank of *barrister* on individuals studying to become lawyers.
inquisitorial manner The method of examination and cross-examination in a *civil law legal system,* whereby an accused person is put on trial and must try to prove his innocence.
instructions The directions given to the jury by the judge concerning the relevant laws that the jury is to apply in deciding the case. See also *charge to the jury.*
insurance See *general liability policy.*
intellectual property Property directly related to the creative human mind, ranging from literary and artistic items, such as books, plays, or musical scores, to computer programs.
interlocutory injunction See *injunction.*
Internal Revenue Code The codified federal tax law of the United States.
Internal Revenue Service The federal *administrative agency* that administers the *Internal Revenue Code.*
interrogation The questioning of an arrested or suspect person by police. See also *Miranda rights.*
interrogatory A form of civil *discovery* in which one party gains evidence outside of court by submitting a list of questions to another party and requesting answers to them.
issue-spotter The most common type of final examination used in law schools. In issue-spotter examinations students are asked to spot multiple legal issues within lengthy hypothetical scenarios and cite the relevant law.
J.D. See *juris doctorate.*
jail A place of confinement, usually run by local authorities (county or city), and used to detain persons convicted of *misdemeanors* or persons awaiting trial. See also *prison.*
joint owners Co-owners; that is, people who own land together.
joint tenants Co-tenants; that is, people who lease land together.
joyriding Stealing a car for a short ride without intending to deprive the owner permanently of the use of his or her property. Sometimes called *use without authority.*
judge See *appellate judge; federal judge; judge of instruction; justices; magistrate; penal judge.*
judge of instruction In a *civil law legal system,* the investigating judge who first considers a case.
judge's chambers A judge's private office within a courthouse, where a judge may carry out research and writing or conduct private meetings with lawyers.
judgment The official, final court decision resolving a legal dispute and determining the parties' rights and obligations.
judgment proof The financial state in which a judgment for money damages is of no practical effect since the defendant cannot be forced to pay, usually because he or she is insolvent.
judgment notwithstanding the verdict See *motion for judgment notwithstanding the verdict.*
judicial activism An "active" judge tends to perceive his or her role as using the law to see that the legal system accomplishes his or her vision of justice. See *judicial restraint.*

judicial conduct organizations Oversight groups that investigate complaints of misconduct by judges. See also *regional judicial councils.*

judicial jurisdiction See *jurisdiction.*

judicial order A written direction made by a judge during a court proceeding, but not included in the final judgment.

judicial restraint A "restrained" judge tends to defer to the legislative and executive branches of government, to focus upon applying the law, and to resist making new law.

judicial review Using the process of judicial review, American courts have the power to decide that the act of another governmental body cannot be enforced since it violates the law of the land as embodied in the U.S. Constitution.

jumping bail See *bail.*

junior partner See *partner.*

jurisdiction The power or authority under which a court can recognize, hear, and decide a particular legal question. See also *executive jurisdiction; legislative jurisdiction; original jurisdiction.*

juris doctorate The standard degree issued by American law schools to students who wish to practice law in the United States; abbreviated as *J.D.* A *Master of Law* degree (abbreviated as *LL.M.*) focuses upon advanced study in a particular field of law.

jurisprudence The philosophy of law aimed at discovering the principles on which legal rules are based. Since each state in the United States has its own court system and its own *precedents,* state jurisprudence differs from state to state.

jury The American legal system has two types of juries. The *trial jury* (or *petit jury*) is the principal decisionmaker in many criminal and civil cases. The *grand jury* meets before a criminal trial ever takes place to decide whether *prosecutors* have gathered sufficient evidence to justify formally accusing a person of a crime and then putting that person on trial.

jury award The amount of compensation a jury grants to a *plaintiff* who has won a *civil lawsuit.* See also *damages.*

jury-box A small enclosed area off to one side of the front of a courtroom. It contains rows of seats where the jury sits to listen to the trial.

jury fees The compensation paid to jurors by a state, the District of Columbia, or the federal government, depending upon the type of court in which the trial takes place.

jury foreman See *foreman.*

jury instructions See *instructions.*

jury room The room in a courthouse where potential jurors wait to be called to serve on a jury. Also sometimes used to designate the room where jurors deliberate at the close of the trial before handing down the verdict.

jury wheel A device for storing and randomly selecting prospective jurors. See also *venire members.*

justice of the peace See *magistrate.*

justices The term that distinguishes the judges serving on the national *court of last resort* from all the other judges in the American legal system. The U.S. Supreme Court is headed by a *Chief Justice,* who has one vote along with each of the *associate justices,* but who also has additional administrative responsibilities. Because of the visibility of the position, the Chief Justice often exercises substantial philosophical influence over the court's decisions. See also *appellate judges.*

juvenile courts State courts that deal with the problems of children who commit criminal offenses. Also called *Family courts.*

landlord or landlady A *landlord* (male) or *landlady* (female) is a person who owns land or lodgings and leases them to another person, called a *tenant.*

larceny The criminal laws of many states recognize two types of *larceny.* In *grand larceny,* an individual has taken and carried away the personal property of another which is worth more than a particular amount of money, perhaps $100. The theft of property worth less than that amount would be considered the less serious offense of *petit larceny.*

lateral movement The hiring of midcareer lawyers, rather than hiring from a pool of law school graduates.

laundering See *money laundering.*

law clerks Recent graduates of law school (or, occasionally, law students) who serve as assistants to judges.

law firm A partnership of two or more persons engaged in the practice of law.

lawsuit See *civil case.*

leading question A question by a lawyer that tries to put "words into the mouth of a witness" by stating what the lawyer would like the witness to say rather than what he or she might freely state.

legal headhunters Slang for professional employment experts who determine the hiring needs of law firms and search for lawyers who might be available to meet those needs.

Legal Services Corporation A government agency that provides financial support for legal assistance to poor people involved in noncriminal matters.

"legalese" Dense legal jargon. Also called "mumbo jumbo."

legislative address A procedure for removing state judges usually for bias, incompetence, or senility on the basis of a vote by the legislature.

legislative courts Federal courts, inferior to the U.S. Supreme Court, established by Congress under Article I of the U.S. Constitution, that have certain administrative and legislative functions along with their judicial functions. Examples include the U.S. Tax Court, the U.S. Court of Military Appeals, the U.S. Customs Court, and the now defunct U.S. Court of Claims.

legislative jurisdiction The ability of a particular group to make binding laws. See also *jurisdiction.*

letter of the law See *loophole.*

letter ruling A written opinion interpreting an ambiguous provision of the tax code, often concerning whether the Internal Revenue Service would allow a particular deduction under a particular set of circumstances.

liability policy See *general liability policy.*

libel A publication that injures the reputation of another.

lien A claim, encumbrance, or charge on property that gives a creditor the right to retain property to secure payment of a debt.

litigants The parties to a *civil case.*

litigation A lawsuit or lawsuits. See also *civil case; political litigation.*

litigator The trial attorney arguing a *civil case.*

litigiousness Willingness to be involved in a lawsuit or lawsuits. See also *civil case.*

LL.M. See *juris doctorate.*

local court A court of limited jurisdiction, which hears cases that involve small amounts of money or property of limited value or less serious offenses (misdemeanors) than do the higher courts in the state system. See also *court of limited jurisdiction.*

loophole Slang for a clever or tricky exception or legal maneuver that complies with the exact wording of a law ("the letter of the law"), but not with the intent of a law ("the spirit of a law").

mafia See *organized crime.*

magistrate A judicial official who is not a judge, but who presides over a minor state court or over minor matters in a federal court and enjoys in limited fashion some of the powers of a judge.

majority opinion See *opinion.*

make partner See *partner.*

malpractice Professional misconduct or unreasonable lack of skill.

managing partner See *partner.*

mandatory minimum sentence See *sentence.*

marshals *U.S. marshals* are law enforcement personnel appointed by the President to each judicial district in order to carry out orders issued under the authority of the United States. Certain states also employ a law enforcement official called the *marshal* that elsewhere might be labelled the *chief of police* or the *sheriff.* In addition, the head of a fire department is sometimes called the *fire marshal.*

Master of Law See *juris doctorate.*

mediation The reference of a dispute to a neutral third party who attempts to assist the adversarial parties in resolving the dispute by negotiation and compromise.

medical examiner See *coroner.*

merit selection system A method of selecting a judge through appointment and election. Customarily, the governor first appoints the judge from a list of candidates nominated by a blue-ribbon panel. After a period has elapsed, the candidate must then gain voter approval in a special uncontested *retention election.* This process is sometimes called the *Missouri plan* after the state in which it was first instituted.

metropolitan court See *municipal court.*

military court system The legal system used by the U.S. Armed Forces to punish offenses committed by soldiers under military law (the Uniform Code of Military Justice).

minders See *rainmakers.*

***Miranda* rights** In the course of any *arrest* police officers are obligated to state to a *suspect:* "You have the right to remain silent; anything you say can and will be used against you in a court of law; you have the right to the presence of an attorney and, if you cannot afford one, an attorney will be appointed for you prior to any questioning if you wish."

misdemeanor A petty offense which under state (and federal) law is classified as a separate group of infractions, less serious than a *felony*. Examples of common *misdemeanors* would be disorderly conduct or prostitution. Some states have created a further category of *petit misdemeanors* for very minor offences.

Missouri plan See *merit selection system.*

money laundering Transferring money derived from criminal activity into legitimate investments in order to keep the original source of the money from being easily traced by law enforcement authorities.

motion An application to a court requesting that some order or ruling be made, usually within the context of an ongoing legal action.

motion for a directed verdict See *directed verdict.*

Motion for a More Definite Statement A preliminary motion that asks the court to declare that a *pleading* is so unnecessarily vague that the other party cannot reasonably be required to respond to it.

Motion for an Order Compelling Production of Documents A preliminary motion that asks a court to declare that one party is wrongfully withholding important documents in a legal matter.

Motion for Judgment Notwithstanding the Verdict A motion brought after a trial that asks a court to declare that no reasonable jury could have reached the verdict announced in the case.

motion for summary judgment A preliminary motion that asks a court to declare that no genuine issue of material fact exists and that as a matter of law the party making the motion (the "moving party") is entitled to prevail.

motion session A period set aside for a judge to rule on preliminary motions that have arisen in different lawsuits.

motion to dismiss A preliminary motion that asks the court to dismiss the case because, even if the plaintiff were to admit that all the facts alleged by the plaintiff were true, the *complaint* still fails to state a legally sound *cause of action* against the defendant. Also called a *demurrer* in certain state courts.

motion to strike One party asks the court to order the other party to delete from a *pleading* improper material that is irrelevant, redundant, prejudicial, or scandalous.

multistate exam See *bar examination.*

municipal corporation When a given area of a state reaches a sufficient population density, the state normally designates that area a *municipal corporation.* Since a township does not always have all the powers of a municipal corporation, it is sometimes called a *quasi-municipal corporation.*

municipal court A local state court that handles a particular set of problems for a particular metropolitan area. An example would be the Boston Housing Court. Also called a *metropolitan court.*

murder The unlawful killing of a person by another, committed so purposely or knowingly or recklessly as to show extreme indifference to the value of human life.

negligence A *tort* theory alleging the failure to use the care a reasonably prudent person, guided by ordinary considerations, would use under a set of particular circumstances.

night court See *police court.*

no bill A document issued by a *grand jury* stating that in its opinion the evidence is insufficient to *indict* a person for an alleged crime. See also *true bill.*

no-fault automobile insurance An insurance plan in which the insurance companies that have insured the drivers in an accident pay for injuries or damage up to a certain limit regardless of who was responsible for the accident.

no-fault divorce A type of divorce that can end a marriage without a showing of fault on the part of either spouse. The reason for the divorce is that irreconcilable differences have developed between the two parties.

nolo contendere A legal term in Latin meaning "I will not contest it." The defendant does not admit or deny the criminal charges, but allows the judge to sentence him or her as though guilt had been admitted or proved.

notary public A public officer who administers oaths, certifies documents, and attests to the authenticity of signatures.

nuisance lawsuit An effort to intimidate, harass, or annoy another individual by filing a lawsuit against him or her.

obiter dictum See *dicta.*

objection The act of formally disputing some matter, often regarding *evidence* or arguments, that has arisen in the course of a trial.

offer of proof Once a judge sustains an objection to a question, the attorney may give the *court reporter* the answer that the *witness* was prepared to give, if he or she had been permitted to do so. The answer to the attorney's question, known as the offer of proof, then becomes part of the written record of the case and can be considered by an appellate court.

omnibus hearing A pre-trial hearing in which a judge considers many unrelated legal issues.

opening statement The first stage in a trial, in which each lawyer introduces the case to the judge and, where applicable, the jury.

opinions An explanation written by a judge of the reasons that he or she arrived at a particular decision. Those *opinions* are then published to provide useful *precedents* for future cases. When a majority of the judges on an *appellate court* agree with a particular opinion, it is known as a *majority opinion.* Any judge who disagrees with that majority opinion is free to write a *dissenting opinion.* A judge who agrees with the majority decision, but for different reasons, may also write a *concurring opinion.* See also *per curiam.*

oral argument The points made by an attorney, spoken out loud and in court, in an *appeal* or *motion* before a judge or judges.

order See *judicial order.*

ordinances Laws passed by cities and counties. See also *zoning ordinance.*

organized crime Crime committed by groups as opposed to individuals. Many criminal gangs are organized within a framework that emphasizes ethnic and family ties, for example, the Italian *mafia,* Japanese *yakuza,* Chinese *triads,* and Jamaican *posses.*

original jurisdiction The power or authority to hear a case the first time that it is argued. *Appellate jurisdiction* means the power or authority to hear a case on appeal.

orphan's court See *probate court.*

out-of-court settlement A private compromise that usually involves compensation paid by one party to another, that settles a legal dispute, and in which both parties voluntarily agree to withdraw a *civil lawsuit* from court.

panel See *appellate judge.*

paralegal A lawyer's assistant who has certain legal skills but is not an attorney.

pardon An act of grace by the executive authority in which a convicted criminal or suspect is made exempt from prosecution and punishment for crimes.

parishes See *counties.*

parole Conditional release of an inmate from a jail or prison, under the supervision of a *parole officer,* after a well-behaved inmate has served part of his or her *sentence.* Parole may be revoked if the prisoner fails to observe the conditions of the *parole order.*

parole officer See *parole.*

partner An attorney who shares in the profits of a law firm after expenses and salaries have been paid. In a *two-track partnership, junior partners* (or *non-equity partners*) do not share profits; rather, they are paid a salary. A *managing partner* both practices law and oversees the administration of a law firm. See also *associate.*

partnership track See *associate.*

patent A formal grant by the government to an inventor giving him or her the exclusive right to make, use, and sell the particular invention for a particular term of years.

penal judge In a *civil law legal system,* the judge who brings the accused person before the court for examination, together with witnesses and others who might contribute useful information about the case.

penitentiary See *prison.*

per curiam A legal term in Latin meaning "by the whole court." See also *opinions.*

per diem basis A fee arrangement in which the client agrees to pay the lawyer a specified amount of money for each day that the lawyer provides the client with legal services.

per project basis A fee arrangement in which the client agrees to pay the lawyer a certain sum of money for all the legal services necessary to complete that legal project. Also called a *straight fee basis.*

peremptory challenge The elimination of a juror by an attorney at a *voir dire* without furnishing any reason for doing so. Although the numbers vary from one state to another, lawyers are normally entitled to a certain limited number of peremptory challenges. See also *for cause challenge.*

perjury A false material statement made under oath in any official proceeding by a person who knows the statement to be untrue.

personal liability policy A type of insurance policy that protects a homeowner against liability for a range of different incidents that might occur on his or her property. See also *general liability policy.*

petit jury See *trial jury.*

petit larceny See *larceny.*

petitioner A party requesting a judge to issue a *temporary restraining order,* even though the *respondent* has not been given notice of the hearing and has not appeared. See also *injunction.*

petty misdemeanor See *misdemeanor.*

plaintiff In a *civil case,* the party who brings the dispute to court for resolution.

plea bargain A negotiation that often occurs between prosecutor and defense counsel in a criminal trial, in which the two attorneys attempt to agree that the defendant will plead guilty to certain charges and that the government will agree to drop other charges, thus settling the defendant's punishment before any trial takes place.

pleadings The written statements presented to the court by the parties, including the *complaint* and the *answer,* that attempt to narrow the dispute to certain legal issues.

pocket part A supplement to a legal source, such as a collection of laws, that is issued periodically to update the bound text. It is usually placed in a pocket on the inside back flap of that text.

police court A minor criminal court that deals with *misdemeanors.* Also sometimes known as a *night court* or *city court.* See also *municipal court.*

police report An internal memorandum prepared by police officers that describes what happened during an *arrest* or other noteworthy incident.

political litigation A lawsuit brought on behalf of an individual or individuals, yet designed to establish a legal principle that will benefit a larger group. See also *litigation.*

political question An issue of a purely political character that a court will refuse to decide in order to avoid encroaching on what are properly considered to be executive or legislative powers under the U.S. Constitution.

posses See *organized crime.*

precedent Legal principles derived from prior decisions in cases resembling the dispute under consideration.

preliminary hearing The stage of a *criminal case* when a suspect is brought before a *magistrate* who decides whether there is sufficient evidence against the suspect and whether the alleged offense is sufficiently significant to justify holding a criminal trial. Also called a *probable cause hearing.* In a *civil case,* this initial proceeding is called a pre-trial *motion hearing.* See also *motion; preliminary motion.*

preliminary injunctions See *injunctions.*

prenuptial agreement A contract entered into before a marriage that determines the property rights of the two prospective spouses. Also called an *antenuptial agreement* or *premarital agreement.*

preponderance of the evidence A standard of proof, summarized as "more evidence for than against," which a plaintiff must meet in order to prevail in a *civil lawsuit.*

presentment A public finding by a *grand jury* after an investigation that concludes that some illegal action may have occurred, but that no *bill of indictment* has yet been issued.

pre-trial conference A private meeting between the judge and the attorneys in a case before the trial begins.

prison A place of incarceration, usually run by state or federal authorities, and used to hold persons convicted of serious crimes. Also called a *penitentiary.*

prisoner's rights lawsuit A *civil case* brought by a prisoner asserting constitutional or statutory rights against the state or national government and their employees who were allegedly responsible for the mistreatment.

privilege One of various narrowly restricted matters about which the court does not require a *witness* to speak because of their private and confidential nature. Examples include communications between attorney and client or doctor and patient.

pro bono Short for *pro bono publico;* a legal term in Latin best translated as "for the public good" or "for the welfare of the whole."

probable cause A legal standard of evidence, summarized as being met when sufficient circumstances exist to lead a reasonably prudent person to believe in the guilt of an accused person. Probable cause is determined at a *preliminary hearing* which decides whether the government may pursue a *grand jury indictment* against the suspect.

probable cause hearing See *preliminary hearing.*

probating a will Proving that a will is valid or invalid in a court proceeding.

probate court The state court that decides inheritance issues. Also called a *surrogate's court* or *orphan's court.*

probation Freedom from incarceration under court supervision so long as no additional offense is committed and so long as any other conditions established by the court are respected by the convicted person.

probation officer The official charged with supervising a prisoner who has been released under specified conditions.

product liability law A body of *tort* law under which those who manufacture, sell, or distribute dangerous products are liable for injuries to consumers and bystanders.

promissory estoppel A legal doctrine stating that when an individual makes a promise that he or she should have expected would induce some definite and substantial action by another, and when the other person relies on that promise, takes that action, and then suffers a serious injustice, a court may declare the promise to be binding.

promissory note A written, signed promise to pay a specific amount to some designated person at a specified time.

property law The body of laws that governs the use, ownership, and sale of real estate and other assets.

prophylactic rule A rule designed to prevent a law from being violated. For an example, see *Miranda rights.*

prosecutor A lawyer representing the government at a criminal trial. A prosecutor for a particular state judicial district is called the *district attorney* (or "D.A."), *state's attorney,* or *county attorney.* The term *district attorney* also describes prosecutors in federal judicial districts. The head federal prosecutor in each federal judicial district is known as the *U.S. Attorney.* He or she is assisted by a staff of *assistant U.S. attorneys.*

prosecutorial discretion A state or federal *prosecutor* is granted the power to determine whether or not to bring criminal charges against an individual.

public defender A court-appointed attorney or one employed by a government agency who defends indigent defendants in criminal cases.

public interest lawyer An attorney who works for a charitable cause.

punitive damages Damages to punish a defendant for wanton, reckless, or reprehensible behavior awarded by the court to a plaintiff, above the amount that would simply compensate for losses suffered. *Treble damages* are set at three times actual damages. Also referred to as *exemplary damages.*

purchase-and-sale agreement An agreement between a buyer and seller of property that states the price and terms of the sale.

racketeering See *criminal racketeering.*

rainmakers Lawyers who spend much of their time bringing clients to a law firm are known in slang as *rainmakers* or *finders;* those who ensure that the clients' affairs are attended to properly are called *minders;* and those who do the legal work for another lawyer's client are called *grinders.*

reasonable doubt The standard, or *burden of proof,* that a defendant must reach in order to be *acquitted* of an alleged offense in a criminal trial. See also *accusatorial system.*

rebuttal evidence Evidence which is offered in order to contradict evidence presented by the other side. Rebuttal evidence is offered in a *reopened case.* That is, it is offered after one side has initially *rested* its case and the other side has presented its case and then rested.

recall petitions In certain states, if a sufficient number of citizens sign a petition, a special election is held in which voters choose whether or not to remove a judge from office.

recidivism Repeated or habitual relapse into crime.

recognition Occurs when one nation-state or government officially and formally takes notice that another nation-state or government exists under international law.

recognize a government See *recognition.*

record See *written record.*

recross examination See *examination.*

recuse To disqualify a *judge* from presiding over a trial or motion because of the judge's potential interest or bias regarding some issue pertinent to the case.

red tape Slang for unnecessarily cumbersome bureaucratic regulations.

redirect examination See *examination.*

regional judicial councils Oversight groups that investigate allegations of federal judicial misconduct. See also *judicial conduct organizations.*

regulations Rules and orders issued under the executive authority by a government department, rather than by a legislature, in order to fulfill the intent of a law and to direct the behavior of those under its control.

relief Redress sought from a court.

remedy The compensation, redress, or enforcement to which someone is entitled whose right has been violated or whose right needs to be enforced. See also *cause of action.*

reopen See *rebuttal evidence.*

repo-man Slang for a person in the business of repossessing cars after the buyer has *defaulted* on automobile-loan payments.

respondent See *appellee; petitioner.*

rest See *case-in-chief; rebuttal evidence.*

restatement of law A reference work that describes American law in a particular field, such as *contracts* or *torts*, and that predicts and recommends changes in the law.

retention election See *merit selection system.*

reversal The overturning of a lower court's decision by a *court of appeals.*

reversible error A mistaken view of the law or a mistaken application of the law to the facts so serious as to warrant reversal of the *judgment* arrived at in the lower court.

ripeness A constitutional doctrine aimed at keeping courts from entangling themselves in premature or abstract disagreements. It states that an appellate court will not review a judicial or administrative decision until all other remedies have been exhausted.

Rule of Four See *writ of certiorari.*

rule on witnesses See *separation of witnesses.*

rulings of law See *trier of fact.*

satisfaction of judgment See *execution of judgment.*

scofflaws Persons who ignore laws that they consider to be of minor importance. The term is often used in relation to persons ignoring laws regarding parking, speed limits, and jury service.

search-and-seizure law The prohibition in the Fourth Amendment to the U.S. Constitution against unreasonable searches and seizures by the authorities and the case law that has developed interpreting the boundaries of that prohibition.

search-warrant A written order, issued by a judge or magistrate, authorizing a police officer to search for and seize any property that constitutes evidence that a crime was committed.

self-incriminate To serve as a witness or furnish evidence against oneself.

senatorial courtesy A senator who belongs to the same political party as the president can ask Senate colleagues not to approve a nominee for a federal judicial appointment who comes from the Senator's home state yet whom the Senator opposes. Usually the other senators will then reject that nominee, anticipating that other senators will return the favor in the future.

sentence The official judgment imposing a punishment upon a convicted criminal defendant. A *mandatory sentence* is one that does not allow the judge to exercise discretion in sentencing a convicted individual.

sentencing guidelines Some legislatures in the United States have diminished the discretion given to judges to sentence convicted criminal defendants to any of a wide range of possible sentences by advising the judges as to what an appropriate penalty might be.

separation of powers The principle that political power in a democracy ought to be set apart among different branches or institutions of government: the executive, legislative, and judicial. See also *division of powers.*

separation of witnesses After an attorney calls for the *rule on witnesses,* the judge will order all the remaining witnesses to be excluded from the courtroom and separated from one another until they are called to take the witness stand.

sequester To isolate jurors from contact with the public during a highly controversial or well-publicized trial. See also *deliberations.*

service of process The act of sending a copy of a *civil complaint* to the defendant to inform him or her of a lawsuit.

settlement See *out-of-court settlement.*

sheriff The popularly elected leader of a police force, especially in a county.

shoplifting Taking merchandise from a store.

sine qua non The indispensable condition; a phrase in Latin meaning, "that without which the thing cannot be."

slip-and-fall case A category of *tort* law that involves a person who slips, falls down, and is injured, and claims that another's *negligence* was responsible for the accident.

small claims court A low-level state court that hears cases involving small amounts of money, usually less than $1,500.

socratic method The manner in which most classes in most American law schools are conducted. Using this method, professors teach by asking questions about law cases that students have been assigned to study.

solicitor general The representative of the U.S. Government before the U.S. Supreme Court.

solitary confinement An area of a prison in which an inmate is totally isolated from human society.

solo practitioners An attorney practicing law alone. Also referred to as *sole practitioners* or *individual practitioners.*

special master An individual with expertise in a specialized field, such as prison reform, who is appointed by a court to help prepare it for trial or to ensure that court orders are properly implemented.

specific performance A legal doctrine that states that if damages would be inadequate compensation for the breach of a contract, a court may order a party to carry through with its obligations as the agreement stipulated.

spontaneous statement A statement made on the spur of the moment and not in response to questioning by authorities.

stand See *witness stand.*

standard of proof See *burden of proof.*

standing to sue The requirement in a *civil case* that a plaintiff must have a legally protectable and tangible interest at stake in the litigation.

standing trial See *defendant.*

stare decisis The judicial doctrine stating that when a court has finally ruled that some legal principle should properly be interpreted as applying to a legal dispute in a particular manner, that court should apply the same reasoning to future cases involving similar disputes and decline to overturn settled points of law.

state courts The courts belonging to any of the fifty American states. See also *federal courts.*

state judge An elected or appointed judge in one of the state court systems.

state supreme court See *court of appeals.*

state's attorney See *prosecutor.*

statute of frauds A law, originating in England many years ago, that declares that certain legal documents, such as a valid contract regarding the sale of land, must be in written form.

statutes See *statutory law.*

statutory laws Laws, also commonly referred to as statutes, passed by the U.S. Congress or state legislatures. See also *ordinances.*

stenographer A person who records everything that is said at a legal proceeding. See also *court reporter.*

stop and frisk A procedure in which a police officer halts someone and pats the person's clothing to ensure that he or she is not carrying a concealed weapon.

straight fee basis See *per project basis.*

subpoena A judicial order to a witness to appear before the court to testify upon a certain matter.

subpoena duces tecum If a witness in a civil case resists producing tangible *evidence* that is pertinent to the issues in controversy, the opposing attorney may have the court issue this order, compelling the witness to produce the evidence in court.

suit See *civil case.*

summary judgment See *motion for summary judgment.*

summation See *closing argument.*

summons A court order notifying the defendant that a lawsuit has been filed against him or her and requiring that defendant to respond to the charges in the *complaint,* either by filing an *answer* within a certain number of days or appearing in court on a specified date.

superior court See *county court.*

supreme court See *court of last resort; U.S. Supreme Court.*

supreme court of appeals See *court of appeals.*

supreme judicial court See *court of appeals.*

surrogate's court See *probate courts.*

suspect A person whom the authorities believe may have committed a crime and, hence, may be brought to trial.

take an exception The act of formally objecting to the court's ruling at the time of the ruling. It is made in order to preserve the right to appeal that ruling at a later date.

take the witness stand See *testify.*

tax court See *U.S. Tax Court.*

tax-exempt status The tax status of property that is used for educational, religious, or charitable purposes and so is not assessed for taxes under the *Internal Revenue Code.*

temporary restraining order See *injunction.*

tenant See *landlord.*

term The time period in which a court is in *session;* that is, the time it is *sitting* to conduct its business.

testify To give a statement, under oath, as a *witness* at a trial. The statement itself is called *testimony.* Witnesses are often said to take the witness stand when they are called to testify. See also *evidence.*

testimony See *testify.*

tort law A body of law that concerns the violation of a legal duty that results in a private injury or wrong committed against another person or the property of another.

townships See *municipal corporations.*

trademark A distinctive mark, symbol, word, or motto used by a manufacturer or merchant to identify goods and distinguish them from those manufactured or sold by others. The federal government has traditionally granted trademark rights for a 28-year period.

traffic court A minor state court that settles traffic disputes, such as speeding or other traffic violations.

treble damages See *damages.*
trespass An unauthorized intrusion on the private land or premises of another.
triads See *organized crime.*
trial attorney A lawyer who represents a client in a court proceeding.
trial courts Courts in which criminal or civil trials take place, as opposed to *appellate courts* in which judges review the records of cases in *trial courts* to determine if errors have occurred.
trial de novo Legal term in Latin, meaning "a new trial." Often, a *trial de novo* occurs in the same court after a fatally flawed verdict or decision. The whole case is retried, as if the original trial had never occurred. Sometimes, a *trial de novo* takes place in a *court of general jurisdiction* after an appeal from a *court of limited jurisdiction.*
trial docket A list of the proceedings scheduled to be tried by a particular court. A similar though more general term is the *court calendar.*
trial jury See *jury.*
tribal courts Tribunals on Native American reservations that share jurisdiction over civil and criminal cases with federal and state courts.
true bill A document issued by a *grand jury* stating that in its opinion the evidence presented by the prosecutor is sufficient to *indict* a person for an alleged crime.
trustee See *fiduciary; trusts.*
trusts Arrangements in which property is transferred from one person to another (the *beneficiary*) with the intention that a third person (the *trustee*) will administer that property in the best interests of the beneficiary. See also *estate; fiduciary; will.*
two-track partnership See *partner.*
under oath Before testifying at trial or in a *deposition, witnesses* must declare that they will speak truthfully. This is most frequently done by placing the individual *under oath;* that is, requiring the individual to swear or to affirm to tell "the truth, the whole truth, and nothing but the truth."
Uniform Commercial Code A standard legal code compiled by a body of experts on the subject of commercial transactions and adopted by all the American states, except Louisiana.
unitary court system A legal system in which a single network of courts hears all the legal disputes that arise in the country.
U.S. attorney See *prosecutor.*
U.S. attorney general See *attorney general.*
U.S. Claims Court A federal court that hears lawsuits against the U.S. government that involve public contracts, patents, and copyrights. It also interprets other federal laws, including those found in the U.S. Constitution.
U.S. Court of International Trade A federal court that hears cases arising under the tariff laws, such as how much customs duties must be paid to import a certain good into the United States.
U.S. Court of Military Appeals The appellate court at the apex of the military court system, staffed by three civilian judges serving 15-year terms. The Court of Military Appeals concerns itself with serious violations of the Uniform Code of Military Justice, which governs the behavior of members of the American armed forces.
U.S. magistrate judge See *federal magistrate.*
U.S. marshal See *marshal.*
U.S. Tax Court A federal legislative court that decides disputes regarding whether an individual or a company has paid sufficient taxes.
use without authority See *joyriding.*
vandalism Willful, ignorant, or malicious destruction of the property of another.
venire member A potential juror called to appear in court.
venue The county or district in which a case may be heard and tried under constitutional and statutory law.
verdict The formal decision about a case made by the jury and reported to the judge.
vice Conduct such as gambling, prostitution, and use of narcotics, that certain laws prohibit because the lawmakers regard it as immoral.
vigilantes Any unauthorized committee of American citizens using extralegal means to maintain order and summarily punish criminals.
voir dire The process of selecting a jury.
warrant See *arrest warrant; search-warrant.*
warrantless arrest An arrest carried out without the authority of a *warrant,* as when police see a crime being committed or have *probable cause* to believe that an individual committed or is about to commit a *felony.*
water courts Tribunals that deal with legal issues arising from the regulated supply of water to a water district and other such matters.
white-collar crimes Nonviolent economic crimes that involve fraud, collusion, or deception.

White House counsel See *attorney general.*

will A written legal document declaring how an individual wishes to have his or her property distributed after death.

witness A person who comes to court to testify as to what he or she personally saw (specifically, an *eyewitness*), heard, or otherwise observed. An *expert witness* testifies as to some technical, and often scientific, matter about which he or she is qualified to speak authoritatively because of special training and experience.

witness protection program A program established under federal law authorizing federal officials to relocate and otherwise protect a witness or potential witness, usually in a case dealing with organized crime.

witness stand A small, fenced-in area in a courtroom, next to the *bench,* where witnesses will sit and respond to questions by the lawyers.

work release An arrangement in which an inmate is permitted to leave prison to continue regular employment during the day. He or she must report back to prison in the evenings and on weekends.

workers' compensation acts State laws that award damages to employees and dependents after work-related accidents without regard to negligence and other causal factors.

workers' compensation boards Tribunals with jurisdiction to review cases arising under state laws that grant fixed awards to employees or their dependents (usually family members) in case of injury during employment. Also called *workmen's compensation courts.*

writ A type of order issued by a court. See also *habeas corpus; writ of certiorari.*

writ of certiorari An order in which a higher court, such as the *U.S. Supreme Court,* requires a lower court to produce the *record* of a particular case for appellate review. Under the so-called *rule of four,* four justices must agree before a *writ of certiorari* to the U.S. Supreme Court will be granted.

written record The official collection of all the court proceedings in a case, including the *pleadings, exhibits, testimony,* and *judicial orders.*

wrongful death A type of lawsuit brought by the survivors of a person who has died alleging that the death was the result of a willful or negligent act by another. All American states now have wrongful death statutes that specify the circumstances under which survivors can sue someone who caused the death of their relative.

yakuza See *organized crime.*

zoning ordinance Rules passed by local governments that specify the permissible uses for particular tracts of land. See also *ordinances.*

About the Author

Michael Ross Fowler currently holds a joint appointment in law and political science at the University of Louisville. A graduate of Harvard Law School, the University of Virginia, and Dartmouth College, Mr. Fowler is admitted to the bars of Maryland, Massachusetts, and Washington, DC. From 1986 to 1989, he practiced law in the Boston offices of Mintz, Levin, Cohn, Ferris, Glovsky and Popeo. He is the author of three books including *Law, Power, and the Sovereign State: The Evolution and Application of the Concept of Sovereignty.* He has served as a Fulbright Scholar to Japan, a Central American Research Fellow for the Institute for the Study of World Politics, and Scholar-in-Residence at the White Burkett Miller Center of Public Affairs. In 1994, the Government of Vietnam and the Program for International Studies in Asia selected Michael Fowler to be the first American lawyer to teach in the Socialist Republic of Vietnam. He has lectured at the Institute for International Relations in Hanoi, Vietnam, and the University of the Ryukyus in Okinawa, Japan, as well as at the University of Virginia, Tufts University, Georgetown University, George Washington University, and the University of Louisville.

Acknowledgments

129, 131, 132, 134, 135, 141, 143, 144, 147, 148, 149, 150, 152, 153, 155, 157, 211

From *The Jury: Trial and Error in the American Courtroom* by Stephen J. Adler. Copyright 1994 by Stephen J. Adler. Reprinted by permission of Times Books, a division of Random House, Inc.

5, 102, 130, 147, 154, 264, 271, 292, 300

From *Courts on Trial: Myth and Reality in American Justice* by Jerome Frank. Copyright 1973 by Princeton University Press. Reprinted by permission of Princeton University Press.

3, 5, 6, 10, 20, 24, 40, 43, 50, 68, 79, 81, 87, 88, 89, 90, 92, 94, 95, 96, 97, 100, 101, 111, 112, 115, 123, 126, 260, 274, 275, 278, 279, 282, 283, 285, 287, 289

Excerpts from *A Nation Under Lawyers* by Mary Ann Glendon. Copyright 1994 by Mary Ann Glendon. Reprinted by permission of Farrar, Straus & Giroux, Inc.

68, 80, 95, 267, 269, 270, 271

From *The Lost Lawyer* by Anthony Kronman. Copyright © 1993 by the President and Fellows of Harvard College. Reprinted by permission of Harvard University Press.

65, 69, 97, 100, 101, 102, 110, 111, 112, 113, 114, 116, 117, 118, 122, 123, 126, 127, 148, 149, 151, 243, 244, 246, 247, 264, 266, 268, 269, 270, 271, 275, 277, 278, 279, 280, 281, 282, 283, 284, 285, 286, 296, 297, 300, 306

Reprinted with the permission of Scribner, A Division of Simon & Schuster, from *The Betrayed Profession: Lawyering at the End of the Twentieth Century* by Sol M. Linowitz with Martin Mayer. Copyright 1994 by Sol M. Linowitz and Martin Mayer.

159, 160, 161, 162, 174, 187, 221, 225, 226, 228, 229

From *Criminal Violence, Criminal Justice* by Charles E. Silberman. Copyright by Charles E. Silberman. Reprinted by permission of Random House, Inc.

4, 10, 99, 101, 207, 208, 211, 213, 214, 215, 217, 218, 244, 271, 285, 292

Excerpted with permission of Simon & Schuster from *The Art of Advocacy* by Lloyd Paul Stryker. Copyright 1954 by Lloyd Paul Stryker. Copyright renewed 1982 by Katharine S. Dunn.

Index

Cases Cited